History of Philosophy

HARPERCOLLINS COLLEGE OUTLINE
History of Philosophy

Dion Scott-Kakures, Ph.D.
Scripps College

Susan Castagnetto, Ph.D.
Pomona College

Hugh Benson, Ph.D.
University of Oklahoma

William Taschek, Ph.D.
University of Michigan

Paul Hurley, Ph.D.
Pomona College

 HarperPerennial
A Division of HarperCollinsPublishers

An American BookWorks Corporation Production

Project Manager: Mary Mooney
Editor Thomas H. Quinn

Library of Congress Cataloging-in-Publication Data

History of philosophy / Dion Scott-Kakures . . . [et al.]
   p.   cm.
  Includes bibliographical references and index.
  ISBN 06-467142-9 (pbk.)
  1. Philosophy—History.   I. Scott-Kakures, Dion, 1957–
B72.H567 1993
190—dc20   02-53291

98 99 00 01   ABW/RRD   10 9

Contents

Preface

More so than in the study of most other disciplines, the study of the history of philosophy is essentially linked to contemporary practice of the discipline. This is so not simply because the systems, problems, and solutions proposed by the philosophers of the past continue to live on—though often in forms not easy to recognize—in current discussions. It is also so because the study of the history of philosophy demands that one *do* philosophy. To study the history of philosophy is to engage, as best one can, in dialogue with the thinkers of the past.

It is for this reason that the history of philosophy is not (or is not merely) the history of ideas; it is not the study of who thought what at some particular time or other. It is, rather, the coming to grips with historically situated philosophical problems and the effort to critically engage the claims of, for example, Aristotle or Rousseau. In what follows we have attempted to emphasize the arguments of the philosophers that students are likely to confront in their study of philosophical texts. We have aimed, whenever possible, to examine in some critical detail various arguments we regard as both historically important and philosophically arresting.

It goes without saying, then, that the doing of the history of philosophy is a partisan affair. This is true both with respect to the nature of our examination of the arguments, and with respect to the philosophers we have chosen to examine in this work. Unlike some other single-volume histories of Western philosophy, we have not attempted to discuss every philosopher a student might conceivably consider. Rather, we have attempted to investigate at some length the thinkers and arguments that students are both likely to confront and ought to consider in their studies.

This is, of course, a collaborative effort. We have divided responsibility in the following way:

Hugh Benson: The Presocratics, Socrates, Plato, Aristotle, the Post-Aristotelians.

Susan Castagnetto: St. Thomas Aquinas, René Descartes, John Locke, David Hume, Thomas Reid.

Paul Hurley: Thomas Hobbes, Locke's Political Theory, Jean-Jacques Rousseau, Hume's Moral Theory, Kant's Moral Theory, the Utilitarians, Karl Marx, American Pragmatism.

Dion Scott-Kakures: St. Augustine, St. Anselm, Francis Bacon, Baruch Spinoza, G. W. Leibniz, George Berkeley, G. W. F. Hegel, Sören Kierkegaard, Friedrich Nietzsche, Jean-Paul Sartre.

William Taschek: Immanuel Kant, the Origins of Analytic Philosophy, Gottlob Frege, Bertrand Russell.

History of Philosophy

1

The Presocratics

*W*estern philosophy begins with the Presocratics, a group of thinkers spread throughout the Greek world. For the most part, they lived and worked (ca. 600–400 B.C.), generally before Socrates. What sets these thinkers apart and makes them philosophers is a difficult question to answer. Prior to these thinkers, the Greek conception of the world—its organization and its operation—was predominantly theocentric and anthropomorphic: The world was what it was and did what it did because of the will of the gods, who differed from humans only with respect to their power. For example, Hesiod (ca. 750–700 B.C.) explained the creation of the ocean-stream as the first result of intercourse between broad-breasted Gaia (Earth) and starry-skied Ouranos (Heaven). The Presocratic philosophers were chiefly concerned with offering explanations of the world and its phenomena that did not rely on such a god-and-human-based conception. They proposed a more scientific and naturalistic cosmology. (Cosmology is formed from two Greek words: cosmos, which means world or universe, and logos, which in this context means science or study of. So cosmology is the science or study of the universe, its structure, and its phenomena.)

A warning is in order before turning to the Presocratic thinkers. Our knowledge of the philosophical views of these thinkers is hampered in two ways. First, our sources for their views are confined to usually brief quotations from otherwise lost manuscripts (fragments) and to reports from later writers concerning what the Presocratics held (testimony). Second, their manner of philosophical exposition (poetry, dense aphorisms, and rarely prose) is very different from our own. Both factors make the task of understanding these thinkers almost impossible. What follows is one brief attempt, focusing on their importance to and influence on subsequent philosophical thought.

THE MILESIANS

The birthplace of Western philosophy is Miletus, a commercial seaport in Ionian Greece (the western coast of present-day Turkey). Here we find a sequence of three thinkers, each of whom offered his distinctive explanation of the world and its phenomena. Despite important differences among these explanations, they all saw natural processes as subject not to the caprice of human-like gods but rather to the order and rationality of a law-governed world. They sought to explain the confusion and variety of the world and its phenomena in terms of simpler and more orderly phenomena. Indeed, each sought to reduce the world, with its profusion of objects and changes, to a single "stuff" which undergoes a variety of transformations. As a result, the Milesians have been frequently labeled monists (from the Latin *mono*, which means one).

Thales

The first of these thinkers is Thales (ca. 624–545 B.C.), of whom we know even less than of the other Presocratics. Thales seems to have held that water is the fundamental "stuff" of which the world is composed. Exactly how the trees, rocks, and animals around us were thought to be composed of water is a matter of speculation (perhaps, by being a complex of water's three states: solid, liquid, and gas). Aristotle conjectured that Thales was led to this view as a result of investigations based on observation. Observations of the births of living things suggest that moistness, whose nature is water, is essential. Thus, Thales offered to explain the world and its phenomena by appealing to a single "stuff," water, whose presence has been observed in the generation of numerous things and whose transformations can be seen as subject to orderly processes.

Anaximander

Anaximander (ca. 610–545 B.C.) appears to have objected to Thales' explanation of the world and its phenomena on the grounds that the four traditional elements (earth, air, fire, and water) are fundamentally opposed. Earth, the dry, is opposed to water, the wet; and air, the cold, is opposed to fire, the hot. This opposition makes it impossible, according to Anaximander, for any one of these elements to be fundamental.

THE *APEIRON*

This led Anaximander to postulate the existence of a fifth element, the *apeiron* or the indefinite, out of which the other elements are composed by means of a process of separation. The *apeiron* is unobservable; but Anaximander believed that we could be certain of its existence by means of an argument from best explanation. Without the *apeiron*, Anaximander maintained, we cannot explain the existence of the other four elements, which are observable. In addition to requiring the existence of the unobserved *apeiron*, the fundamental opposition among the four elements provided Anaximander with a moral model for the lawlike nature of the world. The opposition among the four elements creates a state of strife, with the infringement of one element upon another and the promise of reparation for that infringement sometime in the future.

Anaximenes

Anaximenes (ca. 580–500 B.C.), the last of the Milesians, criticized Anaximander's appeal to the unobservable *apeiron* on the grounds that it is not necessary. Anaximenes appears to have thought that we ought not postulate the existence of anything that is not required to explain the world and its phenomena, especially when the postulate is unobservable. With this we get what looks like an explicit appeal to two principles that will recur in one form or another throughout the history of Western philosophy: the principle of the priority of observation and the principle of ontological simplicity.

OBSERVATION AND SIMPLICITY

The principle of the priority of observation maintains that, all things being equal, it is more reasonable to postulate the existence of observable entities than of nonobservable entities. The principle of ontological simplicity maintains that, all things being equal, the theory that postulates fewer entities is to be preferred. (*Ontological* is formed from two Greek roots: *ont-*, which means a being or existing thing, and *logos*, which in this context means science or study of. So, *ontological* means pertaining to the science or study of being or things that exist).

RAREFACTION AND CONDENSATION

According to Anaximenes, we can avoid the postulation of Anaximander's fifth, unobservable element if we simply deny Anaximander's assumption that the traditional four elements are opposed. Rather, we should think of those traditional elements as simply different states of the single fundamental "stuff," air. Fire is simply a more rarefied state of air, while water and earth are successively more condensed states of that same "stuff." Thus, with Anaximenes, as with his predecessors, we have the attempt to explain the world and its phenomena by appealing to a single "stuff" whose transformations are subject to orderly and lawlike processes.

THE PYTHAGOREANS

From Miletus we move to southern Italy. There, Pythagoras (ca. 570–495 B.C.), after emigrating from Samos, an island in the Aegean Sea off the coast of Ionia, established what was at least in part a religious cult. While the doctrines of this cult are shrouded in secrecy, it is clear that at least some of them are of genuine philosophical interest. Indeed, there are two concerns of Pythagoras and his followers that proved to be very influential in the subsequent development of Western philosophy: their concern for the soul and their concern with mathematics. (Because of the secrecy and cultish nature of the doctrines, it is very difficult to determine which views and influences should be attributed to Pythagoras himself and which to his followers. What follows refers simply to the general views of the Pythagoreans, without attempting to discriminate who said or thought what.)

Concern for the Soul

Unlike the Milesians, the Pythagoreans focused on how one ought to live in the world. Their answer to this question depended substantially on their particular conception of the soul *(psyche)*. The soul, according to the Pythagoreans, is immortal and subject to a succession of reincarnations in other bodies, animal as well as human. This view of the soul, known as transmigration or metempsychosis, prescribes human behavior in various ways. For example, it specifically prohibits the eating of meat, which essentially amounts to cannibalism. More generally, however, belief in transmigration leads to the study of philosophy. Only by practicing philosophy can one properly care for one's soul. Only in this way can one purify oneself sufficiently to eventually escape the endless reincarnations and rejoin the divine soul from which all of our individual souls once came. To see why philosophy contributes to the purification of the soul we need to turn first to the Pythagorean concern with mathematics.

Concern with Mathematics

Pythagoras and his followers are credited with a number of mathematical advances during this period. For example, they apparently discovered that the chief musical intervals of the Greek scale (the octave, the fifth, and the fourth) are functions of fixed mathematical ratios (2:1, 3:2, 4:3). These discoveries and advances led the Pythagoreans to believe that an orderly, rational, mathematical structure can be discovered behind the confusion and variety of the observable world. The attempt to understand this rational order constitutes the essence of the practice of philosophy.

The Practice of Philosophy

Practicing philosophy, then, contributes to the purification of the soul in two ways, according to the Pythagoreans. First, by studying, examining, and eventually understanding the rational structure of the world, the soul gradually begins to take on the features of what it studies. It becomes more rational, more orderly, and apparently purer. Second, and probably more important philosophically, by studying the pure, rational, orderly structure of the world, rather than its dirty, irrational, chaotic matter, one distances the soul from its material counterpart, the body. Thus, unlike the Milesians before them, who focused their attention on the material aspects of the world and its phenomena, the Pythagoreans focused on the structural aspects. Here we find for the first time a distinction between the formal or structural features of the world and the material features of the world. This distinction might also be understood as a distinction between necessary and contingent (or accidental) features of the world, or as a distinction between features of the world that can be known simply as a matter of reason (a priori) and those that can be known only as a result of empirical investigation or observation (a posteriori). It will recur throughout the subsequent history of Greek philosophy, and beyond. (Those who favor the formal, necessary, or a priori features are generally labeled rationalists. Those who favor the material, contingent, or a posteriori features are generally labeled empiricists.)

The Pythagorean Theorem

Probably the most famous of the mathematical advances of the Pythagoreans was their proof of the Pythagorean theorem, namely that the length of the hypotenuse of a right triangle is equivalent to the square root of the sum of the squares of the other two sides. The discovery of this theorem, however, led to the discovery of irrational numbers. (The square root of two, which is the length of the hypotenuse of a right triangle whose other two sides have lengths of one, is not a rational number.) The existence of irrational numbers proved to be a dilemma for the Pythagorean world view. Rather than confirming the orderly, rational nature of the structure of the world, it tended to contradict such a view. It is ironic that the theorem which was most problematic to Pythagorean philosophy should be the one which has come to be most frequently associated with it.

HERACLITUS

With Heraclitus (ca. 540–480 B.C.) we return to the shores of Ionian Greece and a city just north of Miletus, Ephesus. Here Heraclitus disclosed his philosophical views in aphorisms—short, pithy, pregnant sentences, perhaps even intentionally paradoxical or misleading. Indeed, Heraclitus is so difficult to decipher that he was known among the ancients themselves as Heraclitus the Obscure. Nevertheless, at least three general theses seem to stand out.

Logos

According to Heraclitus, all things in the world happen according to *logos*. *Logos* is a Greek word that comes from the verb meaning to say or to speak, and so had the basic meaning of word or thing said. It came, however, to mean much more than this. In addition to meaning word, it also means speech, statement, discourse, reputation, ratio, account, explanation, and reason. (In the Bible, the word translated as *word* in the King James Version of John 1.1 ["In the beginning was the Word and the Word was with God, and the Word was God."] is *logos*.) No English word quite captures the richness of the Greek *logos* and so it is best to leave it untranslated. In claiming that all things happen according to *logos*, Heraclitus seems to have meant that the world and its phenomena exemplify a rational order. Human wisdom consists in grasping this rational order; this wisdom unfortunately has been attained by relatively few people. Indeed, Heraclitus believes that he is revealing this world-governing *logos* to those of us who have not yet grasped it.

Flux

The *logos*-governed world that is revealed to the wise is very different from the common-sense view. According to Heraclitus, common sense is mistaken in thinking that the world consists of stable things. But, interestingly enough, it is mistaken on two accounts: both in thinking that the world is stable and in thinking that the world consists of things. Heraclitus seems to have believed that the world is always in a state of flux. It is constantly changing. What needs to be explained is not change, as common sense would have it, but the appearance of stability.

STRIFE

According to Heraclitus, the stability of the world is to be explained as a result of opposition among the changes, which Heraclitus calls strife. The balancing of these opposed changes produces the appearance of stability and, indeed, the appearance of things at all. Thus, for instance, Heraclitus appeals to the example of a tautly strung bow. Here we have a motion in one direction carefully balanced by a motion in the opposite direction. Cut the string—that is, destroy the balance—and the bow's stability is destroyed. Indeed, the bow itself is destroyed. Thus, for Heraclitus, the unity that is the tautly strung bow is a consequence of strife among changes.

The Unity of Opposites

This unity that results from opposition features in another aspect of Heraclitean philosophy, his particular brand of monism. According to Heraclitus, not only is everything constantly changing, but everything is really one. What Heraclitus seems to have meant by this is that the opposites themselves are in some sense one. Thus, Heraclitus offers the following examples: The good and the bad are one, in that sea water is both good (for fish) and bad (for humans); up and down are one, in that the path up and the path down are one and the same path; day and night are one, in that they are parts of a single day. The unity of the opposites is different in each of these cases, and it is far from clear that Heraclitus recognized this fact. But in offering these examples Heraclitus posed a question which had been looming in the background since Anaximander (recall his argument for the *apeiron* and the Pythagorean distinctions between body and soul, dirty and pure, matter and form, and irrational and rational) and would continue to occupy the attention of subsequent Greek philosophers: How can the same thing be characterized by opposites?

PARMENIDES

With Parmenides (ca. 515–430 B.C.) we begin to move into more familiar territory. Parmenides shows a concern with argument that we have not seen before. It is not that Thales, Anaximander, Anaximenes, Heraclitus, and the Pythagoreans did not have arguments for their views; they did. But apparently they were not concerned to give their arguments. As a result, in discussing their views, we have been limited to simply reporting them and speculating on their arguments. With Parmenides things changed. Parmenides gives us his argument for his view. He does not simply inform us of his view of the world and its phenomena. He wants us to see why he holds this view. He believes that, when we do, the force of the argument will compel us to adopt his view as well. This concern with argument would dominate subsequent Greek philosophy for the next six hundred years.

The Argument

Parmenides unfolds his philosophical view and his argument for it by means of an epic poem. After a prologue in which Parmenides describes his journey to meet the goddess who will reveal to him the "heart of well-rounded truth," the remainder of the poem is divided into two parts, "The Way of Truth" and "The Way of Opinion." The relationship between these parts of the poem is difficult to decipher; but since "The Way of Truth" is more influential for subsequent Greek philosophy (and more accessible to us), we will focus on it.

THREE POSSIBILITIES

While the initial argument that Parmenides offers in "The Way of Truth" is also difficult to decipher, most would agree that its form is that of an argument from elimination. It appears to go something like this:

1. There are only three possibilities, either
    (a) "it is," or
    (b) "it is not," or

       (c) "it is and it is not."
2. "It is not" is neither thinkable nor speakable.
3. "It is and it is not" is confused.
4. So, "it is."

Many questions immediately arise concerning this argument.

It **as a Variable.** First, to what does *it* refer? *It* functions in the way a variable does in modern logic, serving simply as a place holder. For example, we can substitute *Socrates* for *it* in 1 and get the following substitution instance.

There are only three possibilities (for Socrates), either

    (a) "Socrates is," or
    (b) "Socrates is not," or
    (c) "Socrates is and Socrates is not."

Three Uses of *Is*. Second, what is meant by *is*? This second question is more difficult to answer. In Greek (as in English) the verb that gets translated as *is* in this argument has at least three different uses. First, it has an existential use, as when "Socrates is" means that Socrates exists. Second, *is* has a predicative use, as in the sentences "Socrates is tired," "Socrates is heavy," and "Socrates is a human." In certain contexts, "Socrates is" can be used as shorthand for sentences such as these. (Consider, for example, "Socrates is" as a response to the question "Which one of you is tired?" These contexts are more common in Greek.) Finally, *is* can be used to mean the same thing as "is identical with." It is this use of *is* that is employed in the sentence "Socrates is the husband of Xanthippe." This sentence means the same thing as the sentence "Socrates is the same person as the person who is the husband of Xanthippe." Again in context, "Socrates is" can be used as shorthand for "Socrates is identical with the husband of Xanthippe." (Consider, for example, this sentence as a response to the question "Who is the husband of Xanthippe?" Again, these contexts are more common in Greek.) The problem is not that *is* has all these uses. The problem is that Parmenides may fail to distinguish among them. Indeed, the plausibility of this argument and the consequences that Parmenides draws from its conclusion may depend on confusing these uses.

    Thinking or Speaking of "What Is Not." Two further questions are: Why is "it is not" unthinkable and unspeakable? And why is "it is and it is not" confused? "It is not" is unthinkable and unspeakable, according to Parmenides, because to think or speak of "it is not" requires that one think or speak of something that is not. But "something that is not" is not anything at all. It is nothing. And so to think or speak of "it is not" is to think or speak of nothing. It is to fail to think or to speak at all. This is a knot which has entangled a considerable amount of subsequent Western philosophy—how or whether we manage to think or to speak of nonexistent objects (Santa Claus, Pegasus, or a round square). For the present, it is sufficient to note its origin. (W.V.O. Quine, in a famous twentieth century essay, referred to this problem as "Plato's Beard." Perhaps it would be better to think of it as Parmenides' Beard.)

"It is and it is not" is confused, according to Parmenides, because this possibility requires us, at least in part, to think or speak of "it is not." As we have just seen, however, to do so is impossible. Parmenides attributes this possibility to the way of common sense. We can begin to see why by turning to the consequences Parmenides draws from the conclusion of this argument.

Consequences   The consequences that Parmenides draws from the conclusion that "it is" are rather startling. According to Parmenides, it follows that all that exists is one, uncreated, imperishable, unchangeable, motionless, homogeneous, complete, and timeless. Such a world is rather different from the world that appears to common sense. Perhaps we can see how such a view might seem to result from Parmenides' argument by briefly considering the case of change. Change, as the common sense view has it, takes place when, for example, something is heavy at one time, and at another time is not heavy. But this, Parmenides appears to think, requires thinking or speaking of "it is not," either because he confuses the predicative *is* in "is not heavy" with the existential *is*, or because he thinks that to think of Socrates not being heavy is to think of Socrates and of the property of being heavy not existing. In either case, change requires thinking or speaking of "it is not," which Parmenides has argued is impossible.

RESPONSES TO PARMENIDES

The influence of Parmenides' view was so great that it is not uncommon to read the remainder of Presocratic thought (and to a lesser extent the philosophical views of Plato and Aristotle) as various responses to it. The sorts of responses that Parmenides' view generated fall into three basic categories: followers, revisionists, and nihilists.

The Eleatics   The followers of Parmenides—those who shared Parmenides' general philosophical view—are known as Eleatics, named after Parmenides' native town of Elea in southern Italy.

ZENO

The most famous and influential of these followers is Zeno of Elea (ca. 490–440 B.C.) who bequeathed to us his wonderful paradoxes. Zeno's approach was not to defend the counterintuitive consequences of

Parmenides' argument with additional positive arguments, but rather to show that the intuitive, common-sense view is subject to its own rather severe difficulties. While Zeno offered numerous arguments of this sort, his four most famous ("The Dichotomy," "The Achilles and the Tortoise," "The Flying Arrow," and "The Stadium") all aimed at deducing an absurdity from the theories of space and time on which the common-sense view of motion is based. Some have credited Zeno with introducing this type of argument (the reduction to absurdity or *reductio ad absurdum*) to philosophy.

The Pluralists

The second group of philosophers to respond to Parmenides adopted a sort of revisionary approach. They could not accept the Parmenidean conclusions, but they could not ignore the force of his argument either. Nor, unfortunately, could they see what was wrong with the argument. Thus, they adopted a kind of compromise view. They might be thought of as attempting to see how little of the view need be revised to successfully avoid the conclusions, and so save a semblance of common sense. This approach led them to postulate a plurality of fundamental "stuffs," all of which retain the properties of the Parmenidean "One." They did not refute Parmenides' argument for monism. They simply hypothesized that it was false and then attempted to show how much of the rest of the theory could be saved without flying in the face of common sense.

EMPEDOCLES

For example, Empedocles (ca. 492–432 B.C.) held that "it is" is four elemental "stuffs"—earth, air, fire, and water—and two forces—love and strife. Parmenides is correct that there is no creation of and destruction of "it is." Instead there is just mixture and separation of the four elements by means of the two forces: love, which attracts unlike elements into mixtures, and strife, which attracts like elements and so brings about the separation of the less elemental "stuffs."

ANAXAGORAS

Anaxagoras (ca. 500–428 B.C.), on the other hand, held that "it is" is an indefinitely large number of elemental "stuffs." There is a kind of "stuff" for every thing that can be cut into two pieces with each piece remaining the same "stuff." For example, when one cuts a tree into two pieces one is not left with two trees, but with two chunks of wood. Furthermore, every chunk of a particular kind of "stuff" contains a portion of every other kind of "stuff," no matter how small the chunk. (This latter claim may have been offered in order to avoid some of Zeno's reductions to absurdity.) Change, according to Anaxagoras, was simply a matter of mixture and separation of these "stuffs" by means of Mind (*nous*).

LEUCIPPUS AND DEMOCRITUS

Finally, the Atomists, Leucippus (ca. 460–390 B.C.) and Democritus (ca. 460–360 B.C.), postulated a plurality of particles which, unlike those postulated by the previous pluralists, do not differ qualitatively, but only in size and shape. These particles retain the other characteristics of the Parmenidean "One" and are called "atoms" (from the Greek *atomos*, meaning indivisible). The Atomists also rejected Parmenides' argument against the existence of "it is not" and asserted the existence of the void, empty space. The random, mechanical motion of atoms in the void results in clumps of various sizes and shapes, which account for the familiar (common) sensible world.

The Sophists

It is a mistake to think of the Sophists as a group of thinkers all of whom held more or less the same philosophical position. Among the Sophists can be listed such diverse and independently minded thinkers as Protagoras (ca. 490–420 B.C.), Gorgias (ca. 485–380 B.C.), Hippias (ca. 465–390 B.C.), Prodicus (ca. 465–390 B.C.), Antiphon (ca. 485–390 B.C.), Thrasymachus (ca. 465–390 B.C.), and Critias (ca. 450–403 B.C.). We have no hope of doing justice to their views in the space that can be allotted to them here. Nevertheless, there do seem to be two common themes that run through these diverse views and constitute both a response to Parmenides and a preparation for our next major thinker, Socrates.

NIHILISTIC TENDENCY

The first theme is a nihilistic tendency on the part of the Sophists. (*Nihilism* is formed from the Latin *nihil*, which means "nothing." Nihilism, then, is the view that nothing, or nothing of a specific sort, is true or exists.) The Sophists denied the assumption on which the entire preceding tradition had been based—that the activity of philosophical inquiry has a special access to the truth. Some suggested that it is a mistake to view this sort of activity as a method of truth-seeking at all. Rather, it is simply a method of persuasion. Equally good arguments can be given for precisely the opposite conclusions that Parmenides had reached. Thus, Gorgias is reputed to have written a treatise in which he argued that (1) nothing is; (2) if something was, it could not be known; and (3) if something could be known, it could not be communicated. Furthermore, the Sophists appear to have simply denied the gap between the way the world appeared to common sense and the way the world really was—the appearance/reality gap that the philosophical method was employed to bridge. There simply is no hidden world or order that needs to be uncovered. For example, Plato attributes to Protagoras the view that man is the measure of all things, which seems to have meant that the world is for a person just the way it appears to that person to be.

HUMANISTIC TENDENCY

The second theme is a related humanistic tendency on the part of the Sophists—a concern with human activities and institutions. For example, many Sophists professed to teach rhetoric, a skill which was of immense value to a successful citizen in democratic Athens. Indeed, some of the Sophists even professed thereby to teach human *arete*, a Greek word which might be translated as *virtue* or *excellence*. In teaching rhetoric, they could be seen as teaching one to be a better citizen.

IMMORALISM

This humanistic tendency, when joined to the nihilism, tended to breed a sort of immoralism (or at least so their immediate successors seemed to think). Many Sophists were thought to encourage values out of step with the values of traditional Greek morality. For example, Thrasymachus is reputed to have held that justice, one of the traditional virtues, benefits others, while only injustice benefits the agent (the performer of the act); only the weak (because they have no choice) or the foolish (because they do not know any better) would act to benefit others rather than themselves. This immoralism generated a reaction in the philosophical views of Socrates, the subject of our next chapter.

In conclusion, then, we have come full circle. We began with the aim to uncover the hidden order and structure of an apparently chaotic and confusing world. We end with the denial that such an aim can be achieved. In the meantime we have witnessed a variety of philosophical approaches, distinctions, and puzzles. We have seen arguments from the best explanation, arguments from ontological simplicity, arguments from elimination, and reductions to absurdity. We have watched distinctions develop between form and matter, experience and reason, process and object, and reality and appearance. We have encountered puzzles concerning thinking of what is not, possessing opposite characteristics, and bridging the appearance/reality gap. We will meet with all of these again throughout the course of subsequent Western philosophy.

Selected Readings

Barnes, Jonathon. *The Presocratic Philosophers.* London: Routledge & Kegan Paul, 1982.

Guthrie, W. K. C. *A History of Greek Philosophy: The Earlier Presocratics and the Pythagoreans.* Cambridge: Cambridge University Press, 1962.

_____. *A History of Greek Philosophy: The Presocratic Tradition from Parmenides to Democritus.* Cambridge: Cambridge University Press, 1965.

_____. *The Sophists*. Cambridge: Cambridge University Press, 1971.

Kerferd, G.B. *The Sophistic Movement*. Cambridge: Cambridge University Press, 1981.

Kirk, G. S., J. E. Raven, and Malcolm Schofield. *The Presocratic Philosophers: A Critical History with a Selection of Texts*. 2d rev. ed. Cambridge: Cambridge University Press, 1983.

2

Socrates

The next key figure in the history of Western philosophy is Socrates (470–399 B.C.). It is useful to think of Socrates as responding to the challenge posed by the Sophists, among whom he is sometimes grouped. Socrates shares with the Sophists their humanism, but not their nihilism. It may have been for this reason that Cicero credited Socrates with calling "philosophy down from the sky." We have seen in the previous chapter that Socrates is not the first philosopher to have been concerned with human (as opposed to cosmological) activities and institutions. But he may have been the first to subject them to the rigors of philosophical analysis on the assumption that there were objective facts to be learned as a result. More important, Socrates brought philosophy to the person on the street, literally and figuratively. According to Socrates, the questions he asked and the answers he pursued were the most important questions and answers each and every one of us could and should ask and pursue.

THE SOCRATIC PROBLEMS

The First Problem   The first problem we must address in discussing Socrates' philosophical views concerns whose philosophical views we are discussing. The problem arises because Socrates appears to have chosen not to record his philosophical views for posterity; he seems to have viewed philosophy as essentially an oral enterprise. This, in itself, would not be so troublesome since we do have three rather extensive portraits of Socrates from those who knew and heard him: Aristophanes (ca. 450–385 B.C.), a comic poet; Xenophon (ca. 428–354 B.C.), a military general; and Plato (ca. 428–347 B.C.), a preeminent philosopher. The challenge arises, however, because the portraits of Socrates we have from these three authors are substantially different.

Aristophanes' portrait is of a sophistic natural philosopher who offers to teach anyone who will pay how to make the weaker argument the stronger and who denies the existence of the gods of the city. Xenophon's Socrates is a moral instructor who is quick to give advice and who is a model of common morality and religious practice. Plato's Socrates disowns natural philosophy, despises sophistry, denies that he teaches anything, and espouses such non-traditional moral views as "no one ever does wrong willingly," "it is wrong to harm one's enemies," and "knowledge is virtue." With which of these three portraits of Socrates, then, should historians of philosophy concern themselves? This question has come to be called the Socratic Problem.

The Second Problem

Many historians of philosophy have responded to this problem by choosing the Platonic Socrates, sometimes simply because this Socrates appears to be the most philosophically interesting. We will follow their lead. In doing so, however, we have yet to put all of the problems behind us. As is becoming increasingly acknowledged, it appears that more than one portrait of Socrates can be found in Plato.

DEATH IN *APOLOGY* AND *PHAEDO*

For example, in the *Apology*, Plato depicts Socrates' defense speech against the charges of "rejecting the gods of the state," "introducing strange deities," and "corrupting the youth." Near the end of this speech Socrates professes ignorance as to whether death is complete annihilation or the passage of the soul from one place to another. In either case, Socrates maintains, it would be a great blessing—being either the equivalent of a dreamless sleep or the opportunity to converse with the wise and courageous people of old.

In the *Phaedo*, Plato depicts the day Socrates is executed, after having been found guilty of the previously mentioned charges and sentenced to death. Here Socrates' ignorance concerning the nature of death has disappeared. Socrates chides his visitors for lamenting his pending death by proclaiming that death is what true philosophers desire. At death the soul can finally free itself from the body and gain the wisdom that philosophers seek. The bulk of the *Phaedo* consists of four arguments offered by Socrates to prove the soul's immortality. The soul's annihilation is apparently no longer a possibility.

It is difficult to believe that in the month that has transpired between the trial and the execution day Socrates has changed his views concerning death so radically and indeed discovered four proofs of the soul's immortality. It would seem, then, that we have two distinct portraits of Socrates in Plato—one Socrates is ignorant of the nature of death, the other is not. With which of these portraits, then, should historians of philosophy concern themselves? This might be called the Second Socratic Problem.

The Early Dialogues

To respond to this problem we must turn to the Platonic dialogues themselves, the works in which we find the various Platonic portraits of Socrates. Plato chose to reveal his own philosophical views by means of a number of dialogues, in most of which Socrates is his primary spokesman. Research into the order in which Plato composed these dialogues suggests that they fall into the following three periods. (Socrates plays little or no role in the starred dialogues.)

EARLY	MIDDLE	LATE
Apology	*Cratylus*	*Critias**
Charmides	*Phaedo*	*Laws**
Crito	*Phaedrus*	*Parmenides**
Euthydemus	*Republic*	*Philebus*
Euthyphro	*Symposium*	*Politicus**
Gorgias		*Sophist**
Hippias Major		*Theaetetus*
Hippias Minor		*Timaeus**
Ion		
Laches		
Lysis		
*Menexenus**		
Meno		
Protagoras		

Many historians of philosophy have claimed to discover important dissimilarities between the philosophical views expressed by Socrates in the dialogues of the early period and those in the dialogues of the middle and late periods. (For example, the views concerning death, just mentioned above. Notice that the *Apology* appears to have been composed during Plato's early period, while the *Phaedo* appears to have been composed during the middle period.) Once again, we will follow the lead of these historians. In the present chapter, we will be concerned with the philosophical views expressed by Socrates in the dialogues which compose Plato's early period. In the next chapter, we will be concerned with the philosophical views expressed by Socrates and Plato's other spokesmen in the dialogues of Plato's middle and late periods.

THE DELPHIC ORACLE STORY

We can begin to understand the philosophical views of the Socrates of these early dialogues through a story Socrates tells about himself as part of his defense speech in the *Apology*. Socrates explains that his prosecution has been motivated by an enmity he has provoked due to his pursuit of a certain investigation that was spawned by a pronouncement of an oracle. Apparently, a friend of Socrates named Chaerephon approached the oracle at Delphi with the question whether there was anyone wiser than Socrates. This oracle—a priestess who was thought by the Greeks to speak for the god Apollo and so to be infallible—answered that no one was.

Socrates reports that he was puzzled by this answer because he was aware of being wise about nothing, great or small. As a result, Socrates set out to investigate the truth of what the god (through the priestess) said. Whenever he met with someone reputed to be wise he would test their wisdom. Socrates discovered, after examining politicians, poets, and craftsmen, that while some of those reputed to be wise did indeed know things that Socrates did not, they all thought that they knew other things that they did not. To this extent alone Socrates appeared to be their superior. In thinking that he knew nothing, only he avoided thinking that he knew things that he did not. Socrates interpreted the god to mean that only that person who (like Socrates) recognizes the limits of his or her knowledge is wise.

Socrates, thereupon, takes this investigation to be his divine mission: to examine all of those who lay some claim to wisdom; to learn from them if they do know what they are reputed to know; and to make them aware of their ignorance if they do not know what they think they know. Later in the *Apology*, Socrates redescribes this divine mission by saying that he continuously exhorts those he meets to care about "wisdom, truth, and the best possible state of their soul"; whenever he meets with anyone who professes to care about these things he examines them. If it turns out that they do not care about these things, he reproaches them for caring about what is of little value rather than about what is of supreme value.

There are three features of this divine mission that call for further comment: the method which Socrates employs in pursuing his mission; Socrates' professions of ignorance; and his care for the soul. We will see that these three features are all importantly related.

SOCRATIC METHOD

The method Socrates employs in examining the reputed wisdom of those he happens to meet is characterized by two preoccupations: a preoccupation with questions and answers, and a preoccupation with definitions.

The Elenchos

Unlike the Sophists who appear to have engaged in long, polished discourses on a variety of subjects, especially subjects concerning how one ought to live, Socrates seems to have preferred the method of short questions and answers. Indeed in some of the dialogues in which Socrates engages a Sophist (for example, Socrates' exchange with Protagoras in the *Protagoras*), Socrates frequently attempts to restrain the Sophist from engaging in long speeches; instead he urges the Sophist to acquiesce to Socrates' customary method of questions and answers.

This method of questions and answers that Socrates practices is known as the *elenchos*. (*Elenchos* might be roughly translated as *refutation*, *test*, or *cross-examination*.) The *elenchos* involves: (1) encouraging the interlocutor (the individual being examined) to express some belief, usually concerning the definition of some moral concept (e.g., holiness, justice, courage, etc.); (2) getting the interlocutor to express some other beliefs; and (3) showing that these last beliefs negate the original belief. As a result, Socrates concludes that the interlocutor does not know what he purports to know and, therefore, does not care about "wisdom, truth, and the best possible state of his soul." Socrates, thereupon, exhorts the interlocutor to join him in the pursuit of the knowledge they both lack.

LACHES

Consider the following exchange in the *Laches*. Lysimachus and Melesias begin this dialogue by asking Laches and Nicias, two fifth-century Athenian generals, for advice concerning the proper military education of their sons. After receiving incompatible advice from these generals (Nicias advising that the sons ought to be trained in a certain military art, Laches advising to the contrary), the two fathers turn to Socrates to decide the tie. Socrates objects that this is no way to decide such an important issue; he suggests that the fathers ought to follow the advice of the expert, the one who knows. They should not, he maintains, simply follow the recommendation of the majority.

After disavowing his own knowledge of this matter, Socrates sets out to test the knowledge of the generals by asking them to say what courage is. Socrates begins with Laches who offers the following answers: Courage is standing one's ground in battle, and courage is (wise) endurance of the soul. In both cases, Socrates discovers that Laches has other beliefs which are inconsistent with these answers. In the case of the first answer, for example,

Laches also believes that the Spartans were courageous in their retreat at Plataea. (Retreating, of course, requires not standing one's ground in battle.)

The discussion then turns to Nicias, who suggests that courage is the knowledge of fearful and daring things. Socrates, however, discovers that this answer is incompatible with Nicias' belief that courage is a part of virtue. After a series of questions and answers, Socrates discovers that Nicias ultimately understands his answer to mean that courage is knowledge of good and evil, which is the whole of virtue. Socrates concludes that none of them, neither Laches, nor Nicias, nor himself, have the requisite knowledge to advise Lysimachus and Melesias concerning the proper military education of their sons. As a result, he encourages them all to seek out the best teacher they can find on this subject and, most importantly, not to remain as they are, ignorant of this most important affair.

Definition

This exchange from the *Laches* also testifies to the second preoccupation of the Socratic method, definition. In eight of the fourteen early dialogues, a question of the form "What is F-ness?" plays an important role. (*F-ness* stands for a noun that has a corresponding adjective, *F*; for example, *holiness* [F-ness]/*holy* [F], or *temperance* (F-ness)/*temperate* (F).) The primary question of the *Euthyphro* is "What is holiness?"; of the *Charmides*, "What is temperance?"; of the *Hippias Major*, "What is beauty?"; of the *Laches* (as we have seen), "What is courage?"; of the *Lysis*, "What is friendship?"; and of the *Meno*, "What is virtue?". The *Gorgias* and the *Protagoras* begin with the questions "What is rhetoric?" and "What is sophistry?", respectively. In various places and ways throughout the early dialogues, Socrates suggests that what he is looking for in asking these questions is something which, in the case of courage, for example: (1) is possessed by *all* courageous actions and/or people; (2) is possessed by *only* courageous actions and/or people; and (3) makes those actions and/or people courageous.

Thus, in the *Laches*, Socrates finds fault with Laches' definition that courage is standing one's ground because the courageous Spartans did not stand their ground at Plataea. In the *Meno*, Socrates faults Meno's definition that virtue is the ability to rule over men because a child or a slave with that ability is not virtuous. In the *Euthyphro*, Euthyphro's definition that holiness is being dear to all the gods is abandoned because what makes a thing holy is not that all the gods hold it dear, rather what makes all the gods hold it dear is that it is holy. Aristotle explains that what Socrates is seeking with these questions is a universal; he credits Socrates with being the first philosopher to fix his thought on such definitions. We will see that this interest in universals, which the Socratic question prompts, plays an important role in the philosophical views of Socrates' immediate successors, Plato and Aristotle.

SOCRATIC PROFESSIONS OF IGNORANCE

The second feature of Socrates' divine mission—his profession of ignorance—is also apparent in our brief sketch of the exchange in the *Laches*. When Socrates objects to the fathers' request to decide the tie between Laches and Nicias by insisting that they follow the advice only of the expert in the relevant subject matter, the one who knows what courage is, he quickly disavows his own claim to such expertise and knowledge. This disavowal is reiterated at the end of the dialogue.

Socratic Irony

Many readers of the early dialogues have read these disclaimers as examples of Socrates' famous irony. For example, at the end of the *Euthyphro*, after each of Euthyphro's five attempts to answer the question "What is holiness?" has been subjected to the *elenchos* and found wanting, Socrates encourages Euthyphro to try yet again. Socrates assures him that he is confident that Euthyphro knows the answer. Socrates surely does not mean what he says here; he is pulling Euthyphro's leg. But does Socrates mean what he says when he professes his own ignorance?

Many readers of the early dialogues think he does not. Indeed, it has been suggested that Socrates does not merely fail to mean what he says, but he intentionally tries to deceive his interlocutors in order to gain their cooperation in the *elenchos*. This view of Socratic ignorance is encouraged by one of Socrates' own interlocutors. In the first book of the *Republic* (which is believed by some to have been composed during Plato's early period), Thrasymachus explodes at Socrates for what Thrasymachus calls his famous deceit. He says that he knew that Socrates, to avoid having to answer the questions, rather than ask them, would disclaim knowing what justice is.

Genuine Professions of Ignorance

This view that Socrates' professions of ignorance are deceptive is difficult to sustain. Why, for example, would Socrates deceptively disavow knowledge of what courage is at the *end* of the *Laches*, when the discussion is coming to a close? Socrates is no longer interested in encouraging Laches' and Nicias' cooperation in answering his questions. Still more difficult to understand is Socrates' puzzlement concerning the pronouncement of the Delphic oracle, if we understand Socrates' disclaimers as deceptive. Who is Socrates trying to deceive when he tells the jury that he was puzzled by the pronouncement since he was aware of being wise about nothing, either great or small? Surely not himself. The jury? But he has just promised the jury to tell the truth!

It is best, then, to understand Socrates' professions of ignorance as genuine. Not only is Socrates sincere in disavowing knowledge of the nature of courage in the *Laches*, but he is also sincere when at the beginning of the *Meno* he disavows knowledge of the nature of virtue and encourages Meno to teach him if he knows. Similarly, when Socrates suggests his ignorance at the beginning of the *Euthyphro*, encouraging Euthyphro to teach him the nature of holiness if he knows it, and at the beginning of the *Hippias Major*, when he encourages Hippias to teach him the nature of beauty if he knows it, Socrates means what he says. Socrates may be rather skeptical that Meno, Euthyphro, and Hippias actually have the knowledge they profess; he has tested the knowledge of many others who have professed to know and has found it wanting. Nevertheless, he is quite sincere in his desire to test them to see if they know and to learn from them if they do.

Socratic Epistemology

While Socrates frequently and sincerely professes ignorance, especially moral ignorance, we should not take this to mean that Socrates fails to be committed to moral doctrines. Indeed, Socrates is firmly committed to quite a number of non-traditional moral doctrines which we will discuss in the next section. In disavowing knowledge, Socrates *need* not be and indeed *is* not disavowing belief, nor true belief, nor even reasonably firmly held belief. His professed ignorance is perfectly compatible with the acceptance of non-traditional moral doctrines as long as a distinction between knowledge and true belief is a feature of Socratic epistemology. (Epistemology is the branch or field of philosophy concerned with the nature of knowledge and belief. *Epistemology* is formed from two Greek words: *episteme*, which means knowledge, and *logos*, which in this context means science or study of.) Such a distinction is explicitly recognized by Socrates in the *Meno*.

KNOWLEDGE AND TRUE BELIEF

At the end of the *Meno*, Socrates suggests that the difference between knowledge and true belief is that knowledge is more stable than true belief. This greater stability, Socrates maintains, results from the knower's ability to "work out the reason why." Exactly how Socrates understands this distinction between knowledge and true belief, and whether Socrates is committed to even more subtle distinctions (for example, between human and divine knowledge) are difficult questions to answer with which readers of Plato's dialogues have struggled for centuries.

One way to understand what Socrates is disavowing in disavowing knowledge is to recall what he finds lacking in his many interlocutors: the ability to say what holiness, courage, or virtue is without ultimately discovering incompatible beliefs. Thus, one can be truly said to know that prosecuting one's father for murder is holy, or that being trained in a particular art of war will make one courageous, only when one can say what holiness or courage is in a way consistent with one's other beliefs. Only then can one be said to be able to work out the reason why that particular action is holy, or why that particular art makes one courageous. This is a very rare ability—and knowledge, so understood, would be a very difficult thing to obtain. But it is an ability that Socrates never ceases from encouraging his interlocutors to pursue. Nevertheless, however we understand Socrates' epistemological views, we should be certain that they do not threaten his moral ones. Socratic ignorance and Socratic morality are both essential features of Socratic philosophy.

SOCRATES VERSUS THE SOPHISTS

Nor should we confuse Socratic ignorance with the nihilism of the Sophists. The Sophists might be thought to have concluded from the fact that people are persistently unable to answer difficult questions without falling prey to inconsistency or absurdity that such answers cannot be known and that, even if they could be known, they would be of little value. Thus, the course of Presocratic thought leading up to the Sophists may have suggested to the Sophists that the task of discovering the nature of the universe and its phenomena was hopeless; even if it could be discovered, it would be of little value. Who besides Parmenides and perhaps his immediate associates would believe that all that exists is one, uncreated, imperishable, unchangeable, motionless, homogeneous, complete, and timeless?

Disagreement and lack of clear answers was even more pervasive in the moral realm, especially from one city-state or country to another. Herodotus (ca. 484–420 B.C.), a fifth-century Athenian historian, for example, relates that the Greeks found the Indian practice of eating the dead bodies of their fathers morally outrageous, while the Indians found the Greek practice of burning the dead bodies of their fathers equally outrageous. What is important, the Sophists concluded, is not being able to answer these difficult questions consistently or truthfully, but rather being able to persuade others of the answers one gave. Hence, rhetoric proved to be a very valuable tool.

Unlike the Sophists, however, Socrates does not conclude from his and others' inability to answer these questions in a consistent way that the answers cannot be known nor that they would be of little value were they known. Indeed, for Socrates the pursuit of this knowledge is the most valuable occupation one can engage in. Should one obtain such knowledge, one would become an expert in the relevant subject matter, and who would deny the value of medical or military expertise?

For Socrates, moral expertise is the most valuable expertise one can have. The value of this expertise for oneself is an issue we will pursue in the next section when we discuss Socrates' moral views, but its value to others has already been suggested in our sketch of the *Laches*. Just as the advice of an expert in military affairs would prove invaluable when one was about to embark upon a military expedition, so the advice of a moral expert would prove invaluable when one was about to embark upon one's children's education (*Laches*), or the prosecution of one's father for murder (*Euthyphro*), or one's defense of the charge of corrupting the youth (*Apology*). Once again, exactly how Socrates believes that such expertise can be gained (whether, for example, it can be learned from others who already have this knowledge, or whether it can be discovered by means of the *elenchos*) is a difficult question and one which, in the next chapter, we will see Plato addressing. That Socrates believes that the pursuit of such knowledge is of supreme importance should be doubted by no one.

CARE FOR THE SOUL

Finally, we turn to Socratic ethics. (Ethics is the branch or field of philosophy concerned with the nature of good and bad, right and wrong, virtue and vice, and justice and injustice.) Here too Socrates can be usefully compared to the Sophists. Like the Sophists, Socrates appears to abandon cosmological speculation and investigation in favor of a concern for human activities and institutions. It is no accident that Plato depicts Socrates engaging Protagoras and Gorgias in typically Sophistic discussions concerning the teachability of virtue and the power and value of rhetoric in Greek society, while other dialogues concern the nature of courage, holiness, temperance, friendship, and virtue. Nevertheless, Socrates' moral views are quite different from the Sophists'. As we have seen, Socrates believes that there are objective facts in the moral realm and that knowledge of these facts is of supreme importance.

Socratic moral philosophy can be characterized as Socratic intellectualism. Virtue, according to Socrates, is knowledge. This is one of Socrates' moral views which have come to be known as the Socratic Paradoxes. (They are called paradoxes because they seem to be so obviously contrary to common sense.) We can begin to see what Socrates has in mind by briefly considering Socrates' views concerning: (1) the nature of human happiness; (2) the effect of virtuous and vicious actions on the state of one's soul; and (3) one's ability to act contrary to one's perceived good.

Socratic Eudaimonism

Socrates believes that happiness (*eudaimonia*) is the ultimate end of all human action. It is for the sake of happiness that we do all that we do. As the end of all action, then, happiness is the ultimate human "good." But happiness, for Socrates, requires a flourishing and healthy soul. Such a soul is a virtuous soul. Readers of Plato's early dialogues disagree whether

Socrates requires any other "goods" for the attainment of happiness (for example, sufficient wealth to maintain a healthy body), but none dispute that for Socrates the overwhelming requirement for happiness is a flourishing and healthy soul. To know that happiness requires a flourishing and healthy soul—that is, a virtuous soul—is to know one's ultimate "good" (or at least the overwhelming share of it). It is to know the end of one's actions—what will make one happy.

Vicious Actions

Socrates also holds that acting viciously makes the soul vicious. Thus, in the *Gorgias*, Socrates argues for the paradoxical-sounding view that it is worse for the agent to inflict harm than to suffer it. To inflict harm on another is to act viciously. But to act viciously makes one's soul vicious. It harms one's soul, whose well-being we have seen is one's overwhelming concern. To be harmed by another, however, only harms one's body, not one's soul. This is why in the *Crito*, when considering whether or not he ought to escape from jail, Socrates ignores the question whether or not he is being justly punished, in lieu of the question whether or not escaping would be just. The former question concerns the well-being of his body, which pales in comparison to the concern of the latter question, the well-being of his soul.

Weakness of the Will

In response to Meno's fourth definition, that virtue is desiring fine things and being able to acquire them, Socrates objects that the first part of this definition is useless. After identifying fine things with good things, Socrates argues for the paradoxical claim that *everyone* desires good things. The argument that Socrates offers goes something like this:

1. Someone who desires what are in fact bad things either thinks that they are good or thinks that they are bad.
2. When one desires something, one seeks to possess it.
3. When one seeks to possess something, one thinks that that thing is beneficial to oneself.
4. When one thinks that something is beneficial to oneself, one thinks that it is good.
5. So, when one desires something, one thinks that it is good.
6. So, no one desires what are in fact bad things, thinking they are bad.
7. So, someone who desires what are in fact bad things, thinking that they are good, really desires good things.

If this argument is supposed to establish that everyone desires good things, it seems that Socrates must mean by this paradoxical-sounding claim the somewhat less paradoxical-sounding claim that the object of everyone's desire is what they believe to be good (for them). When this is combined with the view that one's actions are determined by one's beliefs and desires, it follows, for Socrates, that no one ever acts contrary to what one believes to be good (for them), that is, their perceived good.

Socratic Intellectualism

When these three views are combined, we can see what Socrates has in mind by claiming that virtue is knowledge. Given that no one ever acts contrary to what one believes to be good for him- or herself, it would appear that no one would ever act viciously except out of ignorance. If one knew that one's own happiness—that is, one's own good—could be obtained only by acquiring a flourishing and healthy soul and that such a soul could be acquired only by acting virtuously, one would believe that acting virtuously is good for oneself and thus desire to act virtuously; therefore, one would act virtuously. Knowledge, then, is *sufficient* for virtue.

But knowledge is also *necessary* for virtue. Without it one is in no position to recognize which acts to perform in order to bring about a flourishing and healthy soul. Without knowledge of one's own good, one may also have no reason to act virtuously rather than viciously. Knowledge, then, is necessary and sufficient for virtue; this is Socratic intellectualism.

TWO COROLLARIES

Two corollaries of the virtue-is-knowledge doctrine need to be mentioned. The first is the Socratic view that wrongdoing is involuntary. If knowledge is sufficient for virtue, it is clear that no one ever does wrong except out of ignorance. It can only be because they failed to know their own good that they acted wrongly. This is the reason Socrates suggests that the wrongdoer is not in need of punishment, but of instruction. All people will willingly act virtuously if they know that doing so is in their own good.

The second corollary is the Socratic doctrine of the unity of virtues. According to this doctrine anyone who is courageous is also holy, and anyone who is holy is just, and anyone just is temperate, and anyone temperate is courageous. Anyone who knows his or her own good and who knows that acting virtuously promotes his or her own good will act virtuously. Such a person, then, will act courageously in military affairs, in a holy way in religious affairs, temperately in personal affairs, and justly in social affairs. Anyone who has one of the virtues has them all.

We have seen that Socrates does have a number of superficial similarities with the Sophists (a less than positive view of his contemporaries' professions of knowledge and a concern with human activities and institutions). But though he is sometimes grouped among them (recall Aristophanes' portrait of Socrates), Socrates in fact is no Sophist. He does not engage in rhetorical displays for the sake of appearances. Rather he engages individual interlocutors in exchanges of short questions and answers in order to test their knowledge, learn from them if they have it, and encourage them to gain it if they do not. Nor is he an epistemological skeptic or nihilist. Despite his own genuine professions of ignorance, Socrates firmly believes in the possibility and, indeed, the value of the knowledge he lacks. Nor is he an immoralist. To the contrary, he argues that acting in accordance with the traditional Greek virtues promotes one's ultimate good. Acting in this way secures one's happiness.

Nevertheless, the Socratic response to the nihilism and immoralism of the Sophists raises certain difficulties of its own, only some of which we have mentioned in passing. How, for example, is the knowledge that Socrates and his various interlocutors apparently lack, and that Socrates continuously exhorts them to seek, to be gained? How plausible is it to think that knowledge is sufficient for virtue? Are there not numerous cases in which we know what would be good for us and yet fail to do it? We shall meet with these difficulties again.

Selected Readings

Brickhouse, T. C., and N. D. Smith. *Socrates on Trial*. Princeton: Princeton University Press, 1989.

Gulley, N. *The Philosophy of Socrates*. London: Macmillan, 1968.

Guthrie, W. K. C. *Socrates*. Cambridge: Cambridge University Press, 1971.

Irwin, T. *Plato's Moral Theory: The Early and Middle Dialogues*. Oxford: Oxford University Press, 1977.

Kraut, R. *Socrates and the State*. Princeton: Princeton University Press, 1984.

Robinson, R. *Plato's Earlier Dialectic*. 2d rev. ed. Oxford: Oxford University Press, 1953.

Santas, G. X. *Socrates: Philosophy in Plato's Early Dialogues*. Boston: Routledge & Kegan Paul, 1979.

Vlastos, G. *Socrates, Ironist and Moral Philosopher*. Ithaca, NY: Cornell University Press, 1991.

3

Plato

With *Plato (ca. 428–347 B.C.) our task becomes both easier and more difficult. Here we have, for the first time, a rather extensive body of work written by the philosopher's own hand. Here, too, there can be no question that what we are dealing with is philosophy. Indeed, as Alfred North Whitehead once remarked, "The safest general characterization of the whole of the Western philosophical tradition is that it consists of a series of footnotes to Plato." This is, of course, an exaggeration. Nevertheless, it does testify to Plato's philosophical importance.*

Although for the first time we have an extensive body of genuine philosophical prose, difficulties remain. First, almost none of Plato's philosophical prose is written in his own voice. As has been mentioned, Plato chose to write dialogues in which the main speaker is frequently Socrates. Plato himself is mentioned only three times in the dialogues (twice in the Apology, as being present at the trial and as being willing to serve with others as a security for a higher fine than Socrates himself was able to pay; and once in the Phaedo, *as being ill and so not present at Socrates' last day). Socrates is commonly taken to be speaking for Plato, at least in those dialogues in which Socrates is clearly the main speaker. But as we have seen in the previous chapter, this does not settle the matter. In Plato's dialogues Socrates does not always espouse the same view. Nevertheless, the views expressed by Socrates in the dialogues of the middle period have come to represent traditional Platonism, and so these dialogues will be the focus of the present chapter.*

Perhaps more challenging, however, is that with Plato philosophy begins to move into deeper waters. The issues become more abstract, the arguments more detailed, and the refinements more delicate. But, for many, this is what makes philosophy fun.

THE THEORY OF RECOLLECTION

Traditional Platonism can be seen as a response to a number of questions that arise concerning the Socratic view that Plato had espoused during his earlier period. One of these questions concerns Socratic method. As we have seen, Socrates concludes his *elenchos* by maintaining that the interlocutor fails to have the knowledge he is reputed to have and by encouraging the interlocutor to join him in the pursuit of the knowledge they both lack. The question is how is such a pursuit to be carried out. We get very little help with this question from the early dialogues themselves. Whenever the interlocutor appears to recognize his ignorance, the *elenchos* either shifts to another interlocutor (e.g., Laches), or the dialogue comes to an end (e.g., Nicias). But in the *Meno*, a transitional dialogue, things are different.

Meno's Paradox

The *Meno* begins just like any other early dialogue. Meno professes to know what virtue is and Socrates sets about testing that knowledge. After a series of failed attempts to say what virtue is, Meno admits to being at a loss (*aporia*). He contends that Socrates' sting has numbed both his mind and his tongue. Thereupon, Socrates, in his customary way, disavows his own knowledge and exhorts Meno to join him in the search for the knowledge that they both lack. But for the first time in the dialogues, Meno questions how such a search is to be carried out. The problem he suggests can be put as follows:

1. Either we know what we are searching for or we do not.

2. If we know what we are searching for, the search is pointless.

3. If we do not know what we are searching for, the search is impossible.

4. So, the search is either pointless or impossible.

The question, of course, is why should we accept 3. Meno argues that if we fail to know at all what something is, we will not know what to set up as the object of our search nor be able to recognize it should we come upon it. We will not know what to look for nor when we have found it.

Two things should be noted about this problem. First, it appears to be a paradox, not concerning learning or coming to know in general, but concerning *directed* learning or inquiry. The problem is not with coming to know something that one fails to know. Rather, it is with coming to know something that one is *trying* to come to know. Second, the paradox appears to depend upon a conception of knowledge in which it is an all-or-nothing affair: Either one knows everything about an object, in which case the search concerning it is pointless, or one knows nothing about it, in which case the search concerning it is impossible.

The Theory of the Priests and Priestesses

This second feature of the paradox seems to be what Plato fastens on in order to resolve it. Plato claims, in the person of Socrates, that the paradox can be resolved by appeal to a thesis espoused by various priests and priestesses. According to this thesis, learning is recollection. The idea seems to be that prior to being joined to a body, that is, prior to birth, the soul knows everything. However, the process of birth for some reason causes the soul to forget what it knows. Inquiry or search, then, is not an attempt to come to know something that one fails to know at all. Rather, it is an attempt to remember what one knows but has forgotten.

How this theory is supposed to resolve the paradox that led to its introduction is a difficult question. How, for example, can one set up an object that one has forgotten as the object one wants to remember? Or how can one recognize that *that* is what one is trying to remember? But Plato appears to take it to resolve the paradox and to do so rather surprisingly not by denying premise 3, but by denying premise 2. Plato leaves unchallenged the claim that trying to come to know something that one fails to know at all is impossible. What he challenges is that it is pointless to attempt to come to know what one knows. One might know it but have forgotten it.

The Conversation with the Slave-Boy

In response to Meno's request to explain this theory of recollection, Socrates proposes to illustrate the theory by means of a conversation. He asks one of Meno's slave-boys a question in the form of "What is F-ness?," only this time it is not an ethical concept Socrates is seeking, but a geometrical one. Socrates asks the slave-boy the question "What is the length of the side of a square that is double the area of a square whose side is two feet long?" The subsequent exchange of questions and answers between Socrates and the slave-boy falls into three parts.

In the first part, the slave-boy offers two misguided answers, that the length of the side of the double square is four feet long and that it is three feet long. After leading the slave-boy to see that neither of these answers will do, Socrates concludes this section by suggesting that the slave-boy is now at the stage where Meno was prior to raising his paradox. The slave-boy now recognizes that he does not know what the length of the side is. Thus,

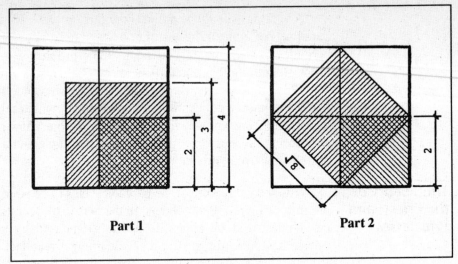

Part 1   Part 2

Fig. 3.1

we should expect the next part of the conversation to be the most relevant
to the paradox and the theory of recollection. In the second part, Socrates
leads the slave-boy through a series of questions and diagrams to see that
the length of the diagonal of the original, four-square-foot square is the
length of the side of the double, eight-square-foot square. At the end of this
part, Socrates concludes that the slave-boy now has a true belief concerning
the length of the side of the double square. He truly believes that it is the
length of the diagonal of the original square (see Fig. 3.1). In the third part,
which Socrates does not illustrate but describes, Socrates maintains that the
slave-boy's true belief concerning the side could be converted into
knowledge by asking him these same questions over and over again and in
various ways.

AN OBJECTION

Despite Socrates' repeated denials that he is teaching the slave-boy
anything and his insistence that the slave-boy unfailingly answers only
according to his own opinion, readers of this conversation have invariably
found fault with it. Socrates, they allege, is leading the slave-boy on with
his questions. What Plato needs to illustrate is a case in which someone, not
knowing, succeeds in the attempt to come to know *on his or her own*. What
Plato illustrates instead, however, is a case in which someone, not knowing,
is taught by someone who does know. It is true that the teaching is by means
of questions and answers, but it is teaching, not genuine inquiry, nonetheless.

This objection is understandable, but it misses an important point. We
would all accept that someone could set oneself the task of coming to know
the length of the side of the double square *on one's own* and succeed;

someone, no doubt, once did. Most of what we know about geometry originally came to be known in this way. Thus, while the conversation with the slave-boy may not succeed in illustrating genuine inquiry, let alone the theory of recollection, the question that Plato uses in this conversation is one which makes the possibility of genuine inquiry quite likely. This is all that Plato suggests he intended it to illustrate. At the end of the conversation, Socrates disowns the details of the theory of recollection and the conversation with the slave-boy; he claims only to be confident that we will be better, braver, and less idle if we search for what we fail to know, than if we believe that such search is impossible.

Phaedo

The theory of recollection also plays an important role in the *Phaedo*. This time, however, it is not introduced in order to solve a problem with searching for what one fails to know, but rather as a premise in one of four proofs for the immortality of the soul. If learning is recollection, Plato claims, then the soul is immortal (or more accurately, as is quickly pointed out by Socrates' interlocutors, Cebes and Simmias, then it exists prior to birth). But learning is recollection. So, the soul is immortal (or more accurately, the soul exists prior to birth).

While Plato refers to illustrations like the one we have considered in the *Meno*, he also offers a quite different argument for the premise that learning is recollection. The idea seems to be that in order to experience equal sticks and stones one must have had knowledge of equality prior to one's birth. The argument goes something like this:

1. If A judges that x is deficient to y at a given time t, then A knew y before t.

2. If A experiences equal things (x), then A judges those things (x) to be deficient to equality (y).

3. So, if A experiences equal things (x) at t, then A knew equality (y) before t.

4. Knowledge of equality is acquired during life only from the experience of equal things.

5. So, knowledge of equality could not have been acquired between the moment of birth and one's first experience of equal things.

6. So, if A experiences equal things (x), then there is some time (t) prior to A's birth at which A acquired the knowledge of equality (y).

7. So, if A acquires knowledge of equality for the first time in this life (i.e., if A learns equality), then A knew equality before (i.e., A recollects equality).

We will return to this argument when we consider Plato's theory of Forms in the next section. For now notice that Plato appears to be restricting the sorts of things that can be recollected. He does not maintain in this argument that we recollect things like equal sticks or equal stones. We did not know prior to birth, and now just recollect, that these two sticks are equal. Rather, what we recollect, and so come to know in this life is equality or what equality is. Plato also mentions in this context things such as the greater and the smaller, beauty, goodness, justice, and holiness. Thus, just as in the *Meno*, Plato maintains that the sorts of things we can recollect, and so inquire into, are the answers to Socrates' "What is F-ness?" questions. Knowledge of this is what the soul has prior to being born, forgets upon being born, and recollects as a result of inquiry.

Republic

The final passage to consider in trying to come to terms with Plato's views concerning knowledge is the end of the fifth book of the *Republic*. Plato distinguishes three kinds of mental states: knowledge, belief, and ignorance. Plato also distinguishes three kinds of objects that correspond to these mental states: "things that are," "things that are and are not," and "things that are not." (Notice that these three kinds of objects correspond exactly with Parmenides' "three possibilities.")

The Epistemological "Two-Worlds" Theory. A common way of reading this passage is that Plato is arguing for a sort of epistemological "two-worlds" theory, according to which knowledge is restricted to one world, the world of the "things that are," while belief is restricted to the other world, the world of the "things that are and are not." (Ignorance, being restricted to the "things that are not," or nothing, has no world corresponding to it.) The "things that are" are things such as equality, beauty, justice, and holiness—once again the things concerning which Socrates raises his "What is F-ness?" question. The "things that are and are not" are common objects that we sense, such as equal sticks and stones, beautiful statues, or just people or actions. One way to understand this restriction is that Plato is denying that one can have knowledge of ordinary contingent facts about the world. (Contingent facts are facts that might have been otherwise.) One cannot know, for example, that Pericles (an object of our senses) is a fine statesman. Facts like this can only be believed. They might have been otherwise. Knowledge is restricted to necessary truths, such as: (1) the length of the side of a square double the area of a four-square-foot square is the length of the diagonal of the original square; or (2) courage is a virtue. These facts can be known, but not believed. Plato might have been led to such a view by confusing the claim that it is necessary that whatever is known is true with the claim that whatever is known is necessarily true.

One difficulty for this understanding of Plato is that it appears to fly in the face of the passage we have just discussed in the *Meno*. As we have seen, Plato there appears to hold that true belief can be converted into knowledge, suggesting that the objects of true belief and knowledge are not distinct. Perhaps Plato has simply changed his view in the *Republic*. The *Meno* does, after all, have many of the features of an early dialogue. Or perhaps we have misunderstood Plato's view in the *Meno*.

A third possibility is that Plato is not committed to an epistemological "two-worlds" theory. Rather, what Plato is arguing for in Book 5 of the *Republic* is the epistemological priority of the "things that are." That is, knowledge of equality, beauty, justice and the rest of the "things that are" is necessary for sensory knowledge—equal sticks, beautiful statues, and just people or acts, but not vice versa. Some confirmation for this possibility might be found in Socrates' apparent endorsement of such a view in the earlier dialogues. Indeed, it may have been one of the motivations for his concern with definitions. But however we understand this passage from the *Republic*, it is clear that for Plato "the things that are" are in some way essential for the pursuit of knowledge.

THE THEORY OF FORMS

What are these "things that are" according to Plato? Remember that in asking the "What is F-ness?" question Socrates is looking for the thing that all things of the relevant sort, and only those things, have in common and that makes those things what they are. For example, in asking the question "What is virtue?", Socrates is looking for the thing that all virtuous actions or people share, that only virtuous actions or people share, and that makes those virtuous actions or people virtuous. One might wonder, however, whether there is any such thing. Meno, for example, at one point suggests that there is not. At the beginning of the dialogue named for him, Meno implies that the thing that makes a man virtuous is different than the thing that makes a woman virtuous, or that makes a child or a slave virtuous. Socrates, however, simply insists that the same thing makes a man, a woman, a child, and a slave virtuous.

Plato's theory of Forms provides the theory behind Socrates' insistence. Plato's Forms are the "things that are." They are what Socrates is looking for in asking his "What is F-ness?" question. Forms provide the objects which are known prior to birth in order to justify Socrates' undefended insistence that once we recognize our ignorance we can successfully search for what we fail to know. Similarly, Forms provide the objects which satisfy the constraints of the "What is F-ness?" question to justify Socrates' undefended insistence that the question he asks has a unique answer.

To begin to see what sorts of things these Forms—which do so much work for Plato—are, we can turn to the *Phaedo*, the dialogue in which Plato depicts Socrates' last day. In this dialogue Socrates offers four arguments for the immortality of the soul (the "Cyclical Argument," the "Recollection Argument," the "Affinity Argument," and the "Final Argument"), the last three of which make essential use of Forms.

"Recollection Argument"

In the "Recollection Argument," Plato distinguishes between sensibles and Forms, the former serving to remind us of the latter. Thus, Plato claims that upon sensing equal sticks and stones we are reminded of Equality. Plato argues for this distinction between sensibles and Forms on the grounds that equal sticks and stones can appear equal to one person and unequal to another, while Equality never appears to be Inequality to anyone. The relationship between the equal sticks and stones and Equality appears to be one of resemblance. The equal sticks and stones strive to be like Equality, but fall short of it. Immediately upon perceiving these sensible equals, we apparently judge them to be deficient to Equality. Plato concludes this argument by claiming that what he has argued for in the case of Equality applies to other Forms as well, for example, to the Greater, the Smaller, Beauty, Goodness, Justice, and Holiness (capitalized to denote Forms).

"Affinity Argument"

In the next argument Plato attempts to prove the immortality of the soul by arguing that the soul is like the Forms and the Forms are immortal, so the soul is immortal. The argument goes something like this.

1. Something is incomposite (not composed of parts) just insofar as it is likely to survive.

2. Something is constant and unvarying just insofar as it is likely to be incomposite.

3. Forms are constant and unvarying; sensibles vary and are never constant.

4. So, Forms are likely to survive and sensibles are not likely to survive.

5. Forms are invisible and sensibles are visible.

6. The soul is invisible and the body is visible.

7. So, the soul is similar to the Forms and the body to the sensibles.

8. The soul studies Forms when not interfered with by the body, otherwise it studies sensibles.

9. So, the soul is similar to the Forms, the body to the sensibles.

10. The soul should be master, the body slave.

11. So, the soul is similar to the Forms, the body to the sensibles.

12. So, the soul is likely to survive, the body is not.

However we judge the particular merits of this argument (and Simmias and Cebes are quick to point out that the analogy is not strict), it abounds with information pertinent to Plato's Forms. For example, the Forms have a number of properties reminiscent of the Parmenidean "One." They are constant, unvarying, incomposite, and immortal. The relationship between Forms and sensibles suggested by the master/slave analogy in (10) is difficult to interpret, but it may suggest (like the "Recollection Argument") that sensibles resemble Forms, in the way in which a copy resembles an original. The idea that the soul studies the Forms when not interfered with by the body conforms to our discussion of the theory of recollection. Apparently, whatever way the soul manages to come to know the Forms when disembodied is blocked when the soul is joined to a body. This is why Socrates claims earlier in the *Phaedo* that the true philosopher should want to die. The true philosopher loves wisdom, that is, knowledge of the Forms. This knowledge, however, can only be easily gained when the soul is disembodied, perhaps through some sort of direct mental perception.

"Final Argument"

Last, in an attempt to respond to Cebes' objection that Socrates has only proven that the soul is long-lasting, not immortal, Socrates offers his final argument for the immortality of the soul. This argument is too long and complex to attempt to summarize here, but it appeals to three features of Plato's theory of Forms that need to be mentioned.

Causation. First, Plato recommends a theory of causation according to which what causes something to be beautiful, for example, is its relationship to the Form of Beauty. We must be careful here because the Greek notion of cause is somewhat broader than our contemporary notion. (We will return to this issue in more detail when we discuss Aristotle's theory of four causes in the next chapter.) But there can be no question that, in some sense of cause, Plato takes Forms to be the causes of things being the way that they are.

Partaking of and Being Present in. Second, Plato indicates that he is unsure how exactly Forms are related to sensibles by offering two possibilities other than resemblance: partaking of and being present in. Thus, sensible equals are related to Equality either in the sense of resembling Equality, or partaking of Equality, or having Equality present in them.

Essentialism. Finally, Plato implies that some things are essentially related to certain Forms and not to others. Thus, for example, snow appears to be essentially related to Coldness (it would no longer be snow if it were not cold), but not to Whiteness (it would remain snow even if it were red).

Putting the Pieces Together

THE PARADIGM MODEL

When we survey these arguments in the *Phaedo*, we begin to get a picture of Plato's Forms that betrays what might be called a paradigm model. (A paradigm is a clear and indisputable example, often used as a standard against which to judge other instances. For example, the standard meter stick in Paris is a paradigm of something a meter long.) According to the paradigm model, Forms are just paradigmatic instances. Thus, for example, Equality is simply the perfect instance of equality. Equality is somehow perfectly equal, and all other things that are equal are approximations of Equality, perhaps in the same way that only the standard meter stick in Paris is exactly a meter long, while all other meter sticks approximate its length. Something is a meter long just insofar as its length sufficiently resembles the length of the standard meter stick in Paris. Similarly, something is beautiful just insofar as it sufficiently resembles the Form of Beauty.

This paradigm model of the Forms is indicated by Plato's repeated suggestion that sensibles somehow resemble Forms. Thus, the idea in the "Recollection Argument" that sensibles strive to be like Forms but fall short and so remain deficient, and the image/original analogy in the "Affinity Argument" both strongly recommend the analogy with the standard meter stick in Paris. But the paradigm model is also suggested in other ways. Consider, for example, Plato's contention that the Forms have the Parmenidean properties of constancy, invariance, incompositeness, and immortality. This suggests that Forms are simply more exalted entities of the same sort as sensibles. The analogy suggested here is with the distinction between the gods and humans or between masters and slaves, one that fits nicely with the image/original analogy suggested by the resemblance relation. Finally, the repeated idea that Forms are in some sense more knowable, having been known prior to birth and recollected in this life, suggests an ontological "two-worlds" view. The one world, the world of Forms, is inhabited by disembodied souls and perfect, paradigmatic instances of Justice, Beauty, and Equality. The other world, the ordinary common sense world, is inhabited by embodied souls and ordinary common sense physical and sensible objects, which pale in comparison with the objects they imitate. This ontological "two-worlds" view is corroborated by various passages from the *Phaedrus*, the *Symposium*, and the *Republic*.

Unfortunately the paradigm model of Forms is subject to a number of difficulties, some of which Plato details in the *Parmenides*. For example, the "Third Man Argument" (discussed below), which purports to refute the theory of Forms, may arise only because Forms are understood as paradigmatic instances. As a result, some readers of the Platonic dialogues have taken the *Parmenides* to testify to Plato's abandonment of the paradigm model of Forms (if not the entire theory). But there are indications already in the *Phaedo* that Plato is not entirely satisfied with such a model.

Consider, for example, the Forms that Plato appeals to in the arguments. They seem to fall into three groups: evaluative notions (Justice, Beauty, Holiness, and Goodness), relational notions (Equality, the Greater, the Smaller, Tallness, Shortness, Hotness, and Coldness), and mathematical notions (Oddness, Evenness, Oneness, and Twoness). Readers of the *Phaedo* have differed over the significance of these three groups, but the examples in the last two groups are especially difficult to square with the paradigm model. It is difficult to imagine, for example, what a paradigmatic instance of Shortness or Evenness could be like. Furthermore, remember that in the "Final Argument" Plato hestitates to endorse the resemblance relation between Forms and sensibles. The two alternative relations he suggests—partaking of and being present in—are again difficult to square with the paradigm model. The standard meter stick in Paris, for example, is in no obvious way present in any other meter sticks, nor do other meter sticks in any obvious way partake of the standard meter stick in Paris.

THE PROPERTY MODEL

These difficulties have led some to suggest that the arguments in the *Phaedo* in fact betray a different model of Forms—the property model. According to the property model, Forms are properties. They are what instances have in common, not instances themselves. Thus, they are objects of an importantly different type than the instances that have them. For example, Oddness is one of the things the numbers one, three, five, and seven have in common.

The property model, however, is incompatible with the paradigm model. According to the paradigm model, Forms are objects of the same type as their sensible instances. Indeed, they are paradigmatic instances. According to the property model, Forms are not objects of the same type as their sensible instances. They are what those instances have in common, not instances themselves. Plato is here struggling, for the first time, with an issue that will occupy a considerable amount of subsequent Western philosophy: the problem of universals. The door to the problem was opened by Socrates' "What is F-ness?" question, but it took the intellectual courage of Plato to attempt to close it.

THE THEORY OF JUSTICE

Let us return once more to Socrates. Recall that Socrates endorsed the thesis that knowledge is sufficient for virtue. We saw that this thesis depended on the undefended claim that happiness, which is the end of all human action, requires a virtuous soul. But why, one might ask, should we think that happiness requires a virtuous soul? Indeed, why should we desire a virtuous soul at all? Put differently, why be virtuous?

This is the question that Plato devotes himself to in the *Republic*, although he does so by focusing more narrowly on the question "Why be just?" In providing an answer to this question, Plato once again builds on and goes beyond his Socratic legacy. In the course of answering this question, Plato manages to sidestep the dubious Socratic claim that no one ever fails to do what one knows is good for one. For Plato, as for many others, weakness of the will (knowing what is good for one and yet failing to do it) is an undeniable fact of human nature.

Thrasymachus' Account of Justice

The *Republic* begins like many other of Plato's dialogues. Socrates is concerned to find an answer to the question "What is justice?," and a number of answers are suggested. After both Cephalus' and Polemarchus' attempts to answer this question are abandoned, Thrasymachus offers the answer that justice is the advantage of the stronger. What Thrasymachus means by this is not completely clear. (Indeed, Cleitophon attempts to explain to Socrates what Thraysmachus meant, and Thrasymachus denies that he meant any such thing.) But the idea seems to be that justice is bad for the agent (the performer of the just act) and good for someone else. It is good for the stronger, who would punish the agent if he or she failed to act so as to benefit the stronger. Only in this rather diluted sense does justice benefit the agent. It keeps him or her from suffering at the hands of the stronger. In every other way it benefits the one who would punish, not the agent him- or herself.

Acting justly, then, for Thrasymachus, is neither admirable nor desirable. It either means that one is weak and so unable to act so as to genuinely benefit oneself, that is, to act unjustly, or that one is freely acting against one's own advantage. Socrates offers three arguments against this definition of justice that suffice to make Thrasymachus succumb. But Plato is apparently not satisfied with them, for the dialogue does not end here. Rather, in the next book of the *Republic*, Glaucon and Adeimantus unenthusiastically enlist in the Thrasymachean cause.

GLAUCON'S AND ADEIMANTUS' CHALLENGE

Glaucon and Adeimantus both express their dissatisfaction with Socrates' arguments against Thrasymachus. They are sympathetic with Socrates' defense of justice but they challenge Socrates to do better.

The Classification of "Goods." Glaucon begins the challenge by distinguishing between three kinds of "goods": (1) "goods" which are desired not because of their consequences but for their own sake, such as joy and harmless pleasures; (2) "goods" which are desired for their own sake and for their consequences, such as knowledge, sight, and health; and (3) "goods" which are desired for their consequences but not for their own sake, such as physical training, treatment for sickness, and various ways of making money. Glaucon and Socrates agree that the second kind of "goods" is the best kind and that justice belongs to that kind. Glaucon claims, however, that the Thrasymachean view, and indeed the common-sense view, is that justice belongs to the third kind of "goods." Claucon challenges Socrates to show that justice belongs, not to this third kind, but to the second kind of "goods."

The connection between Glaucon's classification of "goods" and the Thrasymachean account of justice appears to be this: According to Thrasymachus, people desire to be just only to avoid the consequences that the stronger imposes on those who are unjust. Thus, parents exhort their children to be just in order to avoid the ill repute imposed by the stronger society as a whole or to avoid an unpleasant life in the underworld imposed by the stronger gods on the unjust. A consequence of this view of justice is that all that one really desires is the appearance of justice, not justice itself. For as long as one appears to the stronger as just, one will avoid the unwelcome consequences that actually being just is intended to avoid.

Gyges' Ring. This is why Glaucon introduces the story of Gyges' ring, a ring which reputedly enabled its bearer to become invisible at will. Someone with such a ring can appear to be just while actually being unjust simply by always committing unjust acts while invisible. Such a person can reap the rewards of appearing to be just (for example, avoid the unwelcome consequences that the stronger impose on those who act unjustly), as well as the rewards of being unjust (for example, ill-gotten gain). What Socrates must show in order to satisfactorily defeat Thrasymachus is that such a person will choose to be just, not merely to appear just. What Socrates must show, Glaucon and Adeimantus claim, is that justice is desired not simply for its consequences (which could be accomplished simply by appearing just) but for itself (which could not). This is the challenge that Plato attempts to meet in the remaining books of the *Republic*.

The Definition of Justice

Plato attempts to meet this challenge in a characteristically Socratic way. He has Socrates claim that he must discover what justice is before he can show that justice is a "good" that is desirable both for its consequences and for its own sake.

JUSTICE IN THE CITY

To do this Socrates proposes that it will be easier to look for justice in the city than in the individual (because the former is larger and so easier to "see" than the latter) and sets out to describe the ideal city. This city, as Socrates presents it, is composed of three distinct classes of citizens. First, there are the workers, who provide the city with the goods and services necessary for its proper maintenance. Second, there are the auxiliaries or soldiers, who protect the city against external attack. And, finally, there are the guardians or rulers, who rule the city.

By the middle of Book 4 of the *Republic*, Socrates maintains that he has adequately described the ideal city and proposes to investigate wherein the city's justice lies. According to Socrates, since the city has been rightly founded, it follows that it is completely good. It has all of the virtues. The city is wise, courageous, temperate, and just. Therefore, Socrates maintains, if after having specified what the city's wisdom, courage, and temperance amount to there remains something good in the city, the good that remains is justice.

Wisdom, Socrates contends, is located in the guardian class and is the knowledge of guardianship. Courage is located in the auxiliary class and is the true belief concerning what is to be feared and what is not to be feared. Temperance is spread throughout the city and is the natural harmony and agreement concerning who should rule. What is left, then, according to Socrates, that makes the city good is the fact that each class of citizens performs its own task. This, then, Socrates concludes, is justice in the city. Justice, like temperance, is spread throughout the city and is the performance of its own task by each class of citizens. Justice in the city is the rulers ruling, the soldiers soldiering, and the workers working.

JUSTICE IN THE INDIVIDUAL

Now that justice in the city has been found Socrates proposes next to look for justice in the individual, that is, justice in the soul. Socrates maintains that if the soul consists of three parts in the same way that the city consists of three classes, then justice in the individual will be just like justice in the city. It will be each of the parts of the soul performing its own task. Thereupon, Plato, through the person of Socrates, sets out to show that the soul does indeed consist of three parts in the same way as the city consists of three classes of citizens. The argument that Socrates offers relies on the following principle: Nothing can ever be affected, or be, or act in opposite ways, at the same time, in the same part of itself, in relation to the same object.

Parts of the Soul. First, Socrates points out that individuals sometimes desire, at the same time, to drink and not to drink the same liquid (when, for example, they are thirsty and yet know that the liquid in the glass is poisoned). It follows, Socrates contends, that there must be two parts of the soul: the purely desiring part (the appetite), which desires to drink because it is thirsty, and the reasoning part (the reason), which desires not to drink because it knows that the liquid is poisoned. The reason, as this example makes clear, naturally rules the appetite. Second, Socrates points out that there is yet a third part of the soul that is distinct from the appetite—the spirit. Socrates illustrates the spirit part of the soul by appealing to a certain Leontius who apparently had a strong desire to view dead bodies on a field of battle and yet, at the same time, was angry with himself for this desire. Third, Socrates contends that this spirit part is distinct from reason, although closely allied with it, on the grounds that children are often full of spirit before they possess reason. Thus, Socrates concludes that the soul does consist of three parts in the same way as the city consists of three classes: reason, which is naturally suited to rule; spirit, which is naturally allied to reason; and appetite, which provides for the proper maintenance of the individual. Justice in the individual, then, is each part of the soul performing its own task: reason ruling, spirit courageously defending the dictates of reason against the cravings of appetite, and appetite desiring.

Weakness of the Will. We can see how, in this portion of the *Republic*'s argument, Plato has gone beyond Socrates in making room for the possibility of weakness of the will. For Plato, it is possible, in the case of an individual with an unjust soul, to know what is good for one and yet fail to do it. Someone whose soul is not properly ordered, whose appetite, for example, is ruling rather than his or her reason, may succumb to the desire to drink the liquid even when he or she knows it is poisoned.

The Desirability of Justice

Now that we have discovered what justice in the individual is, Socrates proposes that we return to the question which initiated this discussion, whether justice is desirable for its own sake. At the beginning of Book 5, however, Glaucon and Adeimantus press Socrates to fill in more of the details of the ideal city, and it is not until the beginning of Book 8 that the main question of the *Republic* is broached anew.

THE DEGENERATION OF THE IDEAL CITY

In returning to this question, Socrates begins by recounting the degeneration of the ideal city. Socrates maintains that the ideally just city, in which the rulers rule (a monarchy or aristocracy), first degenerates into a timocracy, in which the auxiliary class rules. A timocracy next degenerates into an oligarchy, in which the workers rule in a controlled way. All workers subordinate their own self-interest to the pursuit of money so that their own self-interest might be more readily obtained. An oligarchy next degenerates into a democracy, in which the workers rule without control. Each worker pursues his or her own self-interest. Finally, a democracy degenerates into a tyranny, in which one worker rules. Five types of individuals correspond to these five types of cities: the wisdom-loving individual (the philosopher), in whom reason rules; the honor-loving individual, in whom spirit rules; the money-loving individual, in whom the appetites rule in a controlled way; the freedom-loving individual, in whom the appetites rule without control; and finally the tyrannical individual, in whom one of the appetites rules (for example, a gluttonous individual). Given this as background, Socrates sets out in Book 9 three distinct arguments for the thesis that justice is desirable for its own sake.

THREE ARGUMENTS

First, Socrates claims that if we keep in mind the happiness of the entire city, the tyrannical city is clearly the most unhappy. So, if we keep in mind the happiness of the entire individual, the soul ruled by one appetite is the most unhappy. The most unjust is the most unhappy and the most just is the happiest. Notice that if this argument is successful the happiness that accrues to the just person (when justice is understood as each part of the soul performing its own task) would not result from the mere appearance of justice. If one merely appeared to have a soul in which each part of the soul performed its own task, but in fact did not have such a soul, one would not be happy. The happiness that accrues to the just person, according to this argument, does not result from the contingent rewards or punishments which might be externally imposed. Rather, it results from the very nature of justice itself. In this sense, then, justice, understood as each part of the soul performing its own task, is desirable for its own sake.

Second, Socrates proposes that corresponding to the three parts of the soul are three unique pleasures. The individual in whom reason rules judges his or her life to be the most pleasant. The individual in whom spirit rules judges his or her life to be the most pleasant, and the individual in whom appetite rules judges his or her life to be the most pleasant. Only the first individual, however, has experienced all three pleasures. Only the first individual, then, is a qualified and expert judge. But the only qualified and expert judge—the individual in whom reason rules—judges his or her life to be most pleasant. Thus, the just individual's life is the most pleasant. Notice again that the pleasure that results from being just results not from the mere appearance of justice, nor from contingent rewards and punishments externally imposed, but from the very nature of justice itself. In this sense, then, justice, understood as each part of the soul performing its own task, has once again been shown to be desirable for its own sake.

Finally, Socrates distinguishes among pleasure, pain, and a middle state that is neither pleasure nor pain. This middle state is the state one is in when one no longer experiences pleasure or pain. Thus, for example, when one removes one's hand from a fire one feels pleasure. But according to Socrates this is not genuine pleasure. It is merely absence of pain. Next, Socrates contends that the pleasure associated with all but the wisdom-loving person is not genuine pleasure, but rather this middle state of absence of pain. Thus, for example, the pleasure of the honor-loving individual is merely absence of envy. Thus, once again, the pleasure that results from being just results from the very nature of justice, and so, once again, justice has been shown to be desirable for its own sake.

CONSEQUENCES OF JUSTICE

At this point, however, one might wonder whether justice, understood as each part of the soul performing its own task, can be plausibly thought to be desirable for its consequences. What reason is there to think that the just person, so understood, would attain the reward of good repute, for example, or avoid various punishments? This may be why, in Book 10 of the *Republic*, Plato has Socrates relate the myth of Er. A feature of this myth is that those who are just, in the sense exhibited in Book 4, will reap numerous rewards and avoid ghastly punishments in the afterworld. By the end of Book 10 of the *Republic*, then, Plato has done what he set out to do. He has shown that justice is a "good" desired both for its consequences and for its own sake. Glaucon's and Adeimantus' challenge has been met.

THE LATER DIALOGUES

Readers of Plato's later dialogues have tended to view them as critical self-evaluations of the theory espoused in the middle period. Thus, for example, dialogues like the *Sophist*, the *Statesman*, and the *Philebus* examine the structural relations that hold among the Forms themselves, which has led some readers to understand those dialogues as modifying the theory of Forms found in the middle dialogues. In the *Theaetetus*, Plato attempts to answer the question "What is knowledge?" in a way that seems to virtually ignore the vital role of Forms in Platonic epistemology. In the *Laws*, Plato offers a more practical solution to the proper founding of a political society. In the *Parmenides*, however, special problems for understanding Plato arise; in it Plato offers a series of quite persuasive arguments apparently designed to refute the theory of Forms, perhaps the most famous of which is the "Third Man Argument."

The "Third Man Argument"

The "Third Man Argument" depends on three theses testified to in our brief sketch of the theory of Forms. The first is the one-over-many thesis, according to which there exists a Form, F-ness, for every set of F-things that makes those things F. For example, in the *Meno*, Socrates postulates the Form of Virtue (F-ness) which makes virtuous people or actions (F-things) virtuous (F). The second is the distinctness thesis, according to which the Form that makes the F-things F is distinct from the F-things themselves. For example, in the *Phaedo*, we saw Plato arguing that the Form of Equality (F-ness), which the sensible equals (F-things) strived to be like was distinct from the sensible equals themselves. Finally, the third is the self-predication thesis, according to which the Form which makes the F-things F is itself F. For example, on the paradigm model of Forms, the Form of Equality is a perfect instance of Equality. Equality (F-ness) is (perfectly) equal (F) and Justice (F-ness) is (perfectly) just (F). Given these three theses, Plato argues that an infinite regress of Forms can be generated.

Assume that there exists a set of men (F-things). It follows from the one-over-many thesis that there exists the Form Man-ness (F-ness), which makes those men, men. From the distinctness thesis it follows that Man-ness is distinct from those men, that is, Man-ness is not itself a member of that set of men, and yet from the self-predication thesis it follows that Man-ness is itself a man. Thus, we have a new set of men, the original set plus Man-ness, which in turn requires the existence of the Form Man-ness^2 that makes these men, men. But Man-ness^2 is distinct from the men it explains and is itself a man. Thus, we have a new set of men and a new Form, Man-ness^3, and so on, ad infinitum.

It is very difficult to assess this argument. Some readers, for example, have taken it as Plato's attempt to warn the reader away from a mistaken understanding of his theory of Forms. Other readers have taken it as testifying to Plato's abandonment of the theory of Forms. Aristotle apparently took the argument to be a persuasive refutation of the theory. However we take it, it serves as a monument to Plato's philosophical subtlety and expertise.

With Plato, then, we have the complete philosophical perspective. Plato has offered us a comprehensive epistemology, metaphysics, and ethics, whose centerpiece is an intricately detailed theory of Forms. He has put forward his philosophy in light of, indeed frequently in response to, his philosophical predecessors, the most influential of whom is his mentor Socrates. Nor has he put forward his views dogmatically. Rather, he has provided them with intricate and subtle arguments and defenses. Indeed, he has even subjected them to his own exquisite critical scrutiny. Perhaps it would not be too much of an exaggeration to regard Plato as the Form of a philosopher.

Selected Readings

Annas, J. *Introduction to Plato's* Republic. Oxford: Oxford University Press, 1981.

Guthrie, W. K. C. *A History of Greek Philosophy: Plato, the Man and His Dialogues: Early Period.* Cambridge: Cambridge University Press, 1975.

_____. *A History of Greek Philosophy: The Later Plato and the Academy.* Cambridge: Cambridge University Press, 1978.

Irwin, T. *Plato's Moral Theory: The Early and Middle Dialogues.* Oxford: Oxford University Press, 1977.

Patterson, R. *Image and Reality in Plato's Metaphysics.* Indianapolis: Hackett, 1985.

Prior, W. J. *Unity and Development in Plato's Metaphysics.* La Salle, IL: Open Court, 1985.

Vlastos, G. *Platonic Studies.* 2d rev. ed. Princeton: Princeton University Press, 1981.

White, N. P. *Plato on Knowledge and Reality.* Indianapolis: Hackett, 1976.

4

Aristotle

Aristotle (384–322 B.C.) is perhaps the most influential of all the ancient Greek philosophers. His influence spans twenty-three centuries and innumerable fields. Descendants of Aristotelian physics and astronomy dominated the science of the Western world up to the Copernican Revolution in the sixteenth century A.D. Aristotelian syllogistic logic was the prevailing logic up to the nineteenth century A.D. and is still being taught in many introductory courses. Portions of Aristotle's philosophy of mind, metaphysics, and ethics have forceful adherents today. In fact his influence is so ubiquitous and far-ranging that he has been known simply as the Philosopher. Given his scope and influence, it will be impossible to deal completely with Aristotle in this chapter. As a result, the focus will be the core of Aristotelian philosophy, Aristotle's ontology. Aristotle's view of what things there are and how they are related to each other—his ontology—both informs and is informed by nearly every other aspect of his philosophy. We will see that this is true in the particular cases of his physics, his theory of the soul (or philosophy of mind), and his ethics.

WORKS

Like Plato, Aristotle published a number of philosophical dialogues. Unfortunately, they all have been lost, except for bits and pieces quoted by later writers. The works from which we must glean Aristotle's philosophical views were not written for public consumption, and, as a result, their nature has been widely disputed. They appear to represent lecture notes (either by Aristotle's own hand or by his students') or textbooks designed to accompany Aristotle's lectures given in his school. In either case, they were clearly subject to frequent revision and were seldom composed with an eye to readability. As a result, they are often difficult to decipher. Nevertheless, they contain a wealth of philosophical wisdom and inspiration.

The sheer size of Aristotle's body of work is enormous, as is the breadth of its scope. Because of the nature of these works (especially the frequency with which they were revised), however, their order of composition is very difficult to determine and hence controversial. As a result, it is preferable to list the works topically rather than chronologically:

I. The Dialogues
   Eudemus
   Protrepticus
   On Philosophy
   On the Good
   On the Ideas

II. Logical Treatises (The *Organon*)
   Categories
   De Interpretatione (On Interpretation)
   Prior Analytics
   Posterior Analytics
   Topics
   De Sophisticis Elenchis (On Sophistical Refutations)

III. Physical Treatises
   Physics
   De Caelo (On the Heavens)
   De Generatione et Corruptione (On Generation and Corruption)
   Meteorologica (Meterology)

IV. Psychological Treatises
   De Anima (On the Soul)
   Parva Naturalia (Short Natural Treatises)

V. Natural History Treatises
   Historia Animalium (History of Animals)
   De Partibus Animalium (On the Parts of Animals)
   De Motu Animalium (On the Movement of Animals)
   De Incessu Animalium (On the Progression of Animals)
   De Generatione Animalium (On the Generation of Animals)

VI. Metaphysics
VII. Ethical and Aesthetical Treatises
  Magna Moralia (The Great Ethics)
  Eudemian Ethics
  Nicomachean Ethics
  Politics
  Rhetoric
  Poetics

THE CATEGORIES

Objections to Platonism

Aristotle began his formal philosophical training as a member of Plato's school in Athens (known as the Academy). He remained there for nineteen years, until Plato's death. After a series of shorter engagements (perhaps the most famous of which was serving as tutor to the future Alexander the Great from 342 to 340 B.C.), Aristotle returned to Athens and formed a rival school (known as the Lyceum). We should not be surprised, then, to discover that Aristotle was very much interested in the same sorts of questions that exercised Plato, nor that Aristotle frequently offers his own distinctive solutions to those questions. Indeed, throughout Aristotle's work, one frequently finds Aristotle raising a problem, describing his predecessors' (especially Plato's) solutions, detailing the difficulties with these solutions, and recommending his own.

UNIVERSALS

One place where both the Platonic influence and the Aristotelian reaction are prominent concerns the problem of universals. As we have seen, one of the questions that exercises Plato (under the influence of Socrates) concerns what sort of thing it is that makes all and only holy things holy or all and only human things human. We have seen that Plato attempts to answer this question by appealing to his theory of Forms. According to this theory, things are holy just in case they are related in some appropriate way to the independently existing Form of Holiness, and things are human just in case they are similarly related to the independently existing Form of Humanity. Aristotle, however, believes that Plato's theory of Forms tends to raise more problems than it solves.

Aristotle maintains that by postulating a distinct world of Forms Plato has only managed to move the problem from one world to another. It is as if, Aristotle proposes, someone who wanted to count things thought it could not be done while there were only a few and so added to their number. Aristotle also seems to think that even with this proliferation of entities there remain questions that the theory on its own terms is unable to resolve.

Essential and Accidental Properties. For example, common sense and Plato's own theory (recall the "Final Argument" from the *Phaedo*) require that the way in which Socrates is related to the Form of Humanity is different from the way in which Socrates is related to the Form of Holiness, or the way in which snow is related to the Form of Coldness is different from the way in which it is related to the Form of Whiteness. Socrates is necessarily human and snow is necessarily cold, but Socrates might not have been holy and snow might not be white. We might say that Humanity and Coldness are essential (or necessary) properties of Socrates and snow, respectively, while Holiness and Whiteness are accidental (or contingent) properties. But how, Aristotle wonders, can Plato's theory of Forms account for this distinction between essential properties and accidental ones? According to the theory of Forms, Socrates is human and snow is cold, and Socrates is holy and snow is white because Socrates and snow are somehow related (either by partaking of, having present in, or resembling) the relevant Forms. Whatever the relationship is between Socrates and Humanity, for example, it is the same relationship that holds between Socrates and Holiness.

The Fourfold Division

The *Categories* is Aristotle's first attempt to find a response to the problem of universals not subject to the objections with which he finds Plato's theory of Forms burdened. In the second chapter, Aristotle maintains that there are four kinds of "things that are." There are, he says: (1) the things that are *said of* a subject but not *present in* a subject (e.g., human); (2) things that are present in a subject but not said of a subject (e.g., an individual knowledge of grammar); (3) things that are both said of and present in a subject (e.g., knowledge of grammar); and (4) things that are neither said of nor present in a subject (e.g., an individual human).

What exactly Aristotle has in mind here is difficult to determine, but it is clear that his fourfold division is a result of postulating two distinct relations that can hold between entities, the said-of (or predication) relation and the present-in (or inherence) relation. The examples that Aristotle provides in this chapter suggest the following picture.

First, some things, such as human, are said of things such as individual humans, but are not present in anything. For example, human is said of Socrates ("Socrates is a human"), but human is not present in anything. Second, things such as individual knowledge of grammar or individual white are present in things such as individual humans or horses but not said of anything. For example, the knowledge that *often* is an adverb is present in Socrates ("Socrates knows that *often* is an adverb"), or a particular whiteness (either a particular shade of whiteness or a whiteness unique to Bucephalus, Alexander the Great's favorite horse) is present in Bucephalus ("Bucephalus is white"), but neither of these things are said of anything. Third, things such as knowledge of grammar or color are both said of things such as individual knowledge of grammar or individual white and are present in things such as individual humans or individual horses. Thus, for example, knowledge of grammar is said of the particular knowledge that *often* is an adverb ("Knowledge that *often* is an adverb is knowledge of grammar") and is present in Socrates ("Socrates knows grammar"), and color is said of Bucephalus' whiteness ("Bucephalus' whiteness is a color") and is present in Bucephalus ("Bucephalus is colored"). Finally, things such as individual humans (Socrates) and individual horses (Bucephalus) are neither said of nor present in anything.

The Tenfold Division

As though things were not difficult enough, in the fourth chapter of the *Categories*, Aristotle draws yet another distinction that must be superimposed on the fourfold distinction in Chapter 2. This new distinction is tenfold. Some things, Aristotle says, are: (1) substances (e.g., human or horse); some are (2) quantities (e.g., four-foot); some are (3) qualities (e.g., white or knowledge of grammar); some are (4) relations (e.g., double); some are (5) places (e.g., in the Lyceum); some are (6) times (e.g., yesterday); some are (7) positions (e.g., sitting); some are (8) "havings" (e.g., having shoes on); some are (9) "doings" (e.g., cutting); and some are (10) "sufferings" (e.g., being cut). These are the so-called Aristotelian categories.

Elsewhere, Aristotle suggests that what led him to the postulation of these ten categories is connected to Socrates' preoccupation with the "What is F-ness?" question. In the *Topics*, Aristotle claims that the categories correspond to the different ways in which one might specify what a thing is. Thus, for example, depending on what is being targeted, one might respond to the question "What is that?" by saying "a substance," or "a quality," or "a place." When we put these two ontological divisions together, the new picture that begins to emerge from the *Categories* looks something like the one found in Fig. 4.1.

Primary Substance

A review of this picture reveals two central features of Aristotle's ontological theory. First, the things that are neither said of nor present in anything else, such as Socrates and Bucephalus, (represented in Fig. 4.1 by bold and italic Xs) are nevertheless such that the other things are either said of them or present in them. In this way Aristotle appears to have made room for the distinction between essential properties and accidental properties, which Plato appeared unable to explain. Indeed, the examples we have used in explicating Aristotle's ontological picture support this suggestion. For example, Socrates may reasonably be thought of as essentially a human

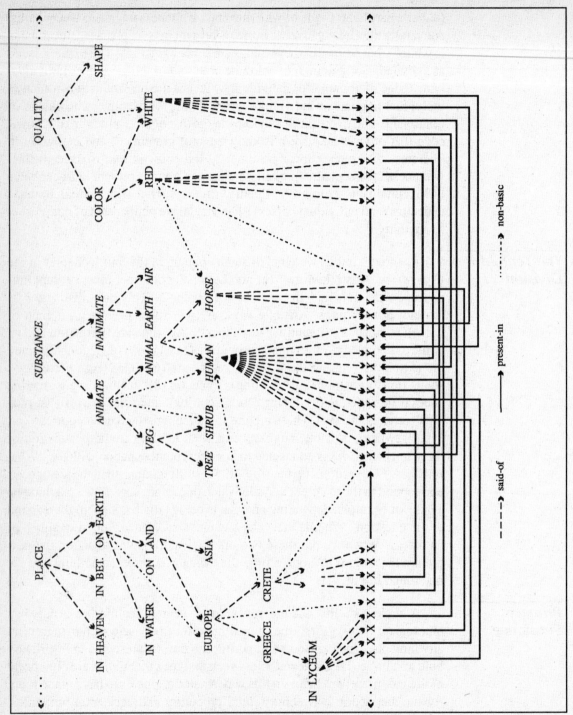

Fig. 4.1   The Ontological Picture of the Categories

(human is said of Socrates) and Bucephalus as essentially a horse (horse is said of Bucephalus), while Socrates accidentally knows that *often* is an adverb (knowledge that *often* is an adverb is present in Socrates), and Bucephalus is accidentally white (white is present in Bucephalus). Socrates would have still been Socrates even if he had failed to know that *often* is an adverb; he, perhaps, would not have still been Socrates if he had failed to be a human. Bucephalus would have still been Bucephalus if he had been brown but, perhaps, not if he had been a cow instead of a horse.

Second, everything else in the ontological picture has arrows running either directly or indirectly to those things that are neither said of nor present in everything else. This reflects Aristotle's view that those things have a certain ontological priority over everything else. In Chapter 5 of the *Categories*, Aristotle names these things (Socrates and Bucephalus, and the like) primary substances, both to distinguish them from the other things in the substance category (the secondary substances) and to underscore their ontological priority. As Aristotle puts it, "if the primary substances did not exist it would be impossible for any of the other things to exist."

Notice how different this ontological view is from the Platonic paradigm model. On the Platonic model, the ontological priority of Forms to the sensibles that partake of them cannot be overstated. Forms are models of which the sensibles are mere deficient copies. They exist independently from their sensibles, in a world inhabited only by other Forms and disembodied souls. Aristotle's picture owes much more to the property model suggested by such Platonic examples as Oddness and Shortness, although even here the emphasis is very different.

For Aristotle things such as Socrates and Bucephalus are the fundamental entities of the universe, not the properties that they have. Without them the properties would not exist. Indeed, many readers of Aristotle have thought that by denying the independent existence of properties or universals, Aristotle manages to avoid many of the objections raised against Platonism. Thus, for example, some have thought that by denying the independent existence of such things as knowledge of grammar, individual white, and human, Aristotle can avoid the "Third Man Argument" we considered in the previous chapter, either by denying the distinctness thesis or the self-predication thesis, or both.

HYLOMORPHISM

The Theory of Change

The ontological theory of the *Categories* also provides Aristotle with the apparatus to resolve one of the fundamental challenges in Greek philosophy. Recall that ever since Parmenides, the philosophers of ancient

Greece had been attempting to respond to his argument that change is impossible on the grounds that change requires reference to "what is not," which is impossible. The pluralists attempted to respond to this challenge by accepting that, in the case of the fundamental elements, change was indeed impossible. The appearance of change, however, could be explained by different mixtures or complexes of the fundamental elements. Plato seems to have responded to this challenge by relegating change to the world of sensibles. The ontologically prior Forms are unchangeable, just as Parmenides would have it.

Aristotle, however, appears to have taken the bull by the horns. In rehearsing the characteristics of primary substance in the fifth chapter of the *Categories*, Aristotle claims that the most distinctive characteristic of primary substances is that they are the only things capable of receiving contrary properties while remaining numerically one and the same. Socrates, for example, can be white at one time and dark at another, hot at one time and cold at another, or virtuous at one time and vicious at another. In the first book of the *Physics*, Aristotle lays out the details of this bold new theory of change.

ACCIDENTAL CHANGE

In Chapters 2 and 3 of Book 1 of the *Physics*, Aristotle attempts to refute the Parmenidean arguments against the possibility of change. In Chapter 7, he offers his own positive account of how change is possible. Aristotle considers a common-sense case of change: Socrates learning to play a musical instrument. This change can be described in any of the following ways:

1. The human becomes musical.
2. The unmusical becomes musical.
3. The unmusical human becomes the musical human.

Only the last description provides us with anything like a complete description. Only in that case are all three elements involved in every change—the two contraries, the *terminus a quo* "end from which" (unmusicalness) and the *terminus ad quem* "end to which" (musicalness), and the thing underlying the change, the *tertium quid* "third thing" (Socrates or the human)—explicitly called out. By noticing that there is a third thing underlying the change, as the third description makes clear, Aristotle purports to resolve the Parmenidean challenge. Change does not require reference to "what is not." Socrates is there all along. He simply goes from not having musicalness present in him to having musicalness present in him. Only the misleading nature of the second (and perhaps the first) description suggests otherwise.

POTENTIALITY/ACTUALITY

Two objections, however, might be raised against Aristotle's theory of change. First, it might be objected that while Aristotle provides us with "something that is" throughout the change, as the Parmenidean challenge requires, he does not completely eliminate all reference to "what is not." In referring to the unmusical or to musicalness not being present in Socrates, reference to "what is not" appears to have sneaked back in. The non-existence of musicalness appears to remain a feature of the change. Aristotle responds to this sort of objection by distinguishing between potential being and actual being. There is a sense, Aristotle claims, that musicalness "is" even at the beginning of the change. Socrates goes from being potentially (but not actually) musical to being actually musical. This is why, in the third book of the *Physics*, Aristotle defines change as "the actualizing of a potentiality as such."

SUBSTANTIAL CHANGE

The second objection which might be raised against Aristotle's theory of change concerns the cases of generation and destruction. Once again Aristotle does not accept the Parmenidean view that generation and destruction are impossible. But how can Aristotle's theory of change account for this kind of radical change? What are the three elements involved when Socrates is created or a tree is destroyed? In particular, what is the third thing underlying these changes?

When Aristotle claims in the *Categories* that primary substances are capable of receiving contrary properties while remaining one and the same, he does not mean that they are capable of receiving *any* contrary properties, at least not if we are correct in taking the said-of relation to represent an essential relation. Socrates cannot receive the contrary of being a human (if there were such a contrary) while remaining one and the same. If Socrates were to lose the property of being a human, Socrates would cease to be. So where is the thing that underlies the change? The ontological picture from the *Categories*, which nicely supplied the three elements required in accidental change, no longer suffices in the cases of generation and destruction.

The Bronze Statue. Aristotle responds to this challenge by considering the creation of a bronze statue of Socrates. The sculptor creates this statue by imposing a particular shape upon a lump of shapeless bronze. The bronze statue, thus, is a composite; it consists of two distinct elements. On the one hand, it consists of the bronze, the material out of which the sculptor creates the statue. On the other hand, it consists of a Socratic shape, the form that the sculptor imposes on the bronze. Notice that the bronze is present both before and after the creation of the statue. The bronze (or the matter) is the third thing underlying this case of change.

Similarly, according to Aristotle, natural primary substances (as opposed to artifacts such as bronze statues) are composites consisting of matter and form. This is Aristotle's hylomorphism. (*Hylomorphism* is formed from two Greek words: *hyle*, which means matter, and *morphe*, which means form. Hence, hylomorphism is Aristotle's matter/form analysis of primary substances.)

For example, Socrates consists of flesh and bones (his matter) and humanity (his form). When an unformed lump of flesh and bones has humanity somehow imposed on it, the primary substance, Socrates, is created. When Socrates somehow loses the form of humanity, when Socrates' flesh and bones lose their form, Socrates is destroyed. Notice again that the flesh and bones (the matter) is present throughout both the creation and destruction of Socrates. It is the third thing underlying the change.

Hylomorphism, then, provides Aristotle with the three elements required for generation and destruction: the privation (or the lack of form), the form, and the matter. Since in the cases of generation and destruction the matter gains and loses (respectively) an item from the substance category, this kind of change is frequently referred to as substantial (as opposed to accidental) change.

The Four Causes

Hylomorphism also plays an important role in Aristotle's doctrine of four causes elucidated in Chapter 3 of Book 2 of the *Physics*. According to Aristotle, we can be said to know a thing only when we know why it is—only, that is, when we know its cause. However, Aristotle maintains that there are four different kinds of causes: the material cause, the formal cause, the efficient cause, and the final cause.

The material cause of a thing is that out of which the thing comes to be. For example, the material cause of the bronze statue is the bronze. The formal cause of a thing is the account of what the thing is. Thus, the formal cause of an octave is the ratio two to one; of the statue, a shape representing Socrates; or of Socrates, humanity or rational animal. The efficient cause of a thing is its primary source of change or rest. For example, the efficient cause of the bronze statue is the sculptor; of Socrates, it is his father. The final cause is what the thing is for. For example, the final cause of walking after eating is health; the final cause of the bronze statue is to represent Socrates.

THE GREEK CONCEPTION OF CAUSE

Two features of this doctrine require further comment. First, Aristotle's notion of cause appears to be broader than our modern notion. Normally we do not think of the matter of something as a cause of it, nor of a thing that results from something (such as what the thing is for) as its cause. Perhaps the easiest way to explain this discrepancy between Aristotle's notion of cause and our own is simply to point out that an essential feature of the Greek word usually translated as *cause* in these contexts (*aition*) is the idea that it is what is responsible for something. Thus, when Aristotle says that to know something we need to know its cause, he means that we need to know all of the factors responsible for it. It seems quite appropriate to think that bronze and representing Socrates are two of the factors responsible for the bronze statue.

COINCIDENCE OF CAUSES

Second, and perhaps more importantly, is Aristotle's claim that in the case of ordinary natural organisms, the formal, the efficient, and the final causes coincide. For example, humanity is the formal, efficient, and final cause of Socrates. The idea seems to be that while being a human or being a rational animal is the form of Socrates, it is also what Socrates is for, in the sense that it is the end or goal of Socrates' being. The end of Socrates' growth or development is to make fully actual his form, just as the end of a developing oak tree is a fully formed oak tree. Humanity is also Socrates' efficient cause, in the sense that a human, Socrates' father, is Socrates' primary source of coming to be.

Teleology. This coincidence of causes suggests that underlying Aristotle's fourfold division lies a twofold division corresponding to his hylomorphism. On the one hand, the matter is responsible for the thing. On the other hand, the form is responsible for the thing (in virtue of its being the thing's form, the thing's efficient cause, and the thing's end). This twofold distinction is important because it provides Aristotle with a teleological view of the natural world. (*Teleology* is formed from two Greek words: *telos*, which means end or goal, and *logos*, which in this context means science or study of.) Since all natural primary substances are matter/form composites, they are all for something. They are for making fully actual their form. This is their function. This is their end.

BROADER IMPLICATIONS

Substance

The hylomorphism which becomes so prevalent in Aristotle's physical works has broad ranging implications outside these works. First, Aristotle apparently recognizes that it is far from clear how the matter/form analysis of concrete individuals such as Socrates and Bucephalus will fit into the ontological picture of the *Categories*. Where, for example, does matter in its various forms (flesh and bones, bronze, etc.) go in the ontological picture we looked at earlier? Perhaps more importantly, part of the argument for the ontological priority of things such as Socrates and Bucephalus in the

Categories seemed to depend on their being "individual and numerically one;" this in turn appeared to require that they were indivisible, without parts. But on the hylomorphic analysis these things turn out to be divisible into form and matter. The question naturally arises then whether these things retain their ontological priority given hylomorphism. Something like this question appears to be the question that Aristotle takes up in the seventh book of the *Metaphysics*.

CANDIDATES FOR PRIMARY SUBSTANCE

In Chapter 3 of Book 7 of the *Metaphysics*, Aristotle says that substance can refer to four things: First, substance can refer to the essence. The essence of something is the property or properties of the thing without which the thing would not be what it is. According to Aristotle, the essence is expressed by a definition of what the thing is. Second, substance can refer to the universal. A universal is something which belongs to a plurality of things. Third, substance can refer to the genus. Genera are things such as animal, which have under them species, such as human, horse, and cow (see Fig. 4.1). Finally, substance can refer to the subject. It can refer to the things that are neither said of nor present in anything else—the primary substance of the *Categories*. The subject, Aristotle maintains, is thought to be substance in the truest sense, but its nature remains obscure because the subject can refer to the matter, the form, or the compound of these two.

The remainder of Book 7 (at least in part) examines the claim of these six things (the essence, the universal, the genus, the subject as matter, the subject as form, and the subject as matter/form composite) to the title of substance in the truest sense, that is, to the title of primary substance. Later in Chapter 3, Aristotle refuses the title to matter on the grounds that, while matter is indeed the subject of all properties, it fails to be an independently existing thing. Still in Chapter 3, Aristotle refuses the title to the matter/form composite on the grounds that it is composed of parts. In Chapters 13 and 14 he refuses the title to the universal (and hence the genus, since all genera are universals) on the grounds that universals belong in common. We are left, then, with the essence and the form, but these two are identical. The form of Socrates is simply what it is to be Socrates. It is to be a human. Thus, form or essence apparently lays claim to the title of primary substance in Book 7 of the *Metaphysics*.

TWO PROBLEMS

Form as Independent Thing. At least two problems arise concerning Aristotle's discussion of substance in Book 7 of the *Metaphysics*. First, while Aristotle does appear to identify primary substance with form, the objection he raises against matter's claim to this title appears to apply to form as well. The form part of the matter/form composite looks, on Aristotelian grounds, to be no more capable of independent existence than the matter part. Indeed, as we will see when we turn to his psychology, Aristotle emphasizes the fact that form is not an independently existing thing. (Insofar as form is capable of independent existence, Aristotle appears to move closer and closer to Platonism.)

Some readers of Aristotle have sought to extricate him from this difficulty by supposing that form, unlike matter, has a separate and independent existence *in thought* only. Others have suggested that Aristotle's claim for the priority of form rests on the fact that form is responsible for the independent existence of concrete objects such as Socrates and Bucephalus, not that form itself is capable of independent existence.

Form as Universal. Second, it is plausible to think that the form aspect of the matter/form composite is a universal. Thus, when earlier we were discussing hylomorphism in the *Physics*, it was maintained that the form of Socrates is humanity. Presumably, this is also the form of the matter/form composite that is Plato. Indeed, do not all humans share the same form? If so, forms would be things that belong in common, that is, universals. But Aristotle refuses the title of primary substance to universals precisely on the grounds that universals *do* belong in common.

This problem has led some readers of Aristotle to deny that Aristotle takes form to be substance in the truest sense in Book 7 of the *Metaphysics*. Others have been led to distinguish between two sorts of Aristotelian forms: universal forms, such as humanity, and particular forms, which can be members of only one matter/form complex at a time. Aristotle calls these latter forms substance in the truest sense. It is not unusual in this context to think of particular forms as the souls of living organisms.

The Soul

This leads us directly to the second implication of hylomorphism. In *De Anima*, Aristotle takes the body/soul distinction in living organisms simply as a special case of the matter/form distinction. Aristotle introduces this idea by considering the case of an eye. To be an eye, according to Aristotle, is to see. To see is an eye's form. Its matter is flesh and blood. When seeing is removed from an eye, when, that is, its form is removed, it ceases to be an eye, except in name. A blind eye, apparently, is an eye only in name, while a mechanical eye that would enable the organism to see would, presumably, count as an eye, not merely in name but in fact. (Notice how the eye's form makes essential reference to the eye's function, just as the coincidence of the formal and final causes requires.)

Similarly, according to Aristotle, to be a living organism is to have a soul of a certain type. The soul enables the organism to perform certain acts depending on its type. The matter of the living organism is its body. When the soul is removed from the organism, it ceases to be a living organism except in name. Socrates' corpse is a human only in name.

SOUL AND BODY UNITY

Two features of this doctrine of the soul call for further comment. First, Aristotle thinks that by employing his hylomorphism to explain the soul/body distinction he has solved the problem of the relationship between the soul and the body. The soul and the body are not two independent constituents that can exist apart. They form an essential unity. The soul is a feature of the body. It makes no more sense to ask about the unity of the soul and the body than it does to ask of the unity of the shape and the bronze or the seeing and the eye.

FUNCTIONAL ACCOUNT OF THE SOUL

Second, since the soul is the form of a living organism and form makes reference to the end or function of the thing, Aristotle provides us with a functional account of the soul. The soul is the feature of the living organism that enables the organism to act in the way that it does. The states of the soul are functional states of the organism. Indeed, Aristotle finds a hierarchy of types of souls according to the behavior that living organisms are capable of.

Hierarchy of Souls. At the bottom of the hierarchy is the nutritive soul, which enables the organism to nourish itself, grow and decay, and reproduce. All living organisms, including plants, for example, possess at least the nutritive soul. Next in order is the sentient soul, which enables the organism to have sensations, including the feelings of pleasure and pain. Having a sentient soul distinguishes the animals from the plants. Within the animal kingdom, however, there are various levels depending on whether the sentient soul is of the sort that enables the organism to experience tactile, gustatory, visual, auditory, or olfactory sensations, whether the soul enables the organism to engage in locomotion, etc. Finally there is the rational soul, which distinguishes humans from the other animals and enables humans to engage in both practical and theoretical reasoning.

Happiness

The final implication of Aristotle's hylomorphism concerns Aristotle's conception of the "good." At the beginning of the *Nicomachean Ethics* Aristotle maintains that every rational human activity aims at some desired end. Sometimes the activity aims at an end apart from the activity itself. For example, studying is done for the sake of taking the exam. Taking the exam is an activity distinct from the activity of studying, which aims at it. Sometimes the activity is done not for the sake of an end apart from the activity but for the sake of the activity itself. Perhaps an example of this sort of activity is reading a bad novel. Presumably, one engages in this activity not for the sake of learning something but for the sake of the activity itself. We might call the former sorts of ends *product ends* (ends distinct from, but *produced* by, the activity) and the latter, *activity ends*. These two sorts of ends, then, are the "goods" that activities aim at.

THE ULTIMATE "GOOD"

According to Aristotle, there is an end of rational human activities that has the following two features. First, it is not itself done for the sake of some end apart from it. It is an activity end. Second, every other rational human activity is done for the sake of it. It is a product end of every other human activity. Thus, there is an end of rational human activity that everything else is done for the sake of but that is not done for the sake of anything else. This, according to Aristotle, is the ultimate or highest "good" of human activity.

Aristotle's argument that there is such a highest "good" is apparently that if there were not such a "good," desire would be futile. If there were not at least one activity end (contrary to the first condition), desiring would go on indefinitely. If there were more than one activity end (contrary to the second condition), these activity ends would be incompatible. (If they were compatible, they could simply be conjoined into a higher compound "good," with each component being done for the sake of the compound.) In both cases, what is ultimately desired would be unattainable.

CANDIDATES FOR HAPPINESS

Most people would agree, Aristotle maintains, that this ultimate or highest "good" of human activity is happiness. (*Happiness* is the most common and probably the best English translation of the Greek *eudaimonia*, but we must be careful here. *Eudaimonia* can also be translated as *flourishing* or *well-being*.) Nevertheless, there is widespread disagreement concerning what happiness consists in.

Some people think that happiness consists in pleasure; others, that it consists in honor; others, virtue; and even some that it consists in money. After refuting the claims of these to the title of the highest "good," Aristotle proposes his own candidate to the title in Chapter 7 of Book 1 of the *Nicomachean Ethics*: Actively using reason well is happiness for a human. The highest "good" for humans, what they do everything else they do for the sake of and what they fail to do for the sake of anything else, is actively using reason well. (More precisely, actively using reason well is the primary component of the highest "good" for humans. Aristotle points out that various external "goods," such as wealth, friends, political power, good birth, good children, and good looks, are also necessary to achieve human happiness.) His argument for this rather startling suggestion relies, at least in part, on his hylomorphism.

The Function Argument. According to Aristotle, the "good" of a thing that has a function is performing that function well. Thus, the "good" of a flute-player is to play the flute well, of a sculptor to sculpt statues well, and of an eye to see well. Thus, if humans have functions, then performing that function well will be their "good." But we have already seen that humans, like other organisms, have functions by virtue of their form, by virtue of what they are. The only question that remains then is what their function is, what makes humans, humans. But this too we have already answered. What distinguishes humans from the other living organisms is their ability to reason. Actualizing this ability, then, is their function, and so actively using reason well is their "good" (or at least its primary component). This, according to Aristotle, is human happiness.

THE ROLE OF VIRTUE

The question remains *how* one is to actively use one's reason well. Aristotle's answer to this question, at least in part, is that one is to act virtuously. According to Aristotle, it is only by practicing the moral virtues, such as courage, moderation, and justice, that one can achieve human happiness. Aristotle explains this by appeal to his thesis that moral virtues are dispositions to desire, feel, or act in a way that is neither excessive nor deficient.

Courage. Consider, for example, the moral virtue of courage. Courage, according to Aristotle, aims at an intermediate state between feeling too much fear, which would divert the agent from the pursuit of rational activity, and too little fear, which would risk the agent's pursuit of rational activity altogether. The courageous attitude is one which fears enough to avoid acting in a foolhardy way but not so much as to act in a cowardly way. Aristotle, however, is quick to observe that virtuous behavior is not necessarily the geometrical midpoint between the two extremes. There may be some circumstances in which courageous behavior requires giving very little weight to one's fears and other circumstances that require giving them much more weight. To determine the appropriate middle in the relevant circumstances is the difficult task of practical reason. Using reason well, then, is both a consequence and component of moral virtue.

CONTEMPLATION

In the tenth book of the *Nicomachean Ethics*, Aristotle endorses yet another way to actively use reason well. Here the idea seems to be that actively using reason well consists in contemplation. (Contemplation, according to Aristotle, consists in theoretical reasoning concerning the immutable first principles of science and philosophy, independent of any concern to apply them in practical affairs.) To contemplate is to fully actualize what is distinctive about being a human. It is to fully actualize one's reason.

Sometimes Aristotle talks as if a life solely devoted to contemplation is the highest "good" for humans. Other times he talks as if it is just one component of a human's happiness, which also includes the moral virtues and the external goods. As Aristotle puts it in Chapter 7 of Book 10 of the *Nicomachean Ethics*, a life solely devoted to contemplation would be a life that would be more than human. It would be a divine life, and so in some sense a life always beyond our reach. But, Aristotle goes on, we ought always strive as much as possible to live a life according to the best part of us. We ought to strive as much as possible to be divine.

Like Plato, then, Aristotle provides us with the complete philosophical perspective. Its centerpiece, however, is not the Platonic theory of Forms but a rival ontological theory that, ultimately, is based upon a matter/form analysis of ordinary concrete objects. Once this hylomorphism becomes fully articulated in his physical works, we see it permeate nearly every other aspect of Aristotelian philosophy. We have seen this in the particular cases of his metaphysics, his theory of the soul (or philosophy of mind), and his theory of the "good," but it can also be found in his biology, his politics, and perhaps even his epistemology.

We have also seen the tremendous influence of Aristotle's predecessors on his philosophy. While Aristotle is quick to criticise and offer his own account, he nevertheless sees himself squarely within the tradition of philosophical thought that began with the Presocratics.

Finally, Aristotle's own influence on subsequent philosophy should not be overlooked. Today, nearly everyone who believes that there are universals considers him- or herself to be Aristotelian in some way. Aristotle's theory of the soul is a distant ancestor of contemporary functionalist theories of the mind, and his ethical theory is a much closer ancestor to contemporary virtue ethics.

Selected Readings

Charleton, W. *Aristotle's* Physics: *Books I and II*. Oxford: Oxford University Press, 1970.

Cooper, J. M. *Reason and Human Good*. Cambridge: Harvard University Press, 1975.

Graham, D. *Aristotle's Two Systems*. Oxford: Oxford University Press, 1987.

Guthrie, W. K. C. *A History of Greek Philosophy: Aristotle, an Encounter*. Cambridge: Cambridge University Press, 1981.

Hardie, W. F. R. *Aristotle's Ethical Theory*. 2d rev. ed. Oxford: Oxford University Press, 1980.

Irwin, T. *Aristotle's First Principles*. Oxford: Oxford University Press, 1988.

Kraut, R. *Aristotle on the Human Good*. Princeton, Princeton University Press, 1989.

Owen, G. E. L. *Logic, Science, and Dialectic: Collected Papers in Greek Philosophy*. Ithaca, NY: Cornell University Press, 1986.

5

The Post-Aristotelians

*F*ollowing the death of Alexander the Great in 323 B.C., Aristotle fled Athens fearing a fate similar to Socrates'. He died the next year. In the centuries that followed, Athens ceased to be the political and scientific center of the ancient world, but it remained the philosophical center. Besides Plato's Academy (which endured a number of transformations until finally being dissolved by the Roman emperor Justinian in A.D. 529) and Aristotle's Lyceum (which declined in influence, from around 269 B.C. until its revival in the first century B.C.), two new schools were established in Athens about this time. Epicurus, the founder of Epicureanism, established the Garden in 307 B.C. and Zeno of Citium, the founder of Stoicism, began conversing in the Painted Stoa around 300 B.C. In addition to the founding of Epicureanism and Stoicism, Athens also found itself home to Skepticism (which did not form its own independent school until the first century B.C.) and Neo-Platonism (sometime in the fifth century A.D., after having been originally founded in Rome over a century and a half earlier). These four new philosophical schools are the subject of the present chapter.

Until recently, this period of Greek philosophy has been belittled as a decline from the heights of Plato and Aristotle. In some sense this cannot fail to be true, given the heights that Plato and Aristotle had achieved. But in every other respect the philosophers of this period are extraordinary.

Part of the explanation for their adverse reputation can be attributed to two historical accidents. First, much of their work has been lost. What we know about their philosophical views frequently comes from secondhand reports. While some are quite sympathetic, others are unabashedly critical. Often we are only able to piece together their doctrines. We are forced to speculate concerning their arguments.

Second, the social and political circumstances of this period may have created a breach in moral guidance in the average individual. While some of these individuals turned to various Eastern religions (which were beginning to influence the Mediterranean world at this time) to fill this gap, others turned to these new philosophical doctrines which tended to emphasize the way a human ought to live in the world. The popularity of these schools and the ways of living they promoted served, on the one hand, to ingratiate their philosophical doctrines into Western culture (notice, for example, that skeptic, epicurean, and stoic have become common nouns and adjectives in English) and, on the other hand, to misrepresent the philosophical doctrines on which these ways of life were based. The doctrines quickly became entrenched and condensed into handbooks accessible to the general public. Their esoteric arguments and theoretical bases were left to the experts and easily forgotten.

EPICUREANISM

The founder of Epicureanism was Epicurus (341–271 B.C.). In 307 B.C., Epicurus arrived in Athens with a group of followers and established the Garden, just south of Plato's Academy. Here Epicurus and his followers lived a communal life, removed from civic strife and dedicated to the principles laid down by Epicurus himself. By the time the Roman poet Lucretius (ca. 99–55 B.C.) wrote his *De Rerum Natura* (*On the Nature of Things*), perhaps our most revealing source of Epicurean doctrine, Epicureanism had spread throughout the Mediterranean world. This seemingly infectious philosophical view can be divided into three parts on Epicurus' own authority: Epistemology (or what the Epicureans called "the Canonic"), Philosophy of Nature (or what the Epicureans call "Physics"), and Ethics.

Epistemology

According to Epicurus, knowledge is based on sense perception. In fact, sensation is the criterion of truth. Sensation enables us to distinguish true views concerning the world from false views. The argument for this seems to have been that sense perception is our only access to the world. As a result, unless at least some of our sensations are true and we can tell which ones, knowledge of the world would be impossible. But knowledge of the world is possible. So, at least some of our sensations are true and we can tell which ones. But there is no way for us to distinguish true from false sensations since sensations are our only access to the world. Thus, since knowledge requires that we be able to tell which of our sensations are true, and if there were some false sensations we could not tell which were true, it follows, according to the Epicureans, that all of our sensations are true. Sensations, that is, are the criteria of truth.

THE DOCTRINE OF EFFLUENCES

To explain how it is that all of our sensations could be true, the Epicureans appeal to the doctrine of effluences (or outflows). According to the Epicureans, sensations are caused by a sort of film of atoms which somehow slough (or flow) off the object and penetrate the perceiver. In this way, the Epicureans explain how it is, for example, that a stick appears straight when out of water, but bent when in water. The effluences which flow off the straight stick are disrupted by the water in reaching the perceiver. The straight effluences, then, become bent by the water.

This doctrine of effluences, however, weakens Epicurean empiricism. (Empiricism is the view that our only or primary source of knowledge is sense perception.) Sensations turn out not to be infallible evidence for the shape of the stick, for example, but rather only for the shape of the effluences of the stick. The Epicureans respond to this problem by distinguishing between sensations and judgments. Sensations, being of effluences, cannot be false. Judgments, however, being of things not directly sensed (such as the stick itself, as opposed to its effluences), can be true or false. According to the Epicureans, those judgments compatible with and confirmed by sensations are acceptable or justified. Epicurus, at least, was well aware that a consequence of his epistemological theory is that there will be times when there is no way to decide between rival judgments. Two rival judgments may both be equally well compatible with and confirmed by sensations.

Philosophy of Nature

What theory of nature, then, is compatible with and confirmed by our sensations? The Epicurean answer is "atomism." Following Democritus, the Epicureans maintained that the world was composed of an infinite number of indivisible atoms moving in the void. These atoms have shapes, movements, weights, and sizes. All other properties and things are to be accounted for in terms of the arrangements, shapes, movements, weights, and sizes of the atoms. It is true, of course, that we do not perceive the void, the atoms, or their properties, but what we do perceive, the Epicureans believe, require them. Only such an atomistic theory is compatible with and confirmed by the sensations we have. (For example, the Epicureans appeal to the sloughing off of atoms from the surface of objects in order to explain how it is possible that all of our sensations are true.)

The "Swerve." While much of Epicurean atomism resembles the atomism of Democritus, at least one important difference should be mentioned. Unlike Democritus, who maintained that the atoms move in the void in random directions, the Epicureans maintain that the atoms move in a single downward direction. To explain the collision, collection, and separation of atoms, the Epicureans postulate the "swerve." This "swerve," which affects the motion of atoms at indeterminate times and places, provides a degree of randomness to this otherwise completely determined world. The "swerve" effectively eliminates any room for Platonic and Aristotelian teleology. The Epicureans maintain that everything can be explained by appeal to the purposeless, accidental, and indeterminate collection and separation of inanimate atoms. The "swerve" may also be thought to make room for some semblance of human free will in this otherwise fully determined mechanistic world.

Ethics

Ultimately, Epicureanism is an ethical theory. According to the Epicureans, the aim of studying nature, after all, is to contribute to human well-being or happiness. Like Aristotle, the Epicureans take the ultimate "good" for humans to be happiness, but, unlike Aristotle, they identify a human's happiness with pleasure. Pleasure is a human's natural state and is nothing other than the absence of pain. There is no middle state between pain and pleasure. Pain is simply the disruption of the natural state. Thus, in seeking pleasure one seeks to live in accord with nature. The moral virtues are necessary for living in accord with nature, but they are not constituents of such a life. They are a means to an end. The end aimed at is pleasure.

In identifying the human "good" or happiness with pleasure, then, Epicureanism espouses a hedonistic ethical theory. (Hedonism is the view that the "good" is pleasure.) It is not, however, the gross hedonism with which Epicureanism is sometimes associated. Simple pleasures are held to be just as valuable and easier to achieve than the more refined and cultivated pleasures. For example, the pleasure of eating a fresh, ripe strawberry is as valuable and easier to obtain than the pleasure of eating a delicately prepared gourmet dinner. In addition, the Epicureans believe that many of the pleasures obtained from gratifying the body often result in greater pain. For example, the pleasure of drinking wine may have the repercussion of a painful hangover. Finally, and perhaps most importantly, the Epicureans maintain that mental anxiety is the greatest pain. Freedom from this anxiety is correspondingly the greatest pleasure. In this respect, the study of nature plays its most important role in the attainment of human pleasure.

According to the Epicureans, the atomistic theory of nature that they espouse serves to discredit the two things most responsible for human anxiety: fear of death and fear of the gods. Humans fear death because they fear the punishment that they may receive in the afterlife. But once they recognize that the soul is completely corporeal—a collection of atoms just as susceptible to decomposition as anything else—they have no reason to fear death and its potential punishments. The atomistic theory of nature assures us, the Epicureans maintain, that neither the soul nor sensation nor consciousness survives death. Death is simply the separation of the atoms of which we are composed. We also have no reason to fear the punishment the gods might impose on us while alive (nor their arbitrary interference). Once again, the atomistic theory of nature assures us that the gods cannot be responsible for any natural event. They are unable to affect anything.

STOICISM

Not far from Epicurus' secluded Garden, in the publicly open Painted Stoa, Zeno of Citium (ca. 333–261 B.C.) began espousing a philosophical doctrine in some ways quite different from Epicureanism. Like Epicureanism, Stoicism maintained that philosophy and the study of nature serve primarily to promote a particular way of life. Unlike that of Epicureanism, the nature that this study revealed was not random and purposeless, but rational and purposeful. The life which such a revelation promoted was not one that aimed at pleasure, but one that aimed at virtue. Stoicism became perhaps the most influential philosophical school of the period. It could claim such distinguished adherents as the conservative Roman senator Cato (234–149 B.C.) and the respected Roman emperor Marcus Aurelius (A.D. 121–180).

The history of Stoicism can be usefully divided into three stages: Early Stoicism, which besides those of Zeno, is represented by the works of Cleanthes (331–232 B.C.) and Chrysippus (ca. 280–207 B.C.); Middle Stoicism, represented by the works of Panaetius (ca. 185–109 B.C.) and Posidonius (ca. 135–50 B.C.); and Late Stoicism, represented by the works of Seneca (ca. 4 B.C.–A.D. 65), Epictetus (ca. A.D. 55–135), and Marcus Aurelius. The following discussion focuses almost exclusively on Early Stoicism. Once again, Stoicism can be usefully divided into three parts (on Stoic authority): Epistemology (or what the Stoics called "Logic"), Philosophy of Nature (or what the Stoics called "Physics"), and Ethics.

Epistemology

Like the Epicureans, the Stoics maintain that all knowledge is built upon and presupposes sensations. But unlike the Epicureans, the Stoics do not believe that all sensations are equally trustworthy. Some are true and some are false, just as common sense suggests. The problem, then, is how to tell which sensations are the true ones if all we have to go on in making this decision are the sensations themselves.

THE CATALEPTIC SENSATION

The Stoic solution to this problem is to postulate a particular kind of sensation which they label "the cataleptic sensations." (*Cataleptic* is formed from the Greek noun *katalepsis*, which means a grasping or seizing.) These sensations, according to Stoicism, are true and, more importantly, carry with them their own mark of truth. Somehow or other, when we have these sensations we cannot help but assent to them. They "seize" our assent. The cataleptic sensations are the Stoic criteria of truth.

Knowledge, according to the Stoics, is assent incapable of being overturned. The cataleptic sensation is its foundation. All of our knowledge is (directly or indirectly) built upon such sensations. The Stoics may have been led to postulate the cataleptic sensation because they believed that knowledge would be impossible without some such self-guaranteeing true sensation.

Philosophy of Nature

The nature that this sensation-based knowledge reveals is one that is subject to a rational order, on which the Stoics bestow a number of different names: nature, *logos*, breath, fate, god, and providence. Like Aristotle, the Stoics maintain that all living creatures are a compound of matter and form. The matter is an indeterminate passive principle; form a determining active principle. Neither can exist apart from the other. The form of the creature is its nature or governing principle. For example, the nature of irrational animals is soul, while the nature of humans is reason or *logos*. Taken as a whole, the world, too, is viewed as a living creature, whose governing principle or nature is *logos*. As a result, humans have the ability to know the rational order.

THE RATIONAL ORDER AND BREATH

The Stoics conceived of this rational order as breath, again by analogy to the individual living creature. The nature or *logos* of an individual living creature is its form, its active principle. It is what enlivens or vitalizes the creature. Following Heraclitus, the Stoics were initially inclined to identify this *logos* with fire (fire being constantly active). Probably under the influence of contemporary physiology, however, they came to view the *logos* as the creature's breath (a compound of fire and air). The rational order of the world taken as a whole (or nature) is also conceived of as breath. It is what activates and vitalizes the world.

The Stoics conceive of the rational order as fate, god, and providence because they maintained that the world is fully deterministic. Everything that happens in the world is such that, given the pre-existing conditions, nothing else could have happened. To think otherwise would be to destroy the rational order of the world. It would be to suppose that what happens is not caused. According to the Stoics, what happens is not just the only possible result of the pre-existing conditions, it is the best possible result of those conditions. To think otherwise would be to suppose that reason, the *logos*, god, or providence does not aim at the "good."

FREE WILL

This determinism raises a problem for the Stoics in accounting for human free will. (Recall that the Epicureans made room for free will by introducing a certain amount of indeterminism with the "swerve.") To respond to this problem, the Stoics distinguish between what they call perfect and proximate causes. Chrysippus illustrates this distinction by means of a rolling drum. The drum's rolling is caused both by the fact that someone gave it a push, its proximate cause, and by the fact that it is round, its perfect cause. The idea seems to be that human actions are caused both by various external conditions (proximate causes), as well as by certain internal conditions (perfect causes). In these internal conditions one can find human free will.

Ethics

As with Epicureanism, the aim of studying nature for the Stoics is human well-being or happiness. Again, like the Epicureans, the Stoics maintain that happiness is a life in accord with nature. But the differences between the theories of nature of the Epicureans and the Stoics result in a different conception about what such a life amounts to. According to the Stoics, a life in accord with nature is not one that aims at pleasure, but one that aims at virtue.

VIRTUE

Virtue according to the Stoics is the perfecting of human nature. It is the perfecting of human reason. The perfection of human reason amounts to knowing the "good" and acting in accord with it. As we have seen, this means knowing the rational order and acting in accord with it. The virtuous person, then, is the person who knows the rational order and lives in accord with it. This is the ideal Stoic sage. But how can one fail to live in accord with nature in a deterministic world of the sort that the Stoics envision? How can one fail to be virtuous?

ACCORD WITH NATURE

To answer this question we need to distinguish between two different perspectives from which a life can be judged to be in accord with nature. A life can be judged to be in accord with nature from the perspective of the individual living creature. Here is room for a life to fail to accord with nature. For example, a life tormented by disease is not a natural life for a particular individual living creature. But from the perspective of the world as a whole, even this diseased life is in accord with nature, because everything happens for the best. The things that fail to accord with nature from the individual perspective are, from the universal perspective, unavoidable consequences of the "good." For the Stoics, failing to accord with nature is necessary in order to successfully accord with nature. For virtue is what is in accord with nature, and virtue cannot exist without vice.

How, then, can one fail to be virtuous? One can fail to be virtuous by seeking things which fail to accord with nature. One will not succeed in achieving these things because everything that happens is in accord with nature, at least from the universal perspective. But it is the intention of the actions that matters, not the result. Thus, one might act so as to promote one's health, believing it to be in accord with nature from one's individual perspective, but not recognizing (through ignorance) that it is contrary to nature from the universal perspective. One fails, then, to be virtuous. But one can approach the virtue of the all-knowing Stoic sage: When things which one seeks from the individual perspective, such as one's health, fail to come about, one accepts them stoically. One accepts that the disease that one had sought to avoid is an unavoidable consequence of the "good" from the universal perspective and embraces it willingly. This is the Stoic way of life.

SKEPTICISM

The third philosophical school of thought to emerge during this period is Skepticism. Skepticism consists of two quite independent branches: the Academic Skeptics, represented by Arcesilaus (ca. 316–242 B.C.) and Carneades (ca. 213–129 B.C.), and the Pyrrhonian Skeptics, represented by Pyrrho (ca. 365–270 B.C.), Aenesidemus (first century B.C. or A.D.), and Sextus Empiricus (sometime between A.D. 150 and A.D. 250). These two branches have much in common. They both deny the possibility of knowledge or certainty and, like all the new philosophical schools of the Hellenistic period (323–31 B.C.), they take their philosophical views to recommend a particular way of life. Nevertheless, they arise from quite different sources and were quite at odds with each other concerning individual doctrines. Furthermore, the Academic Skeptics did not form an official new school but were lodged in an old one (as their name implies), Plato's Academy. As a result, we would do well to think in terms of an ancient Skeptical tradition, from around 365 B.C. to around A.D. 250, rather than an ancient Skeptical school.

Academic Skepticism

ARCESILAUS

In 265 B.C., Arcesilaus became head of Plato's Academy. Arcesilaus, who wrote nothing, apparently believed that the Academy had gradually grown too far away from its Socratic roots. He advocated a return to the

Socratic method, which he understood as reducing an opponent's position to contradictions, and to Socratic wisdom, which he understood not as the possession of knowledge but as the avoidance of error. Arcesilaus appears to have practiced what he preached, for he was a fierce critic of Stoicism.

In particular, Arcesilaus attacked the Stoic criterion of truth, the cataleptic sensation. Arcesilaus apparently agreed with the Stoic doctrines that all knowledge is based on sensation and (unlike the Epicureans) that some sensations are true and some are false. But Arcesilaus denied that any of our sensations are such that we can infallibly recognize them as the true ones. He may have argued for this by pointing to examples of sensations which are as convincingly true while we are having them as any sensations ever are but which, nevertheless, are undeniably false (for example, sensations we have while dreaming or while temporarily insane). Arcesilaus concluded from this that knowledge is impossible and that the proper skeptical attitude is to suspend judgment.

CARNEADES

Carneades, who succeeded Arcesilaus as head of Plato's Academy, agreed with Arcesilaus that knowledge is impossible. He continued the attack on Stoic epistemology (which had undergone revision in light of Arcesilaus' criticism). Unlike Arcesilaus, however, Carneades proposed a substitute for the knowledge that his predecessor had shown to be impossible. Carneades agreed that we cannot attain certainty concerning the truth of particular sensations and that knowledge requires such certainty. But some sensations, he believed, can nevertheless be recognized as more probable than others.

Criteria of Probable Sensations. Carneades proposed three criteria for recognizing probable sensations: First, some sensations are intrinsically credible and clear; their credibility and clarity do provide some evidence for their truth. Unlike the credibility and clarity of the Stoic cataleptic sensation, however, Carneades maintained that a sensation's credibility and clarity are not infallible evidence for its truth. As a result, Carneades proposed a second criterion, in addition to credibility and clarity: the sensation's coherence with other sensations. Here, too, Carneades maintained that a sensation that is credible, clear, and coherent with one's other sensations may, nevertheless, be false. As a result, Carneades proposed a third criterion. The sensation must pass various tests. For example, one can test to see if one is awake, if the object is in water (recall the example of the bent and straight stick, discussed earlier), or if the object is too far away. Sensations of this sort, that is, those that are credible, clear, coherent, and tested, are the most authoritative sensations we can have. Yet even these, Carneades was quick to point out, may be false. Certainty cannot be achieved. But for Carneades, some sensations, those which are credible, clear, coherent, and tested, are more probable than others.

Pyrrhonian Skepticism

The Pyrrhonian Skeptics traced their origins to the mysterious Pyrrho of Elis. Little is known about Pyrrho, but he appears to have been primarily a moral philosopher, advocating a particular way of life. According to Pyrrho, the end or goal of human life, or happiness, is quietude (*ataraxia*), which can be achieved only by the suspension of judgment (*epoche*). The role of philosophy is to bring about this skeptical attitude of suspended judgment so that quietude can be achieved.

TEN TROPES

Sometime around the turn of the millennium, Aenesidemus began to put this doctrine into a systematic form. He did so by codifying the arguments by which suspension of judgment could be achieved into ten different kinds, known as the Ten Tropes. These Ten Tropes, discussed in the writings of Sextus Empiricus, aim at the suspension of judgment resulting from recognition of perceptual relativity—the idea that perceptions of a thing can vary depending on perspectives and contexts.

Each of the tropes aims at showing how sensations can conflict. For example, the first trope points out that differences in the sense organs of animals result in conflicting sensations of the same object among those animals. The ringing of a bell sounds different to a bat than it does to a horse, for example. The fifth trope points out that differences in the distance of a perceived object result in conflicting sensations of that same object. A crow will appear large when one is close to it and yet quite small when it is high in the sky.

These conflicting sensations cannot all be true of the perceived object itself, but there is no non-arbitrary reason to choose one of the conflicting sensations over the other. Thus, all we can say with any certainty is how the object appears to us, not how it really is. Concerning its real nature, we ought to suspend judgment. By recognizing that conflicting sensations can be found for any of our beliefs concerning reality (by means of the Ten Tropes), we are led to total suspension of judgment, satisfaction with appearances, and quietude (which is the goal of human life).

NEO-PLATONISM

Although the last of the four schools of this chapter has its roots in the Hellenistic period, it is in fact of much later vintage. In the third century A.D., Plotinus (A.D. 205–270) synthesized aspects of Platonic and Aristotelian philosophy (both of which had begun substantial revivals in the first century B.C.) into his own distinctive view. Plotinus exhibited his philosophical views in treatises collected by his pupil Porphyry (ca. A.D. 232–305) into six groups of nine, known as the *Enneads* (from the Greek *ennea*, which means nine). Plotinus and Porphyry were headquartered in Rome. Proclus (ca. A.D. 410–485), the third major figure of Neo-Platonic thought, provided a systematic exposition of the doctrine while serving as head of Plato's Academy in Athens.

HYPOSTASIS

According to Neo-Platonism, there are three primary realities or substances (*hypostases*): the One, Intellect, and Soul. The One, which under Platonic influence is identified with the Good, is the ultimate reality. It is what is responsible for the unity of all other things. Without the One there could be no other things. It is grasped by pure intuition, which somehow takes it in all at once, resisting even distinguishing the object of the intuition from the subject of the intuition. Emanating from the One is Intellect. This is the first differentiation, or plurality. The objects of Intellect are the immutable and eternal Platonic Forms which are somehow themselves part of Intellect. Next in order is Soul, which is in space and time. It is Soul's uniting with matter (which under Aristotelian influence is identified with pure negation or non-being) that accounts for the sensible world.

We cannot do justice to Neo-Platonic thought in the short space allotted to it here, but we should not underestimate its influence. Because of its mystical quality, Neo-Platonism was peculiarly susceptible to religious manipulation. It was used both for and against Christian thought, which was at that time beginning to dominate philosophical thought. On the one hand, the Roman emperor Julian the Apostate (A.D. 332–361) attempted to thwart the dominance of Christianity by reintroducing a Neo-Platonic version of pagan polytheism. On the other hand, two writers whose works proved very influential among Medieval Christian theologians were Neo-Platonic Christians, "Pseudo-Dionysius" (sometime after Proclus) and Boethius (A.D. 480–524).

*W*ith *these four new schools of philosophy (Epicureanism, Stoicism, Skepticism, and Neo-Platonism), the history of ancient Greek philosophy comes to a close. In the centuries that follow, Western philosophical thought relocates to the west and to the north. This should not be blamed on the falling off of the quality of the philosophy during this period. As we have seen, all four schools put forward rich, sophisticated, and quite persuasive philosophical systems. In the case of the first three schools, these systems support appealing ways of life. The appeal of these ways of life, along with the mystical quality of Neo-Platonism, made these philosophical systems* *susceptible to popularizing corruptions. But we should not let this obscure the genuine developments made during this period in the areas of epistemology, philosophy of nature, and ethics.*

Selected Readings

Long, A. A. *Hellenistic Philosophy: Stoics, Epicureans, Skeptics*. 2d ed. Berkeley and Los Angeles: University of California Press, 1986.

Rist, J. M. *Epicurus: An Introduction*. Cambridge: Cambridge University Press, 1972.

Sandbach, F. H. *The Stoics*. London: Chatto and Windus, 1975.

Schofield, M., M. Burnyeat, and J. Barnes, eds. *Doubt and Dogmatism: Studies in Hellenistic Epistemology*. Oxford: Oxford University Press, 1980.

Stough, C. L. *Greek Skepticism: A Study in Epistemology*. Berkeley and Los Angeles: University of California Press, 1969.

Wallis, R. T. *Neoplatonism*. London: Duckworth, 1972.

6

St. Augustine

St. Augustine (354–430) is the central figure in the movement from late antiquity to the medieval period. Although the Emperor Constantine had been converted to Christianity in 312, this was still very much a transitional period from pagan past to Christian future.

Augustine was born in the northern African city of Thagaste to a Christian mother and non-Christian father. He traveled, as a teacher of rhetoric, to Rome in 383 and then to Milan. In 386 he was himself converted to Christianity. He returned to north Africa, and shortly thereafter, in 396, become bishop of Hippo. Many of his writings date from this period and are responses to various heretical doctrines.

Augustine was a prolific writer. His major philosophical works are: Contra Academicos *(386),* De Libero Arbitrio *(ca. 390),* The Confessions *(401),* The City of God *(426), and* De Trinitate *(419).*

AUGUSTINE AND PHILOSOPHY

Augustine is chiefly famed for his effort to bring Platonism and Neo-Platonism into concord with Christian doctrine. However, it should be noted that Augustine does not regard the philosophical and Christian lives as essentially in conflict. Indeed, for Augustine, philosophy and religion aim at the same object: the happy or blessed life. This is not an idiosyncratic view. The chief Post-Aristotelian schools of philosophy were at the time regarded as having this same end. Thus, the point of philosophy was regarded as making it possible to live the good life. More than this, Augustine believes that the pagan philosophers had discovered many of the same truths revealed in the Scriptures. What philosophy could not discover on its own was, of course, the particulars of Christian faith: the birth, life, sacrifice, and resurrection of Christ.

Belief and Understanding

This conception of philosophy as essentially religious (or at least ethical) drives Augustine's thinking. For example, he has very little patience with philosophical speculations about the natural world. As Augustine insists, he is concerned to examine only two things: God and the soul. This view of natural scientific investigation is also based, for Augustine, in a Platonic conception of knowledge and reality. What is real, and thus what can be known, in all strictness, is not to be found among the transitory things of the natural world.

But if philosophy or reason cannot bring us to the blessed life on its own, it can nonetheless play an important role in that life. The blessed life must begin with Christian faith and so with belief. To believe something is to judge with assent. Thus, one may well believe something without understanding it. (Such is, typically, the state of the beginning student in a field of study.) One comes to understand something only by having some rational demonstration or by being directly acquainted with that thing. So, while the search for the good life begins with belief, faith comes to its fruition only with understanding. Augustine insists very often that you must "believe in order that you might understand." And here philosophy has a role to play in deepening and fulfilling one's belief in Christian doctrine. What this conception of the relation between belief and the understanding also makes apparent is that, for Augustine, one pursues philosophy in order that one might have a more complete grasp on the objects of faith. Philosophy is not an end in itself. It is a means to the blessed life.

AUGUSTINE ON KNOWLEDGE

Augustine, for a time, was a follower of Manicheism. According to this view, the world is to be understood by appeal to two ultimate forces: the force of good or light and the force of darkness or evil. After rejecting this doctrine, Augustine briefly flirted with Academic skepticism. His *Contra Academicos* is a systematic attack on the Skeptical school. From the *Confessions*, it is clear that Augustine understands Skepticism as holding that everything ought to be doubted and that a human being is unable to apprehend truth.

Response to the Skeptic

Augustine's most important response to the Skeptic is that there is a range of propositions which possess a characteristic such that they cannot be doubted. Famously, Augustine writes, *Si fallor, sum.* "If I am deceived, I am." Thus, I can be certain that I am, that I think, that I doubt, etc. As a result, the unrestricted Skeptical threat has been turned aside.

There can be little doubt that this is an important anticipation of Descartes' "Cogito ergo sum." It is, however, important to note that Augustine's use of the *Si fallor, sum* is a quite limited one; he seeks only to respond to the Skeptic. It is possible for a human being to be certain of the truth of some matter. But this truth is not, as it is for Descartes, the foundation for a vindication of all that we know.

Sense Perception

Augustine has no doubt that through sensory experience we are in contact with an independent world. (Descartes' profound skeptical worries concerning the very existence of an external sensible world are not on Augustine's philosophical agenda.) Still, it can hardly be doubted that we are sometimes led astray by the senses.

Augustine's account of empirical knowledge is difficult. It is made difficult by his Platonic view that there are two worlds: an intelligible world of eternal truths and a sensible world that we perceive by sight, etc. In a strict sense, it seems that the objects of sensory experience can be the objects only of belief and not of knowledge. More than this, knowing is an activity carried out by the soul and not the body. Further complicating Augustine's conception of sense experience is his view that the body cannot causally act upon the soul. So, sensory "knowledge" cannot be a matter of the body's causing, through the senses, certain judgments in the soul.

According to Augustine, the senses themselves are never in error for they do not judge. The senses merely display how it is that things appear in circumstances of some particular sort. It is up to the individual to judge whether they are really thus and so. Judgment is a function of the soul and not the body. As we noted above, such judgments are not, according to Augustine, caused by modifications of the sensory apparatus. What Augustine says about this is obscure. His picture seems to be that such judgment requires the soul's activity on the occasion of sensory stimulation.

Reason

True to his Platonic and Neo-Platonic inheritance, Augustine is less interested in claims we make about the empirical world than he is in claims which are independent of sense experience. These are for Augustine immutable and eternal truths. He has in mind the truths of mathematics and logic as well as moral truths. Such truths are not only necessarily true, they are universally true. They are grasped by all with reason. Such eternal and immutable truths are not grasped on the basis of sensation. Indeed, they are, in strictness, not truths about this empirical world. Rather they are truths of the intelligible world.

ILLUMINATION

These truths of the intelligible realm are "seen." They are however, "seen" by the intellect and not by the eyes. The issue for Augustine here is this: How is it possible for a human being to gain access to this intelligible realm of eternal truths? It will be recalled that Plato sought to explain this by appeal to the doctrine of recollection. In some prior existence, the soul had immediate access to the intelligible Forms. This doctrine had obvious unacceptable theological consequences for Augustine. Thus, in place of recollection, Augustine speaks of "divine illumination."

The source of this doctrine is undoubtedly Plotinus' doctrine of emanation and, ultimately, Plato's own discussion of the Form of the Good as that which illuminates both the Forms and the mind. Unfortunately, Augustine says less about divine illumination than he might. What is, in any case, central to that doctrine is that the divine light is always present in the human soul. And it is this divine light, or illumination, which enables us to "see" truths which possess immutability and necessity. These immutable truths are sometimes spoken of as divine ideas, in which case, in grasping such truths we have access to God's ideas.

PROOF OF GOD'S EXISTENCE

The existence of, and our access to, the eternal and immutable truths is used by Augustine to construct an argument for the existence of God. These truths are independent of our judgments. All of us can grasp them. To recognize them as true, Augustine says, is to recognize that such truths are superior to our minds. But these truths must, according to Augustine, have themselves a foundation. This foundation must be superior to us. Their grounding or basis must be the eternal and immutable Truth, God.

On God and Creation

According to the biblical story of creation, the things of this world are created sequentially. There is addition, the testimony of our own experience that new things are constantly being created. Elsewhere in the Bible, however, is the claim that God created all things together; and this picture is, perhaps, better in keeping with a conception of God as absolutely unchanging. In order to deal with this theological dilemma, Augustine appeals to the doctrine of "seminal reasons" (or causes). Seminal reasons were created by God all at once. These are invisible potentialities which come to realize themselves through time. All of history and the development of the world is present at the creation in the form of seminal reasons.

TIME AND CREATION

Another puzzle concerning creation might be raised in the following manner: If creation is from nothing, what was God doing before he created the world? Such a question has its basis in a worry about whether it makes any sense to speak of absolute beginnings. Surely we can always ask what happened before any arbitrary event?

Augustine's discussion of time in the *Confessions* is justly famous. His response to the above worries is to argue that they are incoherent. Time is not something independent of creation but is, rather, consequent to it. Independently of creation, there is no time, and so the question, "What happened before creation?" is without sense. Augustine argues that time is not a something in which events happen; rather time is just a relation between events.

MORALITY

Morality is central to Augustine's philosophical/theological concerns. Philosophy is, after all, the search for blessedness. Blessedness, the good life, we learn, cannot be found independently of God's grace.

Human beings strive after or desire blessedness or happiness. This desire can, ultimately, only be satisfied in the eternal and immutable, in God. In a real way, Augustine's moral theory is one of love—love of God. Augustine speaks of virtue as correctly ordered love. Like everything else in creation, the human being is driven to seek what will satisfy its longings. However, unlike the rest of nature, human beings have wills. Further, the human will is free. We have the capacity to turn away from the love of the immutable to the love of the mutable and transitory things of this world.

By virtue of our fallen state, our loves (our desires) have become confused. Nonetheless, every human being can recognize his or her moral obligations (to love God). God's will is that we should love him. In the very same way that we have, through divine illumination, access to, for example, the immutable truths of mathematics, so we have access to the immutable truths of morality. So, when we turn away from God, we do so knowingly and freely. However, we cannot by ourselves achieve union with the immutable; for that God's grace is necessary.

EVIL

The human will is, then, the source of evil in the world. That evil exists in the world cannot not be attributed to God's activity. (Augustine's view of what we might term "natural" evils, for example, earthquakes, birth defects, etc., is that these make for diversity in creation and so are ultimately part of the best possible world.) Evil is the consequence of the rejection of God. On the basis of this conception of evil, Augustine hopes to show that evil is not a positive fact in creation. If it were, it would necessarily have to be attributed to God, who created all things. For Augustine, evil is a simple lack, a privation of good. Evil is merely the lack of correct order or harmony in the human will.

THE TWO CITIES

According to Augustine, then, there are lovers of the eternal and immutable God and lovers of the transitory and mutable. The first are citizens of the City of Jerusalem, the second are citizens of the City of Babylon. When Augustine surveys human history, it is in terms of the struggles between these two cities. Augustine's views of human history are, however, considerably more complex then the above might suggest. Unlike Plotinus, who urged the straightforward rejection of things of this world and human history, Augustine recognizes that, since Christ entered this world, human history is of significance. It is for this reason that Augustine must be concerned with the social and the political realm.

The state has, for Augustine, an important role to play in fallen man's salvation. Human history has a goal ordained by God. The state is not, for example, identical with the city of Babylon. Importantly, the state should itself be ordered according to the moral law. In this way it will make for the individual's entrance into the City of God.

*A*ugustine's philosophical views are in the service of his theology. Still, enough has been said here to indicate his brilliance and originality. Working from within a Neo-Platonist framework, he succeeds in marrying the philosophy of the ancient world to Christianity. This achievement was to fix the agenda of philosophy in the West for many hundreds of years.

Selected Readings

Chadwick, H. *Augustine*. New York: Oxford University Press, 1986.

Kirwan, C. *Augustine*. London: Routledge and Kegan Paul, 1989.

Marcus, R. A. *Augustine: A Collection of Critical Essays*. New York: Anchor Books, 1972.

7

St. Anselm

*S*t. *Anselm (1033–1109) was a member of the Benedictine Order. Born in the Piedmont region of Italy, he ultimately became Archbishop of Canterbury. For this reason he is typically referred to as Anselm of Canterbury. His chief works of philosophical interest are the* Monologion, *the* Prosologion, De Veritate, *and the* Liber Apologeticus. *His philosophical fame derives largely from his discovery of the ontological argument. So great an impact has this argument exerted on the thought of the West, it is not easy to imagine philosophy in Europe without it.*

FAITH AND REASON

Some remarks should be made about Anselm's conception of the relation between faith and reason. His views about these matters are largely Augustinian. That is to say, we do not reason—do not engage in philosophical inquiry—in order to have faith. Rather we are first believers in faith; only then do we seek the support of reason. God, Anselm writes, rewards faith with understanding. In this way, we may say that faith comes before the understanding.

NECESSARY REASONS

Since we have been blessed by God with understanding (or reason), we can be said to have a duty to seek reasons for our faith. Anselm calls the reasons so discoverable by the understanding "necessary reasons." Still, the results of reasoning are not independent of one's faith. Throughout his works, Anselm is clearly prepared to test the results of his philosophical search for necessary reasons against the dictates of faith.

Anselm thinks that we can give necessary reasons for our beliefs about God, or at least for some of our beliefs. By necessary reasons Anselm means that, for example, "God exists" is a proposition which is necessarily true. It is a truth the denial of which results in contradiction. Thus, it is no surprise that Anselm's favored form of argument is the *reductio ad absurdum*; this method of argument is encountered in his ontological argument.

Some controversy surrounds Anselm's conception of necessary truth. Many of the difficulties Anselm confronts here are at the center of philosophy on the Continent in the sixteenth and seventeenth centuries. In a nutshell, the question for any believer is this: What is the basis of necessary truth? Is it the case that such truths are true quite independently of God? Or is it the case, in keeping with what seems a straightforward reading of God's omnipotence, that these "necessary" truths somehow depend upon God's will? Anselm's view of these matters is simply not clear. It seems as though he wants to say that it is, at least in some sense, possible that God might have willed these truths to be other than they are. This is a view that René Descartes would later wholeheartedly embrace.

ARGUMENTS OF *MONOLOGION*

The arguments of the *Monologion* are of considerable historical and philosophical interest. Their aim is to show that there must exist some one thing which is the most supreme, or highest, of all existing things. Anselm offers two central arguments for this claim: an argument from considerations relating to goodness and one from considerations relating to existence. We shall concentrate on the first.

Argument from Goodness

This argument begins by noting that certain claims we make are essentially comparative in nature. Thus, we say that X is good; but if something is good it makes sense to say that it is better than something else and that something else is better than X. Clearly, we truly call many things "good." We say that Y is good and that Z is good. These two things may well possess different degrees of goodness, yet they are both good. If this is the case, there must be something that these two things have in common. There must be something by virtue of which they are both good. This thing which is had in common is, according to Anselm, the cause of the goodness of all other things. The goodness of all things then depends upon the existence of this thing. And this thing must itself be good in the highest degree. It is the supreme "good." It is good through itself alone and not because of any other thing.

It is apparent that the argument owes much to Plato. What is of considerable interest is the way in which a realistic account of universals is married to a claim about the causal relation between universals and their particulars.

THE ONTOLOGICAL ARGUMENT

The term *ontological argument* is a relatively modern invention. By earlier thinkers it was referred to as the "Argument of Anselm."

The point of departure of the argument is that faith provides us with a conception of a being than which none greater is possible, or of "a being than which none greater can be conceived." The argument in the *Prosologion* takes something like the form of a dialogue with the fool of Psalm 14 ("the fool hath said in his heart, there is no God"). The burden of the argument is to show that the "fool" is, in a quite literal fashion, not making sense. He is, in fact, uttering a proposition which is necessarily false.

Argument in Outline

For ease of consideration we can schematize Anselm's argument in the following fashion:

1. God is the being than which none greater can be conceived.

2. God exists in the understanding.

3. God might have existed in reality—it is possible that God exists.

4. If something exists only in the understanding and might have existed in reality, then that thing might have been greater than it is.

5. Suppose God exists only in the understanding.

6. God might have been greater than he is (since God, by 3, might have existed in reality).

7. But then, by 1 and 6, the being than which none greater can be conceived is a being than which a greater can be conceived.

8. So, it must be false that God exists only in the understanding.

9. God exists (in reality, as well as in the understanding).

The Argument Considered

It is sometimes said that the ontological argument proceeds from the definition of God alone to the conclusion that God exists. Although there is something to this reading, what the argument importantly and explicitly hinges upon is that if we have a conception of God then we can be certain that God exists. The point is that anyone has or can have a thought the representational content of which picks out God, that is, the being than which none greater can be conceived. (Although Anselm, oddly, given the argument, says later that God is greater than can be conceived.) Of course, God's existence does not depend upon our having the thought of God. Rather, God's necessary existence is made manifest to us given the thought that we have.

Later, St. Thomas Aquinas noted that some would not grant that God is, by definition, the being than which none greater can be conceived. He notes that, among some of the ancients, God was simply identified with the world. However, not much hinges on whether we wish to dispute Anselm's claim that God is, by definition, the being than which none greater can be conceived. (Nor was this suggestion the most important of the worries raised by Aquinas.) If the argument works, it will succeed in showing that, necessarily, there exists a being than which none greater can be conceived. Whether one wishes to argue over the propriety of calling this being "God," is no more than a terminological issue.

The argument, if it succeeds, demonstrates not only that God necessarily exists, but also that one cannot conceive of God's failing to exist. Thus, the fool who affirms in his heart that God does not exist must be a desperately confused fellow. When he asserts that God does not exist, his error is rather like the "error" of someone who asserts the following: "I am now conceiving of a four-sided triangle." Such a thought is, of course, necessarily false. But more than this, the kind of conceptual confusion revealed in such a claim must make us wonder just what this poor soul has in mind. We can properly say, "If you are thinking of something with four sides, then you are not thinking about triangles." Such a fellow is quite incorrect about what it is he is thinking about. You are not having a thought about a triangle if you are having a thought about something four-sided. The same must be true, at bottom, in the case of the fool. If one has a conception of God, then one has a conception of a being who necessarily exists. One cannot have a thought about God if it is a thought about something that does not exist.

Thus, proceeding from a definition of God, which can be grasped in the understanding, and from the assumption that existence is a great-making property, Anselm moves to the central portion of the argument, the *reductio*.

Anselm next invites us to imagine that God exists in the understanding but not in reality. This is just what the fool must be claiming to do when he says that God does not exist. All of us frequently make claims of similar logical form. For example, we say that unicorns and gorgons do not exist.

This claim about the non-existence of God immediately leads to contradiction. Making use of the earlier premises, we can show that the being than which none greater can be conceived is a being than which a greater can conceived. And, since the earlier premises were uncontroversial, we can be certain that the source of the contradiction is the claim that God exists only in the understanding. So in rejecting this claim, we can conclude that God must exist.

The Argument Critically Examined

Though the argument was rejected by Aquinas, it was accepted by St. Bonaventure, Duns Scotus, and by most of the Rationalist philosophers of the sixteenth and seventeenth centuries.

No doubt part of the source of our suspicion about this argument has to do with the fact that the argument seeks to make an existential claim, a claim about what exists in fact, solely on the basis of a priori reasoning, solely on the basis of definition. This has seemed to many thinkers, including Aquinas, an unacceptable way of reasoning.

EXISTENCE

The chief objection to the argument, raised most clearly by Immanuel Kant, but anticipated by Pierre Gassendi, is that existence is not properly conceived of as one property among others. Rather, existence is a presupposition of having any properties whatsoever. The argument hinges precisely on the fact that something with certain properties must have some other property, existence.

One way of seeing the force of this objection in a vivid way is this: Imagine a tall, cool glass of iced tea. Imagine the shape, size, and color of the glass as clearly as possible. Now stop. Next imagine the very same iced tea, only this time add to it another property, existence. It seems reasonably clear that no part of the content of what you are imagining has altered. The point is that existence cannot be understood to be a property like shape, size, temperature, etc. Thus, it is not a great-making property since it is no property at all.

GAUNILO'S OBJECTION

One other objection is of some historical interest. It might seem that if the argument succeeds it proves too much. This worry is raised by Anselm's contemporary, the monk Gaunilo. For if the argument shows that the greatest conceivable *being* exists, why can we not, by the very same reasoning, show that the greatest conceivable *island* exists. But since we know that the greatest conceivable island does not exist, we can be certain that something has gone awry with the argument.

Still, it seems fair for Anselm to respond that what is central to the argument is that we are conceiving of the greatest being *simpliciter* (simply or in and of itself) and not merely the greatest being of some particular species or kind. Thus, it does not seem particularly *ad hoc* to assert that necessary existence is a property only of the greatest conceivable being *simpliciter*.

On the other hand, this sort of response makes clear the importance to the argument of the claim that we do have a conception of the greatest conceivable being. It may well be that we have no such grasp of such a concept. If this is so, the fool may not be so foolish when he asserts that God does not exist.

We have emphasized Anselm's contribution to the history of Western philosophy in the form of his discovery of the ontological argument. Still, we should not forget that his discussion of truth, and his account of the relation between God and creation are also of historical importance. Anselm's discussion of truth emphasizes the fact that if anything is true, this itself is a fact which depends upon the existence of some standard or criterion against which that thing is judged to be true. Just as Anselm speaks of God as the supreme "good" he speaks of God as the supreme "truth." This account of truth is related to Anselm's conception of the relation between God and his creations. The existence of any created thing depends wholly and continuously upon God as the Good and the True.

Selected Readings

McIntyre, J. *St. Anselm and His Critics*. Edinburgh: University of Edinburgh Press, 1954.

Southern, R. W. *St. Anselm and His Biographer*. London: Routledge and Kegan Paul, 1962.

8

St. Thomas Aquinas

*S*t. *Thomas Aquinas (1224–1274) is considered by many to have been the greatest philosopher of the medieval period. He was born near Naples in Italy, into a noble Italian family. He began his studies in a Benedectine monastery when he was five years old. He later attended the University of Naples, where he began to study philosophy, including some works of Aristotle. In 1244, Aquinas entered the Dominican order, which greatly disappointed his family, who had wished that he choose the more prestigious vocation of becoming a Benedictine monk. His brothers kidnapped him and forced him to return home; ultimately, however, he returned to study with the Dominicans. He studied for four years in Cologne under Albert the Great, another of the great medieval philosophers. Having distinguished himself as an outstanding student, Aquinas was sent by Albert to the University of Paris in 1252, where he lectured in theology; he became a full member of the faculty in 1257, teaching there until 1259. For the next nine years, Aquinas lectured on philosophy and theology at various Dominican monasteries near Rome, but returned to the University of Paris in 1268. In 1272, he returned to Italy and taught at the University of Naples. His health began to fail in 1273, and he died in March of 1274.*

Aquinas began his writings when he went to Paris in 1252. His works consist of several long theological treatises, commentaries on the works of others, "disputations" on theological and philosophical problems, and other miscellaneous short works. His most important works are the Summa Contra Gentiles *and the* Summa Theologica.

In a number of his works, Aquinas presents his views in the form of "questions," which are divided into articles. Each article poses a question, generally followed by several objections representing the views of other philosophers, followed in turn by Aquinas' own view, then his replies to the initial objections. To understand Aquinas' view, it is helpful to read the middle part of the article first.

Aquinas' work reflects the influence of a number of other philosophers, including Plato, Augustine, the Islamic philosophers Avicenna and Averroës, and the Jewish philosopher Maimonides. He was most influenced, however, by the works of Aristotle. The major works of Aristotle had come to European universities, via the Middle East, not long before Aquinas began his studies. Aristotle's works were controversial, as some of his views were in conflict with the teachings of the Catholic church—for example, his views that the soul does not survive the death of the body, and that the world had not been created but was eternal. But the works of Aristotle offered to thinkers the exciting possibility of having a systematic understanding of the world. Aquinas himself attempted to reconcile Catholic theology with Aristotle's philosophy. He was concerned with illuminating the relationship between faith and reason. Although he did not think that all articles of faith were demonstrable with reason, he thought many were; thus, he tried to show how the dictates of reason, represented by Aristotle, and those of faith were compatible in the areas in which they intersect. His views were not readily accepted while he was alive, due in large part to the challenge they posed to the established Augustinian theology. However, he later became the official theologian of the Catholic church, and has remained so into the twentieth century.

METAPHYSICAL CONCEPTS

In his metaphysics, Aquinas very clearly employs many of Aristotle's concepts and distinctions, a number of which already had an established place in medieval thought. These are central to Aquinas' views on the nature of creation and its relation to God, and the nature of the human soul. We will examine some of the central concepts here.

Substance

Aristotelian metaphysics was largely concerned with substances and their causes. Aquinas was also concerned with the nature of substances, why they change, and what ends they serve.

One way of understanding a substance is as a thing that can have an independent existence. For example, a cow is a substance, because a cow can exist by itself, while the color red is not, because it can only exist in something else—a substance. For Aquinas, substances are what God created in creating the world and continues to create. Some are corporeal, the things in the material world; others are incorporeal, such as human souls and angels.

MATTER AND FORM

Aristotle held that substances consist of matter and form, neither of which can exist by itself. If you think of a form as a property, Aristotle's view becomes clear. By itself, matter has no properties, although it has the potential to take on properties. Likewise, properties have no existence except in matter; they are what make matter into an actual substance. Also, it is matter that individuates substances—that makes it possible for there to be two of exactly the same kind of thing. For example, consider two copies of the book you are reading. What makes them different books, even though they are exactly alike in their properties, is their matter, not their properties, or form. If there were no matter, there could not be multiple instances of the book, or of anything else.

Substances have both accidental forms and substantial forms. A substantial form is what makes a thing the kind of thing that it is, or without which it would not be that kind of thing. As we will see below, the substantial form of living things is a soul, for it is the soul that makes a living thing be alive, enabling its activities: growth, nutrition, reproduction, perception, etc. An accidental form, by contrast, is a property that a thing happens to have, but could exist without. So, for example, an accidental form that you have is your hair color; you could change the color of your hair, but you would still be you, a human person. Your substantial form is a rational intellect or soul; without that, neither Aristotle nor Aquinas thinks that you would be the kind of substance you are, a human being.

Potentiality and Actuality. Aristotle's distinction between form and matter can be thought of more generally as a distinction between potentiality and actuality. In that matter by itself has no form, it has the potential to take on any form and is thus "pure potentiality." The form it takes on is what enables it to undergo change, thereby becoming actual. Form, then, is what makes matter into a substance, that makes its potentiality become actual, and that brings about change in a substance.

To understand Aristotle's analysis, consider his example of a bronze statue. The bronze out of which the statue is made is like matter; the shape it takes on in becoming the statue is like form. We can say that the bronze out of which the statue is made has the potential to become a statue. The form of the statue—its shape—is what makes the bronze into an actual statue. This example is not perfect because bronze is itself a kind of substance, that is, it can exist by itself. Ultimately, the matter out of which all things are constituted is prime or first matter, which has no properties, but has the potential to take on any property.

Corporeal Substances. Aquinas agrees with Aristotle's analysis of substance as informed matter insofar as corporeal substances are concerned, that is, the material objects that populate the sensible world. Because matter is the basis of corporeal substances, and because corporeal substances are extended, Aquinas thinks of matter as being extensive quantity. Aquinas' notion of matter differs from Aristotle's in this respect, for Aristotle held that matter, pure potentiality without form, had no qualities at all.

Matterless Substances. While corporeal, extended substances consist of informed matter, Aquinas also thinks there are substances that have no matter at all. Such substances are incorporeal, such as angels and human souls. They consist of form only, for they are not extended. Thus, Aquinas agrees with Aristotle that matter cannot exist "by itself," uninformed. However, he does allow that some forms can exist by themselves, insofar as incorporeal substances are form without matter. Human souls have existence independent of the bodies they inform. Incorporeal substances are simple substances. Once created, they are immortal, for having no parts, they cannot deteriorate. Even though they have no matter, though, incorporeal substances still have potentiality. Only God is completely actual. In addition, since it is matter that individuates particular substances, and since incorporeal substances have no matter, there can only be one incorporeal substance of any given kind—for example, there can be only one angel of any given kind. It would make no sense to hold that there are two angels of a kind, for there would be no way of telling them apart.

Essence and Existence

Aquinas wishes to distinguish between *what* a thing is, its essence, and *that* a thing is, its existence or being. The essence of a thing is that which makes it what it is, its "whatness." It is its definition. Clearly, you can understand a thing's essence, what it is, without knowing whether it exists. For example, you can know what a unicorn is without knowing whether one exists or, indeed, even knowing that none exists.

In an early work, *On Being and Essence*, Aquinas tells us, ". . . *essence* . . . designates that through which and in which a being has the act of existing." Aquinas does not mean that to have an essence is to exist. Rather, an essence is what makes it possible for a substance to have existence as that kind of substance. Human beings could not exist, for example, without a rational soul. However, this is not to say that a rational soul causes human beings to exist. In a sense, the explanation is the reverse: Existence causes essences. More precisely, an essence is caused to have actual being by an act of existing; for example, your humanness is caused to exist by your act of existing.

The cause of the existence of an actual being, however, is something beyond it. If a being's own essence could cause its existence, then it would be self-caused; but Aquinas thinks this is impossible for any being other than a necessary one, which is God. Ultimately, the cause of the existence, that is, the coming to being, of substances is God. God himself necessarily exists. In God's case, essence is existence. Thus, Aquinas' distinction between essence and existence serves to distinguish God from the rest of creation.

UNIVERSALS

A problem many medieval theologians and philosophers were concerned with was that of universals. For Aquinas, we could take the problem to be: What is the nature of essences? Following Aristotle's rejection of Plato's transcendent forms, Aquinas holds that essences do not have an existence independent of actual beings, substances. Thus, for example, the essence of being human does not have its own existence, independent of actual humans. It does, however, exist in actually existing humans. Likewise, redness has no existence of its own, independent of red things. But it does exist in existing red things. In general, essences exist insofar as they are instantiated in actually existing substances. Aquinas' view thus echoes Aristotle's view that forms exist in things, not in a transcendent realm as Plato had maintained.

GOD

Aquinas holds that God is the creator of all things—he is the cause of the existence of all finite substances. Such beings need not exist, even though they in fact do exist because of God. In contrast to finite substances, God necessarily exists—God's own existence is not brought about by anything external to God, but by God's own nature. Hence, by his own nature, God must exist, which is to say that God's essence is existence. This idea is central to Aquinas' proofs of God's existence.

Another way of understanding Aquinas' view is that God has more reality than any other being and supports all other beings, causing their continued existence. Created beings may be arranged hierarchically; God, their creator, is at the top, being the most perfect and real. This conception of the relation of God to his creation underlies Aquinas' proofs of God's existence.

Aquinas does not think that we can know God's nature through reason, yet he does think that reason can be used to demonstrate God's existence. He discusses God's existence in several of his works; perhaps the most famous discussion occurs in the *Summa Theologica*. While he thinks that God's existence may be taken on faith, the proposition "God exists" is not self-evident; if it were, then all people would believe it. He thus rejects Anselm's ontological argument for God's existence. The reason God's existence may be taken on faith is that it is demonstrable through reason, hence must be true. In Part I, Question II, Aquinas offers five proofs of God's existence, called the "Five Ways."

"Five Ways"

In the "Five Ways" Aquinas offers causal proofs for God's existence. That is, he argues from facts about existing things to the conclusion that God must exist as their cause. This kind of argument is known as a cosmological argument. It is not surprising that Aquinas argued in this fashion, given the influence of Aristotle on his thought, for Aristotle held that knowledge of substances is knowledge of their causes and had himself offered a cosmological argument to show the existence of an unmoved mover. But Aquinas was no doubt influenced by the cosmological arguments of other philosophers as well.

THE FIRST WAY

Aquinas' first proof is from motion. He begins from the premise that some things are in motion. Like Aristotle, Aquinas understands *motion* in the broad sense of change—change from being potential to being actual. Aquinas' example is that when a fire makes wood hot, the fire causes the wood's potential to become hot to be actualized. In order for a thing to change, something else must cause the change, because to initiate change requires actuality; otherwise, a thing would have to initiate change in itself, which would require that it be both actual and potential at the same time—a contradiction.

Aquinas' example helps to illustrate this. A fire, which is actually hot, causes wood to become hot; if the wood could make itself hot, it would have been hot already, which is impossible. Another way of thinking of it is that in order for something to become hot, it must start off not being hot (otherwise it could not become hot). If it is not hot already, that is, in actuality, then it is hot in potentiality, insofar as it has the potential to become hot. But to become hot in actuality requires that it take on that actual heat from something else. Otherwise, it would have to make itself hot; but then the source of its heat would have had to be within itself, which means that it would have already been hot, contrary to hypothesis.

Perhaps a clearer example is motion, in the sense of change of place. For an object at rest to begin to move requires that something else that is actually moving impart that motion to the object. Thus, an object at rest (which is potentially moving) acquires actual motion by receiving it from a cause that is actually moving.

In short, Aquinas is arguing from the fact that there is change in the world and the premises that things cannot initiate change in themselves and that the analysis of the cause of change cannot be infinite to the conclusion that there must be a first mover to get things started. That first mover is God.

THE SECOND WAY

In the second proof, Aquinas argues that there must be a first cause as an *efficient* cause. He begins by observing that in the natural world all things have efficient causes and that such things are never self-caused. Each cause is itself the effect of another cause upon which it depends for its existence. There must be a first cause because otherwise no effect would ever have occurred, that is, nothing in the natural world would exist. That first cause is God, a cause that is itself not the effect of something external to it.

Commentators, including Copleston, have pointed out that Aquinas is not arguing against the possibility of an infinite series of efficient causes stretching backward in time. (Thus, he is not rejecting Aristotle's claim that the world is eternal.) Rather, he is making the point that all actual beings depend for their existence on beings greater than they are. So, for example, you could cite your parents as the efficient cause of your existence, their parents as the efficent cause of their existence, and so on. But all of the beings in the series that brought about your own birth are dependent on a greater being who is more real than any of them, who makes possible their existence, and who is not dependent on any other being for its existence. (This idea also occurs in Descartes' *Meditations*, particularly in his own cosmological argument.)

THE THIRD WAY

In his third proof, Aquinas argues that everything that exists in the natural world also has the potential to not exist; that is, all existing things are *possibly* existing beings, not *necessarily* existing beings—they could also not exist, just as well as they can exist. In other words, all existing things have the potential to not exist. For example, you exist now; however, you did not exist before you were born. Aquinas also maintains that everything that has the potential to not exist will, at some time, actually not exist (or has actually not existed). If this is the case, then given enough time, there must be some time at which every possible thing is (or was) actually not existing. But if there were a time at which nothing existed, then nothing would exist now, for to begin to exist requires that a thing go from being potential to being actual, which requires a cause. But clearly things exist now. Hence, there must also exist a *necessary* being—one which never does not exist, but must always exist—in order to cause possible things to come into existence at the time when nothing else exists. That is, there must be a being that is the cause of itself, so that its existence does not require a cause other than itself, and that being is God. If there were not such a necessary being, then nothing would exist now.

THE FOURTH WAY

The fourth proof begins by observing that existing things have properties in varying degrees. Aquinas argues that a thing has a property to a certain degree because some other thing has the property in the maximum degree; further, that thing is the cause of the property in all other things that have it to a lesser degree. In his example, fire has the maximum degree of heat and is the cause of heat in all other existing things. Hence, the perfections, such as goodness, that existing things have must also be caused by a most perfect or real being. That being is God.

THE FIFTH WAY

In his final proof, Aquinas begins with the observation that the natural world exhibits design: Things act with a purpose and achieve their purposes or aims through design, rather than accidentally. Yet, things that have no intelligence cannot achieve their aim through design unless there is a designer that so directs them, that has so ordered the world. Hence, an intelligent designer exists, and that designer is God. (This argument is related to the a posteriori argument for the existence of God that Hume discusses in the *Dialogues on Natural Religion*. See Chapter 15.)

THE SOUL AND IMMORTALITY

The nature of the mind or soul and the possibility of an afterlife were important issues for Catholic theology, and for Aquinas as well. To understand Aquinas' views, it is important to understand how he attempts to reconcile Aristotle's view of the soul as the form of the body with Christian theology.

The Aristotelian View

Aquinas accepted the basic elements of Aristotle's view of the soul. According to that view, all living things are kinds of substances. The substantial form of a living thing is a soul, that which makes it grow and change and reproduce, thus developing its potential. When a living thing dies, it loses its soul and hence undergoes a substantial change: It is no longer the kind of substance it formerly was but is merely prime matter with certain accidental properties. For Aristotle, then, the soul is not an entity inhering in the body; rather, it is a *principle* by which a living thing has life, by which it acts and develops its potentiality.

The Human Soul. While the form of any living thing is a soul, the soul of a vegetable is different from the soul of a dog, and the soul of a dog is different from the soul of a human being. Plants have a vegetative soul, enabling them to grow and reproduce. Animals have a sensitive soul, which enables them to grow and reproduce, but also to have sense perception. Humans have a soul that enables growth, reproduction, and sense perception, but which also enables abstract thought, which is what distinguishes humans from other animals. The human soul is thus a rational soul.

Aristotle held that there were different parts of the soul, with different functions: Sense perception is done by the passive soul, thinking by the active soul. Sense perception is dependent on the body, because it requires sense organs, and involves images of corporeal objects. Intellectual thought, however, is not limited to images and does not require corporeal objects; abstract thought is in principle unlimited.

SOME DIFFICULTIES

Aristotle's view of the soul presents the following puzzle: Neither form nor matter can exist independently; they must exist together as substance. Thus it seems that the soul cannot exist independently of the human being that it informs, which means that it cannot exist independent of a human body. Yet Aristotle himself takes abstract thought to be an activity that is independent of any bodily organ for it is not limited by sensory images and is not performed by any of the body's organs. It is difficult to see how any of the soul's activities could be independent of the body if the soul is not in some sense independent of it.

Averroës' Solution. This difficulty led Averroës, an important twelfth-century Islamic interpreter of Aristotle, to postulate that the sensitive soul informs the body, but that the intellect, which performs abstract thought, does not; rather, there is one intellect for all people, which is not a soul. Hence, there is no problem of explaining how there may be individual souls or intellects. There is only one *intellect*, but there are many individual *sensitive* souls informing human bodies.

The Problem for Christian Theology. The Aristotelian conception of the relationship of the soul to the body also poses a problem for Christian theology, which holds that the soul can exist after death. Since forms cannot exist independently of the substances they inform, it is hard to see how a soul could exist independently of a human being. But also, in Christian theology, personal survival of death is possible: You as an individual will survive death because *your* soul will continue to exist after the death of your body. However, in Aristotle's view, it is matter that individuates beings. Without matter, there would be no individuals. So it is hard to see how the notion of an individual soul can make any sense since it is matter that individuates beings, not form.

Aquinas' View

Aquinas adopts Aristotle's view that the soul is the form of the human being, and that it is rational activity that distinguishes the human soul from the souls of other living things. He holds that God gives each body its form, or soul, on creating it. But what happens to the soul on the death of the body? To be consistent with Christian theology, it is of utmost importance for Aquinas to explain how the soul may continue to exist after death, so that personal immortality is possible.

Response to Averroës. Aquinas rejects Averroës' solution to the first difficulty because the intellect Averroës proposed was an impersonal one, the same intellect for all individuals. Aquinas points out that if there is only one intellect for all people, it is difficult to explain why we are not all thinking the same thoughts at the same time, and how it is possible that *I* think when it is the intellect independent of me that is doing the thinking.

Aquinas' Own Resolution. Aquinas' own view is that the soul is the principle of rational activity; as such, it is incorporeal, and it "subsists" independently of the body. Even though it subsists, it is still the form of the body, for it is what gives life, activity, to the body. The soul is incorporeal because if it were not, it would not be able to think abstractly, to know general truths about all bodies. Also, if the intellect operated through an organ of the body, then its knowledge would be limited by the nature of that organ; but intellectual knowledge is not so limited. (This is similar to Descartes' argument in the *Second Meditation* that it is the intellect, not the senses, that have knowledge of material objects. See Chapter 10.)

Aquinas also thinks that if the intellect operates independently of any bodily organ, then it must in some sense "subsist in itself." How is it possible for the intellect to subsist, yet to still be a form? Aquinas answers, in Question 75, Article 3 of the *Summa Theologica*, that the intellect presupposes the body in order to think, in that the body provides the materials for thinking—sensory images, for example. In the same way, in order for any animal to have sense perception, there must be "materials" to sense—material objects. But nonetheless, the animal's own existence is independent of those other objects in the world, which it senses; likewise, the soul is independent of the body, even though it employs the images provided by bodily organs in its activity of thinking. Without the body, then, it could not engage in its activity and is dependent upon it only in that respect.

Aquinas' view that the intellect "subsists" independently of the body has to do with his understanding of form as that which makes a thing actual. As such, the form is itself actual; in acquiring a form—in the case of a human body, the human soul—matter goes from being potential to becoming actual. The form itself, then, "subsists" insofar as it is already actual, by virtue of which it actualizes matter.

Aquinas did not think, however, that a human soul exists prior to the creation by God of the human being of which it is the soul; God creates them together. Nor did he think that the body is merely the "house" for the soul on earth.

PERSONAL IMMORTALITY

Recall that in the Aristotelian analysis of substance as form plus matter, it is matter that individuates substances. So, if the soul is the form of the body, and forms themselves are only individuated by existing in matter to form substances, then in what sense can the soul be an individual? (Aquinas thought, as mentioned above, that there could only be one angel of any kind, for to have multiple entities of a kind requires matter to individuate them.) And in what sense can the soul exist without the body that it informs?

We have already seen something of an answer to the second question, in that Aquinas thinks the rational activity of the soul is independent of the body, hence the soul can itself "subsist." Aquinas' answer to the first question is that the soul is individual by being linked to the body of a particular human being. My soul has a tendency to be united to my body—that is, my form has a tendency to be united to my body, and your form to yours. So, even when my soul is separated from my body, as when my body dies, still it has a tendency to be connected to my body. This fits in nicely with the Christian idea that at the end of the world, the body will be resurrected and rejoined with its soul. Being disembodied is only a temporary state of the soul, and not its natural one.

The success of Aquinas' attempt to reconcile the Aristotelian notion of the soul as the form of the body with the possibility of the soul's ability to survive death is questionable. It is not clear that he can consistently hold that a form can exist without informing anything—or put another way, that sometimes the soul informs the body, yet can also exist as an independent incorporeal substance. What makes an individual corporeal being *that* individual is the matter constituting it. Thus, insofar as you have a body, you are individuated by matter. Is what makes you the individual that you are your body or your soul? Aquinas' view is not very clear on these points.

Aquinas is one of the greatest of the medieval philosophers. His work represents an attempt to synthesize the main principles of Aristotle's metaphysics into a systematic understanding of the world that would be consistent with Catholic theology. Aristotle's views provided Aquinas with a foundation for a rational theology; but whereas Aristotle was concerned with knowing the nature and purpose of substances in the natural world, Aquinas was interested in God and all of creation, viewing the latter as a hierarchy of substances created and sustained by God, some corporeal and some incorporeal.

Aquinas thought that Aristotle's views were correct, hence any disparity with religion must come from a misunderstanding. His work addresses many philosophical issues that go beyond theology. Yet with respect to the latter, he attempted to reconcile Aristotle's philosophy with Catholicism and to show that reason could supplement faith. In that spirit, he offered five proofs of the existence of God. Yet, on other points, he admitted that reason is silent. For example, he agreed that reason cannot show the world must have had a beginning; that must be taken on faith. Aquinas' work is of great importance, in part because of its influence on subsequent philosophers. His followers were known as "Thomists," and there are still many prominent Thomist philosophers. The continuing study of his work is a testament to his greatness.

Selected Readings

Aquinas, T. *Selected Writings of St. Thomas Aquinas*. Translated by R. P. Goodwin. New York: The Bobbs Merrill Company, Inc., 1965.

_____. *Basic Writings of Saint Thomas Aquinas*. Ed. by A. C. Pegis. New York: Random House, 1945.

Copleston, F. C. *Aquinas*. Baltimore: Penguin Books, 1955.

Kenny, A. *Aquinas*. New York: Hill and Wang, 1980.

9

Francis Bacon

Francis Bacon (1561–1626), the central thinker of the English Renaissance, is often regarded as the father of modern empiricism. He is a thinker with whose revolutionary works begin the self-conscious study of scientific methodology and the careful investigation of the powers and limitations of the human being as cognizer.

Bacon's life cannot be easily summarized. He wrote with extraordinary learning about the law, politics, history, and morals. He was also a central figure in the political machinations of the period; he was Attorney General, Lord Keeper, Lord Chancellor, and was, finally, made Viscount St. Albans. Still, there can be little doubt that Bacon is best famed for his efforts to ground the sciences, to clear for them a foundation amid the ruins and confusions of medieval thought.

The chief philosophical works that Bacon composed are The Advancement of Learning *(1605),* Novum Organum *(1620), and* De Augmentis Scientiarum *(1623).*

BACON'S GREAT INSTAURATION

Bacon is deeply pessimistic about the state of the sciences of his day. At the same time, he is deeply optimistic about the capacity of a human being to know, once the human mind is properly directed. At the start of the *Great Instauration* (1620), he writes:

That the state of knowledge is not prosperous nor greatly advancing; and that a way must be opened for the human understanding entirely different from any hitherto known, and other helps provided in order that the mind may exercise over the nature of things the authority which properly belongs to it.

It is in this way that Bacon conceives of his attempt to display the past errors of scientific thinking and to provide for nothing less than the entire reworking of the way in which we are to understand ourselves and the world.

The Structure of the Instauration

The *Instauration*, the plan for the utter restructuring of the sciences was conceived by Bacon to consist of six parts:

1. A Division of the sciences.

2. Bacon's new method for conducting scientific work, called by him the "New Organon."

3. The Phenomena of the universe; the basis in experience, the data, of the sciences.

4. The ladder of the intellect; instances of Bacon's new method at work.

5. Forerunners of the new philosophy; provisional conjectures, and hypotheses, made prior to the use of the new method.

6. The new philosophy; a statement of the science as produced by Bacon's method.

The grandness, the scope, of this project can hardly be overemphasized. It is important to say on Bacon's behalf that he recognized that he could not carry out this plan during his lifetime.

BACON'S DIVISION OF THE SCIENCES

It is in Book 2 of the *Advancement* and Books 2–9 of the *De Augmentis* that Bacon's understanding of the division of the sciences is to be found. Bacon actually claims to be classifying the various branches of learning rather than the sciences (which he calls "philosophy"); and these Bacon calls "poesy," "history," and "philosophy." To these branches of learning correspond the three faculties of the intellect: imagination, memory, and reason.

Bacon is, however, most interested in "philosophy" (science). In the third book of the *De Augmentis* Bacon draws the traditional distinction between revealed knowledge of the divine and sensory, or natural, knowledge. Natural knowledge is divided by Bacon into natural theology and knowledge concerning Nature and Man. Common to all these branches of science is "First Philosophy." Bacon's discussion of first philosophy is not his clearest. It is apparent, however, that it includes certain fundamental logical principles, or canons of good reasoning, for example, the law of contradiction and the law of excluded middle.

Natural philosophy is again divided into the "Speculative" and the "Operative." This division corresponds to our division between the theoretical and applied branches of a given science.

Natural Philosophy

Bacon again divides speculative natural philosophy into "Physic" and "Metaphysic." Corresponding to these on the applied side of the divide are "Mechanic" and "Magic." (This last is so named by Bacon because it is founded upon a deep understanding of nature and so it makes possible great wonders.)

It is by appeal to Aristotle's doctrine of the four causes that Bacon distinguishes between physic and metaphysic. Physic studies efficient and material causes, while metaphysic focuses upon final and formal causes. Ultimately, Bacon's use of this Aristotelian terminology is not helpful. Rather, it is an example of a revolutionary thinker making use of a traditional vocabulary in order to make novel claims. This is a familiar feature of the early modern period in philosophy.

PHYSIC

We can, however, understand what Bacon is after. Physic deals with the "common and ordinary course of nature," and metaphysic struggles with the "eternal and fundamental laws" of nature. Metaphysic gives us a deep understanding of the ways of nature. The laws and principles it discovers serve to explain and to unify the great variety of experiences we confront at the level of observation.

An example will serve to make this clear: "Fire is the cause of induration, but respective to clay. Fire is the cause of colliquation but respective to wax." Thus, physic deals with "variable causes," it notes and examines the correlations which are to be found at the observational level. (It should be emphasized that the discovery of such correlations may require careful observation and experiment.)

METAPHYSIC

Metaphysic is dedicated to the discovery of final and formal causes, or forms. The inclusion of final causes here is quite odd. Bacon is justly famous as one of the first to assert that the search for final causes is one of the chief sources of the distress and stagnation of science. Yet, he at least *says* that there are final causes and that it is appropriate to regard natural phenomena as the intentional product of a superior will. We must simply conclude that

Bacon's inclusion of final causes as a proper object of natural philosophy does not cohere well with the central direction of his thought.

FORMAL CAUSES

Bacon's discussion of formal causes, or forms, is fundamental to his thinking. It also raises some of the most difficult interpretive issues relating to the study of his system. He is clear about the fact that the discovery of forms is the chief aim of science. A reasonable hypothesis as to Bacon's meaning here is the following: While Bacon is no straightforward atomist, he does understand common-sense objects to be composed of particles that are in motion and are arranged in various ways. It seems that the form of a thing is to be understood to denote the structure or organization of these particles. Thus, the form of gold, fire, or lead is some particular manner of the organization of the minute particles of which the gold, for example, is composed.

Bacon's Forms

There are two important issues to emphasize before we leave Bacon's doctrine of forms.

First, forms are unobservable. They are the hidden or real nature of the things of which the universe is made. One simply cannot tell by looking at a particular thing what its form is.

Second, formal causes are not to be understood as causes as that notion comes to be understood in the Humean (named for David Hume) tradition. Rather, Bacon's forms (and here the relation to modern scientific practice is important) show us what it is for a certain property (whiteness, motion, heat) to be instantiated or realized in a particular object. It is this that Bacon means when he says that "the Form of a nature is such that given the form, the nature infallibly follows." Whatever the form of gold is, there will be gold present if and only if that form is present.

Bacon on the Study of Man

Two issues deserve mention here. First, by virtue of Bacon's acceptance of a distinction between the mind and the body, the sciences of the body are to be distinguished from the study of man's intellectual abilities. Second, however odd it seems given Bacon's apparent dualism, he is very clear about the fact that the methods used for studying man should be the same methods used in the study of nature. Bacon is what we would call a "methodological monist."

ATTACK ON CURRENT SCIENTIFIC PRACTICE

This is Bacon's conception of the sciences. But according to Bacon the sciences of his day are in a state of complete disrepair. How has this happened? And how can the situation be remedied? Throughout his writings, he heaps scorn upon the Renaissance Humanists, the Scholastics and the Alchemists.

His chief worries about his contemporaries are aptly noted in the following passage:

> The axioms now in use having been suggested by scanty and manipular experience and a few particulars of most general occurrence are made for the most part just large enough to fit and take these in and therefore it is no wonder if they do not lead to new particulars. And if some opposite instance not observed or not known before chance to come in the way, the axiom is rescued and preserved by some frivolous distinction, whereas the truer course would be to correct the axiom itself.

Bacon is disturbed by the hastiness or rashness of much of the science of his day. From little data, it leaps into the formulation of general principles. Once formulated, these principles are then regarded as true. From these principles one then goes on to construct deductively valid explanations of phenomena. These explanations are protected, in an *ad hoc* way, from contrary data. In virtue of this, Bacon calls this "method" the "anticipation of nature." Here one formulates principles or laws which one regards as necessarily true, and then one goes about looking for phenomena to explain.

Furthermore, Bacon is concerned that the way in which such theories are generated insures that they will be extremely limited; they will apply only to a narrow range of phenomena and will have no observational consequences outside the sphere of their original discovery. Thus, such accounts do not allow us to go on to make surprising discoveries in unexpected places. To give but one example: A theory which explains both the behavior of celestial bodies and the behavior of the tides is just a better theory than one which explains only the behavior of celestial bodies. Such a theory points to an underlying unity and order in what are otherwise diverse and unrelated phenomena. In this way, such a theory is apt to display nature at a more fundamental level.

Bacon's point is that one is unlikely to develop theories of such elegance and explanatory power by making use—uncritical use—of the categories of our common-sense understanding of the world. Bacon writes that "[t]he discoveries that have hitherto been made in the sciences are such as to lie close to vulgar notions." They barely go beneath the surface of observation.

It is for this reason that Bacon condemns the way that the Scholastics and others have divided the natural world into species, genera, etc. If our aim is to understand nature, we must aim to carve nature at her joints. Our aim must be to seek out the causally relevant properties in nature. Only in this way can the distinctions that we draw serve to display nature in a way that corresponds to any real, explanatorily useful distinctions.

The Idols

But how did we come to such a state? More than this, what is the source of Bacon's optimism about our ability to come to understand nature as it really is? Bacon's view is that our minds have become corrupted and that we must take great pains to avoid pitfalls of reasoning.

In Book 1 of the *Novum Organum* we find one of Bacon's most famous doctrines—the doctrine of the Idols. The Idols are certain typical ways in which the human mind is apt to go awry. Bacon points to four classes of idols.

THE IDOLS OF THE TRIBE

These are so called because they have their foundation in human nature itself. Among these are included our tendency to be struck by and to give priority to data which are salient or are otherwise easily recalled; our tendency to pay great attention to evidence which confirms views we hold already; our tendency to ignore or to fail to notice phenomena which disconfirm theories we hold. Included here, as well, is the fact that our senses are limited and in certain circumstances, at least, give rise to illusions.

THE IDOLS OF THE CAVE

These are deficiencies which are the result of idiosyncrasies of habit, education, etc. Some of us may be very good at logic, some very poor. Others of us will be very good at distinguishing between things which are apparently quite similar, others of us will be quite poor in carrying out this task.

THE IDOLS OF THE MARKETPLACE

It is here that Bacon points to the way in which we are led astray in our thinking and reasoning about nature by language. Since we can give names to things which do not exist (e.g., Aristotle's prime mover), words can take us farther and farther away from the things themselves. Second, and perhaps more vicious, a single word can be applied to a variety of what are, in fact, very different properties in different substances. This is a kind of abstraction which seduces us into making claims that have no basis in nature.

THE IDOLS OF THE THEATER

These are ways of thinking which are the result of allegiance to false schools of thought. An Aristotelian, for example, might well be unable to give due consideration to Bacon's own notion of form.

THE IDOLS CONSIDERED

The doctrine of the idols anticipates much that is to be found in contemporary methodology and social psychology. Bacon argues that we have very good reason to be very suspicious of what we find ourselves believing. In this way, the doctrine is part of a tradition to which Descartes' project and Spinoza's effort to improve the understanding belong. More than this, Bacon thinks that the theory of knowledge will be of use to us only if it pays close attention to the peculiarities of human psychology.

BACON'S NEW METHOD

Given this rather dark view of our cognitive abilities, how is it that we are to arrive at a true view of nature? Bacon's own method he terms the "Interpretation of Nature." The method is meant to be a methodical, indeed a wholly mechanical, procedure. From the careful observation of nature, we slowly and deliberately arrive at axioms. We do not, as the old methods did, "fly from particulars to the most general axioms."

The method of induction is a way of moving from particulars to general claims. For example, we might observe that *this* A is F, *that* A is F, the *next* A is F, and so forth; from this we move to the conclusion that *all* As are F. Bacon condemns induction by simple enumeration. It can only seek to confirm hypotheses and, as it has been practiced, is manifestly haphazard.

DATA COLLECTION

Bacon's own method will begin with the gathering of a "complete and accurate natural and experimental history." This stage will provide the data for the interpretation of nature. It is at this stage that critics of Bacon often point out that he fails to understand the role of hypothesis in science. How could one possibly know where to look for the relevant data, and how could one possibly know when to stop without some conception, however tentative, of what it is one is trying to show?

Using the New Method

Once the data are collected, one can then go on to use the method Bacon recommends. Some of the most famous passages of the *Novum Organum* are devoted to Bacon's illustration of the method making use of the example of heat.

We have already suggested that the goal of the method is to discover the form of the nature under investigation, in this case, heat. Toward this end one arranges the natural history of heat into tables of presence, absence, and comparison (for ease we will ignore the last).

HEAT

Table of Presence: rays of the sun, all flames, ignited solids, boiling liquids, etc.

Table of Absence: rays of the moon and other celestial bodies, static electricity, sparks, unignited solids, liquids in their natural state, etc.

Bacon provides many examples such as the above. The aim is to find the form of heat. Thus, we want to discover cases in the table of presence in which heat is, in fact, present but is present in many diverse kinds of substances. If we succeed, we will not be seduced by merely apparent co-present natures. The form of heat must have something to do with what is shared by all the cases in the table of presence.

In the table of absence we look for cases share many of the natures found in the table of presence but in which the nature under scrutiny, heat, is absent. So, all the natures which are present in both tables can be safely ignored as the form of the nature we are studying. It is perhaps surprising that given the meager resources of the method, Bacon, after surveying the tables of heat, suggests that its form is "a motion expansive, restrained, and acting in its strife upon the smaller parts of bodies." Bacon has apparently anticipated the modern notion that heat is molecular motion. Bacon emphasizes that the conclusion is only a "first vintage." Yet, nowhere is Bacon clear about how the investigation should then continue.

Virtues of the Method

In a comparison of the tables, Bacon notes that certain experiments will be suggested. In unclear cases we will need to determine whether the nature under investigation really is present or absent. To resolve such questions, controlled, experimental environments must be constructed. In addition, Bacon's method is properly recognized as anticipating the view that in the sciences one must not seek merely to confirm a theory, one must rather seek data which would disconfirm one's hypothesis. In short, Bacon recognizes the centrality of the negative instance in scientific methodology. And so, while it is true that Bacon can be properly criticized on many fronts, it should not be forgotten that he clearly understands the importance of experiment and the role that disconfirmation must play in the sciences.

Weaknesses of the Method

It is not apparent how, on the basis of the tables, one is to discover the form of a nature. The form is, after all, something unobservable and hidden. This makes it clear that conjecture and hypothesis must be at work if the method is to have any chance of success. Bacon does seem to be aware of the problems here. Nonetheless, he apparently thinks that the method, properly administered, will come to single out some one form.

Bacon is traditionally taken not to have understood the role of mathematics in science. He does understand that careful measurement and quantification is crucial to the making of useful observation. It must be admitted, however, that Bacon views mathematics as a mere "appendix" of science.

We have already noted the chief criticism of Bacon's method: He fails to understand the fundamental role of hypothesis in science. Indeed, the term *Baconian* is, in some contemporary circles, a term of derision. The term points to naive methods which seek to collect all the facts and then, purified of all hypothesis, somehow manage to formulate the single correct account of the phenomena. This is indeed a naive picture—both of scientific methodology and of Bacon's method.

Bacon's central concern is to criticize the *ad hoc* unresponsiveness to the data of the methods of his day. As a result, it is surely not surprising that he would fail to be as clear as he might about the role of conjecture in the method. Yet when Bacon describes his own method, it is apparent that hypothesis is playing a role. Perhaps we should say that, given his justified condemnation of the methods of his time, he quite understandably fails to give due attention to the role of hypothesis in our efforts to explain and understand the world.

The revolutionary quality of Bacon's mind is easy to miss from our current view of the world. He, like many of the philosophers of the modern period, seeks for our sciences a new foundation not in thrall to the claims of the past. He rightly understands that our untutored claims to know are likely to be false. We should then be skeptical of the claims of common sense. In Bacon, we have a clear anticipation of a worry that continues to find its way into philosophy: What is the relation between our common-sense conception of the world and the picture which is produced by our best science?

Selected Readings

Quinton, A. *Francis Bacon.* New York: Oxford University Press, 1980.

Urbach, P. *Francis Bacon's Philosophy of Science: An Account and Reappraisal.* La Salle, IL: Open Court Press, 1987.

10

René Descartes

René Descartes (1596–1650) is the first major philosophical thinker of the modern period—the father of modern philosophy. He was born in La Haye, France, and received a Jesuit education, steeped in scholasticism, at La Flèche. He subsequently studied law at the University of Poitiers, then went to Holland, where he joined the army in 1618. The following year, he traveled to Germany, where on a winter day, isolated in a heated room, he began developing his ideas for how knowledge should be acquired. That he should work on a new unified science was also revealed to Descartes in a series of dreams. Descartes returned to France in 1628, but soon returned to Holland, where he remained until 1649, when he went to Sweden at the request of Queen Christina. He died there in 1650.

As did many philosophers of the modern period, Descartes had many interests beyond traditional philosophy, including physics, physiology, and mathematics (he invented analytic geometry, and the Cartesian coordinate system is named for him). His major works are: The Rules for the Direction of the Mind *(1628),* The World *(1629),* Discourse on Method *(1637),* Optics *(1637),* Meteorology *(1637),* Geometry *(1637),* Meditations on First Philosophy *(1641),* Principles of Philosophy *(1644), and* Passions of the Soul *(1649).*

Descartes' dream was to lay the foundations for acquiring certain knowledge of the world and to proceed to acquire that knowledge through a careful use of the method he prescribed. This was very important for science. Descartes thought that if we use reason carefully, following his method, then we will be able to attain certain knowledge of the truth. He thought that all aspects of nature may be investigated the same way and that, ultimately, we may hope to achieve a unified understanding of the world.

Thus, in his works, Descartes offers a detailed account of his method for acquiring knowledge, as well as his own scientific theories.

DESCARTES' METHOD

One reason Descartes is an important and innovative thinker is that he placed a priority on epistemology—the study of knowledge—and on finding a method of acquiring knowledge. Descartes was skeptical of the so-called knowledge he had learned in his schooling. Yet how can one distinguish true beliefs from false beliefs? How could the false beliefs he had acquired be discounted, and only true beliefs be accepted? This is the subject of Descartes' *Discourse on Method*, as well as the *First Meditation*. Descartes tells us in the *Discourse on Method* that he was "especially pleased with mathematics, because of the certainty and self-evidence of its proofs," and also that he ". . . was astonished that nothing more noble had been built on so firm and solid a foundation."

Knowledge Requires Certainty. Descartes thought that real knowledge requires absolute certainty—the kind of certainty that we find in mathematics. And to achieve such certainty, we need two things. First, we need a solid foundation. Second, we need a way of building from the foundation to other truths. Descartes' *Meditations* is his most important philosophical work, and in it he shows us how certain knowledge may be acquired by following his method. Thus, we will examine the course he takes in the *Meditations*, which leads him to knowledge of important metaphysical principles, such as that God exists, that the material world exists, and so on.

**Descartes'
Foundation**

Descartes describes his foundation for knowledge in the *First Meditation*. His starting point is his collection of beliefs, many of which he suspects to be false. Should he sort through his beliefs, rejecting each one that is false, or at least uncertain, keeping only those that are certainly true? That would be quite an ambitious project, considering all of the beliefs an individual has. Rather, Descartes tells us that he will look for a *ground of doubt* for certain basic beliefs, and if those can be doubted, then all other beliefs based on those will also tumble.

Grounds of Doubt. What Descartes does, then, is to examine his basic beliefs, looking for ways in which they could be false. That is, he looks for grounds for doubting each belief, namely, an alternative explanation, according to which that belief could be false. It is important to note, though, that Descartes does not require that a belief be false in order to set it aside; it is enough that a belief be uncertain, that is, *dubitable*, for it to be set aside. You may well believe some things that are true, even though you cannot be certain that they are true. However, unless you can be certain of a belief's truth, you must set it aside. Thus, Descartes tells us, "I should abstain from the belief in things which are not entirely certain and indubitable no less carefully than from the belief in those which appear to me to be manifestly false. . ." In the *Meditations*, Descartes shows us exactly what such a process of doubting, or withholding belief, is like, and how knowledge can be reconstructed once a firm foundation is discovered.

Doubting Sense Perception. Descartes begins his project by looking for grounds of doubt for the beliefs that he, like most people, accepts the most readily—beliefs based on sense perception. Right now, you have many such beliefs—beliefs of which you are so certain that it would not occur to you to question them. For example, you believe that there is a book in front of you, that you are breathing air, that you are supported by the floor, and so on. Indeed, all of your beliefs about the world around you are based on sense perception.

But can you be sure that such beliefs are true? One way of finding out is to consider whether there is a ground of doubt, an alternative explanation, for the experiences you are having that give rise to these beliefs. Could it be that there is not really a book in front of you? Could your eyes be playing tricks on you? Descartes admits that sometimes the senses "deceive" us. For example, objects sometimes look different from a distance than they do up close. But generally, we take our senses to be reliable indicators of what the world around us is like.

Dreaming. However, Descartes thinks there is another ground of doubt for our beliefs about the world: We could be dreaming. Descartes recognizes that sometimes when we are asleep, we think we are awake. Presumably, you think you are awake right now. But can you prove that you are? How do you know that this is not just one of those occasions when you really are asleep, but think you are awake? Descartes thinks that there are no "conclusive indications" by which sleep and wakefulness can be distinguished. So, you have an alternative explanation, a ground of doubt, for the experiences you are having. You believe there is a book in front of you because you seem to see a book in front of you. But perhaps you seem to see a book in front of you, not because you really see a book in front of you, but because you are dreaming that there is a book in front of you. How will you decide which is true? Descartes maintains that no inspection of the contents of your experience will help you to decide. So, you must put aside your belief that there is a book in front of you until you can find a way to be certain that there really is a book in front of you. Likewise, you must set aside all beliefs based on sense experience until you can be certain that they are true. These include not only beliefs about the particular objects around you but also more general beliefs about the world, including scientific beliefs, as well as the very general belief that there is a world at all!

Doubting a Priori Beliefs. The kind of beliefs we have wondered about above are sometimes called a posteriori—that is, acquired "posterior to," or after you begin to have, experience. Still, we have many beliefs that we believe independently of our experience. These beliefs are called a priori— that is, knowable "prior to" experience. Their truth can be determined independently of experience. Examples are mathematical truths and definitions. Consider the proposition "two plus three equals five." You can tell whether that is true without going out and doing an experiment. Simply by having an understanding of addition and the concept of *two*, you can see that, indeed, two plus three equals five. Likewise, consider the proposition "a square has four sides." Simply by knowing the definition of *square*, you can tell that that proposition is true. You need not go check squares to figure it out, nor does it matter whether or not you are dreaming. In fact, Descartes does think that we have those beliefs "before" we have experience; he thinks that they come from "innate ideas," which we will discuss below.

The Evil Deceiver. Can we be sure that such beliefs are true—that, for instance, two plus three really does equal five? Or is there an alternative explanation for why we believe this, other than that it is true? Descartes thinks so. He asks us to consider that there is an extremely powerful deceiver who brings it about that whenever you think "two plus three equals five," you are wrong. Can you be certain that there is no such deceiver? Another way of thinking about this is simply to suppose that your brain was wired up incorrectly, so that whenever you think a false thought, such as "two plus three equals four," you have a feeling of certainty that it is true, and whenever you think a true thought, such as "two plus three equals five," you have a feeling of certainty that it is false. Now, how do you know that that is not the case? Could an evil deceiver have scrambled your brains, so that you are constantly confused? Can you be certain that this has not happened to you?

Descartes thinks that he cannot be certain of even his seemingly most certain beliefs, such as the truths of mathematics, for he has found an alternative explanation of why he believes them, which he is unable to rule out.

It is interesting to note that Descartes' ground of doubt for a priori beliefs, namely, the evil deceiver, is sufficient to cast doubt on all of his beliefs. So why did he not just start off using the evil deceiver as a ground of doubt? The answer is that Descartes suspects that, in fact, some of the beliefs he has set aside are true, while others are not. Descartes believes that even if there is not an evil deceiver—and he will show us that there is not—there are still good reasons for doubting some of our beliefs, such as those based on sense perception. Hence it is important to be aware of all of the reasons for doubting each set of beliefs.

DESCARTES' STARTING POINT: THE COGITO

Descartes is clearly in a predicament when he begins the *Second Meditation*. He seems unable to be certain of any of his beliefs, hence has put them all aside. He can no longer believe that there is a world around him, nor that two plus three equals five. (Of course, he cannot believe that there is no world either, nor that two plus three does not equal five—he must simply suspend all of his beliefs.) But is there not one thing he can be absolutely certain of—that is, for which there is no alternative explanation?

Descartes' Reasoning

Descartes thinks there is one thing of which he can be absolutely certain, namely, that he exists. For even if there is an evil deceiver, the most powerful ground of doubt Descartes can find, the deceiver cannot be an alternative explanation for Descartes' belief that he exists. Descartes' reason for believing that he exists is that he is thinking, whether that thinking consists of being deceived by the deceiver or not. In order to be thinking, he must exist. Therefore, Descartes cannot be deceived in believing that he exists, for even if he is being deceived, he exists. The prerequisite for his having the thought that he is deceived is that he exists; there is no alternative explanation, no ground for doubting that he exists. Thus, he knows clearly and indubitably that he exists. This line of reasoning is sometimes referred to as the *cogito*.

What Descartes Has Established

With the *cogito*, Descartes believes that he has found an indubitable belief to serve as a starting point, a foundation for a new system of knowledge. But this may seem like very little to work with. All Descartes really knows is that while he is thinking, or engaged in some mental activity, he knows he exists. But what about when he is not thinking? Does he perhaps pass in and out of existence, existing only when thinking is occurring? Does he have to be thinking "I exist" in order to know it, or can he trust his memory? We may even press further to ask whether Descartes is entitled to trust any of his faculties, including reason itself? Certainly it would seem that if an evil deceiver could deceive Descartes into believing that two plus three equals five when it does not, then could not his entire process of reasoning have been the mischievous work of a deceiver?

Of course, if Descartes were to take these worries seriously, he would never be able to get anywhere. What he is really interested in doing is to show how the right use of reason can lead to knowledge; he is not interested in doubting reason itself, although perhaps he has shown us no reason to abstain from such a doubt. But in the interests of understanding his project, we must grant him his reliance on reason, memory, language, and the other tools he needs to proceed.

Some Criticisms of the Cogito

Descartes' reasoning in the *cogito* has been the subject of much discussion. Does it really establish anything? One observation that has been made is that it is not really an argument at all. If it were an argument, then it would have as its premise, "I am thinking," and from that premise alone, it would derive its conclusion, "I exist." But another premise is needed to make such a line of reasoning valid—namely, "Thinking things exist." Yet surely Descartes cannot know that thinking things exist, given that he has doubted everything. But as some philosophers have pointed out, even if he could rely on that second premise, would he really have proved anything? For supposing you saw that argument written in a book somewhere. Upon reading it, would you believe the conclusion that there is someone, whoever the "I" in the argument refers to, that exists?

Jaako Hintikka has offered an interpretation of the *cogito* that avoids this problem. It is that the *cogito* should not be thought of as an argument per se, but as a performance. That is, what Descartes is showing us is that whenever he "performs" the thought "I think," he also knows he exists, for it would be self-stultifying to "perform" the thought "I do not exist." Thus, in Hintikka's view, the *cogito* works, not as an abstract argument, but as an utterance or performance, to show that the performer must exist.

Bertrand Russell offered another interesting criticism of Descartes' reasoning: Perhaps we should not grant Descartes the first premise, "I am thinking," but only grant him, "There is thinking going on." For what is this "I" that is doing the thinking? Can Descartes have knowledge of it? Or does he only have knowledge of the immediate thoughts that are occurring?

A Model for Knowledge

While the *cogito* may seem to establish very little, Descartes proceeds in the *Second Meditation* to show just how much he can learn from it. One thing he knows is that his old beliefs about himself were not correct, or at least were not based on reason. Formerly, he thought he had a body, as well as a soul that was like a wind or a flame, infused throughout his body. Now, he knows that he has grounds for doubting all of that.

THINKING: DESCARTES' ESSENTIAL ATTRIBUTE

What Descartes knows now, through the use of his reason, is that he is a thinking thing, where thinking includes doubting, willing, hoping, sensing, imagining, and any other mental activity of which he is aware. Thinking is the only attribute he can find that he cannot exist without, hence it is thinking that is essential to his being.

THE "LIGHT OF NATURE"

With the *cogito*, Descartes found something that could not be doubted. He thus uses the certainty of the *cogito* as a mark of its truth. Thus, another thing that Descartes draws from the *cogito* is that anything that is as certain as the *cogito* must also be true. He calls the faculty that shows him such truths the "Light of Nature."

The Wax Example

To show how his reasoning about himself can serve as a model for acquiring other kinds of knowledge, Descartes offers what may seem to be a rather curious example. He asks us to consider a ball of wax and how it undergoes change. Now, of course, at this stage, Descartes does not know that anything besides himself exists. But his point is not to show that the wax exists, but rather to show what we would truly know about it if it did. Descartes chooses wax as an example of how material objects in general behave; he formerly thought that he had knowledge of material objects that was even more certain than his knowledge of himself. By examining the wax, Descartes shows that material objects are not as easily known as are our own minds. Moreover, he shows that his own precritical beliefs about the nature of material objects were not well-founded, and it is crucial to the acquisition of scientific knowledge that we get rid of all such beliefs.

Descartes asks us to perform a thought experiment: Consider what a piece of wax is like upon being removed from a beehive. It has a particular color, size, shape, texture, odor, and so on, which properties distinguish it as wax. Now consider what happens to such a piece of wax when it is put near a flame. It melts and, in so doing, loses the particular color, size, shape, texture, odor, and so on, that it had before. But clearly, Descartes tells us, the wax is still there; it just has a different appearance to the senses. But if those properties apparent to the senses have changed, then surely they cannot be what we know when we have knowledge of the wax, or of any other material object. For to have knowledge requires certainty, and certain knowledge is *unchanging*, just as mathematical knowledge is.

THE REAL PROPERTIES OF MATERIAL OBJECTS

How, then, could we possibly have knowledge of material objects? We must look not at the properties that we know through the senses, for sensory information is uncertain and changing; rather, we must look at the properties that are unchanging, that we can detect with the intellect, or reason. Descartes tells us that throughout its change, some properties of the wax remained. Those properties are very general, namely, extension, flexibility, and movability. Although the wax changed size and shape, it still had *some* size and shape, hence had extension. Also, regardless of the state it was in, the wax was flexible and, likewise, could change locations, hence was movable.

THE WAX'S PROPERTIES ARE KNOWN THROUGH THE INTELLECT

Descartes thinks that we arrive at these very general properties through the intellect, or reason, because there is no way that we would be able to understand extension in general, or flexibility in general, or movability in general, by employing the senses alone. The senses can only show us particular appearances of extension; even if we were to have thousands of examples of extension, the senses alone would not give us the concept of extension in general, that property which all particular instances of extension have. Hence, as with his discovery of knowledge of himself as a thinking thing, Descartes finds that it is only through the use of his intellect that he can discover the true nature of material objects.

The distinction Descartes draws between the real properties of material objects—extension, flexibility, movability—and those that have changing appearances to the sense—color, taste, odor, texture, etc.—is sometimes called the primary/secondary quality distinction. We will discuss this further when we look at John Locke in chapter 13.

A PROBLEM WITH THE EXAMPLE

You may notice a flaw in Descartes' reasoning about the wax's properties. Descartes thinks that the properties of the wax that are unchanging are its real, or *essential*, properties, those which real knowledge will be about, and without which the wax would not be wax. But why should Descartes prefer extension, say, to color? It is true that the color of a material object may change under certain conditions; but so may the particular size or shape, as Descartes himself points out with the wax. Could we not say, then, that the general property of having color is a property essential to material objects? Using Descartes' reasoning, it seems that we could. Likewise, you may observe that even if we grant Descartes that extension is known through the intellect, because it is the intellect that finds what is constant in the changing appearances of an object to the senses, that seems to presuppose having observed extension with the senses in the first place. Descartes does not think so, however. He takes extension, unlike color or taste or odor, to be an innate idea, a concept that is somehow in the intellect from the start.

LESSONS FROM THE WAX

Descartes uses the wax example to make several points. Remember, he is not assuming, or even trying to argue, that the wax exists. He is merely showing us how we would go about acquiring knowledge of material objects if they did exist. He is trying to provide a foundation for science, to show what real scientific knowledge of the material world is like.

The Essential Property of Material Objects Is Extension. One important point made by the wax example is that material objects are not really known through the senses. They are known through the intellect, or reason. This discovery conflicts with Descartes' former belief that the senses gave him knowledge of material objects. After considering the wax, he knows that sensory information is changing and uncertain, hence it cannot be the source of knowledge. Descartes' real piece of knowledge about the wax is that it is extended. That is, extension is the essential property of the wax and of material objects in general, just as thinking is the essential property of Descartes.

Material Objects Are Substances. Also, Descartes' judgment that there is some "thing" that remains the same through change is not a judgment derived from the senses, for again, sensory information is in constant flux. Hence, Descartes concludes that his inference that there is some unchanging "thing"—a substance—underlying the properties he observes with his senses can only come from the intellect.

Real Knowledge Requires Innate Ideas. Descartes takes the concepts of extension and of substance to be innate, that is, they are in the intellect at birth and are not derived from experience. (Indeed, it is Descartes' general view that all the concepts used in both mathematics and physics—number, substance, point, extension, etc.—are innate in the mind and are developed through reason.)

Clear and Distinct Ideas. Descartes also talks about his newfound knowledge of the wax, that is, of material objects, as being clear and distinct. By contrast, he thinks that his old beliefs were confused. Descartes will use the criterion of clarity and distinctness throughout the *Meditations* to prove the claims necessary for his foundation. The problem with beliefs that are not clear and distinct is that we simply do not know whether they are true or false. But clear and distinct beliefs must be true. Consider, for example, the claim that there are square circles. Now, Descartes would say that this is not a clear and distinct claim, because anyone who clearly knows what a circle is and what a square is can see that there cannot be square circles. However, he thinks his old beliefs about the wax were precisely like this. Before, he thought the wax was really white, fragrant, and so on; but subsequently, he saw it lose color, shape, fragrance, etc. Hence his initial beliefs were not clear and distinct.

Here is another way of thinking about what a clear and distinct idea is: If an idea is clear and distinct, then to deny it would involve a contradiction. For example, for Descartes to say "I do not exist" involves a contradiction, hence, the statement "I exist" is clearly and distinctly true. Likewise, Descartes takes the statement "Material objects are not extended" to involve a contradiction, for he cannot conceive of a non-extended material object. He can, however, conceive of a material object that does not have color, fragrance, etc., hence his old belief that material objects have color, texture, fragrance, etc., is not clear and distinct. Indeed, sensory experience can never, on Descartes' view, provide us with knowledge that is clear and distinct. It is the faculty of the "Light of Nature" that shows us clear and distinct ideas.

Knowledge of the Mind. One other point that Descartes makes with the wax example is that he knows the intellect—his own mind—much better than he knows material objects. The reason for this is that he has immediate access to his own mind through introspection. Nothing stands between Descartes and his mind; introspection is, as it were, a direct window into the mind. By contrast, material objects do not have that immediate accessibility. But also, by simply going through the process of reasoning about the nature of material objects, Descartes has learned something about his own nature as a reasoning being.

The wax example sets the stage for Descartes' dualism, which is more fully developed in the *Sixth Meditation*. Although he does not yet know whether material objects really exist, if they do exist, they are very different from the kind of substance Descartes himself is. Descartes is a mind, which is a substance whose essential property is thinking. Material objects are substances whose essential property is being extended.

THE PROOFS FOR THE EXISTENCE OF GOD

With the *cogito*, Descartes establishes his first piece of knowledge—that he exists and that he is a thinking thing. The *cogito* provides him with a criterion for knowledge. It is the clarity and distinctness with which Descartes perceives that he must exist that assures him it must be true. He takes that certainty, that clarity and distinctness, as a mark of truth: Anything with that degree of clarity and distinctness will also be true. Still, Descartes has not yet extricated himself from his self-imposed predicament; he still must not believe anything that could be explained away as the work of an evil deceiver. Thus, Descartes must show that he is not being deceived by an all-powerful deceiver, and to do so he proves God's existence.

Descartes holds that anything that is true can be demonstrated a priori by reason, hence it is only fitting that he thinks God's existence can be proved, too. Indeed, he thinks it important to prove God's existence so that nonbelievers will be convinced—for any rational person would have to concede the conclusion of a proof employing reason alone.

Descartes gives two proofs for God's existence in the *Meditations*. Neither is original. The first, in the *Third Meditation*, is a version of the cosmological argument, other versions of which had been given by Plato, Aristotle, and Thomas Aquinas; the second, in the *Fifth Meditation*, is a version of Anselm's ontological argument. In both, Descartes' starting point is his clear and distinct idea of God; from that idea, he infers God's existence.

Descartes' Cosmological Argument

Descartes' version of the cosmological argument is a very intricate one that appeals to certain scholastic ideas about causes, power, and reality. It is an attempt to prove God's existence by causal reasoning. Descartes begins by considering the kinds of ideas he finds in his mind. His intent is to show that there is one idea there—his idea of God—that could only have been caused by God. At the beginning of the argument, he knows only that he is a thinking thing, and that anything with as much certainty as the *cogito* must be true.

As a thinking thing, Descartes has "ideas," which are any objects of thought. Hence, ideas include sensations, images, concepts, and so on. He does not, however, know the cause of these ideas. He could have caused them himself, or he could have been born with them, or they could have been caused by something outside himself—by God, by an evil deceiver, or even by material objects themselves. But Descartes does not know which of the many possible causes of his ideas are the actual causes, and he cannot trust his former beliefs. Further, at this stage he has no way to know that there is anything besides himself that could cause his ideas.

ORDERING HIS IDEAS

In order to see if he can establish the causes of his ideas, Descartes needs a way of ordering them. To do this, he employs two concepts: objective reality and formal reality. Formal reality is the reality that things have and is mirrored in the objective reality that the ideas representing them have.

The Formal Reality of Things. But what exactly does *reality* mean in this context? Formal reality, or power, has to do with a thing's ability to bring about effects—to be a cause. Roughly, Descartes' idea is that some things are more real than others because some things have more power, or more "being," than others. For example, a dog is more powerful than a rock; and a human being is more powerful than a dog; and of course, God is more powerful than anything else since God is infinitely powerful. The more powerful or real a thing is, the more perfect it is.

Ultimately, the most perfect things are mental substances since they have within them a principle of activity: They can think, and they bring about changes in other things. Material things, by contrast, are inherently inert—something must move them because they cannot act on their own. Thus, an ordering can be established of all things, according to the degree of formal reality that each has.

Objective Reality. To order his ideas, Descartes appeals to another kind of reality—objective reality—which characterizes ideas. The objective reality of an idea is the reality it has in virtue of what it represents, its object. Hence, the objective reality of an idea corresponds to the formal reality of the object it represents. So, for example, since the formal reality of a human is greater than the formal reality of a rock, likewise the objective reality of the idea of a human is greater than the objective reality of the idea of a rock.

The Idea of God Has the Most Objective Reality. The idea that Descartes finds within himself that is the most real is, of course, his idea of God. Since the idea represents an infinite substance that is infinitely powerful, good, wise, and so on—i.e., a thing with infinite formal reality—the idea itself must have infinite objective reality. Of course, Descartes does not know that God does exist, but only that he has an idea of a being with infinite formal reality. However, to show that God must exist, Descartes argues that an idea with that much objective reality could only have been caused by God.

Descartes' Causal Principles. To do this, Descartes appeals to two causal principles, which he takes to be clear and distinct, shown to him by the "Light of Nature." One is that there must be at least as much reality in a cause as in its effect (otherwise, something could arise from nothing). The other, related to the first, is that the cause of an idea must have at least as much formal reality as the idea itself has objective reality. So, for example, your idea of a tomato must be caused by something with at least as much formal reality as a tomato. (Descartes also assumes that all of his ideas are caused, since otherwise, he tells us, an idea could arise from nothing.)

Of course, some ideas could be caused by other ideas—that is, they could be composed of other ideas. For example, you may have an idea of a unicorn, even though there are no unicorns to cause your idea of a unicorn. Nonetheless, you have an idea of a horse and an idea of a horn, and you can put them together to get the idea of a unicorn. Still, you got the idea of the horse from a horse, and the idea of a horn from a horn. Thus, Descartes maintains that even if one idea can give rise to another, something must exist to cause the very first ideas out of which all others are composed.

But could not that cause be Descartes himself? Descartes admits that he has enough formal reality to cause many of his ideas. He thinks that by comtemplating himself, he can get the idea of substance, for he is a mental substance. Also, many of his ideas are not clear and distinct: For example, he is not sure whether his idea of cold is simply an idea of the absence of heat, or whether, conversely, his idea of heat is an idea of the absence of cold, so he cannot be sure which has more objective reality. Because these ideas are confused, he thinks it possible that he conjured them up himself. Hence, it seems that he could have conjured up his ideas of God's infinite attributes, since his idea of the infinite could simply be the negation of his idea of the finite.

Only God Could Have Caused the Idea of God. Descartes rejects himself as a cause of his idea of God, though. He takes his idea of God to be clear and distinct, hence he cannot be mistaken in taking it to have infinite objective reality. And Descartes, being finite, does not have enough formal reality to have caused that idea in himself. In fact, the only thing with infinite formal reality is God, therefore God must exist.

Descartes also considers the possibility that his idea of God had several causes. According to his idea of God, God is an infinite substance that is omniscient, omnipotent, everlasting, unchanging, and the creator of all things. But it is easy to conceive of there being several deities, each of whom has some one or more of these properties. Then the idea of God could simply be a composite of each of the ideas these deities had caused: For example, one could be an omniscient deity, one an omnipotent deity, one the creator of everything, and so on. But Descartes argues that his idea is of a perfect God, implying that God is simple and unitary and that God's perfections are inseparable. Hence only a single deity could have caused Descartes' idea of God.

THE EXISTENCE OF GOD EXPLAINS DESCARTES' EXISTENCE

Having proved God's existence, Descartes is able to explain his own existence. For he now understands God to be the source of his existence, both having created him and sustaining him from moment to moment. Prior to discovering God's existence, Descartes had no idea of why he existed, for he could find no power within himself to bring about his own existence. Indeed, he finds himself to be imperfect—finite and dependent. Also, he now recognizes that God created him with all of the tools necessary to discover that God exists: God gave him reason, as well as a clear and distinct idea of God (which he takes to be his clearest and most distinct idea), the latter being like the mark of an artisan upon his work. Descartes also concludes that he has been made in God's image and likeness. Like God, Descartes is a rational, mental substance, but unlike God, Descartes is finite; yet, Descartes has been given the faculty of reason, which will enable him to increase his own perfection through the attainment of knowledge, thereby bringing him closer to God.

THE ROLE OF THE ARGUMENT IN DESCARTES' PROJECT

Of course, there are many problems with Descartes' argument. Perhaps the most obvious are his reliance on the causal principles, his acceptance of his previous scholastic beliefs about the degrees of reality of ideas and of things, and his claim that his idea of God is clear and distinct. But what is important to note is that Descartes' project in the *Meditations* is to show that all knowledge can be derived from reason, together with clear and distinct ideas. He is on a voyage of rational discovery: He begins with the *cogito*, which shows him that he exists as a thinking thing. From the *cogito*, he knows that what he clearly and distinctly perceives by the "Light of Nature" must be true. Thence, he discovers certain clear and distinct principles which, together with a clear and distinct idea of God, enable him to derive

God's existence. And once he has proved God's existence, he is able to remove the evil demon as a ground of doubt, since an even more powerful, benevolent, perfect deity exists. Descartes thereby reinstates a priori truths. He no longer must doubt that two plus three really equals five. And he is on his way out of the abyss into which he was plunged by his doubts.

The Ontological Argument

Descartes offers one other argument for God's existence. The argument occurs in the *Fifth Meditation*, and is a variation on an argument given much earlier by St. Anselm. It is a much simpler argument than the argument of the *Third Meditation*, but like the latter, it is an a priori argument: From a clear and distinct idea of God, Descartes derives God's existence.

DISTINGUISHING ESSENCE FROM EXISTENCE

In the previous argument, Descartes showed that God could be derived as the cause of his idea of God. In this argument, Descartes shows that existence is included among the essential properties of God in his clear and distinct idea. Descartes begins by acknowledging that the essence of a thing is distinct from its existence. The essence of a thing is that property without which it could not be what it is. His example here is that the essence of a mountain is to have a valley. Thus, a thing could not be a mountain unless it had a valley. Descartes' point is that this does not prove that mountains and valleys exist, only that being a mountain is inseparable from having a valley. Similarly with God: From Descartes' clear and distinct idea of God, many things about God can be derived.

But of course, it need not follow that God exists, only that God is inseparable from those essential properties that follow from the idea of God. However, Descartes argues that since, according to his clear and distinct idea, God is supremely perfect, existence *is* one of God's essential qualities—for existence is a perfection. Hence, just as it follows from his clear and distinct idea of God that God is benevolent, omniscient, omnipotent, and so on, so it follows that God has existence.

Existence as a Perfection. That existence should be taken by Descartes to be one of God's perfections may seem like a trick; indeed, many philosophers, beginning with Kant, have objected that existence is not a property at all, hence cannot be derived from the concept of God in the same way as God's benevolence or omnipotence—or as a fact about a triangle can be derived from the definition of triangle. Indeed, if you were asked to list the properties of the book you are reading, you might give the dimensions, the number of pages, the color, the weight, and so on, but it would be very odd to add, "and it exists."

It is easier to understand why Descartes conceives of existence as a perfection, though, if we think back to the conception of perfection that Descartes employs in his cosmological argument. Descartes equates perfection with reality, or being. The more perfect a thing is, the more real it is, hence the more "being" it has. As one moves up the scale of reality, the entities one finds are more active—more actual, hence less potential. A completely active being is one that depends on nothing but itself for its existence, hence, unlike Descartes, it is an infinite, independent substance. Descartes himself has both actuality and potentiality. His potentiality is developed into actuality through activity (the use of his intellect and will). However, Descartes is not fully actual; his existence is limited, and he is imperfect.

In the ontological argument, Descartes conceives of a being that is infinitely perfect—a thing that is at the top, so to speak, of the reality scale. But that thing would be fully actual, by definition, since it has infinite reality, which means that it would *necessarily* exist. It is dependent on nothing, hence is the cause of its own existence. If it did not exist, it would be less than perfect, hence would not be the most perfect being, contrary to the clear and distinct idea with which Descartes starts.

Some Other Critical Considerations. Of course, as with the cosmological argument, we can question Descartes' claim that his idea of God is clear and distinct. Perhaps the idea of a supremely perfect being contains a contradiction that is not immediately apparent. And even if we were to grant Descartes that reality, or existence, is a property, why should we think that there is a most perfect being—that is, that there is a top to the scale, at which complete actuality is reached?

The ontological argument has been the subject of fascination ever since Anselm formulated it. A variety of criticisms of it have been made, and perhaps that is why Descartes does not rely on the ontological argument as his main argument for the existence of God. Also, however, the project of the *Meditations* is to lay the groundwork for the discovery of knowledge, and part of that project is to go about discovering the true causes of phenomena. Descartes' doubts in the *First Meditation* were largely causal doubts—that is, grounds for doubting his beliefs consisted of alternate hypotheses about how they could have been caused. Hence, it is natural that Descartes' first proof for the existence of God should be a causal one, showing that there is a true cause—something beyond his own mind that causes, not only his idea of God, but Descartes himself to begin to exist and to have a continued existence. The more interesting question is, perhaps, why Descartes thinks it worthwhile to even include the ontological argument in the *Meditations* at all.

The Cartesian Circle

With the knowledge of God's existence, Descartes has removed the doubt raised by the possibility of an evil deceiver. Thus, he can once again trust that a priori truths, such as mathematical truths, are indeed true. But there is something puzzling about the development of Descartes' project.

For it seems that the possibility of a deceiver has cast doubt on the veracity of a priori truths, that is, truths that had formerly seemed to be clearly and distinctly true. Yet, Descartes must assume that what he clearly and distinctly perceives is indeed true in order to prove God's existence. (Recall that Descartes' reason for accepting the causal principles used in the cosmological argument was their clarity and distinctness. He also had to be sure that his idea of God was clear and distinct—that he was not confused about it and that the idea of an infinite substance was not just the negation of an idea of a finite substance.)

So Descartes seems to have engaged in a bit of circular reasoning. For until God's existence is proved, Descartes cannot be sure that he is not being deceived about what he seems to clearly and distinctly perceive. Yet, he must believe that what he clearly and distinctly perceives is true in order to prove God's existence. This predicament is known as the Cartesian Circle.

Could Descartes have really engaged in such viciously circular reasoning? It would seem odd that he would not have noticed this flaw. One possibility is that once Descartes finds a firm footing with the *cogito*, he does not really think that he can be confused about his clear and distinct perceptions. One thing the *cogito* provides him with is a criterion of truth: Anything with as much clarity and distinctness as the *cogito* must also, like the *cogito*, be true. Hence, that an evil deceiver could really be deceiving him about his clear and distinct perceptions becomes a very remote possibility—as Descartes calls it, a mere "metaphysical" doubt.

A RESOLUTION

But why, then, does Descartes tell us at the end of the *Fifth Meditation*: "But after having recognized that there is a God, and having recognized at the same time that all things are dependent upon him and that he is not a deceiver, I can infer as a consequence that everything which I conceive clearly and distinctly is necessarily true"? Descartes goes on to say that now that he knows that God exists, he can be sure that what he remembers to have clearly and distinctly understood is indeed true—in other words, he can know that his memory is reliable.

This suggests that all along Descartes has trusted what he clearly and distinctly perceives *while he is perceiving it*. However, an evil deceiver could have been playing tricks on his memory, causing him to think he knew something, or had derived something, when in fact he had not. So, for example, before having proved God's existence, he could have been sure that two plus three equals five as long as he was contemplating it and thus perceiving it clearly and distinctly. But when he was not contemplating it, he could not be sure about it. Now that God exists, he can be sure that two plus three equals five, whether he is contemplating it or not. But even if this is what Descartes intends, it still does not relieve him of the problem completely. This is because the entire line of reasoning in the *Meditations* thus far, including the proofs for the existence of God, requires that Descartes correctly remembers what he has done—that he can trust his memory.

Whether soluble or not, the predicament of the Cartesian Circle underscores the difficulty of engaging in the kind of task that Descartes has undertaken, of trying to construct a foundation for knowledge from a position of extreme skepticism.

TRUTH AND ERROR

Descartes' quest in the *Meditations* is to build a firm foundation for knowledge, in particular for science. His worry at the start is that some of his beliefs are false; he wants to have a way of distinguishing truth from falsehood. By following reason, the "Light of Nature," he can be sure that what he clearly and distinctly perceives is true. But how has error occurred in the first place? This question is particularly pressing since Descartes has proved the existence of a supremely perfect God, who has created him. If God is supremely perfect, though, why would God make humans such that they make errors? Should not God's creations be perfect, too, even if they are finite?

Descartes sets out to answer these questions in the *Fourth Meditation*. He begins by claiming that error does not proceed from a faculty of error—that is, God, being benevolent, would never have made humans with such a faculty. Rather, Descartes believes that God has given humans all they need to acquire knowledge; it is only misuse of those faculties, not the presence of a faculty of error, that causes humans to err. So why does error occur?

Belief

To make an error is to have a false belief, and Descartes thinks that belief is the product of two faculties, the will and the understanding. To believe something involves both having a perception of it, and choosing to accept that perception as true, which is performed by the will. So, for example, suppose you look at the moon and perceive it to be about one inch in diameter. On Descartes' view about belief, you can either will to accept that perception, that is, you can believe that the moon is one inch in diameter; or you can reject that perception, having learned from other sources that the moon is much bigger than it looks; or you can simply suspend belief, neither accepting nor rejecting that perception. The last is precisely what Descartes himself has done in the *Meditations*: Despite his inclination to accept his perceptions as true, he has suspended his will to believe them, accepting only perceptions that he clearly and distinctly perceives, that is, only those that are produced by the understanding. Hence, Descartes' practice of his own method in the *Meditations* is in keeping with the view expressed in the *Fourth Meditation* that we can separate the content of a belief from our acceptance of it.

THE CAUSE OF ERROR

This view about belief enables Descartes to explain error as a product of the two faculties of understanding and will. While each works perfectly well when considered alone, sometimes they do not work well together. God has given Descartes an infinite will, that is, an absolutely free will. In placing no restrictions on his will, God has made Descartes like himself. But also, God has given Descartes only a finite understanding. Thus, there is a limit to the knowledge Descartes can acquire. Error, then, occurs when the infinite will chooses to believe something that is not clearly and distinctly perceived by the understanding. And since the understanding is finite, it cannot provide us with clear and distinct perceptions of everything there is to know. But on Descartes' view, humans need not err; in fact, they can avoid making errors by restricting what they will to believe to those clear and distinct perceptions given by the understanding. This analysis allows Descartes to maintain that God is perfect and that he has made humans perfect, even though they are liable to err.

Still, one could ask, why did God not just make humans so that they never err? To do so would have required either that God give humans a finite will—one that is not absolutely free but can only accept those perceptions that are clear and distinct—or that God give humans an infinite intellect, so that all of their perceptions are clear and distinct. Descartes argues that it is better to have an infinite will than a finite one. As to not having an infinite intellect, Descartes argues that having only a finite intellect, he cannot hope to understand God's reasons for giving him a finite intellect, especially since to understand those reasons could require taking into account what is best for the entire creation, not just for humans. Even so, God has given humans the potential to develop their finite intellects, thereby approaching perfection.

A PROBLEM WITH DESCARTES' ACCOUNT

As described above, Descartes' account of error rests on his account of belief. While Descartes' account of belief has a certain appeal, it is also problematic. Consider, for example, your belief that two plus three equals five. On Descartes' account, you first perceive that two plus three equals five, then you will to accept that perception as true, whence it becomes a belief. But on what basis, other than believing it to be true, would you will to accept a perception as true? But then, of course, Descartes' account would be circular, because we would have to believe something to be true in order to will to believe it. This problem is linked to the difficulty you may have had in allowing Descartes that he could doubt two plus three equals five in the first place.

Descartes' Response. Descartes has an answer to this problem. He says that the reason we will to accept that two plus three equals five is not that we already believe it; rather, it is that ". . . the great clarity which was in my understanding produced a great inclination of my will. . . " Still, he also admits that he has a great inclination to believe what his senses tell him, even though he wants to refrain from accepting those beliefs. So why should a great inclination alone be sufficient reason to accept a perception as true? Also, sometimes we make mistakes even in our a priori reasoning. Mathematicians frequently make errors in constructing proofs. But presumably the feeling of certainty a mathematician has in constructing a proof that has an error in it is indistinguishable from the feeling of certainty in constructing a proof that is correct. So how can Descartes explain the error in the first case? Should the mathematician simply never believe that he or she has constructed a proof that is correct? A feeling of certainty seems to be an insufficient guarantee, since mistakes do occur.

The Significance of Descartes' Account. Whether we accept Descartes' account or not, the important thing is that Descartes has offered an explanation of how we can avoid error. This is important for two reasons. One is that Descartes can be certain that real knowledge, error-free, is possible—he is not on an impossible mission. The other is that there is no incompatibility between God's being perfect and human beings' being imperfect—that is, holding false beliefs, or in the moral realm, sinning. God has made humans not fully perfect in actuality, but perfect in their potential, if they only use their faculties wisely by restricting the will only to accept clear and distinct perceptions.

THE MATERIAL WORLD

As should be clear by this point, Descartes thinks we can have real knowledge only through our understanding, through using reason. He does not think that our senses are a reliable source of information about the world. Indeed, he attributes past errors to a failure to restrict belief to what is clear and distinct, and sensory information certainly is not that, as he showed with the wax example. But how, then, can we have any knowledge of the material world, perhaps most fundamentally, that it even exists?

The basis of Descartes' former belief that material objects existed was that he perceived them—or so he thought until he considered the possibility that he was dreaming. In the *Third Meditation*, he tells us:

> I have . . . previously accepted and admitted several things as very certain and very obvious which I have nevertheless subsequently recognized to be doubtful and uncertain. What, then, were those things? They were the earth, the sky, the stars, and all the other things I perceived through the medium of my senses.

THE REPRESENTATIVE THEORY OF PERCEPTION

On his old view of how perception works, Descartes took material objects to cause sensations in the mind, which together formed images of those objects. By perceiving the images, we have knowledge of the objects that cause the perceptions. The images are like little pictures of objects. This is sometimes called a *representative theory of perception*: Material objects cause ideas, or images, in us; those ideas, in turn, represent the objects that cause them. Or in Descartes' words, "that there were things outside of myself from which these ideas came and to which they were completely similar." (We will see this view again in chapter 13.)

DOUBTING THE REPRESENTATIVE THEORY OF PERCEPTION

But Descartes thinks that there is no reason to believe this: ". . . the principal and most common error which can be encountered here consists in judging that the ideas which are in myself are similar to, or conformable to, things outside of myself. . ." The possibility that he is dreaming showed Descartes that he had no reason to believe that the causes of his ideas of material objects are material objects themselves; furthermore, even if his ideas of material objects were caused by material objects, he points out himself in the *Third Meditation* that there is no reason to suppose that they are like little pictures of objects:

> Even if I should agree that the ideas are caused by these objects, it does not necessarily follow that they should be similar to them. On the contrary, I have often observed . . . that there was a great difference between the object and its idea. Thus, for example, I find in myself two completely different ideas of the sun: the one has its origin in the senses, and must be placed in the class of those that . . . came from without, according to which it seems to me extremely small; the other is derived from astronomical considerations—that is, from certain innate ideas—or at least is formed by myself in whatever way it may be, according to which it seems to me many times greater than the whole earth. Certainly, these two ideas of the sun cannot both be similar to the same sun, and reason makes me believe that

the one which comes directly from its appearance is that which least resembles it.

The wax example, too, showed that the real nature of material objects is not what it appears to be through the senses.

Proving the Existence of the Material World

Descartes seems to have no reason to believe that the senses inform him of the properties of material objects. But does he even have reason to think that material objects exist at all? To know that material objects really exist as the causes of his perceptions would require certainty, that is, knowing that no alternative explanation is possible.

POSSIBLE CAUSES OF OUR IDEAS OF MATERIAL OBJECTS

To show that the material world exists, Descartes argues that only material objects can cause our perceptions, or ideas, of material objects—a strategy similar to the one used in the cosmological argument to show God's existence. Thus, he rules out several other possible causes, or alternative explanations, of those perceptions.

Descartes Is Not the Cause of His Ideas of Material Objects. One possible cause of his perceptions of material objects is Descartes himself. However, Descartes does not think that he is the cause of those ideas, for he is not aware of the power by which he would conjure them up. Indeed, he generally seems to have little control over his sensations. For example, when he opens his eyes, visual sensations just come to him, whether he wants them or not.

God Is Not the Cause of Our Ideas of Material Objects. Another possible cause of his perceptions of material objects is God. By the causal principle that Descartes appealed to in the *Third Meditation* to prove God's existence, it seems that God could cause all of our ideas, for God, having infinite formal reality, has more than enough reality to cause any of the ideas we find in our minds.

Descartes is not content to accept that God could be the cause of our perceptions of material objects, though. One thing that troubles Descartes is that if God were the cause of our perceptions of material objects, we would have no way of knowing it. Indeed, anything with enough formal reality, from God down to material objects themselves, could cause our ideas of material objects. But not being able to know the exact cause of our ideas would doom Descartes' project of building a foundation for knowledge.

Only Material Objects Can Cause Our Ideas of Them. Oddly enough, Descartes uses this observation to prove that material objects exist and are the causes of our apparent perceptions of material objects. His reasoning is that if humans could not ever know that their ideas of material objects are, indeed, caused by those material objects, then they would be in a permanent state of ignorance, of having to suspend belief, just as Descartes himself was in the *First Meditation*. However, being supremely perfect, God would not have created humans to be unable to attain knowledge, that is, to be in a permanent state of ignorance. Moreover, God has created humans with a great inclination to believe that their ideas of material objects *are* caused by material objects. Thus, unless God is a deceiver, material objects must exist and must be the cause of our ideas of those objects. Descartes hastens to add, though, that material objects need not be exactly like our perceptions of them—as, for example, when the sun looks small, but turns out to be very large.

A PROBLEM WITH DESCARTES' REASONING

Descartes' proof that material objects exist is a little shaky. It relies on arguing that since God gave us an inclination to believe something—that material objects cause our perceptions—we should be able to trust that inclination, because otherwise God would be a deceiver for having created us with an inclination to believe something that is false. Yet, Descartes earlier discounted our very great inclinations to believe as good reasons to believe. Indeed, he himself notes that we have a very great inclination to believe that our sense perceptions accurately represent material objects, even though he knows that at least sometimes they do not, as his examples of errors in perception show.

Of course, in the latter case, Descartes thinks we have a way to find out that our inclination is wrong, whereas in the case of believing that material objects exist as the causes of our perceptions of them, we would have no way to find out that they do not. Also, God has given us a way of finding out what the nature of material objects really is, hence reason to doubt our inclination to trust our senses. (It is interesting to contrast Descartes' view here with Berkeley's. While Descartes thought that God could not cause our sensations of material objects without being a deceiver, Berkeley thought that he could prove God *is* the cause of our sensations of material objects. Having proved that God must be the cause of our sensations, it was then easy for Berkeley to prove that God exists.)

Knowledge of the Nature of Material Objects

Descartes' foundation for knowledge provides us with a proof that the material world exists and that material objects are the causes of our perceptions of material objects, our sensations. But he also holds that sense perception does not show us what material objects are really like. How, then, can we know the true nature of the material world, which is the subject matter of physics?

One of Descartes' main aims is to provide a foundation for scientific knowledge. Descartes thinks that physics, like geometry, is an a priori science. The materials are innate ideas, and the faculty is reason. In several passages in the *Meditations*, he contrasts knowledge of material objects gained through reason, using innate ideas, and the beliefs we acquire by sensation. For example, in the passage from the *Third Meditation* quoted above, he contrasts our idea of the sun, gained through astronomy, as being a very large body, with our belief, from looking at the sun with the naked eye, that it is not very large at all. Of course, we cannot acquire any idea of the sun without doing some kind of empirical observation of it. But as he describes in the wax example in the *Second Meditation*, Descartes thinks that using the intellect, we abstract what is constant and unchanging about material objects, and that the materials we use to do so are not found in the objects themselves, but rather are innate within us.

In Descartes' physics, material objects are beings that have as their essential property extension. In contrast to the mind, which is thinking, hence active, material objects are in themselves passive. The ultimate constituents of material objects are extended corpuscles that are in motion, whirling about in an ether. Descartes thinks that all of the other properties of objects can be derived from the extension—size and shape—of the ultimate constituents and their motion. For example, an object looks blue or feels warm or has a length of two feet because of the size, shape, and motion of its ultimate constituents. Descartes thought that physics would ultimately turn out to be like mathematics—that we could derive knowledge of the world just as we could derive theorems in geometry, using innate ideas and reason. One problem for Descartes' physics, though, is explaining how material objects are set in motion and kept in motion. God provides the obvious answer.

The Dreaming Argument Reconsidered

You may have wondered what happened to Descartes' dreaming argument. At the end of the *Sixth Meditation*, Descartes dismisses dreaming as a ground for doubting that the material world exists by noting that he now knows how to distinguish dreams from his sense perceptions while awake. He maintains that when he is awake his perceptions cohere with one another and with the rest of his life, which is not generally true of dreams; further, since God is not a deceiver, he could not be confused about this.

This is not a very satisfactory reply to the dreaming quandary, for the doubt rested on his observation that sometimes dreams are coherent, just like the experiences of our waking lives. However, having proved that material objects must be the cause of our waking perceptions, Descartes does not seem to be worried about occasionally making a mistake about whether he is dreaming. He is convinced that he can never make such a mistake when he is really awake.

CARTESIAN DUALISM

One of the aspects of Descartes' metaphysics for which he is very well known is his view on the nature of the mind and its relation to the body. In the *Second Meditation*, Descartes establishes that he exists and that his existence is constituted by thinking. He takes himself to be a thing, a substance, whose essential property—that without which it could not exist—is thinking. Material objects are also substances, but of an essentially different kind—that is, the essential property of material substance is being extended. Because Descartes thinks that there are two essentially different substances, his view is called dualism.

From his argument in the *Second Meditation* that he exists, it seems that Descartes thinks his existence is dependent on thinking, not on having a body. At that stage of the *Meditations*, however, he cannot be sure that his existence is not dependent on a body—all he knows is that at the very least his existence is dependent on thinking. Still, from his analysis of the wax, he concludes that if material objects exist, then their essential property is extension. So, it would seem that mental things and physical things have different requirements for their existence. Once Descartes proves in the *Sixth Meditation* that material objects exist, he knows that he does have a body. He must consider, then, how mind and body exist together. Do they necessarily exist together, even though they have different essences? Descartes does not think so. One reason he is inclined not to think so is that he wants it to be possible for the mind, or soul, to exist independently of the body after death.

Mind and Body Can Have Independent Existences

To show that the mind and body may, in principle, exist independently, even though they happen to exist together here on earth, Descartes argues as follows. Anything that he can clearly and distinctly conceive can be made by God just as he conceives it. Now, he has a clear and distinct idea of what the mind is—it is a thinking, unextended thing—and he has a clear and distinct idea of what the body is—it is an extended, unthinking thing. So, God can make minds without bodies. But if God could make minds without bodies, then clearly the existence of minds does not require the existence of bodies, even though they happen to exist together on earth. It is not out of the question, though, that God could have created minds without bodies, or bodies without minds. In fact, the existence of other animals illustrates just what happens when God creates living bodies without minds. Likewise, presumably heavenly creatures such as angels would be examples of minds without bodies. Thus Descartes concludes that mind and body are indeed two separate substances, which could, in principle, have separate existences as well.

The Nature of Mind

For Descartes, what makes humans special is that they have minds. The mind is an extensionless, thinking substance. This thinking is uniquely characterized by the use of reason, language, and free will.

REASON AND LANGUAGE

The kind of thought that characterizes humans, and sets them apart from other animals, is reason. In this respect, humans have been created to be like God; but unlike God, humans do not have all knowledge, but only the potential to acquire knowledge through the use of reason, becoming more real, more actual, as they do. Language, also, is a function of the intellect and is, in addition, beyond the capacity of other animals. Thus, Descartes thinks that only minds have reason and language; machines, which are part of the material world, do not.

FREE WILL

One other feature that characterizes human minds is the possession of free will, which Descartes discusses in the *Fourth Meditation*. Like God, humans possess absolutely free will. Our choices are unconstrained by the laws of nature. It is possible for Descartes to maintain that the mind is free, even though the body, being a machine, is subject to the laws of nature, because mind and body are different kinds of substances.

It is important to note, though, that Descartes thinks we are most free when we are making choices according to knowledge provided by the understanding. To be free is not to exercise "the liberty of indifference"— that is, to simply choose arbitrarily among the various alternatives. Rather, we are most free when the understanding shows us which of the alternatives we have is the most rational. Thus, we become more free, more like God, as we acquire more knowledge. Indeed, if we had God's knowledge, we would never have to worry about making a wrong choice, that is, about sinning or choosing to believe what is false. And as we acquire more knowledge, we become more and more independent of our bodies—that is, we become less and less dependent on our bodies, on sensation, for knowledge, and we become increasingly self-determining through the knowledge we gain about the world. To be free is to have power, to be active (which is to be thinking or reasoning), to be independent of external causes acting upon us.

The Mind-Body Connection

Still, we are connected to the material world through our bodies, and indeed sensation does help us to navigate in the world by telling us what is happening in our bodies and what relation they are in to other material objects. Descartes argues that sensation is not essential to his existence as a mind, since he can conceive of himself existing without sensation and without imagination, which is a sort of picturing objects to one's self as they would appear to the senses. Since Descartes takes sensation to be a purely mechanical function of the body, he can allow that other animals have sensation even though they do not have minds—indeed, they are mere automata in his view. Nonetheless, sensation does link the mind to the body. But if mind and body are essentially different substances—one an actively thinking and unextended substance, the other an inert, unthinking, and extended substance—then how does the connection occur?

TWO VIEWS OF THE CONNECTION

In the *Sixth Meditation*, Descartes offers two different ideas about how the mind and body are connected.

The Mind Permeates the Body. One view Descartes offers is that the mind is intimately connected with the body, permeating it. The mind's relation to the body is not like the relation of a sea captain to his ship; if it were, then the mind would be able to perceive the occurrences in the body through intellect alone, and there would never be any error or confusion. Rather, the mind feels sensations throughout the body, and thus a unity of mind and body is produced. Descartes says, ". . . all these feelings of hunger, thirst, pain, and so on are nothing else but certain confused modes of thinking, which have their origin in the union and apparent fusion of the mind with the body."

The Mind Is in the Brain. In another place, though, Descartes suggests that the mind is somehow located in a part of the brain—the "common sense," or pineal gland. This enables Descartes to explain how sensations are produced in the mind. His idea is this: The body, like other objects in the material world, is a machine, operating according to mechanical principles. That is, objects stimulate the sense organs through the motions of their corpuscles, and the resulting motions in the sense organs initiate a set of motions that get sent along the nerves to the brain. Descartes envisions the nervous pathway between sense organs and brain to be something like an elastic cord. Pulling on the cord at one end causes motion at the other. When the motion initiated at a sense organ reaches the brain, or more specifically, the pineal gland, a sensation gets produced in the mind. To each motion produced in the pineal gland there corresponds a unique sensation. So using one of Descartes' examples, suppose you step on a nail; the nail causes nerves in your foot to be pulled, which causes a pulling of the nervous cord between foot and brain, and ultimately produces a motion in the pineal gland, which gets translated into the pain-in-the-foot sensation. Thus, you receive a sensation of pain in your mind as though the pain were in your foot, which in turn leads you to remove the cause of the pain, thereby enabling your survival. Note that Descartes' dualism sets up a certain awkwardness about how to describe sensations—a pain in the foot, strictly speaking, is a pain-in-the-foot sensation in the mind.

How, though, is it that the motions in the pineal gland are correctly correlated with sensations? For example, why is it that when the nerves in your foot get pulled by your stepping on a nail, the corresponding motion sent to the pineal gland gets translated into the pain-in-the-foot sensation and not, say, a hunger-in-the-stomach sensation? Or a sensation of the color blue? Or a sensation of the sound of a trumpet? Descartes' answer is that God, being supremely benevolent, has set up the best possible matching of motions in the brain with sensations, necessary for our self-preservation. God could have made it so that the motion which now corresponds to the pain-in-the-foot sensation had instead corresponded to the hunger-in-the-stomach sensation. But that would not have served a very good purpose, for then, instead of tending to the foot, or removing the nail, you might have gone in search of a pepperoni pizza.

ERROR IN PERCEIVING OUR OWN BODIES

Despite the connection God has established between motions in the brain and sensations in the mind, sometimes errors do occur in our perceptions of our own bodies. Descartes' account enables him to explain this. Like all machines, the body is subject to breakdown or malfunction. Hence, sometimes the motions sent along the nerves will go awry. But also, nervous motions may be initiated at any place along the cord leading from sense organ to brain. So, suppose the cord stretching between your foot and your brain gets pulled at the halfway point. A motion will be sent along the cord, just as if the motion had been initiated at your foot, and the resultant motion in the brain will also be the same. But since that motion is correlated with exactly one sensation, the pain-in-the-foot sensation, that sensation will be produced.

The Phantom Limb Phenomenon. This explains the phantom limb phenomenon—that is, how people who have lost a limb may continue to have sensations of pain in that limb. The nerve cords that had originally ended in the limb still exist, hence, motions will sometimes be sent up the remaining parts of the cords to the brain, just as if they had been initiated in the original limb.

What We *Can* Know: Seek Pleasure, Avoid Pain. It is not surprising that we may sometimes make errors in perceiving our own bodies, since we know sensation to be fallible. Still, Descartes thinks that we are more often right in those perceptions than not. Further, he thinks that one thing we can be certain of with respect to sensation is that in general we should seek pleasure and avoid pain, as God has set up our sensations so that pleasurable sensations indicate what to seek out for our survival, and painful sensations show us what to avoid.

Problems with Descartes' Dualism

Descartes' conception of the nature of the mind has been an extremely influential one in Western thought. Many religions assume the existence of a substantial soul, which can have a continued existence after the death of the body. There are some problems with Descartes' dualism, though, that are worth considering.

CONNECTING A NON-EXTENDED THING TO THE BODY

Descartes' characterization of the mind as a thinking substance gives rise to certain problems. One is explaining how a substance that has no extension can be connected to a substance that does have extension, the body. If the mind has no extension, then it is difficult to see how it can have a location at all. Likewise, it is difficult to see how there could be any causal interaction between mind and body. For mind acts by thought, and body acts by extension. How can thought affect an extended, unthinking thing? How can extension affect a thinking, non-extended thing?

THINKING MAY NOT BE UNIQUE TO MINDS

Another problem is Descartes' view that thinking is unique to minds. He holds that only minds can reason or use language; a machine never could. Now, one reason he thinks this is because he takes thinking to be an activity; minds have a principle of activity within them, which initiates thinking and willing. By contrast, material objects are inherently passive—if they act, or move, it is only because an external force has acted upon them.

But is this really right? With the advent of computers that perform all manner of rational functions—indeed, some much better than any human could—we must wonder whether being able to reason is indeed unique to a human mind.

Similar criticisms have been made of Descartes' view that the capacity to use language is unique to the human mind. Experiments in training chimpanzees to use sign language have suggested that in the animal kingdom language use may not be singularly human. More generally, both language and reason can now be considered as the production of mechanical processes which, in theory, a computer could perform. There is little reason to think that mental processes cannot be generated by material things, that is, that the material brain cannot produce all mental processes. Also, Descartes thinks that minds generate knowledge through the operation of reasoning on innate ideas. So if computers were supplied with those materials, presumably they, too, could generate the kind of knowledge Descartes had in mind.

THE TRANSPARENCY OF THE MIND

Another questionable aspect of Descartes' view of the mind is that it is transparent to us—that through introspection, we can see directly into the mind. Recall that in the *Second Meditation*, he argued that the mind is better known than the body, for precisely this reason. Research in psychology, however, suggests that introspection is in many ways not very reliable in revealing the workings of the mind. Examples of this come from experiments done with "split brain" patients—people who have had the membrane separating the right and the left hemispheres of the brain cut in order to relieve epileptic seizures. While such patients generally seem normal in their daily activities, psychologists have designed experiments to show that sometimes the left half of the brain does not know what the right half is doing. Similarly, such experiments throw into question Descartes' assumption that the mind is a unity. Indeed, one psychologist has proposed that perhaps we each have more than one mind, even though there is only one that is self-conscious, in control.

Descartes offers no very good reason for thinking that there is only one mind; he takes the notion of substance to be innate and hence assumes that what underlies the mind's multiple activities is a single substance. But can we really be sure that there is only one mind?

THE MIND MAKES US SPECIAL

Finally, we can question Descartes' view that what makes us essentially human is the mind and that the body is an artifact God has given us so that we can exist in the world. This conception of human nature clearly devalues the importance of the body to our existence and ignores the importance of the body in giving us the consciousness we have. It also underlies the view that work of the intellect is more valuable and desirable and puts us closer to God than does work of the body, manual labor.

In general, Descartes' dualism sets up a questionable hierarchy of beings, with humans clearly at the top, and those who engage in intellectual work superior to those who do not. This kind of hierarchy has been used to assign simple laborers and animals an inferior status. Also, consistent with his view that mind is superior to matter, Descartes thought that God had given humans reason in part so that they can understand and consequently control nature.

DESCARTES' EPISTEMOLOGY

As should be clear by now, Descartes' goal was to establish a firm foundation for knowledge. Descartes changed the emphasis in philosophical inquiry from metaphysics to epistemology, ushering in a new philosophical era—the modern period. He attended to metaphysical issues, such as whether God exists, whether the material world exists, what the nature of the self and of the material world is, whether we have free will, and so on, only after having established what real knowledge is like. His views on those issues provide the foundation for his science. Descartes thinks that reason is what distinguishes the human mind from everything else in the world and, likewise, that reason is the source of real knowledge. Only by using reason can we achieve the kind of certainty that is required to truly have knowledge. Thus, as we have seen, Descartes discounts sense experience as a source of knowledge. Likewise, real knowledge is a priori: It is in principle achievable independently of sense experience, just as mathematical knowledge is. Just as mathematical knowledge can be derived, using reason, from basic axioms and definitions, so knowledge of ourselves, God, and the material world can be derived from innate ideas and principles using reason alone, as Descartes shows us in the *Meditations*.

Some Questionable Assumptions About Knowledge

While Descartes' attempt to use reason alone to establish the foundations of knowledge is impressive, some of his views about the sources and acquisition of knowledge are problematic.

THE REJECTION OF SENSE EXPERIENCE

Sensation, Descartes thinks, is not a good source of knowledge—indeed, he thinks that we should really only trust it as a means to our own bodily survival. Sensation too often causes us to make errors of judgment, such as when we judge that a stick partially submerged in water is bent when it is really straight, or that the sun is really only a few inches in diameter.

Our Senses Do Not Err. In fact, though, our senses rarely make errors. Rather, we err in the conclusions we draw from the information they provide. Our ability to detect information about the world around us through the senses is in fact very remarkable, perhaps more remarkable than our ability to reason. It is possible to program a computer that can in some ways reason as well as we can. Indeed, computers are much more consistent than humans in performing calculations and have even been able to find proofs of theorems that humans could not (e.g., the Four-Color Problem). But computer scientists have found it extremely difficult to program a computer that can pick up information about the world around it the way humans and other animals are able to do.

One reason Descartes rejected the senses as a source of real knowledge was that he thought we could never have certainty that our senses are not misleading us. A machine can always break down; an inference about the material object we seem to be perceiving can always be wrong. Demonstrative reasoning, by contrast, seems foolproof. We simply cannot be wrong that two plus three equals five. Hence, only the conclusions of pure reasoning can be considered real knowledge. In fact, Descartes thought the errors of past philosophers and scientists had resulted from a failure to require absolute certainty for knowledge and in trying to explain why objects behave the way they do, from trusting too much the way they appear to the senses. Descartes was hopeful that physics would turn out, like geometry, to be an a priori science whose development required only a careful use of reason. But in rejecting the senses as a source of information about the world, Descartes went too far in the opposite direction. By using mathematical knowledge as the standard for what all knowledge should be like, Descartes set a standard that cannot be met; with such a standard, we must remain skeptics about the nature of the material world.

KNOWLEDGE AND THE INDIVIDUAL

One other important assumption Descartes makes is that the pursuit of knowledge can be, in principle, an isolated process. In fact, the *Meditations* is itself a model for how knowledge may be acquired: To start down the path towards knowledge, one need only go through the process that Descartes has gone through. Acquiring knowledge is like learning geometry by working through a textbook—one can do it on one's own, and anyone pursuing knowledge will arrive at the same result. But these assumptions, too, are highly questionable. Knowledge seems to be in part the product of one's community and culture. It is significant that Newton lived in England in the seventeenth century, and Descartes in France in the seventeenth century. Both thinkers were heavily influenced by the ideas of their day. Also, scientific knowledge often reflects the interests of the knower and the knower's society; it is not simply waiting "out there" to be discovered, independent of culture.

*D**escartes was truly one of the great modern thinkers. He set an important precedent in viewing epistemology, the study of how we can have knowledge, as the fundamental concern for philosophy. He showed the importance both of method and of questioning how one knows to the advancement of knowledge. With his method, he attempted to distinguish superstitious or unsupported belief from a sound understanding of real causes, which gave him a basis for rejecting the former. In the* Meditations, *Descartes shows us exactly what the application of such a method is like: He uses it himself to prove that he exists, that God exists, that the material world exists, that the essential property of mind is thinking and the essential property of material objects is extension, and that mind and body are distinct substances. By applying his method, Descartes thought that he had secured a firm foundation for the sciences and that scientific progress would henceforth be unimpeded by false assumptions and ignorance—real knowledge of the workings of the natural world was just around the corner.*

Descartes was also an important representative of the rationalist approach to knowledge. He thought that knowledge is the product of reason alone. He rejected sensory information as uncertain, hence unreliable;

indeed, even by the end of the Meditations, *his doubts about the reliability of his sense experience as an accurate source of information about the material world remained unchallenged. So, for Descartes, real knowledge about God, the self, and the material world is a priori, just as mathematical knowledge is. It is attainable independently of experience and only through reason.*

Many of the details of Descartes' views now seem silly and outdated, and his faith in reason overly optimistic. But for his time his project was an awe-inspiring one. His views on the nature of knowledge and mind have been highly influential in Western thought, hence, understanding them is very worthwhile.

Selected Readings

GENERAL

Curley, E. M. *Descartes Against the Skeptics.* Cambridge, MA: Harvard University Press, 1978.

Descartes, R. *Discourse on Method and Meditations.* Translated by L. J. Lafleur. New York: Macmillan Publishing Company, 1960.

Kenny, A. *Descartes: A Study of His Philosophy.* New York: Random House, 1968.

Wilson, M. *Descartes.* London: Routledge & Kegan Paul, 1978.

ON DOUBT

Frankfurt, H. *Demons, Dreamers, and Madmen: The Defense of Reason in Descartes' Meditations.* Indianapolis: Hackett, 1970.

ON DUALISM

Churchland, P. M. *Matter and Consciousness.* Cambridge, MA: The MIT Press, 1988.

Ryle, G. *The Concept of Mind.* New York: Barnes & Noble, 1949.

11

Baruch Spinoza

*B*aruch (Benedict de) Spinoza (1632–1677) produced works that must certainly be counted among the most difficult in philosophy. He was born in Amsterdam, into a Marrano family. Marranos were Jews living on the Iberian peninsula who were forced to profess Christianity by the Spanish Inquisition. Spinoza's ancestors had left Portugal for the relative freedom of Holland. He was himself excommunicated by the Jewish community of Amsterdam in 1656 for his heretical thinking.

Spinoza has long been viewed as having led something like the exemplary philosophical life: solitary and alone with his ideas. Although commentators have been quick to note that Spinoza was, for example, very much at home with the works of Descartes, the ancient Stoics, and medieval Jewish philosophers, he is still typically viewed as an isolated thinker. Friedrich Nietzsche called him a "sick hermit." The very great complexity of Spinoza's philosophical work has added to the view that he was a thinker whose work emerges from solitary philosophical reflection.

Still, of the Rationalist European philosophers of the period, Spinoza is perhaps the one who has most in common with our own secular, physicalist conception of the cosmos. According to Spinoza, all that there is, is of this world. Whatever order is found in this world—whether causal or moral—is not to be explained by appeal to facts beyond this world; in particular, it is not to be explained by appeal to the free acts of some transcendent God. Since there is no transcendent realm, whatever salvation or liberation there is to which a human being can aspire must be found within this world.

All of this Spinoza can be said to embrace in his assertion that all that there is, is God or Nature (in his famous words, "Deus sive Natura")—the one eternal and infinite substance. For Spinoza, human freedom amounts to *coming to understand this God or Nature. In Spinoza's work, one encounters, even if not in a straightforward fashion, a naturalistic voice. He embraces mechanistic explanation, argues for mind/body monism, rejects revealed religion as a source of knowledge, and advocates political and religious tolerance. In these ways, Spinoza is an important harbinger of modernity.*

Spinoza published only two works during his life: the Principles of Cartesian Philosophy *(in which the chief points of Descartes'* Principles *are set out according to the geometrical method) in 1663 and the* Theological-Political Treatise, *published anonymously in 1670. His most important and most difficult work, the* Ethics, *was published shortly after his death. It is upon the central aspects of this work that we will concentrate.*

THE ETHICS

The *Ethics* is not a work which invites easy comprehension. It is divided into five parts.

1. "Concerning God." Here, Spinoza sets out his central metaphysical claims: the nature of substance and the relations between substance, attribute, and mode. In addition, it is here that he draws startling consequences from his claims: that besides God nothing can be or be conceived; and that everything that is, is in God.

2. "Concerning the Nature and Origin of the Mind." Here Spinoza offers a brief account of his physics. More importantly for our purposes, he prepares the way for his denial of Descartes' claim that there can be causal relations between minds and bodies.

3. "On the Origin and Nature of the Emotions." This is Spinoza's account of human nature and, in particular, Spinoza's account of the relation between an individual and the infinite substance that is God.

4. "On Human Bondage and the Strength of the Emotions." Spinoza outlines the ways in which, when subject to the emotions, which imply passivity, we are slaves. Part Four contains brilliant and provocative characterizations of various emotional states.

5. "On the Power of the Intellect or on Human Freedom." Here Spinoza characterizes how it is that in his fully deterministic universe, in which contingency is but an illusion, we can aspire to a kind of freedom which is identical to an understanding of God or Nature.

THE GEOMETRICAL METHOD

The *Ethics* is set out in the geometrical method. Spinoza proceeds from definitions to the proof of various propositions. It has and is meant to have the look of a proof in Euclidean geometry. Now, whatever one thinks of the validity—not to mention the soundness—of Spinoza's various arguments, that the *Ethics* is set out in the geometrical method is fundamental to the work. That the structure of the cosmos *can* be set out in geometrical fashion, that the world is and can be understood by appeal to self-evident claims bound by relations of logic, is the basis of a fundamental presupposition of Spinoza's vision: The world is such that it can be wholly grasped as an expression of the logically necessary. Just as a conclusion of an argument depends on its premises, and just as a conclusion of a valid argument follows with logical necessity, so the things of the world are bound together in this way. There is, ultimately, no distinction between "cause of" and "reason for." The cosmos is an intelligible system, a rational order. There is no difference between adequate conception and reality.

Spinoza on Substance

At Definition III of Part I of the *Ethics*, Spinoza characterizes his notion of substance: "[B]y substance, I understand that which is in itself and is conceived in itself; in other words, that, the conception of which does not need the conception of another thing from which it must be formed." This definition of substance is clearly related to the Cartesian notion that a substance is a thing which does not depend on any other thing. What does Spinoza mean by the claims that a substance is "in itself," and that it is "conceived through itself?"

What Spinoza means by saying that something is a substance only if it can be conceived through itself is reasonably clear. For at Scholium 2 of Proposition VII, Spinoza writes that substance is such that knowledge of it "does not need the knowledge of another thing." Thus, if one can have complete knowledge of a thing without having knowledge of any other thing, one may be certain that that thing is a substance.

But what does it mean to say that a substance "is in itself?" At Axiom 4, Spinoza writes that to have knowledge of something is to have knowledge of its cause. (There Spinoza says that knowledge of an effect requires knowledge of its cause, but there seems no good reason to limit this claim about the requirements of knowledge to effects alone.) But Spinoza accepts the Principle of Sufficient Reason in a particularly strong form: There must be a reason or cause for the existence or nonexistence of anything. This suggests, as E.M. Curley points out, that to say that substance exists in itself is to assert that substance is causally or logically independent of any other thing.

If knowledge of substance is such that it requires no conception of or knowledge of any other thing, and if knowledge involves knowledge of causes or reasons, then substance must be such as to contain its own cause or reason for being. In this sense, a substance *is* in itself; it is wholly independent of anything else. In this way, we already begin to see the ways in which, for Spinoza, adequate conception mirrors reality or being. Anything which can be conceived through itself must in fact be independent of anything else.

Consequences of Spinoza's Account of Substance

Spinoza draws numerous consequences from this account of substance. An immediate result is that no substance can cause another substance to exist. There is nothing by which a substance can be caused to exist. If this were not so, then one could not know a substance without having knowledge of something independent of substance, and this is of course contrary to the definition of substance. This argument can be schematized in the following way:

1. Suppose a substance could be caused by something independent of that substance.

2. By Axiom 4, knowledge of an effect "depends upon and involves" knowledge of the cause.

3. But from 1 and 2, we can conclude that the knowledge of this caused substance would require knowledge of some other thing (substance).

4. But by Definition III, knowledge of substance requires no conception or knowledge of anything else.

5. Thus, such a substance is both conceived through itself and is not conceived through itself. But this is a contradiction.

6. Since 1 leads directly to a contradiction, it must be rejected; and we can conclude that a substance cannot be caused by anything else.

From this, Spinoza claims at Proposition VII that it "pertains to the nature of substance to exist." As Spinoza had foreshadowed at Definition I, a substance must be a *causa sui*, a cause of itself. This result would appear to follow straightaway from the just demonstrated conclusion and the principle of sufficient reason. For if some thing cannot be caused to exist, and yet there must be some cause or reason for the existence or non-existence of anything, we can conclude that that thing is a cause of itself. This is just to admit that that thing is a necessary being, that its essence involves existence.

Additionally, Spinoza claims that any substance must be infinite. If a substance were finite, it would have to be limited by something else of the same nature. According to Spinoza, this is impossible since there cannot be two substances of the same nature or, in Spinoza's terminology, with the same attribute. (There may be a more straightforward argument in defense of the claim that any substance must be infinite. If something is finite, it is limited by some other thing. The first substance is, then, limited by that second thing. If this is so, then it would seem that knowledge of that first substance could not be had independently of knowledge of the second substance. This is contrary to the definition of substance.)

DEUS SIVE NATURA

Armed with the above results, Spinoza shows that, necessarily, God exists. Spinoza presents an argument for this claim that is meant to echo the ontological argument. The conclusion that God exists follows from Spinoza's conception of substance, along with his claim at Definition VI that by God, he means, "substance consisting of infinite attributes." Since this God is a substance, just by recapitulating the argument for the claim that any substance is such that its essence involves existence, we can show that God is such that his essence involves existence. Thus God is a necessary being.

At Proposition XIV, Spinoza makes his famous claim that "[b]esides God, no substance can be nor be conceived." It is to the investigation of this claim that we now turn.

Spinoza's Argument for Substance Monism

Spinoza arrives at this conclusion by means of a *reductio ad absurdum*. Using terminology that we will discuss below, the argument is as follows:

1. [Definition VI] God is a being absolutely infinite, a substance consisting of infinite attributes.

2. [Proposition XI] God is a substance whose essence involves existence; that is, God necessarily exists.

3. Suppose that some substance other than God exists.

4. This substance other than God would have to be explained by appeal to some attribute of God.

5. But then two substances would possess the same attribute and by Proposition V this is impossible. Therefore, since the supposition that there is another substance in addition to God leads to contradiction, there is but one substance.

Much of this argument is puzzling. Still, what is fundamental is again the notion that substance must be absolutely independent of anything else. Since God possesses infinite attributes, any substance other than God would necessarily possess some attribute or other in common with God.

The chief worry about this argument is the claim Spinoza makes at 4 above. Why is it that two substances having an attribute in common are such that there must be an explanatory relation between the two? At Definition IV, Spinoza says that an attribute is that which "the intellect perceives of substance, as if constituting its essence." If this is so, and if God and some other substance share an attribute (as must be the case if some other substance exists), then it seems as though Spinoza may well be claiming that to conceive of this other substance is necessarily to conceive of God.

This, however, violates the claim that substance is such that it must be conceived through itself alone. Thus, whatever exists must exist in God. (Already we can see that an adequate understanding of anything must involve knowledge of God.) But this God, Spinoza is at pains throughout to emphasize, is not the familiar transcendent God of religious orthodoxy; rather, this God (or Nature) is the cosmos. We have arrived at the familiar charge that Spinoza is a pantheist.

Attribute and Mode

Some of the most difficult interpretative issues in Spinoza are encountered in an effort to characterize his notions of attribute and mode. We will of necessity be brief here.

We have already encountered the notion of attribute in one of Spinoza's arguments. An attribute is that which the intellect perceives of substance as if constituting its essence. Only through the attributes can human cognizers conceive of substance. We know from what we have said above that God must have infinite attributes. But Spinoza identifies only two of the attributes of God: thought and extension. We have no access to the others, and so about them we must be silent. It must be admitted that it is not at all obvious how both thought and extension (let alone the infinitude of other attributes) could be attributes of God or Nature. It is clear that according to Spinoza, God or Nature can be understood, under the attribute of extension, as the system of extended bodies *and*, under the attribute of thought, as the system of ideas. Perhaps Spinoza's claim that the attributes are themselves infinite can be understood in the following manner: Anything whatsoever can be understood under the attribute of extension, at one time, and under the attribute of thought, at another time.

Some remark should be made about the fact that in some interpretations of Spinoza's metaphysics, attributes are themselves substances. Thus, the substance, God or Nature, consists simply of its infinitely many attributes. It is nothing over and above these. The issues here are difficult, but it should be noted that the language that Spinoza uses when discussing attributes throughout the *Ethics* does recall his earlier remarks about substance. For example, he seems willing to speak of attributes as conceived through themselves and in themselves. These issues will return when we come to a consideration of Spinoza's discussion of the mind-body relation.

Spinoza's account of modes is this: "By mode, I understand the affections of substance, or that which is in another thing through which it is also conceived." All modes, then, are in God. Making use of our earlier results, we may say that modes causally depend on attributes, and that they are conceived through the very same attribute upon which they depend causally.

All finite modes (particular finite minds and particular finite bodies) exist in God and are caused by and conceived through one of the attributes of God. There are also infinite modes. We will focus below on the infinite modes of extension.

INFINITE MODES

One intuitive way of generating Spinoza's notion of the infinite modes is this: When we come to a consideration of the physical universe, we ultimately come to note certain regularities or uniformities. According to Spinoza, "motion and rest" is the immediate infinite mode of substance under the attribute of extension. The mediate infinite mode is something Spinoza calls "the face of the entire universe." At proposition XXIII, Spinoza distinguishes between immediate and mediate infinite modes: "Every mode which exists necessarily and infinitely must necessarily follow either from the absolute nature of some attribute of God, or from some attribute modified by a modification which exists necessarily and infinitely."

Thus, according to Spinoza, "motion and rest" follows immediately from the nature of extension. The "face of the universe" follows as well from the nature of that attribute, once modified by "motion and rest." These infinite modes are eternal. They serve to characterize the unchanging nature of the physical universe. Spinoza has in mind here the Cartesian conservation laws, but his point is that the laws of nature, the nomological facts about the physical universe, are the infinite modes of the attribute of extension.

FINITE MODES

Finite modes, as we might expect, are particular things and particular facts. Individual things are, for Spinoza, nothing but modes of God's attributes. Such individual things "express" God's attributes "in a certain and determinate manner." Thus finite modes are necessarily as they are. At Proposition XVII, Spinoza writes that the finite modes "flow" necessarily from God's infinite nature. Just as it follows from the nature of a triangle that its interior angles are equal to two right angles, so all things and facts follow from God's nature. Thus, all facts about the cosmos are necessarily as they are.

NATURA NATURANS *AND*
NATURA NATURATA

However, Spinoza is willing to speak of God or Nature as "free." But, at Definition VII, he has warned us about what he means by "free." ("That thing is called free which exists from necessity of its own nature alone, and is determined to action by itself alone.") All things exist in God, causally depend upon God, and flow necessarily from God's nature or essence. For this reason, Spinoza speaks of God as the immanent rather than the transient cause of all things. God does not cause from the outside; he is not the "remote" cause of things, since all things are joined to and are in God.

Insofar as we consider God or Nature as a "free cause" in this sense, we consider it as that infinite substance which is in itself and conceived through itself. This is *natura naturans*, "nature naturing." This is God or Nature as the active principle from which all things flow necessarily, from its essence alone. For this reason, all things find their explanation in God alone.

But we can also consider God or Nature as that infinite system of modes which flow necessarily from the infinite substance. In this way, we speak of one finite mode causing another, and that mode being caused by yet another. This is *natura naturata*, "nature natured." Here, we conceive of nature through the infinite and finite modes. This is the realm of science. What must be emphasized is that this is a conception of nature as passive, as a chain of causes and effects stretching back into eternity. But it is a conception of the very same thing that we conceived as *natura naturans*. They are two conceptions of the very same infinite substance.

Thought and Extension

DESCARTES' VIEW

Descartes took the universe to suffer from a great metaphysical divide: The real distinction between the mind and the body. The essence of mind was thought, the essence of body extension. These two substances were, however, related to each other as cause to effect.

SPINOZA'S VIEW

Spinoza rejects this dualistic picture. Any conception of a thing under the attribute of thought has a corresponding conception under the attribute of extension. These are both conceptions of the same infinite substance. This is to say that God or Nature can be conceived under the attribute of extension or under the attribute of thought. Every finite mode and the relations between them can be described and explained either in terms of thought or in terms of extension. Spinoza writes that "the order and connection of ideas is the same as the order and connection of things." Again, there is but one infinite substance from which all things necessarily flow, but this one system can be understood in two quite different ways.

It may be useful to consider an example. We might seek to describe and to explain why it is that a certain round peg will not fit into a square hole. Imagine that we have a geometer and a super-physicist. The geometer might produce a detailed account of the situation in geometrical terms. The super-physicist might produce an explanation in complicated micro-physical terms. They explain and describe by making use of radically different vocabularies and principles. Yet each gives us an adequate account of what is going on in the situation. Still, there is only one situation here, now described in geometrical terms, now described in micro-physical terms. Perhaps, in *something* like the same fashion, the one infinite substance can be accounted for now in terms of thought and now in terms of extension.

MIND AND BODY

This claim might strike us as exceptionally odd. How, for example, is a rock's smashing a window to be represented in terms of the attribute of thought? Clearly, we do not possess the ideas adequate for such an understanding. Yet in the case of one finite mode, we do have some understanding of the way in which one thing can be apprehended under the two attributes. This one thing is the human being.

Spinoza claims that the *object* of the idea that is the human mind *is* a mode of extension, a body. The idea is complex rather than simple. The point here is that to each of the ideas that we have there corresponds some mode of extension (we would presumably say some neural process). Spinoza calls this mode of extension the "object" of the idea.

This may seem to us an odd way of speaking. When we speak of the object of an idea, say the idea of London Bridge, we mean that London Bridge is the object of the idea. But this is not Spinoza's terminology. Recall that for Spinoza the connection between ideas and things is the same. The mode of thought which is the idea of London Bridge is or corresponds to some mode of extension.

Spinoza's Denial of Mind-Body Interaction

Spinoza attacks Descartes' dualist interactionism. At Part III, Proposition II, Spinoza puts it this way: "The body cannot determine the mind to thought, neither can the mind determine the body to motion nor rest . . ." In arguing for this Spinoza appeals to Proposition IV of Part II, which reads: "The modes of any attribute have God for a cause only insofar as He is considered under that attribute of which they are modes, and not insofar as He is considered under any other attribute."

The time we have spent coming to grips with Spinoza's metaphysical machinery will now pay dividends. Spinoza says that each attribute is conceived through itself and without any other attribute. He then concludes that the modes of any attribute must be conceived under that attribute and no other attribute. With some plausibility, this second claim can be seen to follow from the first in the this way: If a mode of the attribute of thought needs to be conceived through the attribute of extension, then some fact about the attribute of thought (its mode, some idea) will involve the attribute of extension. But then the conception of the attribute of thought would involve the attribute of extension. This is, however, contrary to the conclusion that a conception of an attribute depends upon itself alone. Granting our earlier views about the relation between knowledge of a thing and knowledge of causes, we can conclude that modes can be caused only by other modes of the same attribute or by that attribute itself. Thus, modes of thought cannot cause or be caused by modes of extension. This is simply to agree that causal interaction between the mind and the body is not possible.

The Mind-Body Relation

Spinoza's positive account of the relation between mind and body is difficult. We know that, fundamentally, there is but one thing here and not two. For Spinoza, mind and body are one thing which can be conceived of in two ways.

Every mental event, a mode of thought, corresponds to some physical event—a mode of extension. For this reason, Spinoza's view of the relation between mind and body has been called "parallelism." But this term is not particularly helpful here. There are not two things or events which run in parallel. Rather there is one thing. One understanding of it is to be had in a mentalistic vocabulary or conceptual framework; another understanding of it is to be had in the framework of the physical sciences.

But if we seek an understanding of the world and of ourselves within it, any successful explanation must be wholly within the framework of the attribute of thought or wholly within the framework of the attribute of extension.

The Human Person

We are all modes of God; in Spinoza's terminology, we exist in God. In this sense we are not real individuals at all. Under the attribute of thought, we are a part of God's mind; under the attribute of extension, we are a part of God's body. According to Spinoza, all things necessarily follow from God's essence. Thus, there is no room for anything like a familiar account of human freedom.

CONATUS

Still, Spinoza is willing to speak of a way in which finite modes may be said to "be in themselves," "[e]ach thing insofar as it is in itself endeavors to preserve its being." This is a thing's *conatus*, its striving to express itself. This causal principle of a thing, its striving to persist, is its essence. We, as human beings, are conscious of this striving. When related to the mind, this *conatus* is called the "will." When related to both the mind and the body it is called "appetite."

ON THE UNDERSTANDING

All ideas are in a sense true since they have objects, modes of extension, to which they must correspond. Falsity, for Spinoza, is a matter of confused or inadequate ideas. The *conatus* of human beings, insofar as the essence of mind is thought, is a striving to have adequate ideas of things.

Three Kinds of Understanding

In the *Ethics*, Spinoza identifies and describes three grades of knowledge, three kinds of understanding.

IMAGINATION OR SENSE PERCEPTION

The first kind of understanding is sense perception or imagination. However useful sense perception is, the ideas generated by sense perception are inadequate to their objects. Sense perception is not up to the task of representing the causal structure of the world. The fundamental source of the confusion of sense perception is that all the objects of such sensory ideas are states of our own bodies. We assume our ideas adequately represent the world, but they do not. Our knowledge at this level is knowledge of things only insofar as our bodies are affected by those things. Such knowledge can only be confused knowledge of our own bodies and of external things. The ideas generated by sense perception come by happenstance; they are the result of things impinging on us. Thus, they are inadequate.

REASON

The second kind of understanding has much in common with Descartes' view of how we arrive at an adequate representation of the world. We can call this second kind of understanding "reason" or "science." Spinoza's point is that such understanding makes use of "common notions," ideas which are adequate to an understanding of the structure of nature. By "common notions" Spinoza means notions like extension, and "motion and rest." These are possessed by all things. Only by making use of these notions, which are not the result of sense perception, are we able to display the world as it is—something which has the kind of logical structure mentioned early in our discussion of the *Ethics*.

SCIENTIA INTUITIVA

Spinoza calls the third kind of understanding *scientia intuitiva* or intuitive knowledge. Here, Spinoza is both obscure and semi-mystical. Intuitive knowledge is a kind of union with God or Nature. In this union we move from "an adequate idea of the formal essence of certain attributes of God, to the adequate knowledge of the essence of things." The illustration that Spinoza provides, that of a mathematical proof, implies that with intuitive knowledge we directly grasp the truth of things immediately.

According to Spinoza, there is continuity in moving from understanding of the second kind to that of the third kind. In understanding of the second kind, we possess wholly adequate explanations, displayed in deductively valid form, of the events and states of affairs of the world. Intuitive knowledge makes use of these explanations, yet understands them in a new way. In intuitive knowledge we come to see the way in which particular things (ourselves included) that have already been adequately explained at the second level of understanding, express God's essence through immanent causation.

Human Freedom

There is an intimate connection between Spinoza's account of *scientia intuitiva* and the way in which a human being can be free. Much of *Ethics* concerns the way in which, in the grip of inadequate ideas, we are passive. Spinoza's brilliant discussion of the ways in which this is true of the emotions makes for compelling reading. We become active when we free ourselves from the emotions, when our understanding is not the result of how we happen to be affected on some occasion, but rather the result of an adequate understanding of things.

Recall that Spinoza says that a thing is free when and only when "it" exists from the necessity of its own nature alone. In this sense, only God is free. But I am a mode of God. With intuitive knowledge I clearheadedly come to understand the way in which I express God's essence.

Why is this a kind of freedom? With this knowledge I recognize my own essence in God's essence. I am wholly self-realized in that I come to see that I am just as I, necessarily, must be. Insofar as I recognize myself as necessarily expressing the essence of God or Nature, I rightly see that there is no question of my being moved by something external to me. I see the unity of God or Nature with me. This is blessedness. It is the condition of the wise man.

Spinoza's system is spare and beautiful. Whatever it is that we think of his arguments, and there are few Spinozists today, we must marvel at the achievement. Making use of the geometrical method and seeing that method as a model of the universe itself, Spinoza produced an extraordinary meta-physical system. Furthermore, Spinoza exerted great influence on many of the thinkers who continue to exert a direct impact upon our world: Leibniz, Kant, Hegel, Nietzsche, and Freud among them.

Selected Readings

Bennett, J. *A Study of Spinoza's Ethics*. Cambridge: Cambridge University Press, 1984.

Curley, E. *Spinoza's Metaphysics*. Cambridge, MA: Harvard University Press, 1969.

Donagan, A. *Spinoza*. Chicago: University of Chicago Press, 1988.

Loeb, L. *From Descartes to Hume*. Ithaca: Cornell University Press, 1980.

Scruton, R. *Spinoza*. Oxford: Oxford University Press, 1986.

12

G. W. Leibniz

Gottfried Wilhelm Leibniz (1646–1716) is one of the outstanding intellectual figures in the history of the West. He possessed a mind of extraordinary breadth and depth. In addition to his philosophical works, he made important discoveries in the sciences and mathematics. (In a nasty dispute, he and Newton quarreled over the discovery of the infinitesimal calculus.) Leibniz was active politically as well. He was attached to the House of Hanover, and was much distressed when the elector of Hanover did not bring him to England upon assuming the English throne as George I.

Unlike many philosophers of the period, Leibniz does not present his philosophical views in a systematic fashion. Many of his important views are found in his correspondence. His chief philosophical works are The Discourse on Metaphysics *(1686) and* The Monadology *(1714); these are the texts upon which we shall concentrate. These works are sometimes referred to as Leibniz's "popular philosophy." It is often suggested that his considered, and strikingly original—not to say bizarre—philosophical views are set out clearly only in his non-public works.*

APPROACHING LEIBNIZ

More so than most philosophers, Leibniz's work has given rise to a strikingly diverse range of interpretations. For some, Leibniz and his use of the Principle of Sufficient Reason are simply a particularly clear embodiment of the spirit of the Enlightenment. Others argue that Leibniz can be best understood as being chiefly motivated by his concerns in logical theory. Still others insist that Leibniz is a deeply religious thinker whose work must be seen as a defense of a certain traditional conception of God. Last, there are those whose view is that Leibniz is fundamentally interested in the difficulties of Cartesianism and Spinozism.

This great range of views stems, in part, from the difficulty of Leibniz's work. But in part the difficulty is also the result of trying to bring unity to a body of philosophical work which, in fact, may be fundamentally fragmented. In any case, we are able to note some of the major issues with which Leibniz is concerned.

INFLUENCES ON LEIBNIZ

We know that as a very young man Leibniz avidly read the works of thinkers such as Hobbes, Descartes, Kepler, and Galileo. We also know that he was much impressed by the way in which these works apparently devastated the old teleological explanatory ways of the Scholastics and, along with this, the traditional conception of God. According to that earlier system, the order found in the world was to be explained by appeal to the *purposes* of things in the world, and, ultimately, by appeal to the goals of God. Leibniz regarded one effort to deal with the conflict between teleology and the mechanism of the new sciences—Descartes's dualism—as patently frivolous. Given Descartes' own conception of substance—a thing which depends on nothing else—mind-body interaction is obviously impossible. In this way it is accurate to say, as many commentators do, that Leibniz regarded Spinoza's odd pantheism as the only way in which to render Cartesianism consistent. And given the straightforward unacceptability of Spinoza's doctrine, it is not surprising to see Leibniz urging more radical measures. These measures are, in part, Leibniz's effort to save tradition—God and teleology—from mechanistic science.

THE PRINCIPLE OF SUFFICIENT REASON

One way to approach Leibniz's philosophical work is by way of the principle of sufficient reason. The principle is this: For everything that is as it is, there is a sufficient reason for its being and for its being as it is. Early in the *Discourse on Metaphysics* we see this principle at work. Here Leibniz is concerned with Descartes' doctrine that the eternal truths are as they are only by virtue of the will of God. God, that is, might have arbitrarily willed the truths of, for example, arithmetic to be other than they are. Leibniz's point in Section II of the *Discourse* is that God must have a reason for his choice; it is not a matter of will alone but of rational will.

Leibniz's invocation of the principle of sufficient reason is complex. If it is true that for any true proposition there must be, in all cases, some sufficient reason for its truth, this will not be the same sort of reason in all cases. In particular, Leibniz draws an important distinction between *truths of reason* and *truths of fact*. Truths of reason are true by virtue of the law of contradiction (for any arbitrary proposition p, both p and not-p cannot be true). Truths of fact are true by appeal to God's choice of the best.

Leibniz's appeal to the latter principle can be seen in his claim that God has produced the system which, by making use of the simplest means and order, produces the greatest richness of effects. Here we have displayed in clear form Leibniz's commitment to the view that the cosmos is a harmonious and elegantly unified whole. It operates according to principles ordained by God.

Truths of Reason and Truths of Fact

Here we must begin to examine Leibniz's logical views. For Leibniz, all true propositions are true in virtue of some sufficient reason. Now we must note that for Leibniz all propositions which assert some truth possess the same logical form—the subject-predicate form. All true claims assert that some property or other can be predicated of some substance or other. Thus, the truth of fact, "Caesar crossed the Rubicon," predicates the property, "crossed the Rubicon," of the individual substance "Caesar." Still, even if all propositions have the same form, there are important distinctions to be drawn. In particular, some propositions are truths of reason and some are truths of fact.

In the *Monadology*, Leibniz observes that truths of reason are necessary, by which he means that their opposite is impossible. He goes on to claim that truths of fact are contingent, by which he means that their opposite is possible. Elsewhere, Leibniz refers to the distinction as that between absolute necessity and necessity *ex hypothesi* (by hypothesis). Still elsewhere, he characterizes the distinction as one between the admittedly certain and the fully necessary.

The distinction, as drawn by Leibniz, certainly seems to be the familiar distinction between the necessarily true and the contingently true. As a way of coming to grips with Leibniz's distinction consider the following two propositions:

1. A triangle has three interior angles.

2. Caesar crossed the Rubicon.

Leibniz notes that propositions like the first are necessary. They are true by virtue of the law of contradiction; one cannot deny such a truth without being involved in a contradiction. Furthermore, one can demonstrate the truth of such claims a priori by means of some finite proof; according to Leibniz they amount to an assertion of identity. (This should be clear in the case of 1 above; to say that a triangle has three interior angles is to say no more than what is fully grasped when we say that something is a triangle.)

As for propositions like 2, Leibniz says that their contradiction is possible. One can deny them without being involved in a contradiction. There is no *finite* proof to which we can appeal in demonstrating their truth. Such truths are certain but not necessary; they are contingent. Such truths are made true by virtue of God's free choice. They are, nonetheless, true by virtue of the principle of sufficient reason—God's choice of the best. Furthermore, such truths include all existential claims (with one important exception, the claim that God exists).

What demands our attention is the basis of such truths. Truths of reason are true by appeal to the law of contradiction. While truths of fact must also be true by appeal to the principle of sufficient reason, we must appeal to God's choice of the best (or the principle of the best or perfection).

A DIFFICULTY WITH THE DISTINCTION

This apparently familiar distinction is complicated by another doctrine of Leibniz's. According to Leibniz the "concept of an individual substance [for example, Caesar] includes once and for all everything which can ever happen to it and that in considering this concept one will be able to see everything which can truly be said concerning the individual, just as we are able to see in the nature of a circle all the properties which can be derived from it." How then is Leibniz able to draw a distinction between the necessary and the contingent?

LEIBNIZ'S RESPONSE TO THE DIFFICULTY

Leibniz recognizes that this view seems to threaten the familiar distinction between the necessary and the contingent. He notes that all truths about any arbitrary individual substance can be seen to follow a priori from the nature of that substance (even if in practice only God can do this). At various places in his writings Leibniz seeks to respond to this difficulty by appeal to the distinction between what is certain and what is necessary. Thus, while it is necessarily the case that the triangle has three interior angles or that two plus two are four, it is certain—but not metaphysically necessary—that Julius Caesar will cross the Rubicon. Here Leibniz simply asserts his original claim that truths of reason depend only upon the principle of contradiction, while truths of fact depend instead on God's choice of the best (the decision to create Caesar), and Caesar's choice (to cross the Rubicon).

However, we cannot yet accept this reasoning. For Leibniz, God is the greatest conceivable being. And since Leibniz accepts a version of the ontological argument, we know that for Leibniz, necessarily, God exists. God is omnipotent, omniscient, and omnibenevolent. Given this conception of God, we can say that God only wills the best possible world and that whatever God wills, is. If this is so, then we know that this actual world is the best possible world. It is a simple matter, on Leibniz's view, to show that God always does everything for the best. With these views now in hand, it seems as though we can construct the following argument:

1. Necessarily, God exists.

2. Necessarily, God is omnipotent, omniscient, and omnibenevolent.

3. Necessarily, God wills the best. Therefore, necessarily, this actual world, the world willed by God, is the best possible world.

The consequences of this are fairly easy to see. Since Caesar did exist and since he did cross the Rubicon, we know that these are facts about the best possible world. That is, if Caesar did not exist or did not cross the Rubicon, the world would not have been the best possible. And, on Leibniz's view, this supposition does seem to involve a contradiction. That is, the existence of this other possible world (the one in which Caesar did not exist, or did not cross the Rubicon) looks to be incompatible with the existence of God. But we know that, necessarily, God exists. Thus, this reasoning suggests that every feature of the actual world is necessary, not just certain. In this way, the distinction between the necessary and the contingent must have, at best, an uneasy place in Leibniz's system.

Human Freedom

In ways that are not hard to see Leibniz will have difficulty making sense of the possibility of human freedom. In fairness to Leibniz, this difficulty is in many ways just a version of the old problem of reconciling God's foreknowledge of future events with human freedom. Yet in some ways the difficulty is more serious because of Leibniz's view of God's role in the cosmos.

Leibniz raises these worries in a discussion of Judas' free act to betray Jesus. Of such human decisions Leibniz wants to argue that God inclines our souls without at all necessitating them. Much of Leibniz's point here is that God has made it the case that human beings choose in accord with what we might term the "law of practical reason": Human beings always choose the apparent good. So what human beings must do is to be on guard against appearances; we must decide or act only after mature deliberation. But given Leibniz's views about the nature of God's choice of the best, whatever decision Judas makes has "been assured from all eternity."

What Leibniz wants to urge here is the following. We should not ask why Judas chose to betray Jesus, rather the real question is why God chose to create a world with Judas. As we saw above, once Judas is created, everything he will ever do, any predicate which can ever be assigned to him, is assured. Yet, if our above argument concerning Leibniz's effort to distinguish the necessary from the contingent is right, it would seem as though it is necessarily true that Judas betray Jesus. If this is on the right track, it is not at all clear that we can give sense to the claim that Judas' action is free.

Human Choice   Still, it must be emphasized that much of Leibniz's discussion of this problem has a profoundly contemporary ring. According to Leibniz, to say that we are free is to say no more than that what we do depends on what we choose to do. If we weigh reasons and can act in accord with our reasoning, then we are free. This rather neatly anticipates much of what contemporary compatibilists have to say about freedom and determinism. For even if Judas' choice is determined, indeed determined from eternity, it is still true that Judas chose to betray Jesus; what he does and what we do depends upon our choices, at least when we are not compelled or coerced to act as we do.

In fact, if there is a special problem with what Leibniz has to say about the freedom of the will, it is not merely his claim that freedom is compatible with causal determinism. In one way or another, this view is familiar to all students of philosophy since Hume. Rather, the problem is that all truths for Leibniz may turn out to be necessary truths. If this is so, our freedom does seem to be an illusion.

SUBSTANCE AND PREDICATE

As we mentioned in our discussion of Leibniz's distinction between truths of reason and truths of fact, it is one of his deepest metaphysical/logical commitments that every true predication is such that the predicate is contained in the subject. Leibniz's notion of "containment" has startling consequences. He writes:

> The concept of the subject must always include that of the predicate in such a way that if one understands perfectly the concept of the subject, he will know that the predicate appertains to it also. This being so, we are able to say that this is the nature of an individual substance or of a complete being, namely, to afford a conception so complete that the concept shall be sufficient for the understanding of it and for the deduction of all the predicates of which the substance is or may become the subject.

One of the consequences of this view is that a complete understanding of any individual substance makes possible our understanding of the truth of all predications which will ever be truly made. So, God, looking at the individual substance Alexander the Great, can see a priori that Alexander will defeat Porus at the Indus river, and that he is the conqueror of Darius.

Leibniz is never clear about why he thinks this doctrine true. There are occasionally suggestions that he takes it to follow from the principle of sufficient reason. In other places, it seems as though Leibniz takes the fact that individual substances persist through changes to imply that all predicates must be contained in the subject.

For our purposes, what is most important is not why Leibniz takes this doctrine to be true, but rather what else he understands it to imply.

Leibniz on Causal Relations

It is one of Leibniz's most important claims, an understanding of which is essential to an accurate appreciation of his views, that, with the exception of God, there are no causal relations between individual substances. Each individual substance is, in this way, a world by itself. In the language of Leibniz's mature metaphysics, *monads* (individual substances) have no windows or doors through which anything may pass. Thus, strictly speaking, there are no external causes other than God.

Why does Leibniz hold this extraordinary view? The only clear argument for the claim to be found in his writings comes early in the *Monadology*. There Leibniz notes that if something is to count as an individual substance, it must be a simple unity; it can have no parts. He then goes on to claim that causation, or rather some change being brought about in some substance by some external substance, must be understood to involve the transposition of parts. Here the picture in reasonably intuitive. If A brings about some change in B, that must be because the action of A has altered B in some fashion which must be understood to involve the addition, subtraction, or alteration of some parts of B. But if this is what such causation involves, it cannot be a relationship which holds between individual substances, simply in virtue of the fact that nothing is an individual substance if it has parts. Since individual substances are simple unities, they cannot engage in causal relations with each other.

This argument is, however, deeply at odds with much of the rest of Leibniz's metaphysics. Throughout the *Discourse*, indeed throughout much of his writing, Leibniz clearly says that earlier states of a monad are at least a partial cause of later states of the monad. Yet, if the above argument were taken seriously, this would result in a deep inconsistency in Leibniz's thought. Since monads are simples they could not cause later states of themselves. We must look elsewhere for an account of Leibniz's reasoning behind his claim that there can be no causal relations between individual substances.

Causation and the Subject-Predicate Conception of Truth

It seems likely that Leibniz is led to make his odd claim about causation in virtue of his thinking that a complete conception of an individual substance contains any predicate which will ever be true of the subject. Thus, if the pencil now in your hands is at some point in the future to have no eraser, then it is true now that a complete conception of the pencil now is such that it contains this fact about the pencil. How do we get from here to the claim that there are no causal relations between individual substances?

Leibniz's reasoning may be this: If a complete understanding of an individual substance is such that it contains all of that substance's predicates, then nothing that is ever true of that substance can ever depend on anything external to that substance. In particular, if a complete conception of the pencil is such that it can be seen that it will someday have no eraser, then the fact that it will have no eraser cannot depend on the action of anything else (for example, your chewing it off). Thus, it may be that Leibniz's thinking is just that all the predicates of a substance follow from its concept alone and so cannot depend on anything external to it. So, it seems that we can conclude that all the states of an individual substance depend causally on that substance alone—once that substance has been willed into existence by God.

INDIVIDUAL SUBSTANCES

We move now to Leibniz's account of the nature of monads. For Leibniz, monads are the simple things of which the whole of the universe is composed. Monads are simple unities, and they do not engage in causal relations with other individual substances. Perhaps even more strikingly, monads are, fundamentally, psychological entities which are hierarchically organized. Extension is, on Leibniz's account, relative to our perception and not a fundamental attribute of real things. Leibniz's reason for claiming that monads must be conceived of as rather like souls is that extension is inconsistent with simplicity and unity. Anything which is extended, which takes up space, must have parts; and since monads are simples—atoms—they cannot be extended. Thus, extension, one of Descartes' two sorts of substances, is banished from Leibniz's universe.

More on Monads

Just as extension was the essence of material substance in the Cartesian picture, so force is the essence of substance on Leibniz's picture. Monads, we know, depend on nothing else, yet monads do change. Since the alteration cannot be the result of causal relations between monads, it must be conceived of as a kind of internal self-development. Monads, we might say, desire to become what they are; they are driven to change as they do.

COMPOSITE BODIES

In addition, as we might expect, monads combine to constitute composite bodies.

> There are everywhere simple substances, separated in effect from one another by activities of their own which continually change their relations; and each important simple substance of monad which forms the center of a composite substance (as, for example, of an animal) and the principle of its unity, is surrounded by a *mass* composed of an infinity of other monads, which constitute the body proper of this central monad; and in accordance with the affections of its body the monad represents, as in a *center*, the things which are outside of itself. And this *body* is *organic* though it form a sort of automaton or natural machine . . .

Composite bodies are hierarchically arranged collections of monads. These monads are arrayed about a dominant monad; and this dominant monad fixes the sort of thing that the composite substance is. Importantly, Leibniz here notes that monads represent or perceive each other. It is this relation of representation or perception which is the fundamental relation between monads. Some monads, of course, represent or perceive more adequately or clearly than others. But all monads—even the dimmest— are such as to have perception, though only a few are such as to be fully conscious—have "apperception" in addition to perception. It is this relationship of perception or representation by which Leibniz will seek to explain what, for all the world, looks to be causation between substances.

In any case, we can now clarify our earlier remark that extension is not a real attribute of substance. On Leibniz's view, that we perceive aggregates of monads as extended bodies in space is just a matter of how it is that we represent or perceive these collections of monads. This is not to say that extension is an illusion; it is rather to say that extension is reducible or is to be explicated by appeal to the perceptions of monads.

TELEOLOGY

Leibniz understands himself to have shown that both teleological and mechanistic explanations have their proper place. Each monad is, for Leibniz, a little entelechy, each develops according to its own nature. And each monad is in harmony, pre-established by God, with other monads so that each monad fits into an arrangement with every other monad. And since the only relationship between monads is that of perception or representation, each monad mirrors the whole of the rest of the universe. This relationship is not causal; rather it has been ordained by God.

> It is most true that the perceptions and expressions of all substances intercorrespond, so that each one following independently certain reasons or laws which he has noticed meets others which are doing the same. . . . It is God alone . . . who is the cause of this correspondence in their phenomena and who brings it about that that which is particular to one is also common to all, otherwise there would be no relation.

This statement clearly presents Leibniz's doctrine of the pre-established harmony. One monad can affect another only through the mediation of God. Thus, one simple substance mirrors or perceives another. This relationship is brought about by God's making it the case that the two individual substances, wholly independent of each other metaphysically, are in harmony with each other.

The Mind-Body Relation and Pre-Established Harmony

It is sometimes suggested that Leibniz's doctrine of the pre-established harmony is especially adapted to concerns about Descartes' doctrine of mind-body interaction. This suggests that Leibniz is concerned about how it is that a substance whose essence is thought could causally interact with a substance whose essence is extension. It should be clear from the above that one cannot even raise the mind-body problem, as it is traditionally conceived, from within Leibniz's metaphysics. For Leibniz, all substances are to be understood as mental substances; there are, as a matter of fact, no extended substances.

Leibniz's Account of Mind and Body

Leibniz's view of the mind-body problem takes the following form: What is the relation between the dominant monad and the infinitude of other monads which together form the human being? It is crucial to see that this is no longer the mind-body problem, as it is standardly conceived. Instead, the question is about the relation between simple mental substances. Leibniz's answer to this problem is ingenious.

Leibniz's answer appeals to his notion of pre-established harmony: The states of the dominant monad run in parallel with the states of the other monads in a way established by God. But how are we to make sense of what certainly appears to be the case (and which makes for the intuitive basis of Descartes' mind-body interactionism)—that the mind appears to act upon the body and the body upon the mind? Leibniz does have a way of, at the very least, explaining the appearances here. According to Leibniz, we can say that one thing acts upon another when we find in the first the a priori reason for what occurs in the second.

For example, we may wish to say that I (or my will) act upon my body in such a way as to raise my arm. Leibniz would say that the a priori reason for the alteration of the monads which constitute my arm is to be found in a state of my soul—the dominant monad which constitutes me. Ultimately, God makes it the case—or rather it has eternally been the case that this would be so—that there is a harmony between the states of the dominant monad and the other monads which constitute the human being that I am, without there being causal interaction between them.

Leibniz's doctrine of the pre-established harmony is the result, not of a particular Cartesian worry about mind-body interaction, but of far more fundamental metaphysical concerns about the nature of substance and the relation between substances.

Teleology and Mechanism

One of Leibniz's chief philosophical aims is to show that the cosmos is a teleologically organized system. It is as it is, it behaves as it does, by virtue of the activity of God. His system, as outlined above, surely does make a place for teleological explanation. Not only is the universe as a whole such a system, but, in addition, every portion of that universe is a teleological system.

Leibniz's goal is to show that mechanism and teleology are not explanatory competitors. Each kind of explanatory strategy has its proper place; and each is important to our comprehension of the cosmos. The mechanistic accounts of, for example, Newton or Galileo, quite obviously cannot be fundamental. Indeed, since extension is not a fundamental attribute of things, and since these explanations range over extended things, they must be understood to be an organization of the way in which the phenomena appear to us. Yet, this is the way that God has ordained that things appear to us. As a way of ordering and predicting the phenomenal realm, mechanistic accounts are dazzlingly successful.

Yet even if we grant that mechanistic explanation is very good at what it does, Leibniz insists that it cannot be the whole story. Along with mechanistic explanation and efficient causes, we must appeal to teleological explanation and final causes. Part of Leibniz's point is that without appeal to final causes our understanding of nature would be far more difficult and laborious. (See especially his discussion of Descartes and Snell's Law at Section 22 of the *Discourse*.) More fundamental is Leibniz's view that this world is organized as it is according to God's choice of the best. Newton's laws are only one of a possible infinitude of ways in which the world might have been organized. In order to account for this, we have no recourse but to appeal to final causes at the fundamental explanatory level.

God

Needless to say, God plays a fundamental role in the Leibnizian system. Unsurprisingly, Leibniz provides a number of arguments for the existence of the entity upon which so much depends.

THE ONTOLOGICAL ARGUMENT

"God alone," writes Leibniz, "has this prerogative that if he be possible he must necessarily exist." This is a familiar appeal to the consideration that since God is the absolutely perfect being, he must exist. Leibniz, more so than most who have adopted the argument, does betray some sensitivity to the fact that the ontological argument will work only if it can be established that God is a possible being. And Leibniz is concerned to show that God is a possible being and thus necessarily exists.

THE ARGUMENT FROM TRUTHS OF FACT

Since every truth of fact needs a sufficient reason for its truth, we must ultimately, according to Leibniz, appeal to a necessary being, God, in order to account for such truths of fact. This, in essence, is an appeal to the cosmological argument.

THE ARGUMENT FROM HARMONY

According to Leibniz, there is no causal interaction between created things. And yet when we look at the world, we find a well-ordered, elegant, and harmonious system. This would be inexplicable but for the existence of God.

LEIBNIZ ON INNATE IDEAS

Leibniz responded to John Locke's attack on innate ideas. As the dispute between those who accept and those who deny innate ideas or knowledge is often regarded as a fundamental Rationalist/Empiricist division, we should briefly consider the nature of Leibniz's response.

Given that Leibniz thinks that there are no causal relations between individual substances, we might expect him to say that all our ideas are innate—indeed, in some strict metaphysical sense this must be the case. Yet this is not what Leibniz says. He seems willing to speak, in the common manner, of some ideas, for example, bitter and sweet, having an external source. Leibniz cannot mean by this what an empiricist would mean. What Leibniz means is that the source of an idea can be said to be external when the a priori reason for its presence in a person's thoughts can be found in some other individual substance.

When Leibniz considers what is to count as innate, he provides a rather sophisticated dispositionalist account. That is, he speaks of ideas or knowledge as being in us in a *virtual way*. Leibniz constructs a quite famous metaphor. He compares the mind to a block of marble. The block is veined in certain ways such that, although the figure of Hercules cannot be seen, it emerges easily from the stone. On Leibniz's view, we are strongly disposed to have certain ideas. So, for example, Leibniz would say that our grasp of the law of contradiction is innate. It is not necessary that in order for this to be so we must actually assert "not both p and not p." Rather our virtual grasp of this necessary truth is revealed in our assent to such claims as "the rectangular is not the circular."

Leibniz produces an elegant and compelling system. His aim is to demonstrate that God and teleology are not at all passé in a mechanistic universe. And in order to make these claims, Leibniz's metaphysical doctrines became predictably radical: He denies the fundamental reality of extension and argues that there are no causal relations between created substances; and in order to explain the cosmos he appeals to pre-established harmony. In this way, Leibniz's system, like George Berkeley's, emerges from the clash of science, tradition, and common sense.

Selected Readings

Broad, C. D. *Leibniz, An Introduction*. Cambridge: Cambridge University Press, 1975.

Frankfurt, H. (ed.). *Leibniz: A Collection of Critical Essays*. New York: Anchor Books, 1972.

Jolley, N. *Leibniz and Locke*. Oxford: Oxford University Press, 1984.

Loeb, L. E. *From Descartes to Hume: The Development of Continental Metaphysics*. Ithaca: Cornell University Press, 1982.

Russell, B. *The Philosophy of Leibniz*. London: George Allen and Unwin, 1900.

13

John Locke

John Locke (1632–1704) is the first of a trio of famous British empiricist philosophers, the forerunner of Berkeley and Hume. Locke was born in Somerset, England. In 1652 he went to study at Oxford, became a master there, and eventually studied medicine, although he did not practice as a physician. He was also a statesman and a diplomat and was very interested in politics, making important contributions to political philosophy. He traveled a good deal and had many friends, among them some of the most important thinkers of the day. In England he became closely associated with Lord Shaftesbury, who fell out of favor during political conflicts in England; Locke, likewise, fell under suspicion and fled to Holland in 1683. He died in 1704 at Oates, England, where he had enjoyed residency for a number of years and had produced a number of lesser known works.

Locke's most important works are the Essay Concerning Human Understanding *and the* Two Treatises of Government. *The former was published in 1689 and went through four editions. In the opening "Epistle to the Reader," Locke describes the development of the* Essay *as having been sparked by a discussion with a few friends in his chamber. In the course of trying to examine the "objects our understandings were, or were not, fitted to deal with," Locke began to write the* Essay, *which was finished only twenty years later. What had begun as a chance piece became one of the most important works in modern philosophy; when it was published, it was well received and much discussed.*

Like Descartes, Locke was critical of the scholastic philosophy he had learned in his schooling, and he became very interested in Descartes' work. Also like Descartes, Locke wanted to separate real knowledge from mere opinion; similarly, his philosophical views were a reflection of the scientific revolution of the seventeenth century. For Locke, as for his contemporaries, philosophy was nearly inseparable from the sciences. He knew and was greatly influenced by many important scientists of his day, including New-ton, Clark, and Boyle. From Boyle he learned about a model of the natural world called the corpuscularian view, according to which nature operates in a machine-like fashion, following mechanical laws.

Locke's main task in the Essay Concerning Human Understanding *was to explain what it is to know something in a way that would be consistent with seventeenth-century science. To do this, he proposed to examine the objects of knowledge, which he took to be ideas, and the faculties of the mind that operate on those ideas. Part of Locke's task was to investigate the ideas that are the elements of knowledge, to see how they derive from experience, and whether they are truly found in experience. As we will see, this is a strategy followed by later empiricists, most notably Hume.*

IDEAS

Locke follows Descartes in taking the mind to have ideas, and in taking ideas to be the immediate objects that we know about, think about, perceive, etc. That is, Locke thinks that when we know something, the immediate thing we are thinking about is an idea. In Book II, Chapter i, Section 1 of the *Essay*, he says:

> Every man being conscious to himself that he thinks; and that which his mind is applied about whilst thinking being the ideas that are there, it is past doubt that men have in their minds several ideas,— such as those expressed by the words whiteness, hardness, sweet-ness, thinking, motion, man, elephant, army, drunkenness, and others.

Just as Descartes used the term *perceive* generically, to describe mental acts, so Locke uses the term *think* to describe the mental activities by which we have knowledge. He thinks that there are two components to thinking: an act of mind, such as sensing, imagining, believing, judging, and so on, and an object of that act, an idea. You can see, then, that Locke's use of the term *idea* is very broad indeed.

Two Sources of Ideas. Being an empiricist, Locke holds that everything we know about, all of our ideas, must come originally from experience. There are two forms of experience: sensation, which provides ideas of the external world, and reflection, which provides ideas of the workings of our own minds. We cannot, on Locke's view, have an idea that is not traceable to one of these two forms of experience.

Simple and Complex Ideas. Some of our ideas are simple ideas—ideas such as whiteness, hardness, etc. Others are complex, such as elephant and army. Complex ideas are analyzable into simple ideas. Some of our ideas, like the idea of a unicorn, may not seem to come from experience; however, Locke thinks that if we look at the simple ideas composing the complex ones, we will find that all of those originate in our experience, either in sensation or reflection.

Ideas Are the Materials for All of Our Thinking. The ideas that we get through experience are the materials that the rest of our faculties work with: When we remember, we call up an idea we have had before; when we use a word, the meaning is an idea; when we judge, we compare ideas; and so on. In general, thinking, in the generic sense, is manipulating ideas, or having them present in the mind. Thus, Locke's philosophy has sometimes been called "the way of ideas." With it, he sets the stage for the views of Berkeley and Hume.

The Rejection of Innate Ideas

You may recall that Descartes took substance, extension, number, being and the other basic concepts of his metaphysics to be innate; they are not learned through experience. Likewise, Descartes took a number of principles, such as those employed in his proof of the existence of God, to be innate. By contrast, Locke holds that there are no ideas that are not acquired through some experience or other. Before having experience, the mind is a *tabula rasa*, or blank slate. Hence, Locke rejects innate ideas and principles.

TWO REASONS FOR REJECTING INNATE IDEAS

Locke gives two reasons for thinking there are no innate ideas or principles. First, if there were innate principles that we use for reasoning, then everyone would have them. However, he observes that people think very differently, and indeed many people would not assent to the principles that Descartes took to be innate. Also, like Descartes, Locke takes consciousness to be transparent—a window into the mind—which means that we should be aware of any innate principles that exist in the mind. However, we have no awareness of such principles until we are taught them. It makes more sense, Locke thinks, to hold that we discover such principles through the use of reason than to think that reason somehow activates innate principles that had been hidden in the mind all along.

This is not to say that Locke takes nothing to be innate. What he takes to be innate are the faculties by which we acquire knowledge, not the objects of knowledge. One of the main purposes of the *Essay* is, in fact, to show how we acquire knowledge through experience, using the faculties we have.

Sensation: The Source of Ideas of the Material World

The source of all of our ideas, hence all knowledge, of the material world is sense perception: "the *first* step and degree towards knowledge, and the inlet of all the materials of it . . . " Without sensation, we would have no knowledge of the material world; hence, explaining sense perception is fundamental to Locke's epistemology. This, you may notice, is in stark contrast to Descartes' view that sense perception is confused, hence cannot provide knowledge of the material world.

THE REPRESENTATIVE THEORY OF PERCEPTION

Locke thinks that "ideas of sensation" are caused in us by the actions of material objects on our sense organs. The sensations that result from those actions form a complex idea, or image, of the object. What you perceive is that image, and the image represents the object to you. Thus, there is a two-way relationship between the material object and the image of it that you perceive: The material object causes the image in you, and the image, in turn, represents the object that caused it. So, for example, suppose you are looking at a tomato. The action of the object on your eye causes sensations of color, size, and shape to be produced in your mind, and together those form a tomato image. What you see immediately is the image caused by the tomato, and that image represents the tomato.

The Primary/ Secondary Quality Distinction

But how does this image of the tomato represent the actual tomato to you? One possible answer is that the image of the tomato resembles the tomato itself—that it is like a little photograph of the tomato in your mind. On that view, the image of the tomato shows you what the tomato really is like, in the same way that looking at a photograph of an object shows you what that object really looks like.

Primary Qualities Resemble Properties of Material Objects. Locke does not quite accept this view, though. He thinks that some of the sensations we receive do really resemble the object's qualities, but others do not. The sensations that do he calls ideas of "primary qualities." Primary qualities are motion, size, shape, and mass.

Secondary Qualities Do Not Resemble Properties of Material Objects. There are other sensations, however, that do not resemble anything in the object. Locke calls these sensations ideas of "secondary qualities." Secondary qualities are color, taste, texture, odor, temperature, sound, and so on.

Primary Qualities Are Real Qualities of Material Objects. Locke holds that primary qualities are the real qualities that material objects have, while secondary qualities are not. So, for example, when you perceive the tomato to be red, you have a sensation that does not resemble any real quality of the object. However, when you perceive it to be round, you have a sensation that does resemble a real quality of the tomato—the tomato really is round.

THE CORPUSCULARIAN VIEW

Why should Locke think that primary qualities are real qualities of objects, while secondary qualities are not? The primary/secondary quality distinction was one that was held by many great thinkers of his day. It is based on a view of the ultimate nature of material objects that is sometimes called the corpuscularian philosophy. On that view, material objects consist of tiny atoms, or corpuscles. Corpuscles are colorless, odorless, tasteless, soundless bits of matter moving about in space. The only properties that corpuscles really have are size, shape, mass, and motion or rest—the primary qualities. All of their actions can be explained by knowing these properties.

The only way that corpuscles can affect each other is by impulse. Hence, all explanations of events in the material world are mechanical explanations, appealing to the primary qualities of objects. These qualities are taken to be the true objects of science. Locke says, "The particular bulk, number, figure, and motion of the parts of fire or snow are really in them,—whether any one's senses perceive them or no . . . " (*Essay*, II, viii, 17)

Corpuscles Are Like Billiard Balls. On the corpuscularian view, the universe is something like a huge billiard table. Corpuscles are like billiard balls moving about and colliding with one another. The behavior of each ball can be explained by its real properties—weight, size, shape, motion—together with those same properties of the balls that collide with it. Indeed, we could specify a set of laws in terms of these properties that completely predict the behavior of a billiard ball.

By contrast, the billiard ball's secondary qualities have no role in explaining its behavior. For example, the path a billiard ball takes is unaffected by the color it happens to have. In fact, if the analogy of corpuscles to billiard balls were really accurate, the billiard balls would not have color at all.

Of course, ordinary objects are in fact collections of corpuscles tightly bound together, not individual corpuscles; but the billiard table analogy gives a rough idea of this conception of the objects' properties and how they interact. Nature, like the balls on a billiard table, operates according to mechanical laws.

Perception Is a Mechanical Process. Even perception is a mechanical process. It is the result of the actions of the corpuscles of an object on our sense organs: ". . . bodies produce ideas in us . . . manifestly by impulse, the only way which we can conceive bodies to operate in." (*Essay*, II, viii, 11) The idea is that material objects act on our sense organs by means of their constituent corpuscles, those motions get transmitted to our brains, and there sensations are produced.

Thus, we can see why Locke would say that the tomato in the example above really is round but is not really red. When you look at the tomato, you receive an image of it consisting of sensations of roundness, redness, etc.

Your sensation of its roundness is caused by the real shape of the tomato; however, your sensation of its redness is caused by the actions of the tomato's corpuscles affecting your eyes in a particular way. Thus, sensations of secondary qualities, such as color, are caused by particular configurations of the object's primary qualities. Secondary qualities, insofar as they exist in objects, are really only such configurations of primary qualities. They are powers to produce sensations of color, taste, sound, etc., in you. Primary qualities, by contrast, really do exist in material objects.

LOCKE'S SUPPORT FOR THE PRIMARY/SECONDARY QUALITY DISTINCTION

Locke offers several reasons for making the distinction between primary and secondary qualities. Here are the principal ones.

Primary Qualities Are Present in All Material Objects. One of Locke's ways of distinguishing primary from secondary qualities is that primary qualities are "inseparable from every particle of matter," whereas secondary qualities are not. He considers what happens when we divide a material object into parts:

> Take a grain of wheat, divide it into two parts; each part has still solidity, extension, figure, and mobility: divide it again, and it retains still the same qualities; and so divide it on, till the parts become insensible; they must retain still each of them all those qualities. . . For division. . . can never take away either solidity, extension, figure, or mobility from any body, but only makes two or more distinct separate masses of matter, of that which was but one before. (*Essay*, II, viii, 9)

Locke's reasoning is that certain apparent qualities of objects—color, sound, taste, odor, texture, temperature—disappear as we divide them into smaller and smaller parts, hence those qualities cannot be the real qualities of objects. Only the qualities that remain regardless of how far we carry the division are the real qualities. If we could get to the ultimate constituents of objects, perhaps using a microscope, we would be able to perceive real qualities:

> Had we senses acute enough to discern the minute particles of bodies, and the real constitution on which their sensible qualities depend, I doubt not but they would produce quite different ideas in us: and that which is now the yellow colour of gold, would then disappear, and instead of it we should see an admirable texture of parts, of a certain size and figure. This microscopes plainly discover to us; for what to our naked eyes produces a certain colour, is, by thus augmenting the acuteness of our senses, discovered to be quite a different thing. (*Essay*, II, xxiii, 11)

The Relativity of Perception and Secondary Qualities. Locke offers another reason why secondary qualities are not real qualities of objects. He reasons that our sensations of an object's secondary qualities may undergo change as the conditions under which we perceive the object change, even though the object itself does not change. For example, our sensations of the color of an object will disappear when we turn off the light, but will reappear when the light returns. Like Descartes, Locke holds that the real properties of objects are unchanging. We cannot think that a property really disappears from the object when we turn off the light and reappears when we turn it back on. So, the change must be in us, not in the object. It is our sensations of color that change, and since they are changing, they cannot resemble the real unchanging properties of the object. In other words, Locke thinks that if a sensation of color really resembled a quality of color in the object causing it, then our sensations of color would not change, despite any change in the conditions of perception. So how can we think that anything resembling our sensation of color is really in the object, given that the sensation disappears as soon as we turn off the light?

Another example Locke uses to make this point is that the same water may feel cold to one hand and warm to the other, according to the temperature of your hands when you put them into the water. It is difficult to explain how this could be if we take those sensations to resemble actual properties in the water, for water cannot be both hot and cold simultaneously. Hence, our sensations of hot and cold cannot resemble real qualities in the water. However, this phenomenon can be explained by the primary qualities of the corpuscles in the water and in your hands:

> But if the sensation of heat and cold be nothing but the increase or diminution of the motion of the minute parts of our bodies, caused by the corpuscles of any other body, it is easy to be understood, that if that motion be greater in one hand than in the other; if a body be applied to the two hands, which has in its minute particles a greater motion than in those of one of the hands, and a less than in those of the other, it will increase the motion of the one hand and lessen it in the other; and so cause the different sensations of heat and cold that depend thereon. (*Essay*, II, viii, 21)

Note the similarity between Locke's reasoning and Descartes' reasoning in the wax example of the *Second Meditation*; Descartes, however, thought that primary qualities are really innate ideas.

Identifying Sensations of Secondary Qualities with Pleasure and Pain. Locke uses another clever observation to argue that secondary qualities are not the real qualities of objects. He argues that sometimes our sensations of secondary qualities are indistinguishable from sensations of pain or pleasure; since we do not think anything like pain or pleasure is really in a material object, then neither are the secondary qualities with which pain and pleasure are identified. To make this argument, he considers sensations caused by a fire:

> He that will consider that the same fire that, at one distance produces in us the sensation of warmth, does, at a nearer approach, produce in us the far different sensation of pain, ought to bethink himself what reason he has to say—that this idea of warmth, which was produced in him by the fire, is *actually in the fire*; and his idea of pain, which the same fire produced in him the same way, is not in the fire. Why are whiteness and coldness in snow, and pain not, when it produces the one and the other idea in us; and can do neither, but by the bulk, figure, number, and motion of its solid parts? (*Essay*, II, viii, 16)

Locke's point is that we would readily accept that the same property, heat, can cause two different sensations in us, depending on our closeness to the fire: If we are very close to it, it will cause sensations of great heat, which is pain; however, if we keep our distance, it will merely make us warm. We are quite willing to say that pain is not in the fire but is only a sensation produced in us by a property of the fire—there is nothing resembling pain in the fire. So should we not also be willing to accept that a mild sensation of heat is also only in us—that there is nothing resembling it in the fire? Again, this is not to say that there is no heat in the fire; but to say there is heat in the fire is a shorthand way of saying that the corpuscles in the fire move in a certain way so as to sometimes produce pain sensations in us and at other times to produce sensations of mild heat in us, depending on how close we are to the fire. There is nothing resembling pain or heat, however, in the fire.

HOW SENSATIONS ARE PRODUCED

You may have wondered how the motions of corpuscles produce the sensations that they do. Why, for example, does one power in an object produce the sensation of red, while another produces the sound of a trumpet? Locke's answer to this question, like Descartes', is God: God attaches the appropriate sensation to each motion produced in the brain. He says,

> A violet, by the impulse of such insensible particles of matter, of peculiar figures and bulks, and in different degrees and modifications of their motions, causes the ideas of the blue colour, and sweet scent of that flower to be produced in our minds. It being no more impossible to conceive that God should annex such ideas to such motions, with which they have no similitude, than that he should annex the idea of pain to the motion of a piece of steel dividing our flesh, with which that idea hath no resemblance. (*Essay*, II, viii, 13)

Thus, God has set up a correspondence between motions in the brain produced by the powers of objects and sensations. So while your sensations of secondary qualities do not *resemble* anything in the object, still they *represent* the powers that cause them, in that there is a one-to-one correspondence between the powers of objects and the sensations they cause. This may lead you to wonder, though, why sensations of primary qualities are not produced in the same way—by God's annexing sensations of primary qualities to certain motions in the brain. Let us turn, then, to a consideration of whether Locke's distinction really holds up.

PROBLEMS WITH LOCKE'S DISTINCTION

There are a number of problems with Locke's reasoning in arguing for the primary/secondary quality distinction, many of which were pointed out by Berkeley in his attack on material substance. Let us briefly consider some of those. First, consider Locke's contention that primary qualities are ever present in bodies, regardless of how much we divide them. Could not the same argument be made for some secondary qualities? Consider, for example, texture. Do not objects continue to have some texture regardless of how small they are? Do they not feel like something? And what about color? It is hard to conceive of being able to see an object without observing some color, even if it is transparent.

Another difficulty arises with Locke's contention that our sensations of primary qualities of objects really do resemble those qualities in the objects, while sensations of secondary qualities do not. If we look closely at Locke's reasoning, it seems that it can be made to apply to primary qualities as well. For example, consider the size of an object. You may recall Descartes' observation that when you look at the sun, it looks very small. If you know nothing about astronomy, you may take it to be only a few inches in diameter. In what sense does your sensation of size, then, resemble the sun's actual size? Also, consider Locke's argument that sensations of secondary qualities change, even though the object does not, hence there is nothing like those sensations really in objects. The same case can be made for sensations of primary qualities. For example, when you turn off the light, your sensation of the size of an object "goes away," just as color sensations do. But surely, the size of the object does not go away. On Locke's reasoning, though, we should conclude that size is not a real quality of the object. Of course, Locke could argue that even in the dark, we have a way of perceiving size: we can feel the object to see how big it is. We cannot do that with color.

Consider his other argument, though. As you approach an object, your sensations change—the image you have of it gets larger. But using Locke's reasoning, an object cannot have two different sizes. So, why think that our sensations of size really resemble anything about the object? That is, why think that size really is in the object? This is an argument that Berkeley used to show that primary qualities do not really exist in material objects but are only sensations in our minds.

Determinates and Determinables. Locke's arguments often trade on blurring a distinction between what are sometimes called "determinates" and "determinables." "Determinables" are very general properties—properties such as size, shape, color, taste, and so on. "Determinates" are more specific properties—properties such as being six feet tall, being spherical, being chartreuse, tasting sweet, and so on. They are instances of the determinable properties. Now, consider Locke's contention that sensations of secondary qualities change as the conditions of perception change, while our sensations of primary qualities do not. What in fact change are our sensations of secondary quality determinates—particular colors, temperatures, tastes, etc. But sensations of primary quality determinates also change as the conditions of perception are altered. As we approach an object, its particular size may seem to get larger; likewise, if we view an object from different angles, its particular shape may seem to change. Of course, the object will have the determinable of shape regardless of the angle from which we view it, or how far we divide it, and in this sense, its primary qualities are constant. But likewise, it will have the determinable of color regardless of the extent to which we alter it or the conditions under which we perceive it.

Our sensations are sensations of ordinary objects, not corpuscles. Hence, our ideas of primary qualities cannot, strictly speaking, resemble the real primary qualities of corpuscles and often do not even accurately resemble the primary qualities of the macroscopic objects we are perceiving. But what Locke may mean in claiming that ideas of primary qualities resemble those qualities is this: We have primary quality ideas that have real shape, and objects have real shape; insofar as sensory images are describable in the same terms that objects are, the images resemble the objects; and the terms in which both are describable are primary quality terms. Thus, for example, your image of the sun has a shape, and the sun itself has a shape—moreover, the corpuscles of the sun also have shape. In that sense, then, your image of the sun resembles the sun itself. However, your image of the sun has color, while the sun, if considered in terms of its ultimate corpuscles, does not. Hence the color you perceive resembles nothing in the sun; rather, that color sensation is the product of the sun's corpuscles acting on your eyes.

THE INEVITABILITY OF SKEPTICISM

Locke's acceptance of the primary/secondary quality distinction reinforces the representative theory of perception: If material objects really are very different from what we perceive—they have no color, taste, odor, sound, etc.—then we must be immediately perceiving something other than the actual objects. And that something is an image in the mind. And if the objects of sense perception are ideas in the mind, and those ideas are the materials on which all other faculties operate, then all objects of knowledge must be ideas. However, by taking the immediate object of sense perception to be an idea, or image, in the mind, Locke has essentially removed the perceiver from any direct connection to the world. Without any direct access to the world, there is no way of knowing what the world is really like—how can we know that our images of material objects do resemble them in certain respects unless we have immediate access to those objects so that we can make a comparison? As long as we can only know material objects through images, we have no grounds for asserting that the images resemble the objects—or indeed, that the objects are there at all. Skepticism about the existence of the material world, hence, seems inevitable. This is precisely the predicament that Berkeley took advantage of to argue that there are no material objects outside the mind—only ideas in our own minds.

SUBSTANCE

On Locke's theory of sense perception, material objects cause sensations in us, and what we immediately perceive are images, composed of those sensations. But what makes a bundle of sensations an image of an object, and not just a random assortment of sensations? Moreover, why is it that material objects are objects and not just collections of properties?

On the corpuscularian view, the ultimate things in the world are corpuscles—bits of matter, or material substance, with properties. The substance is what the properties "subsist" in. Properties do not just float about; they are properties of some "thing." But what is this thing, or substance? And how can we know it? Can we have an idea of it?

Our Idea of Substance

Locke's answer to these questions is that, ". . . not imagining how these simple ideas *can* subsist by themselves, we accustom ourselves to suppose some *substratum* wherein they do subsist, and from which they do result, which therefore we call *substance*." (*Essay*, II, xxiii, 1) So, the tomato is not just roundness plus redness. It is a substance in which roundness and redness "subsist." But the idea of substance is itself not very clear. Indeed, it is not, to use the traditional terminology, "clear and distinct" but is rather "relative and confused," insofar as we have no direct experience of substance and can know it only in relation to the qualities of which we do have direct experience. If pressed on what this thing is in which qualities inhere, Locke answers that it is the "solid, extended parts"— corpuscles. But as he points out, the question may be continued: What do solidity and extension inhere in? And to that question, Locke says it is a "something, I know not what."

It is interesting to compare Locke's view of substance with Descartes'. You will recall that in discussing his own existence in the *cogito*, and the changes in the wax, Descartes assumes that we know there is some "thing" that thinks, or that has extension. Moreover, ultimately he tells us that it is an innate idea—it is not gotten from anything we experience, but is rather in the intellect. But Locke has rejected innate ideas, which puts him in a bit of a bind with respect to substance. He has restricted all knowledge to ideas that ultimately originate in sense perception. Yet, we never get an idea of substance per se—that is, we never get an idea of whatever it is that holds all of the qualities of a thing together. We only get ideas of the qualities themselves. So why think that we have knowledge of substance, or that there is even such a thing? These are precisely the questions Berkeley would later raise.

Locke's answer is that we cannot help but think otherwise: We cannot help but think that qualities cannot exist by themselves—that red, for example, can only exist in something. Likewise with the mind: Presumably there is something holding together all of the thoughts you are having, a *you*. Yet, you can only perceive the thoughts themselves, never the thing that is doing the thinking. Locke observes that we would not give up the idea of spiritual substance, or spirit, just because we have no idea of it; thus, he argues, we should not think we must give up the notion of material substance, or matter, just because we have no experience of it. (It is interesting to note that Berkeley was not moved by this observation. However, Berkeley thought that we could have the "notion" of spirit, while rejecting the possibility of an idea of material substance.) Still, given Locke's restriction of knowledge to that of which we can have experience, he does not very adequately explain how the concept of substance is possible or meaningful.

MATTER VS. SUBSTANCE

An important element in Berkeley's criticisms of Locke's views is his attack on matter. Strictly speaking, Locke does not take the terms *matter* and *substance* to mean the same thing. Locke takes matter to be extended solid substance. He also says, "The primary ideas we have *peculiar to body*, as contradistinguished to spirit, are the *cohesion of solid, and consequently separable, parts*, and a *power of communicating motion by impulse*." (*Essay*, II, xxiii, 17) Thus, matter is more than just what holds a collection of properties together. In his book on Berkeley, J. O. Urmson points out that matter and substance have very different meanings for the corpuscularians. Substance is that unknown something that holds qualities together—a substratum in which qualities "inhere." Matter, however, is an imperceptible cause of ideas. Strictly speaking, then, arguments against substance need not work as arguments against matter. As you will see, in rejecting material substance, Berkeley rejects more than he is entitled to, and less than he should: He rejects the properties of matter along with substance; yet he rejects substance only insofar as material substance is concerned, not insofar as spiritual substance is.

PARTICULAR SUBSTANCES

In addition to the general idea of substance, we also have ideas of particular substances, such as tables and chairs, apples and oranges, mountains and molehills. An idea of a particular substance is just

> A collection of a certain number of simple ideas, considered as united in one thing. . . Thus the idea which an Englishman signifies by the name swan, is white colour, long neck, red beak, black legs, and whole feet, and all these of a certain size, with a power of swimming in the water, and making a certain kind of noise, and perhaps, to a man who has long observed this kind of birds, some other properties: which all terminate in sensible simple ideas, all united in one common subject. (*Essay*, II, xxiii, 14)

A particular substance, then, is a collection of properties, or "ideas," as Locke refers to them here, that are united together. But another important characteristic of substances is that they have powers.

POWER

What characterizes objects, or particular substances, as opposed to random collections of properties, is that they can bring about changes in other objects, and to do that is to exercise power. A fire can melt wax; one billiard ball can move another by hitting it; a cat can kill a mouse. In bringing about these effects, all of these objects are exercising power. They are acting. To have knowledge of a particular substance is to know its qualities, which are powers:

> He that will examine his complex idea of gold, will find several of its ideas that make it up to be only powers; as the power of being melted, but of not spending itself in the fire; of being dissolved in aqua regia, are ideas as necessary to make up our complex idea of gold, as its colour and weight: which, if duly considered, are also nothing but different powers. For to speak truly, yellowness is not actually in gold, but is a power in gold to produce that idea in us by our eyes, when placed in a due light . . . (*Essay*, II, xxiii, 10)

The task of science is to understand substances, and their powers, which ultimately requires understanding their primary qualities.

Thus, for particular substances, Locke has answered the question of what substance is. A thing is a substance insofar as it has powers resulting from its constituent corpuscles, as Locke describes with the example of gold.

So, it is really only at the level of corpuscles that Locke must face the question, what is it that qualities inhere in? His answer is a "something, I know not what." Minds also exercise power. When you raise your arm, you feel a control over the motion of your arm; you exert a certain power, and voilà, your arm rises. With material objects we can get an idea of power only by observing their effects. However, Locke thinks that in our own minds, we get an idea of power directly, when we perform actions.

Active Power vs. Passive Power. Consistent with his epistemology, Locke refrains from discussing power itself; what he is interested in is our idea of power, that is, how we have knowledge of power. He finds that our ideas of particular substances include the idea of power, hence he wants to discover the source of the idea. Whenever we notice a change, we have an idea of power—either the power to bring about the change, or the power to receive the change. The power to receive a change from something else Locke calls a "passive" power, while the power to bring about a change he calls an "active" power. Thus, the power of fire to melt wax would seem to be an active power, while the power of wax to be melted would seem to be a passive power. The power of a rose to cause the sensation of red in us would seem to be an active power, while the power of the mind to receive the sensation of red would seem to be a passive power.

In fact, though, Locke believes that material objects really only ever have passive power—or rather, from material objects, we get an idea only of passive power. He observes that the idea of power can come from two sources: thinking or motion. We do not get the idea of thinking from material objects, but from our minds. And while we do get the idea of motion from material objects, this is due to their being moved by other material objects. That is, material objects would never move, or bring about changes in other material objects, unless a force or power were first impressed on them. They do not have the power to spontaneously move, uncaused by the power of something else. Locke says:

> A body at rest affords us no idea of any active power to move; and when it is set in motion itself, that motion is rather a passion than an action in it. For, when the ball obeys the motion of a billiard-stick, it is not any action of the ball, but bare passion. Also, when by impulse it sets another ball in motion that lay in its way, it only communicates the motion it had received from another, and loses in itself so much as the other received: which gives us but a very obscure idea of an active power of moving in body, whilst we observe it only to *transfer*, but not *produce* any motion. (*Essay*, II, xxi, 4)

Thus, when a material object causes sensations in you, it is not really exerting active power; it is merely transferring motions that it has acquired from the impact of something else to your sense organs. A rose would not have the power to produce the sensation of red in you had something else not caused its corpuscles to move in the first place. The solidity, shape, and size of those corpuscles, moving as they are, cause motion to be generated in your sense organs in such a way that ultimately a sensation of red is produced in you. But that is really only a transferral of motion that the corpuscles of the rose must have received from elsewhere.

This account of our idea of power is consistent with the corpuscularian view. Matter is inherently inert. It is extended and solid, but motion does not follow from either of these qualities. To move, material objects must first be moved by something else; and if moving other objects, they are only transferring motion that they have received from other objects. Real power to initiate motion lies only with minds, or spirits; we observe this power directly in ourselves, in reflecting on our own thinking or willing. For example, suppose you are writing a philosophy paper. In the course of doing so, you entertain various ideas, reflect on the reading you have done, and so on. In doing this thinking, you are bringing about ideas in yourself, hence you are exerting active power. Likewise when you will to do something. Suppose you want to ask a question in class. You raise your arm so that the teacher will notice you. In raising your arm, you are initiating a motion in a material object, your arm. That act of willing and causing your arm to move gives you an idea of active power. Hence, our idea of active power derives from observing our own mental activity.

The implication of this view is that if one traces the motions of material objects back through a causal chain, one must eventually get to a power that is a real active power, that can set matter in motion. This must be some kind of spirit. In the billiards analogy, it is the human player who sets the balls moving in the first place. The balls do not initiate their own motions. On the Newtonian view of nature, it is God who sets the material world in motion in creating it.

It is also interesting to note that Locke's account of passive and active power provides us with a hierarchical view of the world similar to Descartes'. In Locke's view, material objects are inherently passive and have no real active power. Humans have both active and passive power: The power to receive sensations is a passive power, whereas the powers to will and to use the intellect in thinking are real active powers. Hence, real activity and power lie in having will and intellect. God is, of course, fully active and not at all passive, consistent with Descartes' view that God is infinitely perfect, self-causing, and actual. (Not having passive power means that God receives no motion from other sources but is fully self contained and fully active, or actual, and also unchanging; God is not at all potential.) Also, humans have free will: ". . . so far as a man has power to think or not to think, to move or not to move, according to the preference or direction of his own mind, so far is a man *free*." (*Essay*, II, xxi, 8) Material objects are not free, for they have no minds, hence, no will nor choice. They cannot initiate motion, but only transfer it, according to the laws of nature.

Locke's discussion of power is important in that it provides part of the epistemological underpinnings of the corpuscularian view, but also because it sets the stage for the discussions of power by Berkeley and Hume. Berkeley agreed with Locke that only spiritual substances have real active power; but then, Berkeley thought, there is no reason to attribute to material objects the power to cause ideas in us. Only an active cause can be a real cause, hence the real cause of our ideas must ultimately be a spirit. So why not just hold that God causes ideas of material objects—sensations—in us directly, without using material objects as intermediaries? Then we have no reason to suppose that there is such a thing as matter causing our ideas of material objects. Hume took Berkeley's position one step further. He argued that even in reflecting on our own thinking or willing, we find no idea of active power. We have only successions of ideas. Hence, Hume concluded that there is no real power in minds either. And consistently with that view, Hume also concluded that there is no spiritual substance.

ABSTRACTION

Locke thinks that all faculties of the mind "operate" on ideas. When we think, remember, perceive, hope, or imagine, the immediate object of that mental activity is an idea in the mind. As we have interpreted *ideas* in Locke's theory of sense perception, ideas are images composed of sensations. However, it is not clear that Locke always uses *idea* to mean "image." When he describes the ideas we get in experience, his examples are often examples of ideas that are rather general: whiteness, hardness, sweetness, thinking, motion, man, elephant, army, drunkenness, etc. But what kind of idea is an idea of whiteness, or an idea of elephant? Is it a collection of sensations, a sensory image? Berkeley thought so and mounted a powerful attack on abstraction, based on that assumption. However, in such uses Locke does not seem to have in mind sensory images. Rather, he is talking about concepts derived from the ideas we receive in sense perception.

Forming Abstract Ideas   Locke thinks we have a faculty, which he calls "abstraction," that enables us to extract what is common to our ideas of particular things, so that we may form more general, or abstract ideas—concepts. He describes the process of forming such an idea, which he calls an "abstract idea," in this passage:

The Mind makes the particular Ideas, received from Particular Objects, to become general, which is done by considering them as they are in the Mind such appearances separate from all other Existences, and the circumstances of real Existence as Time, Place, or any other concomitant Ideas. This is called ABSTRACTION, whereby, Ideas taken from particular Beings, become general Representatives of all of the same kind and their Names general Names, applicable to whatever exists conformable to such abstract Ideas. Such precise naked Appearances in the Mind, without considering, how, whence, or with what others they came there, the understanding lays up with Names commonly annexed to them as the Standards to rank real Existences into sorts as they agree with these Patterns, and to denominate them accordingly. Thus the same Colour being observed to-day in Milk, it considers that Appearance alone, makes it a representative of all of that kind and having given it the name of Whiteness it by that sound signifies the same quality wheresoever to be imagin'd or met with; and thus Universals, whether *Ideas* or Terms, are made. (*Essay*, II, xi, 9)

Locke's suggestion seems to be that we start with sensory images of particular things, and from those images we abstract, or make general ideas, corresponding to the different features of the idea. So, to use his example, suppose you are looking at a glass of milk. Some of your sensations will be sensations of white. Thus, you consider the appearance of white—the white sensations—separately from everything else about the image, and you name the resulting idea "white." When you use the term *white*, you are using it to name that idea of white, which represents all white things. This illustrates Locke's general view of how language acquires meaning: Words immediately name ideas in the mind, which in turn represent objects.

BERKELEY'S CRITICISM OF ABSTRACT IDEAS

There has been much discussion about how to understand abstract ideas. In his famous attack on abstract ideas, Berkeley argued that there could be no such things. For what is it to have an idea of just white? Presumably any appearance of white will not be just white—an appearance of white has to have size and shape, otherwise it would occupy no space in your visual field. Likewise, even if we could have an idea of just white, it would still have some particular intensity and hue. But Berkeley takes Locke to mean that an abstract idea of white is just that, an idea with no feature in it but whiteness, so that it would represent what all white particulars, or images, have in common. Berkeley's argument is that it is impossible for an appearance to be that general.

ABSTRACTING AS SELECTIVE ATTENTION

However, one need not interpret Locke's description of abstraction as Berkeley does. Indeed, when Locke says we "consider" the whiteness in the image of milk, he may mean that we simply attend to the whiteness selectively, that is, to the exclusion of other features of the image, and use that as our general idea, representative of all other white things or ideas. Thus, an abstract idea of white could just be an image with white in it, in which we do a sort of mental pointing to the whiteness. We do not, however, in an attempt to get an image of just whiteness, literally strip away everything in the image but the whiteness. That would be impossible. If this interpretation is correct, Locke's view of abstraction turns out to be not very different from what Berkeley himself proposed as a theory of what general terms like *white* mean (described in more detail in chapter 14).

A CIRCULARITY IN LOCKE'S ACCOUNT

There is a more significant problem with Locke's account of abstraction than the one posed by Berkeley. Locke intends his account of abstraction to explain how it is that we can recognize which general term or concept to use to describe an object (or strictly speaking, an image of the object). That is, an abstract idea of white should help us to classify other things that we meet, or ideas that we perceive, as white. Thus, he describes abstract ideas as "standards to rank real existences into sorts as they agree with these patterns." This suggests that to decide whether a thing is correctly described as white, we call upon the abstract idea of "white." If the object matches the abstract idea, then we classify it as white. However, this description actually presupposes that we can already tell whether the object in question is white, for otherwise, we would not know which idea to use for the comparison. Hence, the abstract idea seems to be redundant in accounting for how we are able to think generally—how we are able to recognize general properties of objects and to use general terms to describe them.

PERSONAL IDENTITY

Another problem to which Locke contributed an interesting and important view is that of personal identity. You may recall a famous expression of the general problem of identity in Heraclitus' wondering how he could ever step in the same river twice. The problem is about change: If a thing changes, then is it really the same thing after the change? And if it is not, how can we even sensibly talk about it? One way to try to solve the problem is to say that what is changing are a thing's properties; the thing itself, the substance, does not change. This was Descartes' solution. Recall that despite all of his doubts, Descartes never doubted that the same self existed from one moment to the next. And in considering the changes that the piece of wax could undergo, Descartes assumed that it was still the same piece of wax, the same substance.

Locke's View of General Identity

Locke has a different kind of answer to the general question of what constitutes the same object over time. He avoids talk of substance. For Locke, our idea of identity is a relation between the parts of a thing. To explain identity, he distinguishes mere masses from organisms, or things with a particular structure and organization. For a mass, a mere collection of atoms, that collection will stay the same as long as no atoms are added or subtracted. But for an organism, identity is different. Locke wants to hold that an acorn that has grown into an oak tree is still the same thing, even though its atoms have changed; its identity lies in its organization. Although an acorn acquires new particles of matter as it becomes an oak tree, it shares identity with the oak tree as long as it has the same life:

> That being then one plant which has such an organization of parts in one coherent body, partaking of one common life, it continues to be the same plant as along as it partakes of the same life, though that life be communicated to new particles of matter vitally united to the living plant, in a like continued organization conformable to that sort of plants. (*Essay*, II, xxvii, 5)

The Problem of Personal Identity

Locke's most interesting view about identity, however, is about persons: That is, what makes a person the same person over time. Locke rejects the Cartesian idea that what makes a person the same person over time is sameness of immaterial substance, spirit, or soul. However, if it is not the same soul that binds one's changing thoughts and perceptions together into one person, then what is it?

On Locke's view, identity of person means identity of consciousness. Thus, he is concerned to explain what makes a stream of consciousness one consciousness over time. He thinks that the question of whether a person has the same spiritual substance is irrelevant, for there is no reason that the same spiritual substance could not have more than one stream of consciousness; or indeed that one stream of consciousness could not be associated with different spiritual substances, in the same way that one animal body is associated with changing material substances—atoms. (Locke even considers that two persons—two different consciousnesses—could conceivably switch bodies.)

LOCKE'S ACCOUNT OF PERSONAL IDENTITY

In his view of personal identity, Locke tries to capture our intuitions about our continued existence as persons, namely, that we remember our own past experiences and that we look forward to our own future experiences. We feel a continuity with our own pasts, and we anticipate a continuity with the future. That is, when you think about who you are, you do not, or need not, think about whether you have the same body, and, for that matter, you do not think about whether you have the same immaterial substance, or substances, either, for you have no immediate experience of those. What is important, what gives you a sense of continued existence is that you are conscious of, or remember, your own past, and you anticipate your own future. You are related to and interested in your own past and future in a different way than you are related to or interested in the past and future of anyone else.

Memory Connects States of Consciousness. For Locke, to ask what makes a person the same person over time, then, is to ask a question about whether states of consciousness belong to the same person, the same stream of consciousness. To have the same consciousness over time means that one's states of consciousness are related in a special way, namely, by memory. Locke says:

> For as far as any intelligent being can repeat the idea of any past action with the same consciousness it has of any present action; so far it is the same personal self. For it is by the consciousness it has of its present thoughts and actions, that it is self to itself now, and so will be the same self, as far as the same consciousness can extend to actions past or to come; and would be by distance of time, or change of substance, no more two persons, than a man be two men by wearing other clothes to-day than he did yesterday, with a long or a short sleep between: the same consciousness uniting those distant actions into the same person, whatever substances contributed to their production. (*Essay*, II, xxvii, 10)

The states of consciousness that you now remember are part of the same stream of consciousness you now experience; likewise, in the future, your states of consciousness will include memories of your present state and hence will be parts of the same consciousness. Your consciousness achieves continuity, hence sameness, over time through memory links between the states. Locke says, "as far as this consciousness can be extended backwards to any past action or thought, so far reaches the identity of that person."

PROBLEMS WITH LOCKE'S ACCOUNT

Accounting for a Person's Continued Existence. Although Locke's view captures our special interest in our own futures and pasts, there are problems with it as an account of personal identity. One is that we believe that we have a continued existence despite the fact that there are many moments in our lives that are inaccessible to memory. For example, it is doubtful that you can remember events in your life that occurred before you were two. Yet, you probably would want to hold that it was you who existed before your second birthday, not somebody else.

Reid's Criticism. It is also not clear how Locke's view could handle cases such as one suggested by Thomas Reid. Reid asks us to suppose that a boy is flogged for stealing apples, that that boy grows up to be an officer who commits an act of bravery, and that in old age the officer is made a general. Now suppose that the brave officer remembers the flogging, hence is the same person as the boy. Also suppose that the general remembers the act of bravery as an officer but does not remember the flogging. Then the general is not the same person as the young boy but is the same person as the brave officer. But since the brave officer is the same person as the boy, the general both is and is not the same person as the boy, hence, a contradiction seems to arise. Similar counterexamples can be generated from actual cases of people suffering various kinds of memory loss.

*W*e have touched on only a few of the themes of Locke's great Essay. *Locke wanted to give an account of knowledge, and specifically, of how knowledge of the material world is possible. He thus provided an epistemological basis for the science of his time, the corpuscularian view, according to which the natural, or material, world consists of tiny particles that interact by impulse, according to mechanical laws. It is the primary qualities of objects—shape, size, motion, etc.—that determine their behavior, and hence those qualities are the "real qualities" of objects.*

An important part of Locke's project was to provide accounts of the mental faculties by which we have knowledge of the material world. He gave an account of sense perception consistent with the corpuscularian view, according to which sense perception is a mechanical process, resulting in the production of an idea, a mental image, in the mind. This idea is the immediate object that we perceive, and represents the material object that caused it. However, the idea does not represent the way the object really is, for it includes sensations of secondary qualities—sensations of color, temperature, taste, sound, etc.— and corpuscles do not really have those qualities.

The ideas we get in sense perception are the source of all of our ideas about the material world. They are the objects of the mental acts by which we know the material world. Locke is thus an empiricist, rejecting the possibility of innate ideas. To have knowledge, hence ideas, requires experience. Likewise in investigating the mind, he sets an important precedent in limiting his investigation of the mind to experience, conducting "experiments" on the mind by introspection. This is in keeping with the new scientific method and foreshadows the later empiricism of Hume.

Locke's investigation of our knowledge thus focuses on our ideas, the source of knowledge. As part of his account of how knowledge of the material world is possible, Locke investigates our ideas of substance and power. By distinguishing active and passive power, Locke points out what he takes to be an important difference between material things and spiritual things, for material objects can only transfer motion to other objects, but can never initiate it.

Locke's "way of ideas" is not without its problems. One is that by accounting for all knowledge in terms of ideas, Locke puts a barrier of ideas between the mind and the material world. Berkeley observed this, and argued that we cannot have knowledge of a material world beyond our ideas. Another problem is that Locke's analyses of the faculties of the mind as manipulations of ideas ultimately suggests a rather passive mind: to perceive is to have sensations; to remember is to have certain kinds of ideas; and so on. This tendency becomes full-blown in Hume and would be later sharply criticized by Thomas Reid.

Selected Readings

GENERAL

Aaron, R. I. *John Locke*. Oxford: Oxford University Press, 1971.

Bennett, J. *Locke, Berkeley, Hume: Central Themes*. Oxford: Clarendon Press, 1971.

Locke, J. *An Essay Concerning Human Understanding*. New York: Dover Publications, 1959.

Mackie, J. L. *Problems from Locke*. Oxford: Clarendon Press, 1976.

ON THE CORPUSCULARIAN VIEW

Urmson, J. O. *Berkeley*. Oxford: Oxford University Press, 1982.

ON PERSONAL IDENTITY

Perry, J. "Introduction," *Personal Identity*, ed. by J. Perry. Berkeley: University of California Press, 1975.

14

George Berkeley

George Berkeley (1685–1753) was an Irishman of English descent. He entered Trinity College, Dublin, at the age of fifteen. By 1707, he was a Fellow of the College and had taken Holy Orders; he was later to be a Bishop in the Anglican Church. In 1709, he published his An Essay Towards a New Theory of Vision, *in 1710, his* Principles of Human Knowledge, *and in 1713, his* Three Dialogues Between Hylas and Philonous. *Thus, by the age of twenty-eight, Berkeley had assured his place in the history of Western philosophy.*

BERKELEY'S PHILOSOPHICAL MOTIVATIONS

Berkeley is much the antagonist of Robert Boyle's corpuscularian science and Locke's corpuscularian philosophy. Indeed, if we regard this as Berkeley's chief target we will not be forced into asking whether his philosophical motivations are chiefly theological, epistemological, or metaphysical.

Berkeley, unlike many other thinkers—especially in Britain—of the period, is legitimately a devout believer. For familiar reasons, he regards the corpuscularian, mechanistic picture of the cosmos as a threat to religious orthodoxy. At best, it gives God a role as creator of the universe; but it renders pointless the view that God is immanent in the world—that he actively sustains the universe. In addition, and in obvious ways, it suggests that the mechanistic picture might be extended to the realm of the mental—

as Locke recognized—wholly undermining the picture of ourselves as immaterial, immortal creatures.

But the issue that emerges most clearly in Berkeley's attacks on corpuscularianism is his claim that the Boylean-Lockean picture is one among the latest of philosophical views that commits us to a thoroughgoing skepticism. If we accept the corpuscularian picture, then most of our commonsense claims about the ordinary objects of experience will turn out to be groundless.

Locke and Berkeley

On Locke's account, we perceive material objects only mediately—we perceive material objects, those things which exist independently of us, only by means of ideas. Here we need emphasize only two aspects of the view: (1) The Lockean is committed to an indirect or representative account of perception. On that picture, as Berkeley understands it, since we are never in contact with the things themselves, our experiences can give us no good reason to make claims about how the things, in fact, are. (2) The primary/secondary quality distinction, as Berkeley understands Locke's account of that distinction, makes it the case that very many of the claims that we make about the world are in fact false. The sky is not really blue, nor is sugar really sweet, etc.

BERKELEY AS DEFENDER OF COMMON SENSE

We must take Berkeley seriously when he claims to be a defender of common sense. What he means by this is that he will defend the view that we are directly in contact with real things and that the best evidence about how things are is how they seem or appear to us in perception. But in order to defend common sense and religion, Berkeley must argue that there is no difference between how things appear and how they, in fact, are. That is, Berkeley will argue that the claim that real things exist independently of minds cannot be sustained. Real things are just collections of ideas in minds. This is the core of Berkeley's immaterialism.

BERKELEY'S ATTACK ON ABSTRACT IDEAS

It is important to be clear about why it is that Berkeley devotes his lengthy introduction to the *Principles* to an attack on illegitimate abstraction. The thought that objects can exist outside of all perception is taken by Berkeley to involve illegitimate abstraction. This understanding of the realist or materialist "mistake" recurs throughout Berkeley's work. Why does Berkeley think that this is the case?

LOCKE'S ACCOUNT OF ABSTRACTION

As Berkeley understands Locke's account of abstraction, a single word, say, "man," comes to stand for the genus *Man* by coming to be associated with an abstract idea, *man*. How does an idea come to be "abstract" on Locke's account? Berkeley cites Locke:

> For example, the mind having observed that Peter, James, and John resemble each other in certain common agreements of shape and other qualities, leaves out that . . . which is peculiar to each, retaining only what is common to all, and so makes an abstract idea, wherein all the particulars equally partake; abstracting entirely from and cutting off all those circumstances and differences, which might determine it to any particular existence.

This is the way our general terms come to signify a multiplicity of particulars. It is apparent that this process of abstraction is, by and large, one of substraction; that is, one arrives at abstract ideas by means of subtracting the idiosyncratic features of my ideas of Peter, James, and John, leaving only an abstract idea of man—man in general. It is in this way that one arrives at the abstract idea, *man*.

Berkeley's Chief Objection to Locke's Account

According to Berkeley, this account of abstract ideas involves an incoherence. The ideas described by Locke are in a quite literal fashion impossible. Berkeley admits that there is nothing problematic about a certain kind of abstraction. Thus, even if I have never encountered a human eye detached from a human head, I can, in a sense, abstract the eye from my concept of a human head, and thus arrive at an idea of a human eye apart from the human head. But this will not be an abstract idea in a Lockean sense.

Berkeley's main worry is this: If I am to form an abstract idea of man, then it quite obviously cannot be an idea which, as part of its content, has some particular shape. Men come in very different shapes; and if the abstract idea of man includes some particular shape, then it will not pick out all men in a fully general fashion, which, of course, is what we expect the abstract idea of man to do. But neither can it be the case that the abstract idea of man can include no shape whatsoever. Shape—as a "determinable" and not a "determinate" quality—is quite apparently something that all men have in common. We can be fully certain that if a thing has no shape whatsoever, it is not a man. What then are we to do? Our idea must include in its content some shape, but it can include no particular shape. Berkeley takes this idea to be an impossible one.

The thought here is clear: What would an idea be like which included some shape but no particular shape? Berkeley's point is that there are no such ideas. "Try," we can imagine him to ask, "to arrive at the idea of man, an idea which includes some shape but must not include any shape in particular."

BERKELEY ON ABSTRACTION

Historians of philosophy have, by and large, rejected Berkeley's dismissal of abstract ideas on the grounds that it assumes an imagist conception of ideas and of thought. In short, it may be that if we construe ideas as little mental pictures, forming a picture of a man which includes some shape but no particular shape is impossible. But then, we may ask, why think that ideas are pictures? And if ideas are not little mental pictures, why can I not have an idea the content of which includes some shape but not any shape in particular? After all, I do seem to have an idea of a chiligon, a thousand-sided figure, and yet, most certainly, my having that idea does not depend upon my having a mental image of a figure which has, as a matter of fact, one thousand sides.

Even if Berkeley does assume the imagist conception of ideas, it is just not obvious that his point depends upon this. For it is surely appropriate to ask of the defender of abstract ideas: What in particular is the content of the abstract idea, *man,* by virtue of which it applies quite generally to all men? If it is the case that it is the content of the idea which, by itself, fixes its generality, it is not at all clear that it could be such that it could include some shape but no particular shape. Yet it is not clear how it could apply to all men unless it did just this.

The Relevance of Abstraction to Immaterialism

Our interest here is why it is that Berkeley takes abstraction to be intimately implicated in the view that real things exist independently and outside of all minds. Here, as we shall see, Berkeley's thought is straightforward. To be a realist, in the sense in which we are interested, is at least to claim this: It is coherent to claim that real things—houses, apples, etc.—exist independently of all perception and outside of all minds. If this is so, it seems that the realist must have a conception of such real things; he or she must be able to conceive coherently of the state of affairs he or she is claiming to be true. But this state of affairs seems to involve the vicious sort of abstraction raised above. "This apple exists independently of all perception," says the realist. By this he or she means that he or she can have a grasp on the claim, "the apple exists," wholly abstracted from any of its sensible qualities. But apples do, of course, have shapes, colors, etc.; nothing would be an apple without such qualities. So the apple that exists must have some shape, color, etc. This is just the sort of abstraction Berkeley claims to be incoherent.

BERKELEY'S OWN VIEW OF GENERAL IDEAS AND WORDS

Having ruled out abstract ideas, Berkeley does not, of course, deny that we do sometimes make general claims, for example, "The apple is a fruit." Berkeley's claim is that we do not need the mediation of Lockean abstract ideas to accomplish this. According to Berkeley we do have "general ideas" (see *Principles*, "Introduction," Section 12). We arrive at general ideas by what we may call a process of "selective attention." That is, I can make an idea general simply by attending to certain features of an idea of a particular apple. In this way, a particular idea is made to stand for all apples or triangles, etc. The crucial claim is that an idea or a word can be made to stand for a whole class of objects without the mediation of some special, and odd, abstract idea. (It should be noted that a number of contemporary commentators claim that Locke himself held this selective attention view of abstraction. See G. Pitcher's *Berkeley*.)

What is to be emphasized here is that Berkeley's account of general terms permits us to make quite general claims, without the need for abstract ideas. This is important, for, according to Berkeley, it is just the alleged ability to have an idea, a conception of something independent of experience, that is the source of the realist error.

BERKELEY'S IMMATERIALISM

Berkeley famously characterizes his immaterialism about sensible things by means of the slogan, *esse est percipi*, "to be is to be perceived." It is important to be clear about the fact that Berkeley is here giving us an account of what it means for a sensible thing—a house, an apple, etc.—to exist. According to Berkeley it can mean nothing other than that certain sensible qualities—redness, a certain shape, etc.—are before some mind. "The table I write on I say exists; that is I see and feel it." There is nothing else for the term *existence*, applied to sensible things, to mean.

It must be emphasized, as we begin our investigation of Berkeley's immaterialism, that Berkeley is *not* denying that houses, apples, trees, real things, exist. Real things, for Berkeley *are* collections of sensible qualities, of ideas. He does not deny that real things exist, rather he gives us an account of what the claim, "real things exist," amounts to.

An Argument for Immaterialism

At Sections 22–24 of the *Principles*, Berkeley produces an argument (an argument which is repeated in whole in the *Dialogues*) which we may call the "conceivability argument." It is here that Berkeley tries to show that the realist claim—that objects exist "absolutely," or outside of all mind—is meaningless. Berkeley argues that it is inconceivable that objects exist outside of minds, and therefore, it is impossible that objects exist independently of their being perceived. Thus, the fundamental point is that one cannot conceive of objects having an absolute existence. To this supposition the realist will certainly respond: "But of course I can imagine objects existing independently of any perceiver. Indeed, I am now conceiving of the dark side of the moon." Berkeley has a ready reply to this.

> But, say you, surely there is nothing easier than for me to imagine trees, for instance, in a park, or books existing in a closet, and nobody by to perceive them. I answer, you may so, there is no difficulty in it. . . . [But this] only shews you have the power of imagining, or forming ideas in your mind; but it does not shew that you can conceive it possible the objects of your thought may exist without the mind. To make out this, it is necessary that you conceive them existing unconceived or unthought of; which is a manifest repugnancy.

What emerges is that Berkeley understands the realist to have made a horribly obvious blunder. For in supposing that objects have an absolute existence, and in supposing that he or she has a grasp of what this supposition amounts to, the realist asserts that he or she has a conception of an object which is unconceived. And this, according to Berkeley, is a contradiction. It is not a possible thought.

BERKELEY'S CONCEIVABILITY ARGUMENT EXAMINED

This argument has the appearance of devastating elegance. It has, however, been regarded as something of a horrible blunder itself. There is, of course, a truism which it would serve the realist ill to dispute. No one can, independently of minds, conceive of anything, let alone unconceived objects. It is obvious that any thought had is had in some mind or other, that is, that thought is itself mind-dependent. So the realist should certainly admit that in having the thought "x exists unconceived" he or she is in some mental state; and if it is true that he or she is in some mental state, that fact is obviously mind-dependent.

All this shows is that the having of any thought is a fact which involves the mind. Berkeley must do more than this to demonstrate that the realist is involved in contradiction. Consider two possible thoughts which we might represent in the following way:

1. I am thinking: I am conceiving of something which is unconceived. Compare this with:

2. I am thinking: There exists something which exists unconceived.

These are two different thoughts; the contents of the two thoughts—what follows the colon—are different. What Berkeley must show, if he is to claim that the realist supposition involves a contradiction is that 2 is not a possible thought, since it is this thought which constitutes the realist supposition. But all his argument establishes is that 1 is—and perhaps obviously so—not a possible thought. The content of 1 claims to represent something as both conceived and unconceived. The content of 2 does not claim to do this. With the content represented in 2 there is no suggestion, as well there should not be, that the object's being conceived is part of the very content of the thought.

If this is why the argument fails, we should note that given what Berkeley will say later, he should be happy that it fails. Berkeley, as we will see, will claim both that God and other minds (in addition to his own) exist. If we took the above argument seriously, then this would show that the thought that God exists or that other minds exist would, as well, involve contradiction. That argument hinged on claiming that there was repugnancy involved in any thought which purported to represent something as existing independently of my thought. The argument does not involve the special nature of material objects. Thus, if the argument worked it would establish, not immaterialism, but a thoroughgoing solipsism.

THE CONCEIVABILITY ARGUMENT RECONSIDERED

It may be that there is a reading of the argument under which important conclusions are, in fact, reached. Kenneth Winkler, in his *Berkeley: An Interpretation*, suggests that the argument should be read, not as an independent assault on realism, but as a response, which makes use of earlier Berkeleian assumptions, to a certain kind of realist challenge. Thus, imagine a realist who holds: (1) that to conceive of something is to entertain an image before one's mind's eye; and (2) that a thought represents, or is about, some state of affairs by virtue of resembling that state of affairs. Now imagine that our realist says to Berkeley: "What! I cannot conceive of an object's existing outside of all minds? But I am doing that right now—nothing is easier."

Berkeley's response to this is, rightly, puzzlement. For how can the idea the realist claims to be enjoying represent something which is mind-independent? What part of the content of the idea resembles and thus represents mind-independence? Thus, if the realist, as characterized above, claims to have an idea of mind-independence and founds her realism on that idea, then the Berkeleian argument may well hit its target.

BERKELEY'S TOUR DE FORCE

Berkeley, luckily, does not need to rely upon the conceivability argument in order to establish his claim that *esse est percipi*. Early in the *Principles* he produces an argument which also attempts to establish that conclusion. At 1 through 7, but especially at 4, Berkeley can be understood to argue in the following manner:

1. Sensible objects (houses, apples, etc.) are things that we perceive by sense.

2. The things that we perceive by sense are ideas.

3. Ideas cannot exist unperceived. Therefore, sensible objects cannot exist unperceived.

Two Responses to the Argument

We would do well to consider how it is that realists of different stripes might respond to this astonishingly brief argument.

First, consider what a direct realist might say. A direct realist holds that we perceive physical objects directly, without the mediation of ideas which represent those objects. It is obvious then that the direct realist will object to premise 2 of the argument.

Next, consider what the indirect, or representative, realist will say. The representative realist holds that we perceive physical objects only mediately, by means of ideas which represent (at least some aspects of) those objects. It is apparent that such a thinker will argue that premise 1 is profoundly ambiguous; in order to make the argument run it must be read as asserting that sensible objects are the things that we *directly* perceive by sense; but read in this way it will be rejected by the representative realist.

What Berkeley must do is argue that the immediate object of perception is always an idea, something in the mind. In this way he will have dispatched with the direct realist. He must also demonstrate that the representative realist's claim that we perceive physical objects mediately is to be rejected. This is just what Berkeley does.

The Burden of the "First Dialogue"

It is in the first of the *Three Dialogues Between Hylas and Philonous* that Berkeley argues that what one is immediately aware of in perception are "ideas of sense," things that exist only in minds. It is of importance to note that the dialogue begins with Hylas (from the Greek for "matter") and Philonous ("lover of mind") agreeing to count as true that position which is farthest from skepticism. It is clear that Hylas takes Philonous' idealism to be a form of skepticism, insofar as it denies the existence of material substance, or matter, and so apparently denies the reality of things. Berkeley's goal in the "First Dialogue" can then be regarded as twofold: (1) He will show that the immediate objects of perception are ideas, and that sensible objects exist only in minds; and (2) that it is Hylas' realism that results in skepticism.

Especially with regard to 2 above, we must note that near the start of the dialogue Hylas is compelled by Philonous to put forward what we might term his standard of reality. We learn that for Hylas something will count as real, and a property will count as a real property of some thing, only if it is independent of perceivers. It is this familiar realist conception of the real together with Hylas' direct realism that will produce the unlikely result that it is the realist who is the skeptic.

Against Direct Realism

Hylas, armed with his account of what it is for some thing to be real, agrees, in familiar direct realist fashion, that sensible objects (trees, houses, etc.) are the things immediately perceived by sense. Of course, sometimes one perceives objects to be hot, that is we wish to claim that objects have heat. On Hylas' account of real, if heat is a real property of objects, then it must exist outside of all minds.

HEAT CANNOT EXIST OUTSIDE THE MIND

Philonous produces the following argument:

1. Pains and pleasures exist only in perceiving minds. (It makes no sense to say that there is a pain unfelt, etc.)
2. All degrees of heat are equally real. (Just in virtue of being more or less intense, heat does not count as more or less real.)
3. The most intense heat is a very great pain. (Berkeley here draws on the following: When you put your hand in a fire, you experience a single uniform sensation; one does not experience heat and pain.)
4. By 1 and 3, the most intense heat can only exist in a perceiving mind.
5. By 4 and 2, all degrees of heat exist only in perceiving minds.

There is an additional conclusion here that Berkeley is concerned to draw. For given Hylas' account of the real, he is forced to conclude that heat is not a real property of objects. And this, indeed, does have a skeptical ring to it. "What," we can imagine someone protesting, "the fire is not really hot!" This form of argument is then applied to tastes and odors.

AN OBJECTION TO THIS ARGUMENT

There is an obvious objection to the argument, and it is one that Hylas later raises. We can imagine someone saying in response to Philonous' argument: "If what you mean by "heat" is heat-as-experienced, then of course *that* can only exist in perceiving minds. But heat itself is something different, a real property of bodies." (This will have a familiar Lockean gloss: Heat, as an idea of a secondary quality exists only in minds, but the "power," the secondary quality itself has real existence in the object.)

In response to this objection, Philonous retorts that it is irrelevant. And he is right. Recall that Hylas is defending direct realism, that we are directly aware of sensible qualities and sensible objects. But heat, in the sense now being discussed, is never the direct object of perception, according to Philonous. Heat, in this new sense, is not a sensible thing. In any case, in drawing the distinction, we are already on our way to representative realism.

The Argument from Perceptual Relativity

Berkeley produces another argument against Hylas' realism. This argument from perceptual relativity has a long philosophical history. And it is chiefly used by Berkeley, like the above argument, to establish that what we are directly aware of, sensible objects and qualities, cannot exist outside of all perception. The perceptual relativity gambit is made use of in the *Principles* against heat, taste, color, as well as Lockean primary qualities. Consider the following:

1. Under certain conditions, an object may appear to be different colors or shapes at the same time. (Sometimes the premise appears in the following form: An object can appear to be different colors or shapes at different times *when the object itself has suffered no intervening alteration.*)

2. But an object cannot be two different colors (red *and* blue all over) or two different shapes (circular and elliptical) at the same time.

3. So, by 1 and 2, the sensible qualities of which I am directly aware are not in the objects.

4. The object of direct awareness: colored and shaped surfaces, etc., must be something mental.

One might quibble about the move from 3 to 4, but, in Berkeley's defense, we can note that when I see colored or shaped surfaces, surely I am aware of *something* that has that color or shape, and if not the physical object then surely an idea of sense.

EVALUATING THE ARGUMENT FROM PERCEPTUAL RELATIVITY

This argument is utilized by Berkeley in many ways throughout his writings. We can note that as deployed against Hylas, it appears to establish that one is never aware of objects, and so one cannot say that objects have the colors or shapes that they appear to have. Again, this is the result of the realist conception of the real, and again it leaves the realist in the embarrassing position of being a skeptic. Hylas is committed to concluding that on the basis of experience, he cannot say what sensible qualities objects possess.

There is, of course, the stronger metaphysical conclusion as well, namely, that sensible qualities, colors, shapes, etc., exist only in minds. The relativity gambit seeks to establish this by noting that if one took such qualities to inhere in objects, then one would be forced into contradiction—into claiming that objects have contradictory properties. But is the realist forced into this conclusion?

Let us imagine that a particular object appears circular to you, while at the very same time it appears elliptical to me. Are we forced to conclude that we are aware of mental objects, ideas, and that objects are not really shaped, or colored, or what have you?

It is important to note that we are not so forced. The obvious move to make here is to say that the object really is circular, and that the other claim—that it is elliptical—is false. And here the point seems obvious: How can we draw metaphysical conclusions from facts about the perceptual situation?

There is an additional point: Even if we grant that we have, on the basis of experience alone, no good reason to assert that the object is either circular or elliptical, it is quite another thing to go on to claim, on the basis of facts about perceptual relativity, and as Berkeley at least sometimes seems to do in the *Dialogues*, that shape or color cannot be properties of objects. Here we must draw a distinction between "determinate" and "determinable" properties. We may not be able, on the basis of perception, to ascertain the "determinate" shape (circular, elliptical, etc.) of an object, but this seems to give us no reason to deny that the object has any shape whatsoever; that is, shape—in the sense of some shape or other as a "determinable" quality—might still be a real property of objects.

It is important to emphasize that in the *Principles*, Berkeley seems well aware of these difficulties. At Section 15, he notes that the argument cannot, of itself, show that there is no extension or color in ojects, but rather proves only that we cannot know by perception which is the real color or shape of the object. It is to be emphasized that this is, in any case, an important skeptical result to hang on the realist.

AGAINST LOCKEAN REALISM

We have, for a while now, been considering direct realism. The arguments just canvassed are meant to establish that the objects of immediate awareness are mental objects. But this will not trouble the indirect or representative realist. Someone like Locke (at least Locke as Berkeley understands him) agrees that the objects of direct awareness are mental. But he claims that such mental objects are caused by outward objects which, at least in some respects, resemble the ideas to which they give rise. It is this position to which Hylas is finally pushed by the end of the "First Dialogue." Sections 8 through 21 of the *Principles* are devoted to an examination of this brand of realism.

Berkeley and Locke on Perception

It will be useful to compare the accounts of the perceptual situation as characterized by Locke and Berkeley. Here the chief question will be: What is wrong with Locke's account that is not wrong with Berkeley's structurally similar account?

In Locke's view, there are objects which exist independently of all minds. These objects, in the proper circumstances, cause ideas in human cognizers. The ideas, which are the direct objects of awareness, are of two important kinds. Ideas of primary qualities resemble primary qualities—resemble properties of objects—while ideas of secondary qualities do not resemble properties of the objects. Rather, secondary qualities, though real properties of objects, are powers which are had by objects by virtue of their primary qualities. So there are four important claims: (1) We are directly aware of ideas; (2) there are independently existing substances; (3) at least some of our ideas resemble properties of objects; and (4) these objects or substances cause our ideas.

In Berkeley's view, the ideas of which we are immediately aware are caused by God's volitions. God plays, on this account, something like the role of Locke's material objects. Whether Berkeley conceives there to be a relation of resemblance between God's ideas and ours is not clear. In any case, we turn now to Berkeley's attack on the indirect realist picture.

Arguments Against the Primary/ Secondary Quality Distinction

Berkeley's arguments here are of uneven quality. In Sections 9 and 10 of the *Principles* he argues that one cannot conceive of objects with primary qualities but not with secondary qualities. Berkeley moves from the inconceivability claim to the impossibility claim—it is impossible that objects exist with primary qualities alone. It seems, however, that a realist might grant that we cannot conceive of objects without some color, shape, etc., and still insist that objects do not really, at bottom, have colors. Still, in Berkeley's defense, we should note that he is clearly relying on his earlier attack on abstract ideas.

Next, Berkeley notes that considerations relating to perceptual relativity establish that all sensible qualities exist only in a perceiving mind. At Section 14 of the *Principles*, Berkeley seems to suggest that philosophers like Locke argue for the claim that objects do not really have color or heat on the basis of perceptual relativity phenomena. He then rightly points out that perceptual relativity affects our ideas of size, shape, etc. Here the conclusion, cannot be that such qualities must exist only in the perceiving mind, but rather that if one argues for the non-resemblance of ideas of secondary qualities and properties of objects, then one is committed to saying the same about primary qualities. But Locke, it is reasonably clear, does not argue in this way.

Berkeley then moves to an attack on the notion of *substratum*, or substance. The notion that Berkeley is attacking is just the one that Locke considers in his *Essay*: some stuff or other which supports accidents, or in which all properties, extension, size, etc., inhere. Berkeley clearly thinks that Locke is an advocate of the *substratum* view. In Sections 16 and 17 of the *Principles*, however, he sounds very much like Locke himself in pointing out that when we say *substratum*, no meaningful idea attaches to the word. The proper conclusion, it seems, is that an indirect realist should not advocate the *substratum* view.

Resemblance, Causation, and Substance

If the preceding arguments are misdirected against Locke or simply fail, there is a powerful series of arguments that does connect with Locke's brand of realism.

It is crucial to Locke's view that we have good grounds for thinking that some of our ideas do, in fact, resemble properties of objects. About this Berkeley claims that only ideas can conceivably be said to resemble one another. The claim here is straightforward. If I assert that X resembles Y, or that things relevantly like X resemble things relevantly like Y, then I must have access to both X and Y. What can it mean to say that two things resemble each other if one of those things is, in principle, never open to inspection? Yet according to Berkeley, this is just the position of the indirect realist. Further, since only our ideas are perceivable, that must mean that real objects are not perceivable. Berkeley concludes that this is to say that real things are invisible; but how, Berkeley asks, can something invisible resemble something visible (our ideas)?

Berkeley is pressing an issue which has come to be known as the *veil of perception* problem. We may economically state this as follows: All we have access to are our ideas; we never have direct access to objects. Since this is so, how can we go on to make claims about the things themselves when we never have access to those things? Berkeley is, then, not just making for an internal problem for the indirect realist, he is, even more importantly pointing out that if you argue that there are things which exist independently of all minds then you make skepticism about our knowledge of that independently existing world unavoidable.

Further Remarks on Causation

On the indirect realist picture, material substances cause ideas in minds—spiritual substances. And since Descartes first clearly enunciated mind-body causal interactionism, such causal relations were viewed with suspicion. In Section 18 of the *Principles*, Berkeley objects to the claim that material substances cause ideas in minds, on something like the following familiar grounds. The objection here has a less and a more subtle reading. In a straightforward way, it simply points to the fact that such causal relations are very difficult to make sense of, and yet the indirect realist—any realist in fact—is committed to the coherence of such causal relations (so long as he views mind as immaterial substances). But there is more at work here. As is clear from the passage, Berkeley recognizes that the indirect realist will claim that his view is explanatorily superior. That is, he will claim that we want an elegant explanation of how and why it is that in certain circumstances we undergo certain sensory states—ideas of redness, or of warmth, or of circularity. A Lockean/Boylean account of the perceptual situation promises such an explanation. Here, Berkeley points out that if what we are trying to explain is my having a certain idea of redness, a state naturally describable as the conscious awareness of redness, then realism has no explanation. On the corpuscularian picture, particles strike my eyes, for example, and this causes particles in my brain to move about and so on, but we have no explanation of the *idea of redness*. On this issue, even Locke could say no more than that God could "annex" to certain motions certain ideas; but this, it should be clear, is no explanation of a sensory idea. Thus, Berkeley points to the fact that realism cannot claim to be superior to immaterialism from the point of view of explanatory considerations.

Berkeley's Account of Causation

Berkeley, however, has a positive view of causation, the result of which is that material substances, even if they existed, could not cause ideas. According to Berkeley, only spirits can be causes. Thus, neither material substances nor ideas can be causes. Berkeley's views on this matter are not at all clear, but it is apparent that he takes only the volitions of spirits—God and finite spirits—to possess the kind of activity, or power, or efficacy, which is properly termed "cause." Ideas and material substances (if they existed) are wholly passive; they are inert. There is nothing of activity or power in them.

So far, Berkeley's claim—if not the argument—is clear. But why does he think that only the volitions of spirits can be causes? Berkeley is impressed by the nature of volitional activity. Think for a moment about what it is like to will to move your arm. One wills this: "I will move my arm so." And then, under normal circumstances, one's arm moves just so. There is a connection between the content of the will and what it is that one wills. Thus, the content of one's will, we might say, "looks forward to" or foreshadows the event that it causes. Berkeley finds in this intelligible connection between the content of one's will and the event that one wills, the power, or activity, that is missing in ideas (or material objects if they existed).

The Material Object Hypothesis Is Unnecessary

Last in our consideration of Berkeley's fusillade against Locke are remarks that suggest that the supposition that there are material objects does no explanatory work, and that Berkeley's own idealist account should be preferred on the basis of theoretical elegance and economy.

At Section 18 of the *Principles*, Berkeley notes that even if material objects existed, we could never know this. If we had knowledge, it would have to be on the basis of the senses or on the basis of reason. But no evidence from the senses can, according to Berkeley, establish that something exists outside of all minds—since whatever is perceived is perceived by minds. Reason—by which Berkeley means demonstrative argument—cannot establish the existence of material objects since even the advocates of material substance agree that our experiences might be just as they are now and yet there might be no material objects. Berkeley thus claims that his idealism can explain all the phenomena that the material object hypothesis seeks to explain. And since there is no good reason to hold that material objects exist—even independently of Berkeley's arguments that that supposition is incoherent—we should prefer Berkeley's idealism as the simpler, more elegant explanation.

BERKELEY ON SPIRIT

While Berkeley argues that there are no material substances, he does not think that there are no substances. There are spiritual substances; there are minds, in addition to ideas. According to Berkeley, as we have foreshadowed in our discussion of Berkeley's views on causation, spirit is, fundamentally and essentially, activity or will. What Berkeley means by *activity* in the case of ideas of imagination is clear. At will, I can excite in myself the idea of a rainbow trout or of Notre Dame. But he seems also to think that there is activity, though not a "like dependence" on my will, in the case of ideas of sense. And, of course, I also will and am active—with God's concurrence—in the case of altering certain ideas of sense: those which constitute my own body.

Spiritual Substance

Berkeley argues that material substances—if they existed—are unknowable. How can we know that spiritual substances exist? Berkeley's most straightforward account of these matters is to be found in the *Third Dialogue*. There, he writes that my knowledge of my own mind is immediate and direct. By this means, I come, indirectly, to have knowledge of other spirits.

Later, Philonous remarks that he knows that he exists—that is, his soul, the mental substance that he is, exists—by "reflection." He knows immediately, not just that he has certain ideas, but in addition, he is aware of the active principle that has ideas, his mind. Thus, Berkeley's view is the rather Cartesian one that, in introspection, I am made immediately aware of my mind—something in addition to my ideas. This, according to Berkeley, is how we come to talk meaningfully about spirits.

PROBLEMS WITH SPIRITS

Problems with this account abound. For example, in Berkeley's view, ideas are passive, essentially inert. By virtue of their status, then, ideas cannot represent minds, which are essentially active. We can have no ideas of minds or spirits, Berkeley says. What this suggests, and what Hylas in fact presses, is that Berkeley, or in this case Philonous, should say about "spiritual substance" what he says about "material substance"; namely, that we have no understanding of the term, and that it does not exist. Philonous' response is that the idea of material substance involves a contradiction or incoherence, while spiritual substance does not involve a contradiction. And unlike the case of material substance, we do have reason to believe in the existence of spiritual substance—my own case provides me with all the evidence that I need.

But it is ideas which are incoherent or contradictory, and as this is so Hylas insists:

> Notwithstanding all you have said, to me it seems, that according to your own way of thinking . . . it should follow that you are only a system of floating ideas, without any substance to support them. Words are not to be used without a meaning. And as there is no more meaning in spiritual substance than in material substance, the one is to be exploded as well as the other.

That Berkeley presses this objection against his system must be counted a testament to his philosophical honesty. The point raised by Hylas clearly anticipates, neatly, what David Hume in his *Treatise* would say about these matters.

What Berkeley does say about these matters, both in the *Principles* and the *Dialogues*, is that though we have no idea of spiritual substance, we have a *notion* of such substance. So in this special case, at least, words can have meaning without being linked to an idea. Berkeley seems convinced that we have a notion of spiritual substance, but how we arrive at it is, it must be admitted, a matter of obscurity.

The Problem of Other Minds

Let us grant that we have a notion of spiritual substance, which is somehow derived from our own first-personal awareness of ourselves. How is it that we come to have knowledge of other minds? Berkeley's official answer is a form of the argument from analogy. I behave in certain ways as a result of my will, and I have access, in my own case, to the fact that I am a spiritual substance. I see others behave in certain ways, ways in which I behave, and so I can rightly conclude on the basis of analogical reasoning that they, too, are spiritual substances.

But really, how strong is the analogy? Indeed, in order to make any sense at all of my having a notion of spiritual substance, Berkeley, as we saw above, is forced to emphasize the special first-personal nature of that awareness. It is that awareness that gives sense to the term *spirit*. But it is obvious that I have *that* kind of awareness only in my own case. I am never aware of your conscious states, or your activity. What gives me a notion of self is, in principle, limited to my own case.

GOD

God, as we have seen, plays an enormous role in Berkeley's system. It is his volitions which cause our ideas of sense, and it is his standing volitions that the world behave in certain ways that permit us to understand the cosmos. In this way, at each moment, the cosmos depends upon the will of God.

Arguments for the Existence of God

Here, we need only note that Berkeley's idealism allows him to formulate some relatively novel arguments for the existence of God. The first we may call the *dependency* or *passivity* argument. Just as Locke argues that the fact that I am passive in the perception of ideas of sensation, so Berkeley argues that my passivity with respect to ideas of sense—that they do not depend in their reception on my will—argues in favor of the existence of God. Thus the argument:

1. I enjoy a succession of ideas of sense.
2. These ideas are caused by (a) material substance or (b) spiritual substance or (c) ideas.
3. Ideas and material substances (if they existed) cannot cause anything (see above discussion on causation).
4. I know that this spiritual substance (me) is not the cause of the succession of ideas of sense.
5. Therefore, some other spiritual substance, God, is the cause of the succession of ideas of sense.

This argument would seem to inherit all the difficulties which traditionally plague the cosmological, or first cause, argument.

There is, additionally, another argument for God's existence which some claim to find in Berkeley. Since this argument will neatly raise the issues to be considered in the next section, it is worth considering. Given Berkeley's view that, in the case of houses, apples, etc., to be is to be perceived, we might conclude that when no one is around to perceive that apple or that house it pops out of existence. In the *Dialogues*, the following argument is, at least implicitly, present.

1. For sensible things, to be is to be perceived.

2. But some sensible things continue to exist when there is no finite spirit about to perceive them.

3. Therefore there must be some infinite spirit, God, who perceives such sensible things.

It can rightly be objected that, as an argument for the existence of God, this argument begs the question. For consider: What possible reason could Berkeley have for thinking that 2 is true? Given his view that in the case of sensible things, *esse est percipi*, no reason at all. Unless, of course, Berkeley already thinks that there is an infinite spirit, God.

ON THE NATURE OF REAL THINGS

In the last section, we asked what, no doubt, seems an odd question: What reason could Berkeley have for thinking that sensible things exist when not perceived by finite spirits? Odd because we, of course, all do think that real things continue to exist when not perceived. This is only one of the puzzles that Berkeley's idealism raises.

First, note that Berkeley has an immediate response to the objection that, on his view, there is no distinction between real things and mere fancies or imaginings (both, of course, exist only in minds, the objector will say). For Berkeley, real things (your house, your car, etc.) are collections of ideas which are excited in your mind by "the Author of nature." They are caused by God. Fancies or imaginings are caused by you.

Here, then, are some difficulties to which Berkeley's view may be thought prey.

1. The problem of intermittently observed objects.

2. The problem of wholly unobserved objects.

3. The problem of the "surface."

4. The problem of distinguishing between appearance and reality.

Intermittently Observed Objects   Does my desk pop out of existence when I turn out the lights and shut the door? Do things continually spring into and out of existence? At Section 48 of the *Principles*, Berkeley writes: "For though we hold indeed the objects of sense to be nothing else but ideas which cannot exist unperceived, yet we may not hence conclude that they have no existence except only when they are perceived by *us*; since there may be some other spirit that perceives them though we do not." And since, in Berkeley's account, God is always perceiving objects, it is not the case that they constantly spring in and out of existence.

Wholly Unobserved Objects

We think, for example, that it is true that the earth existed before any finite observers. And we think that it is false that computers existed before any finite observers. Why, in Berkeley's account, is the first true and the second false?

These issues are crisply raised by Berkeley very near the end of the *Third Dialogue*. It, no doubt, seems as though Berkeley should appeal to the very same considerations as he made use of when considering intermittently observed objects. But there is a problem with that account, and there are added complications in the case of wholly unobserved objects. For if we say simply that God perceives the earth before we exist, we may wonder whether Berkeley himself is forced into a representative account of perception. "Do our ideas resemble real things (God's ideas)?" is a question which will now seem important to ask. And we will seem to have a new version of the veil of perception problem.

But worse is the fact that on Berkeley's very traditional theological views, God is absolutely changeless. So what can it mean to say that at some point God *created* the world before finite perceivers? It cannot be the case that at some point God does not perceive the earth and then at some later point he begins to—this would be to claim that God undergoes alteration. Berkeley's theological views commit him to the view that all ideas have existed in God's mind from eternity. And there is more to consider, since when we say that God perceives something we cannot mean the same thing as when we say that we perceive some sensible thing. We are passive in the reception of ideas of sense, and God is wholly active. God cannot perceive as we do.

If there is a solution to these problems, we must claim that although all ideas exist in God from eternity, it is true only of some of them that God wills that they shall become the objects of awareness of finite spirits. This is to gloss Berkeley's claim that God perceives sensible things when we do not, as the claim that God intends that under certain circumstances finite creatures will have certain ideas of sense. So creation is a matter of God's intending that certain ideas should become perceptible to finite creatures. And the existence of wholly unobserved objects (the existence of moons surrounding some distant star) is a matter of its being true that God now intends that certain ideas of sense will be enjoyed should finite perceivers venture there.

The Surface Problem

If the existence of sensible things is a matter of their being perceived, what is the point of the complicated and minute, but usually unobserved, insides of things? Open a human being, and one sees a rich and complex organic system; look at living tissue under the microscope, and one sees immensely complex structures. But again, if to be is to be perceived why would empty husks not serve as well? Of course, the realist has in mind a particular view: It is these minute mechanisms and structures that cause and thus explain the observable phenomena. Berkeley, as we know, regards this as incoherent since material things, even if they existed, could not be causes.

But Berkeley's final response to this worry is ingenious and demands attention. His view is that the complex and minute organization of nature permits us to come to understand and to better predict the course of experience. God has established certain regularities in our experiences, and when we probe what is unseen to the naked eye we come to deepen our understanding of these regularities. It is for this reason that Berkeley sometimes refers to the order of nature as "the language of God." Indeed, God speaks to us in the very fact that he has willed to organize our experience in ways that permit understanding.

Appearance and Reality

In common-sense talk about the world, we distinguish between how things look and how they are. Thus, consider the oar in water; we say that it appears bent but is, in fact, straight. What makes trouble here for Berkeley is that the idea of the oar as bent does not depend upon one's will, the way ideas of imagination do. One of the important facts about perceptual illusions is that they strike us with the force of real things. They are caused quite independently of one's will.

Berkeley, of course, cannot reconstruct on his terms the common-sense distinction between appearance and reality. This is just the distinction between how things seem to us and how they are, independently of perception. It is just this distinction that Berkeley rejects as the source of skeptical worry. What he says about the case of what we call "perceptual illusion" is that there is nothing false about the perception of the oar as bent. We go wrong only if, on the basis of that idea of sense, we go on to make predictions about the course of future experience. For example, I might think that the oar would make a bad baseball bat since it is so bent. Thus, Berkeley's view is that the idea of the oar as bent is part of the collection of ideas that constitute the oar. That is the way God intends our experience to be. I err only if I go on to make predictions of a certain kind.

We have spent considerable attention on Berkeley's complex system. No doubt, many of his claims continue to strike us as odd, even bizarre. Still, we must recall that Berkeley is fundamentally concerned to turn back the skeptic; and in order to do this he claims that what must be rejected is the distinction between what is available in experience and how things are absolutely. With a keen eye, he noted that the sciences threatened not just a traditional conception of God but also most commonsense knowledge claims.

Selected Readings

Bennett, J. *Locke, Berkeley, and Hume: Central Themes*. Oxford: Oxford University Press, 1971.

Dancy, J. *Berkeley: An Introduction*. Oxford: Oxford University Press, 1987.

Foster, J. and Robinson H. (Eds.) *Essays on Berkeley*. Oxford: Oxford University Press, 1985.

Pitcher, G. *Berkeley*. London: Routledge and Kegan Paul, 1977.

Winkler, K. *Berkeley: An Interpretation*. Oxford: Oxford University Press, 1989.

15

David Hume

*D*avid Hume (1711–1776) is the third of the great British empiricists and a foremost thinker of the Scottish Enlightenment. He was born in Edinburgh and studied at the University of Edinburgh, although he left at age fifteen without earning a degree. He studied law briefly; however, philosophy and literature were more to his liking.

Hume published his first work, A Treatise of Human Nature, in 1739. The Treatise was an empirical investigation into the workings of the human mind, inspired by Newton's scientific method. It was not well received; indeed, in Hume's own words, it "fell dead-born from the press." Several years later, Hume published two much shorter works, An Enquiry Concerning the Principles of Morals and An Enquiry Concerning the Human Understanding, in which he presented some of the same ideas as in the Treatise. He also wrote Dialogues Concerning Natural Religion, which was published after his death.

Hume was very disappointed at the failure of his work to excite philosophical enthusiasm; however, many of his contemporaries were concerned with the skeptical conclusions that seemed to follow from Hume's views, as well as his apparent rejection of religion. He was rejected for appointments in philosophy at both the University of Edinburgh and the University of Glasgow. However, as a man of letters, Hume was highly regarded. He wrote the acclaimed History of England while serving as Keeper of the Advocates Library at the University of Edinburgh. He also held several positions as a statesman, and he counted many important people, including Adam Smith, among his friends.

HUME'S METHOD

In the *Treatise*, Hume seeks to found knowledge of the human faculties on an experimental investigation of the human mind, much as Newton had investigated the nature of the material world through observation and experiment. One of Newton's rules for philosophizing was to "feign no hypotheses"—that is, to refrain from offering explanations of phenomena that could not be supported with experimental evidence. To an empiricist, speculation and a priori reasoning about nature is the bane of science.

Hume thought that he could construct a science of the mental by following Newton's method—making no unfounded assumptions and recording only what he truly observed. Just as Newtonian science seeks generalizations that accurately describe the phenomena of the natural world, so Hume seeks generalizations that accurately describe mental phenomena. The result in the *Treatise* is an account of knowledge and belief, the passions (including love, hatred, pride, humility, beauty, fame, vice, and so on, as well as free will), and morality. Hume also shows why the views of his predecessors on these subjects were not right—why they are not founded in experience, namely, what we find in the mind. In *An Enquiry Concerning Human Understanding*, Hume presents a condensed discussion of knowledge, belief, and free will. We will focus primarily on this discussion in this examination.

Ideas and Impressions

Hume's first task is to find the basic elements, or "atoms," that the mind works with in all of its operations. He notes that when we introspect, we find "perceptions," and those are of two kinds. First, there are "impressions." Impressions are feelings or sensations: feeling heat, feeling pain, seeing red, hearing a loud noise, and so on. Notice that Hume calls these "impressions," suggesting that they are impressed upon us, or perhaps, on our sense organs.

But introspection also reveals another kind of perception. Hume calls these "ideas," which are less vivid than impressions. So, for example, when you think about something, or remember something, or imagine something, you are not exactly having sensations—rather, you are having "ideas."

IDEAS ARE COPIES OF IMPRESSIONS

Hume thinks that all ideas are copies of impressions. Like Locke and Berkeley, he thinks all of the materials of knowledge come from experience. Thus, it is not surprising that he thinks ideas derive from impressions. However, unlike Locke and Berkeley, Hume refrains from telling us where the initial impressions come from. For all we know, the mind may generate them itself, or they may come from external objects. But Hume does not postulate the source or cause of our impressions, for he has no evidence about that. All he knows is that he has impressions, and he has ideas which come from and are copies of impressions.

How Ideas Differ from Impressions. Hume also considers how ideas are different from impressions, and how they are related. Impressions and ideas differ in force or vivacity or "liveliness." "The most lively thought is still inferior to the dullest sensation," Hume tells us. Hence, the difference between impressions and ideas is a matter of degree—it is a quantitative difference, not a qualitative one. Likewise, ideas are related to impressions by being copies of them, like pictures of them. And since ideas derive from impressions, it is clear that Hume thinks there are no innate ideas, that is, ideas preceding corresponding impressions.

Hume's Arguments. Hume offers two reasons that ideas must be copies of impressions, not vice versa. The first is that if we consider our ideas, it is always possible to trace them, or their components, to impressions. But the reverse is not true. For example, consider imagining a unicorn. Hume thinks that even though you may have never seen a unicorn, you can analyze your idea into simpler ideas—say, a horse idea and a horn idea—and you will find that at some point in your life, you have had an impression of each of those.

So, while you cannot have an idea that is not traceable to some impression or set of impressions, Hume thinks it is possible to have a new impression, of which you have never before had an idea. Consider, for example, hearing a musical instrument played that makes sounds you have never heard. Once you have heard them, you can have ideas of them. This happens, for example, when you remember the sounds. However, Hume thinks that you cannot have the ideas until you first have had the sound impressions. And what if you think otherwise? Hume challenges you to find an idea that you think is not traceable to some impression, then it will be up to him to try to find such an impression.

Hume's other argument, perhaps more persuasive, is that people who are missing a sense will not have ideas corresponding to the missing sensations. For example, if you have never had a visual impression, you will not have ideas corresponding to visual impressions. You will not, for example, have an idea of the color blue—or at least, if you do have such an idea, it will not be copied from an impression of blue, for you never have had a blue impression.

The Missing Shade of Blue. Is Hume's thesis, that all ideas are copies of impressions, correct? Oddly enough, Hume himself offers a counterexample to his claim. He asks us to suppose that a person has seen every color except a particular shade of blue; in Humean terminology, that person would be missing a certain blue impression. Yet, if presented with a color spectrum excluding that shade of blue, that person would, Hume thinks, be able to form an idea of the shade that is missing. So is this not a case of having an idea with no corresponding impression?

Interestingly, Hume dismisses the example, saying "it is scarcely worth our observing, and does not merit, that for it alone we should alter our general maxim." However, the example is not so out of the ordinary, nor should a scientist dismiss possible counterexamples to his hypotheses. Perhaps more important, our ability to extrapolate from the shades of blue on either side of the missing one may indicate that we can recognize what is similar about those two shades, which is to be able to abstract. However, Hume, like Berkeley, rejected abstraction and abstract ideas.

Other Problems with Hume's Claim. There are some other problems with Hume's claim that all ideas are copies of impressions. One is that even if ideas are derived from impressions, not all ideas seem to be literally copies of the corresponding impressions. When you remember an event, for example, it is not like rerunning a movie of it in your mind. Or when you remember a person, your memory need not be like a photograph of him. It is not at all clear that the idea you have when you remember something differs from the original impression by only a degree of vivacity. Hume's description suggests that having an idea is like turning down a dimmer switch on an impression, but this simply does not account for the variety of ideas we have and how they contrast with corresponding impressions.

Hume's Account of Meaning. Hume's claim that all ideas are copies of impressions enables him to establish a criterion for the meaningful use of terms. Like Locke and Berkeley, Hume thinks that words are signs for ideas. So to check whether a word has meaning, one need only find the idea that it names. And to see whether there really is such an idea, one need only look to one's experience to see if there is an impression from which the idea was copied.

This test of meaningfulness is of utmost importance in Hume's epistemology. Hume does a thorough investigation of metaphysical terms such as *power*, *substance*, *soul*, and *free will*. His investigation consists of looking for the ideas corresponding to those terms. Thus, if philosophers use a term meaningfully, they should be able to produce the idea, hence the impression, that it signifies.

RELATIONS AMONG IDEAS

Having categorized the objects of the mind, Hume must discover the laws that best describe their operations. Ideas do not just occur randomly in the mind, just as material objects and the atoms they are made of do not behave randomly. Thoughts are not chaotic: Ideas occur in the mind in certain patterns. Hume finds three relations in particular that characterize the behavior of ideas: resemblance, contiguity, and cause and effect.

Resemblance. Hume's first relation is resemblance. Sometimes an idea will be followed by another that resembles it. Hume's example is that when we see a picture, we immediately think of, have an idea of, the object pictured. Or suppose that your alarm clock is like the sound a truck makes when it goes into reverse. When you hear your alarm, that impression may be followed by the idea of a truck. Often impressions will remind us of things we have perceived before: Thus, ideas are called to mind that resemble those impressions in the relevant respects. These examples are associations of impressions with ideas; but when Hume uses the phrase "association of ideas," he seems to be using the term *ideas* generically, to include impressions.

Contiguity. The second relation Hume describes is contiguity in time and place. Ideas or impressions that have been associated temporally or spatially in the past tend to subsequently occur together. Suppose, for example, that you always eat lunch at noon, and that every day at noon, you hear church bells chime. Your eating lunch is temporally contiguous with the chiming. Hence, when you hear the church bells chime, you immediately think of lunch. Hume also tells us that to think of one item in a place will lead you to have ideas of the surrounding, or contiguous, things. Thus, if you think of your bedroom, you may also think of adjacent rooms.

Cause and Effect. The third and perhaps most important relation between ideas is cause and effect. Hume's example of this relation is that wounds cause pain, hence having an idea of a wound may be followed by having an idea of the pain it causes. For example, if you broke your leg when you were young, it is probably difficult to think of it, have an idea of it, now without also thinking about how painful it was. If you think about standing near a fire, you probably also think about the warmth it causes. Or if you think about dropping a ball, you probably also think about the ball's falling to the ground and bouncing. These are all examples of ideas that are associated by the relation of cause and effect.

In setting forth these relations, Hume sees himself as doing what Newton did in finding the laws that describe the behavior of bodies, such as the principle of gravitation. Hume does not claim to have necessarily found all of the laws that describe the patterns of our thoughts. But likewise, scientists cannot prove that they have found a complete set of laws that describe the operations of nature. Hume thinks that to satisfy ourselves that these three laws are exhaustive, we need only repeat our observations, just as a scientist would:

> All we can do, in such cases is to run over several instances, and examine carefully the principle, which binds the different thoughts to each other, never stopping till we render the principle as general as possible. The more instances we examine, and the more care we employ, the more assurance shall we acquire, that the enumeration, which we form from the whole, is complete and entire. (*An Enquiry Concerning Human Understanding*, III)

POWER AND CAUSALITY

One of Hume's main aims in *An Enquiry Concerning Human Understanding* is to examine the notion of causality. Causality is of utmost importance for science, and Hume's intent is to show precisely what it is to have knowledge of causes. The notion of causality is associated with the notion of power. You will recall that Locke thought that substances have powers to produce changes in other substances, but that strictly speaking, only minds have active powers. Material substance has merely passive power, the power to be changed by impulses from other material substances, and to transfer, thereby, the impulses it receives to other substances. Material substance is hence essentially inert. In taking minds to be the only truly active substances, Locke followed Descartes.

Berkeley took Locke's conclusions a step further. He thought that if only mental substances have active power, then there is no reason to postulate that material substances cause ideas in us. They have no real power to do so. You, a mental substance, exhibit real power when you conjure up ideas in your own mind, as happens, for example, when you imagine or remember something. And those ideas over which you seem to have no control—sensations of material objects—must also have a real cause, namely, a mental substance. Berkeley took the cause of those to be God.

Using the empiricist principle that all knowledge must be founded in experience, Hume takes Berkeley's reasoning a step further. He argues that in fact, we have no idea of power at all. Hence, Hume thinks, there is no such thing as causality, either in material substances or spiritual substances. (For that matter, Hume thinks we have no idea of substance either, which we will consider below.) Rather *causality* is simply a term we use to describe a relation of ideas in our minds. To show this, Hume considers what it is that we know when we have causal knowledge.

The Objects of Knowledge

To consider what knowledge of a causal relation is, Hume observes that the objects we know about, or reason about, divide into two classes: relations of ideas and matters of fact.

RELATIONS OF IDEAS

Relations of ideas are propositions whose truth can be known by simply inspecting the ideas to see if the asserted relation holds. Hence, they are true or false a priori. Examples of such are definitions and mathematical propositions. For example, "a square has four sides" is a proposition whose truth you can determine just by understanding what *square* and *four sides* mean. Likewise, "two plus three equals five" is a relation of ideas. Another way of thinking of relations of ideas is that if such a proposition is true, then to deny it would involve a contradiction. To say, for example, "a square does not have four sides" contradicts the meaning of *square*. Or to say, "two plus three is not equal to five" contradicts the meaning of *two, three, five,* and *addition.* In fact, mathematical proofs are often performed in precisely this way: The opposite of what is to be proved is assumed, and a contradiction is generated.

MATTERS OF FACT

The other kind of object of knowledge Hume calls "matters of fact." Matters of fact are propositions whose truth can only be known by experience—by making an inspection of the world to see if they are true or false. Examples of such are, "the book is heavy," or "today is Tuesday," or "heavy objects fall when dropped." You cannot determine whether these statements are true simply by inspecting the meanings of the terms. Rather, you have to check: You have to examine the objects, or in the last case, perform experiments. Thus, matters of fact are true or false a posteriori.

Another way of thinking of matters of fact is that such propositions may be true, but it is possible that they could have been false. Unlike relations of ideas, there is no contradiction involved in denying a true matter of fact. For example, while it may be true that today is Tuesday, the statement "today is not Tuesday" does not involve a contradiction, whereas "two plus three does not equal five" does involve a contradiction. In fact, sometimes the statement "today is not Tuesday" will be true.

It is interesting to note that relations of ideas are the kind of proposition that Descartes doubted by introducing the possibility of the evil deceiver. Moreover, ultimately, Descartes thought that all real knowledge consists of relations of ideas, including knowledge of the material world. Knowledge of the material world is causal knowledge—it is about why things happen the way they do. Descartes thought that physics would ultimately turn out to be, like geometry, an a priori science. What Hume wants to show, though, is that science is not at all a priori, and indeed that knowledge of causal laws is not very certain at all.

Causes and Effects Are Matters of Fact

Having divided objects of knowledge into relations of ideas and matters of fact, Hume shows that a piece of causal knowledge is really a matter of fact. He notes that when we reason about matters of fact, we employ causal principles. For example, you study for a test, reasoning that you will perform better if you study. Why do you reason that way? Because in the past studying has improved your performance on tests. In this case, you are reasoning about the future, based on your observations about the past. You are reasoning from a cause, your studying, to an effect, your good performance on the test.

Sometimes we also employ causal reasoning to figure out what must have happened in the past. Suppose, for example, that you have arrived at the professor's office to pick up your graded test. You notice that your best friend got an *A* on the exam. You reason that your friend must have studied for the test. That is, from the effect, the good grade, you reason to the cause.

Now, you may notice that your conclusions in both cases could be incorrect. Perhaps despite your studying, you do not get a good grade on the test. There is certainly no guarantee that you will. Or perhaps your friend got an *A* because she got lucky. This is precisely what Hume will argue about our reasonings concerning causes and effects: They are never certain, and could always be wrong. They are not a priori truths.

To convince us that conclusions of causal reasonings are not relations of ideas, but are merely matters of fact, Hume asks us to consider whether we could discover causes and effects by employing reason alone. Suppose, for example, that you had never seen a heavy object fall. Would you be able to tell, simply by inspecting it, that it would fall if dropped? Of course, we are tempted to say yes; however, that is probably because we have seen so many objects fall in the past. But suppose you were suddenly transported to the moon. There, a heavy object would not fall, at least not the way it does on earth. You could not have predicted its behavior by deducing it from an inspection of the object; so "knowing" that heavy objects fall when dropped is not like knowing that two plus three equals five. It is not a process of reasoning that leads you to your conclusion—otherwise, you would have been able to tell a priori how the object would behave on the moon. Likewise, if you were to see someone drop what looked like a heavy object, but it did not fall to the ground, you would, no doubt, be surprised. But you would not think it to be impossible or to involve a contradiction. Hume himself says:

> We fancy, that were we brought, on a sudden, into this world, we could at first have inferred, that one Billiard-ball would communicate motion to another upon impulse; and that we needed not to have waited for the event, in order to pronounce with certainty concerning it. Such is the influence of custom, that, where it is strongest, it not only covers our natural ignorance, but even conceals itself, and seems not to take place, merely because it is found in the highest degree. (*Enquiry*, IV, i)

Hume is saying that because we are so used to seeing objects behave in certain kinds of ways, we think we could have known how they would behave without ever having witnessed their behavior. But that is simply not the case. When presented with new objects or circumstances, we do not really know what to expect.

The Problem of Induction

Hume is concerned to find the foundation of our reasonings about matters of fact. We seem to appeal to causal relations to draw conclusions about what has happened in the past and what will happen in the future. But is there any basis for appealing to causality? What makes us think that causal relations that have held in the past will hold in the future?

CAUSAL REASONING IS NOT DEMONSTRATIVE

A partial answer to this question is negative: It is not demonstrative reasoning that makes us think causal relations will hold in the future. To see why not, let us consider one of Hume's examples, that bread nourishes. In the past you have found that eating bread nourishes you. Now, suppose you are hungry and decide to have a piece of bread. Can you be certain that this time it will nourish you and not poison you instead? You probably give the latter possibility no thought whatsoever. But if asked, you might reason, "Well, bread has nourished me whenever I have eaten it in the past, so this piece will do so as well." That is, you might express your thought process as follows:

Premise: Whenever I have eaten bread in the past, it has nourished me.

Conclusion: When I eat bread in the future, it will nourish me.

Now, to see that this is not a piece of valid demonstrative reasoning, all one need do is consider whether the premise could be true and the conclusion false. For in a valid demonstration, like a mathematical proof, if the premise is true, the conclusion must also be true. But clearly, it could be true that bread has always nourished you in the past, but the piece of bread you are about to eat will not. It could be laced with arsenic. Or you may have developed an allergy to wheat. Or it could simply not nourish you. So even though the premise is true, the conclusion could be false. As Hume says, ". . . it implies no contradiction that the course of nature may change, and that an object, seemingly like those which we have experienced, may be attended with different or contrary effects." (*Enquiry*, IV, ii)

At best, the conclusion of the above argument is probable, but not certain. Put another way, in demonstrative reasoning, the conclusion is somehow contained in the premises—it does not tell us anything new. But the conclusion in your reasoning about the bread does tell us something new, something that is not contained in the premise.

THE MISSING PREMISE

There is a way of making the above argument demonstratively valid. All we need do is insert an additional premise: "The future will resemble the past." Then we would have the following:

Premise 1: Whenever I have eaten bread in the past, it has nourished me.

Premise 2: The future will resemble the past.

Conclusion: When I eat bread in the future, it will nourish me.

Now, if both premises are true, then the conclusion has to be true. For otherwise, one of the premises would be contradicted.

Begging the Question. But how do we know that Premise 2 is true? To assume that it is would beg the question at hand—for after all, we are trying to show, to prove, that the bread will nourish, that future bread will be like past bread.

We could try to prove that the future will resemble the past, but to do so, we would again find ourselves going in circles. For to do that would require the same kind of argument as the argument above:

Premise: In the past, the future has resembled the past.

Conclusion: In the future, the future will resemble the past.

This argument is clearly not valid, for the premise could be true and the conclusion false, with no contradiction whatsoever. And to make it valid, we would have to insert as a premise the very conclusion we are trying to prove, that the future will resemble the past:

Premise 1: In the past, the future has resembled the past.

Premise 2: The future will resemble the past.

Conclusion: In the future, the future will resemble the past.

Premise 2 is clearly the same as the conclusion, for the phrase "in the future" could be dropped from the conclusion with no loss of meaning. So, we are stuck. There seems to be no way of proving anything about the future, for we cannot be certain that the causal relations that seem to have held in the past will continue to hold. Like all other matters of fact, they could turn out to be false in the future, without contradiction.

This problem is sometimes known as the problem of induction. It is an important problem for scientists, and Hume was the first to give it a clear articulation. If you consider how science proceeds, it will be clear why it has this problem. Science proceeds through experiment. Experiments provide evidence for hypotheses, and scientists test hypotheses with experiments. But when has a scientist conducted enough experiments to know that a hypothesis is right? There is always the possibility that the next experiment will not conform to the hypothesis. Indeed, a scientist can never *prove* that a hypothesis is true. Rather than deduce that particular events will happen from general principles and innate ideas, scientists induce general hypotheses from particular events. But no matter how many particular events are observed, an induction is never certain, as Hume has shown.

Thus, Hume's conclusion poses a serious problem for rationalists like Descartes and Leibniz, as well as empiricists like Locke and Newton. With respect to the former, he has argued that scientific knowledge is not like mathematical knowledge. It is not demonstrably certain but proceeds from observation. Reason is not the faculty by which we have knowledge of the laws of nature. However, if we accept that science proceeds by generalizing from observation, as Locke and Newton among many other empiricists and scientists held, we still are faced with the problem that the generalizations we form can never be certain. The future need not resemble the past. So we can never really be said to know anything about the future, if knowledge requires certainty. Thus, the problem of induction lands us in a position of deep skepticism.

Hume's Solution

As a philosopher, Hume knows that he cannot be certain of what will happen in the future. We have a faculty for knowing a priori truths—reason—and we have faculties for knowing past and present matters of fact—memory and sense perception, respectively. Yet we have no faculty for knowing future matters of fact. Still, we operate on the assumption that we do know what will happen in the future; we continually make predictions, and indeed if we could not, we would be in a rather sorry state. For example, how would you be able to take a step if you could not be sure that the floor would support you?

CUSTOM

Hume has an answer to the question of why we think the future will resemble the past, that is, why we trust our causal "reasonings" about future matters of fact. It is not reason that provides this trust, but rather custom or habit. Having experienced a causal relation over and over, we come to expect that the particular cause we have observed will bring about the particular effect. Having enjoyed bread over and over, we come to expect that we will enjoy it when we eat it in the future. Of course, there is no reason why many experiences give more weight to our expectation than a single experience. But those many experiences make us accustomed to expect that in the future the causal relation will also hold. As Hume says, regarding custom:

> This hypothesis seems even the only one, which explains the difficulty, why we draw, from a thousand instances, an inference, which we are not able to draw from one instance, that is, in no respect, different from them. The conclusions, which it draws from considering one circle, are the same which it would form upon surveying all the circles in the universe. But no man, having seen only one body move after being impelled by another, could infer that every other body will move after a like impulse. All inferences from experience, therefore, are effects of custom, not of reasoning. (*Enquiry*, V, i)

His point is that if our causal reasonings truly were a product of reason, then they should occur after only one experience. But the contrary is true: We need much experience before we are confident of our expectations. Hence, it cannot be reasoning that leads us to our conclusions about future matters of fact.

Hume also points out the great value of custom:

> Custom, then, is the great guide of human life. It is that principle alone, which renders our experience useful to us, and makes us expect, for the future, a similar train of events with those which have appeared in the past. Without the influence of custom, we should be entirely ignorant of every matter of fact, beyond what is immediately present to the memory and senses. (*Enquiry*, V, i)

In other words, without custom, we would not know how to act in the future, for we would not have the expectation that the future will be like the past. Reason is not the operative faculty in our beliefs about the future, contrary to what Descartes and some other rationalists thought.

THE PSYCHOLOGY OF BELIEF

Part of Hume's epistemological task is to investigate what happens when we know or believe something. It is an interesting observation that what we take to be knowledge of future matters of fact is not really knowledge at all, but results from custom. So, we believe that the future will resemble the past, but we cannot be certain that it will. But what is it to have a belief?

Recall from above that Hume thinks all mental objects resolve into either impressions or ideas. Hence, belief, too, must be analyzable in terms of impressions or ideas. To understand belief, suppose that you are watching someone light a firecracker. As you see the fuse burn, you have a firm expectation, based on your past experience, that there will be an explosion. Now consider imagining a firecracker exploding. How is your belief that the firecracker will explode different from imagining it explode? Hume thinks that both include an idea of a firecracker exploding—a faint copy of impressions you have had in the past of firecrackers exploding. However, the belief has something else: It has an impression attached to it, which Hume names "belief." Belief gives us a "more vivid, lively, forcible, firm, steady conception of an object, than what the imagination alone is ever able to attain." (*Enquiry*, V, ii)

Thus, when we receive impressions of objects we have seen before, they are often followed by ideas of the effects with which they have been associated, together with a belief impression. When you have an impression of a firecracker burning, it will be followed by an idea of an explosion, together with a belief impression that makes the explosion idea more vivid. Thus, Hume has found a law describing the occurrence of belief in terms of the basic mental entities he has postulated, ideas and impressions. Other mental states can be analyzed similarly, and on Hume's view, this is precisely how the science of the mind should proceed: by "experimenting" on the mind, observing it through introspection, followed by giving a law-like description of what we find.

Our Idea of Necessary Connection

In addition to finding the laws that describe our mental states, Hume wants to explain where philosophers have gone wrong in the past. For example, why did Descartes think that causal relations were discoverable by reason alone? Was there something about the idea of causality that he had gotten wrong? Should we think that there really are causes just waiting to be discovered by us? Or that objects have powers, as Locke thought? Where does the idea of substance come from? Following Berkeley and Locke, Hume thinks that to find the meaning of a term, one need look only at the idea to which it corresponds. Thus, to see what *power* or *necessary connection* or *substance* means, we must look for the corresponding idea.

One of the ideas Hume wishes to investigate is that of power, or necessary connection. His reason is that *cause* had been used synonymously with *power* and *necessary connection*. Other philosophers had thought that if a thing can cause something to happen, it is because of a power it has—the power necessarily brings about the effect. Thus, Locke thought that material objects have powers—determined by their primary qualities—to bring about effects in other objects. When a billiard ball strikes another billiard ball, for example, it will cause the second ball to move; the motion of the second billiard ball is necessarily connected to the motion, mass, etc., of the first. The power of the first ball causes motion in the second.

WE HAVE NO IMPRESSION OF NECESSARY CONNECTION

Is there really any power in the first ball, though? Is the motion of the first necessarily connected to the motion of the second? Hume does not think so. Indeed, he thinks that if we look for an impression of power in the motion of the ball, we find none. And if we look for an impression of connection in the motions of the two balls, we again find none. All we can find in our experience is the motion of the first ball, followed by the motion of the second. There is nothing about the motion of the first that tells us the motion of the second must follow. Indeed, even if we could analyze each ball into its corpuscularian constituents and their primary qualities, we still would find no necessary connection between those of the first ball and those of the second. Nor would we get an impression of power.

Hume considers that our idea of power may come from elsewhere, though. Locke thought that we really have no idea of power in material objects. He thought that our idea of real power—active power—comes from ourselves, spiritual substance. We feel power when we conjure up ideas out of nowhere, or when we move parts of our bodies. Hume dismisses introspection, too, as a source of an impression of power. He considers two sources of such an impression: the mind's ability to bring about ideas, and the mind's apparent power over the body.

An Impression of Power Cannot Come from Mental Activities. Hume's reasons for rejecting the mind's activities as a source of an impression of power, or necessary connection, are as follows. First, if we consider that to bring up an idea is to make something from nothing, that would seem to require a very great power. However, we have no sense of that power but only of a willing to produce the idea, followed by the idea. We do not know how the idea is produced. Second, the mind has only a limited control over its states and ideas, yet we have no idea why. If we did get an impression of necessary connection from its conjuring up ideas, we would certainly see why some can be produced and others not—indeed, it would follow, necessarily, that some can be and others cannot. Third, our ability to control our ideas changes according to different conditions—whether we are sick, or distraught, or in some other state. Yet we have no sense why it should. Hence, again, there is no impression of necessary connection between our willing an idea and its production. We really have no impression at all of how ideas occur.

An Impression of Power Cannot Come from the Mind's Control over the Body. Hume also dismisses the view that our control over our bodies produces an impression of power. First, we have no idea of how mind and body are connected. However, if we did get an impression of necessary connection when we will to move parts of the body, we should certainly understand how they are connected. Second, we also have no understanding as to why we can move certain parts of our bodies and not others. You can will to wiggle your toes, and your toes wiggle; but if you will to stop your kidneys, nothing happens. But certainly, if we did have an impression of necessary connection from such action, we would see why toes' wiggling follows from willing them to move, but kidneys' stopping does not follow from willing them to stop. Finally, moving a body part involves many motions in between—the sending of nerve signals, muscle movement, etc., of all of which we are unaware. But surely if we had an impression of necessary connection from such an occurrence, we would also see why all of the intervening motions occur.

In general, Hume's arguments amount to showing that in cases where we think there is a power, or a necessary connection, there really is only one event followed by a completely independent event: one billiard ball moving, followed by another billiard ball moving; the willing of an idea followed by the occurrence of an idea; the willing that a part of the body move, followed by motion in that body part. In none of these sequences of events do we have an impression of what connects them. We have only an experience of the conjunction of objects or events. Hume thinks that we can never find a connection between two events, even if we think of them as causally related.

Strictly speaking, they are completely independent. The one never follows from the other, for we can always conceive of something entirely different happening, with no contradiction whatsoever.

The Real Source of the Impression of Necessary Connection. So why do we think there is a power in objects, or that causally related events are necessarily connected? Why do we think the first billiard ball has the power to move the second, and that the second's motion is necessarily related to the first's? Hume thinks the answer lies in ourselves. We expect that the second billiard ball will move when the first one strikes it. Thus, our own expectation, or belief, that it will move provides the connection. But the connection is one that we make—there is no connection in the events themselves, nor any power in the ball. The impression of necessary connection really is just the impression that is our own belief, on observing the first event, that the second will follow. Hume notes that if we had never before observed the impact of one billiard ball upon another, we would not have the impression we take to be one of power. It is only after experience in the world that we have the belief that we mistakenly take to be an impression of power. But if the power really were in the ball, we should have an impression of it the very first time we observe it strike another ball.

The Cause/Effect Relation

What, then, is it for one event to cause another, if there is no such thing as power or necessary connection beyond our own beliefs? In Section VII of the *Enquiry*, Hume offers three definitions of cause. The first is, "an object, followed by another, and where all the objects, similar to the first, are followed by objects similar to the second." He adds, "Or in other words, where, if the first object had not been, the second never had existed." Supposing we consider the simple causal rule, "The impact of one billiard ball on another causes it to move." On Hume's definition, this merely means that when one billiard ball strikes another, the second ball will move. That is, the first event will be followed by, or conjoined with, the second. However, note that there is no mention of necessary connection or power.

Hume's additional phrase, however, has a different meaning. Considering the billiard ball rule again, what it says is that if the first billiard ball had not struck the second, the second would not have moved. But is this true? Perhaps all other things being equal, it is. But consider that another billiard ball could have struck it instead. Then we would have a case in which the first event did not occur, yet the second occurred anyway. There need not be only one thing that can cause an event to occur. The first definition really says, "A causes B means that if A occurs then B will occur." The addition says, "A causes B means that if B occurs then A must have occurred." If we put them together, we get, "A causes B means that A occurs if and only if B occurs." Of course we are not able to prove that A will always be followed by B, or B always preceded by A. But Hume is saying that this is what we mean when we say "A causes B."

Hume's third definition is very different from the first two. It is "... an object followed by another, and whose appearance always conveys the thought to that other." While the first two are about events in the world, the third is about our psychological states: To say firecrackers cause explosions means that, for example, when we see a firecracker we think of, or expect, an explosion.

FREE WILL

Another of Hume's important contributions to philosophy is his discussion of free will. As with other philosophical issues, Hume approaches the problem of free will by examining the meanings of the terms employed, *liberty* and *necessity*. Hume thinks that when the actual meanings of the terms are understood, the problem will disappear.

The Problem   Briefly, the problem of free will versus determinism, or in Hume's terms, liberty versus necessity, is this: We seem to act freely, that is, to determine our own actions and hence, to be responsible for them. However, the scientific view of the natural world—that underlying the corpuscularian model—is that all events are determined. On that model, the natural world can be thought of as being like a huge billiard table, with balls moving about and striking one another. The motion of each ball is completely determined by its primary qualities. If we knew enough about each ball, and the laws of physics, we would be able to precisely predict how it would move. Hence, given a state of the world at a particular time, and the laws of nature, we could derive any other state of the world. Hume puts it this way:

> It is universally allowed, that matter, in all its operations, is actuated by a necessary force, and that every natural effect is so precisely determined by the energy of its cause, that no other effect, in such particular circumstances, could possibly have resulted from it. The degree and direction of every motion is, by the laws of nature, prescribed with such exactness, that a living creature may as soon arise from the shock of two bodies, as motion, in any other degree or direction than what is actually produced by it. (*Enquiry*, VIII, i)

Then should human behavior not be completely determined as well? But if it is, how can humans be held responsible for their behavior, if they cannot do otherwise, that is, cannot contradict the laws of nature? On the other hand, if human behavior is not subject to determinism, then is it not uncaused, or random? And how can we hold a person responsible for his actions if they are just random?

Hume thinks that the solution to this dilemma is to observe that liberty is in fact compatible with necessity. Indeed, to act with liberty, or freedom, requires necessity. Hume thinks it is easy to see this if we consider our ideas of necessity and of liberty. We can see that both characterize human actions.

NECESSITY CHARACTERIZES HUMAN BEHAVIOR

Our idea of necessity comes from our observation of the uniformity of events. "A causes B" just means that A's tend to be followed by B's. But this same uniformity is evident in human behavior, as well as the behavior of material objects. Actions are constantly conjoined with motives, in the same way that causally related events in the natural world are conjoined. A person's character and motives are associated with his or her behavior in a highly predictable way. Indeed, we interact with others on the assumption that human behavior is predictable and not random. Hume says, ". . . this experimental inference and reasoning concerning the actions of others enters so much into human life, that no man, while awake, is ever a moment without employing it." (*Enquiry*, VIII, i) We believe that human nature can be studied—the disciplines of psychology, political science, anthropology, and sociology are based on that assumption.

Human Behavior Exhibits Regularity. So, if we believe determinism is true in the natural world because there is regularity in the relations of events, then we have every reason to think that determinism is true of human behavior as well, for human behavior is just as regular. Indeed, we could have developed our idea of cause from observing the regularity in human behavior even if we had never observed constant conjunctions of events in the material world.

Determinism Does Not Require Perfect Predictability. This does not mean, however, that we can predict everything that a human will do, or that such predictions are perfectly accurate. But then, our predictions about material objects are not perfect either. Hume offers the following example:

> Were a man, whom I know to be honest and opulent, and with whom I live in intimate friendship, to come into my house, where I am surrounded with my servants, I rest assured, that he is not to stab me before he leaves it, in order to rob me of my silver standish; and I no more suspect this event, than the falling of the house itself which is new, and solidly built and founded.—*But he may have been seized with a sudden and unknown frenzy.*—So may a sudden earthquake arise, and shake and tumble my house about my ears. (*Enquiry*, VIII, i)

If a material object does not behave precisely as we think it will, we do not conclude that determinism is not true, but only that our knowledge about the causes of its behavior is lacking. Similarly, if a person's behavior seems surprising given our expectations, that need only mean that we did not have adequate knowledge of the person's character, motives, etc., or of an unusual occurrence—having a fit, for example—that may have caused different behavior than expected.

THE MEANING OF *LIBERTY*

Having examined the notion of necessity and argued that it applies to human action as well as to other events in the natural world, Hume considers what the term *liberty* means. According to Hume, to have liberty does not mean that one's actions are uncaused, or that actions do not follow predictably from "motives, inclinations, and circumstances." Rather, liberty is "the power of acting or not acting, according to the determinations of the will; that is, if we choose to remain at rest, we may; if we choose to move, we also may." (*Enquiry*, VIII, i)

Liberty Is Being Unconstrained. You are at liberty, then, when you want to do something, and you are not prevented from doing it, or when you do not want to do something and are not forced to do it. You are not at liberty when you are prevented from doing what you want by an external constraint, or forced to do something you do not want by an external constraint. So, suppose you want to eat a piece of pizza. You do so freely if nothing is stopping you from doing so: You are not locked in your room; there is a pizza parlor open; you have money to buy it, etc. There are certain things, though, that you are not free to do because of the constraints on you. For example, even though you may want to fly to the moon on your own power, you cannot. No matter how hard you try, there are external circumstances that will prevent you from doing so.

Liberty and Necessity Are Compatible. Thus, liberty is not incompatible with being determined. In fact, to act freely requires that your acts be determined by your own desires. You freely get a slice of pizza when you do so because you want to, not when you do so because someone is holding a gun to your head. In both cases, though, your act is determined, caused, by *something*. Those acts are free which we will to perform, not which we are forced to perform by factors beyond our control. Further, if we were to take the position that to act freely is incompatible with being determined, then we would have to accept that some acts are uncaused. But we could not hold a person responsible for actions that are uncaused, that is, that have no connection with a motive, character of the agent, etc. Such acts would have to be random. Hume says:

According to this principle . . . which denies necessity, and consequently causes, a man is as pure and untainted, after having committed the most horrid crime, as at the first moment of his birth, nor
is the character any wiser, concerned in his actions; since they are
not derived from it, and the wickedness of the one can never be used
as a proof of the depravity of the other. (*Enquiry*, VIII, ii)

Hume also observes that the degree to which we hold people responsible
is related to how carefully planned their acts are. We tend not to hold people
responsible for more random, unplanned acts—that is, where the connection
between motive and action is not very regular. However, when an act follows
from a person's character, we hold that person responsible. It is not accidental, or random, or free in the sense of being uncaused. Because Hume takes
free will and determinism to be compatible, the position he takes has come
to be called compatibilism.

The Source of the Problem

Hume thinks that everyone will accept compatibilism when the meanings of the terms of the debate are understood. So why should there have
been any confusion to start with? Hume's answer is that we start at the
"wrong end" of the question. That is, we start off with introspection, taking
our own acts to be undetermined because we cannot perceive the connection
between an act and its cause. However, if we start at the other end of the
question and consider objects in the material world, we also find that we
cannot find a necessary connection between events—yet we do not take
events in the material world to be undetermined. And if we consider, not our
own actions, but those of others, we see causal regularities that indicate that
human behavior is as subject to determinism, that is, as law-like, as are
material events.

A Problem with Hume's Account

Hume does seem to capture some of our basic intuitions about free will
and responsibility. However, there is an important problem with his account.
If we pursue the causes of a person's behavior very far, we ultimately find
that the causes are not within the person's control. For example, suppose
you choose to rob a bank. We could look at your action and your character,
your motives, your desires, etc., to see if there were a connection. If there
were, you would have acted freely. (If, by contrast, someone else had
threatened to kill your family if you did not rob the bank, your action could
be said to have been caused by circumstances beyond your control.) But
suppose that you did want to rob the bank, that you knew that doing so
invited arrest and punishment, and so on, yet you decided to rob the bank
anyway. What caused these desires? Was it your wicked character? And if
it was, then what caused you to have that character? Was it in your genes?
Was it determined by early childhood experiences? If we trace a causal chain
back to discover the source of your character, we will ultimately find that

your character was caused to be what it is by factors beyond your control. Hence, you are constrained to have the character you have, so you could not have acted freely in robbing the bank—or in performing any other action, for that matter. So it seems you are also not responsible for any of your actions.

Hume's response to this objection is not very satisfying. He finds no objection to this reasoning per se. However, he observes that in fact we do praise and blame people for actions they commit that are caused by their characters, and indeed, society depends on it. Just as it is in our nature to expect that the future will resemble the past, so it is in our nature to blame people for actions of which we disapprove and to praise people for actions we like.

OUR IDEAS OF SUBSTANCE AND THE SELF

Like Berkeley, Hume thinks that we have no real idea of material substance. When we look for an impression of substance, we find only impressions of particular qualities, but nothing underlying them. For example, when you look at an apple, you have impressions of red, round, shiny, smooth, and so on, but you do not have an impression of stuff or substance holding those qualities together. However, Hume goes a step beyond Berkeley in his analysis. For while Berkeley accepts that we have a notion of spiritual or mental substance, Hume rejects that as well. Just as we have no impression of what holds the qualities of material objects together, so we have no impression of what holds our thoughts together.

Berkeley associated substance with causal power; he thought that the only things with any real power are minds. One of his reasons for rejecting material substance is that it is not needed as a cause of our sensations, and furthermore, it would have no real causal power within it anyway. But Berkeley adhered to the Cartesian and Lockean tradition in maintaining that minds do have causal power; we cause ideas in our own minds when we imagine, remember, hope, etc., and God causes ideas in us when we have sensations.

Given Hume's rejection of the idea of power, it should not be surprising that he rejects the idea of substance as well. Not only do we have no idea of how we produce ideas (power), we also have no idea of what holds those ideas together (substance). So our idea of the mind is not an idea of mental substance. But what is it then?

The Nature of Mind

Hume had some unique ideas and perceptions about the nature of the mind. In the *Treatise* Hume says:

> The mind is a kind of theatre, where several perceptions successively
> make their appearance; pass, re-pass, glide away, and mingle in an
> infinite variety of postures and situations . . . They are the successive
> perceptions only, that constitute the mind . . . (*Treatise*, I, iv, 6)

Thus, Hume thinks that there is no one thing which is the mind; rather, the
mind is just a sequence of perceptions—ideas and impressions. Still, we
have a sense that there is some unity to the sequence—that something holds
them together and makes them into one person. Why should we think so?

THE SOURCE OF UNITY AMONG OUR PERCEPTIONS

Using his usual strategy of looking for the impression that gives rise to
the idea of "self," Hume finds none. But he does offer a reason as to why
we think that there is a single person over time to whom all of the perceptions
belong. Strictly speaking, perceptions are each distinct—none is the same
as any other, and there is no reason to think they are connected. But
perceptions *are* related, by contiguity, resemblance, and cause and effect. It
is these relations that give us the sense that there is a necessary connection
among our perceptions that makes them perceptions of one person.

Skepticism

As you would expect, Hume agrees with Berkeley's arguments that we
have no reason to believe that there is a material world beyond our perceptions. In the *Treatise*, he shows that we have no perceptions corresponding
to *substance*, *existence*, etc. Still, Hume admits that we have a natural
inclination to believe there are material objects outside of us, and that those
objects cause our perceptions which in turn resemble them—the representative theory of perception. In the *Enquiry*, he argues that there is no
evidence that this is the case, and indeed that no evidence could ever be
acquired. In the first place, we have no way of knowing that our perceptions
do not simply arise from some power of the mind.

THE EXISTENCE OF THE MATERIAL WORLD CANNOT BE VERIFIED

Hume also notes that causal questions are empirical; they can only be
settled by making observations. Yet the observations that would be necessary to determine whether material objects cause our perceptions are in
principle impossible to make. To verify that material objects cause our
perceptions, we would need to observe material objects constantly conjoined
with perceptions of material objects. But all we can ever observe are our
perceptions, thus, "here, experience is, and must be entirely silent." Hence,
the belief that material objects cause our perceptions may be instinctive, yet
it is not a scientific one. It is mere speculation.

Thus, Hume is a severe skeptic in that he thinks that we cannot know
that the material world exists. Indeed, it was Hume's skepticism about our
knowledge of causality that Kant alleged awakened him from his "dogmatic

slumbers." Berkeley was not a skeptic, for he claimed that the material world did not exist independent of our perceptions—there was no doubt about it. The notion of "matter," Berkeley argued, was an impossible one. But Hume merely claims to not know, pointing out that we can never know because of the impossibility of acquiring evidence.

When we consider Hume's views on causality and substance, he may seem very extreme. After all, what do exist in his view are perceptions—that is all. However, it is important to keep in mind that Hume's aim is to rid philosophy of unsupported or unsupportable speculation. He wants to make philosophy like Newtonian science, offering law-like descriptions of the observable data, doing mental experiments to find the regularities that characterize our perceptions. Thus, he is often doing a kind of psychology. But also, Hume raises important questions about the foundations of our beliefs in causality, substance, the material world, and so on, some of which remain problems to this day. Hume acknowledges that he himself has instincts to believe in causes, the existence of material objects, etc., when he is not in his study doing philosophy. Part of his point, though, is that these beliefs are the result of instinct, not reason, as many of his predecessors had thought. (Indeed, even Berkeley thought he could show through reason that God causes our ideas, a claim that Hume would argue is unverifiable.) Thus, if knowledge is thought of as requiring certainty, then we have real knowledge of very little indeed. Reason is not what helps us navigate in the world. It is instinct. And it is Hume's purpose to describe what those instincts are.

ON RELIGION

Hume's last work, published posthumously, was the *Dialogues Concerning Natural Religion*. Through the views of the characters in the dialogues, Hume examines the arguments that had been advanced to prove God's existence. The term *natural religion* in the title refers to religious beliefs that are based on evidence, in contrast to revealed religion, which is based on God's supposed revelations to humans. Hume himself thought that to prove the existence of something, whether it be God or material objects or the mind, requires evidence, that is, experience. He did not take a priori arguments for the existence of God, such as Descartes', very seriously, and most of the *Dialogues* is devoted to the argument from design, which does indeed appeal to experience to argue for God's existence. It is, hence, an a posteriori argument. It argues from the existence of an effect (a designed universe) to the existence of its cause (God, the designer). Therefore, it takes God's existence to be a matter of fact.

The Argument from Design

The argument from design, offered by the character of Cleanthes, is a teleological argument—that is, it argues that the universe has a final cause, or purpose, or design, that reveals to us something about the designer. It is an old argument, going back at least to Aristotle. It reflects an anthropocentric view of the universe, that God made the universe for the purposes of humans. Every animal, plant or mineral has a purpose which may be seen in the use to which it is put by humans. Like all causal inferences, its conclusion can at best be probabilistic, not certain.

As Cleanthes presents it, the argument from design is roughly as follows:

1. The universe exhibits design: a) its parts are adapted to each other (e.g., legs work together) and b) means are adapted to ends (e.g., legs are made for walking).

2. These two properties make the universe resemble a humanly designed machine.

3. Like effects very probably have like causes.

4. Therefore, *very probably* the cause of the universe is like the cause of a humanly designed machine—namely, the cause of the universe is a designer, with the attributes that enable humans to design machines: thought, wisdom, and intelligence. Moreover, those qualities are present in the Designer of the universe in proportion to the grandeur of the universe.

The conclusion of the argument from design is thus twofold: The universe very probably has a designer, God; and the designer's qualities are like the qualities that enable humans to design machines.

Problems with the Argument

Once Cleanthes presents the argument, the character of Philo begins to attack it in a variety of ways. His aim is to show that it is simply not very good experimental reasoning. To do this, he shows that the analogy between the universe and a human design is very weak, that the God whose existence is inferred need not be very much like the traditional Judeo-Christian conception, that the argument leads to an infinite regress, that there are alternative hypotheses that explain the data equally well, and that the conclusion is incompatible with the existence of evil. Let us look at each.

THE WEAKNESS OF THE ANALOGY

One problem Philo cites with the analogy is that the effects are not very much alike. However, the strength of the conclusion depends on the strength of the analogy. If two things are not very much alike, then it is hard to conclude that their causes are alike. Philo offers a number of reasons why the effects—the universe and a humanly designed machine—may not be very much alike.

First, we only observe a very small part of the universe—the part we inhabit—and we only observe it for a very short time. Can we really know what the rest of the universe is like, or that what we see now is what it has always been like or will always be like? Philo asks, "Can a conclusion, with any propriety, be transferred from parts to the whole? Does not the great disproportion bar all comparison and inference? From observing the growth of a hair, can we learn anything of the generation of a man?" (*Dialogues*, II) Furthermore, since we do only observe the universe for a very short time, we do not know that what we are observing is the finished product; it could be the embryo of a universe. Perhaps we should reserve judgment until we can know that it is finished.

Second, thought is only one of the "springs and principles" that operate in the universe. Why should we choose thought as the cause of the universe over the others that we observe?

Third, there are certain analogies that are even stronger—for example, perhaps the universe is more like an animal, or a vegetable, than it is like a humanly-made machine.

Fourth, to have a strong analogy, we would have to have much experience of the cause-effect relationship that is proposed. Scientists do not make causal inferences after having made only one experimental observation. Hence, we would have to observe the making of universes to draw a conclusion about the cause of our own. But in fact, we have only this one experience, and that is not even of the origin of the universe.

GOD'S NATURE

Another important weakness of the argument is that the God whose existence is inferred need not have the perfect qualities traditionally associated with God: infinity, perfection, and unity. The argument takes God's qualities to be the cause of the design in the world, and concludes that God has those qualities in proportion to the grandeur of the design. First, this means that God need not be infinite. What we can observe is not infinite, hence, the designer need not be either. Second, God need not be perfect, for nature is not itself perfect. Also, even if the universe were perfect, it may be that the designer is merely a "stupid mechanic," mimicking the work of previous gods. Perhaps many worlds had been "botched and bungled" before this world was made. Third, God need not be unitary, for perhaps more than one designer created the world. It is more often the case that great works of humans are created by more than one designer, hence, why not think the same of the universe? Finally, if the designer were exactly like humans, then why not think the designer has eyes, a nose, and so on? Could the designer be a doddering old fool?

Philo's point is that even if we accept the premises of the argument from design, it establishes very little about the designer—that the designer is infinite, perfect, unitary, or incorporeal is pure conjecture. As Philo says to Cleanthes:

> A man who follows your hypothesis, is able, perhaps, to assert, or conjecture, that the universe sometime, arose from something like design: But beyond that position he cannot ascertain one single circumstance, and is left afterwards to fix every point of his theology, by the utmost licence of fancy and hypothesis. (*Dialogues*, V)

ALTERNATIVE HYPOTHESES

Just as a good scientist would consider alternative explanations of the data in an experiment, Philo argues that Cleanthes should consider alternative explanations for how the world was designed. One of the hypotheses was considered briefly above: that the world is more like an organic thing, an animal or vegetable, than it is like an artificial machine. Hence, the universe could perhaps be brought about by reproduction, and perhaps God is the soul of the universe—a pantheistic suggestion.

A more interesting suggestion is the Epicurean hypothesis, that the design in the universe is only apparent and is, in fact, the result of the accidental configuration of atoms. Suppose that there are infinitely many atoms in motion, and they happen to eventually hit on a stable configuration, in which they remain. If that were the explanation for why the universe is the way it is, then there would be no purpose to the universe at all. This suggestion is an interesting, although unintentional, foreshadowing of the Darwinian hypothesis. We really have no reason, no data, to prefer the explanation that an anthropomorphic designer created the universe than to think that the universe developed by reproduction or by chance.

AN INFINITE REGRESS

Philo also points out that the argument leads to an infinite regress. The order in matter is explained by appealing to the plan of an intelligent designer. But if we think that the order in matter requires an explanation, then why do we not think that the order in the designer's thoughts, which produce the design, requires an explanation, too? Also, if mind is the principle of order in matter, then why not think that the order in the mind's ideas should be explained by appealing to another mind as the principle of order, and so on ad infinitum? Philo argues that from our experience alone, we have no more reason to think that ideas are naturally ordered than to think that matter is.

THE PROBLEM OF EVIL

The last major objection that Philo raises is the problem of evil. There is one observation about the design of the universe that Philo thinks Cleanthes has overlooked: the existence of evil. There are two kinds of evil, natural and moral. Natural evils include illness, natural disasters, famine, poverty, pain, the "disorders of mind," and so on. Moral evils include crime, gluttony, war, tyranny, and so on. If we accept that the universe was designed, then it seems that we must also accept that it was designed to include evil. But it is difficult to reconcile the existence of evil with God's perfect but humanlike qualities of wisdom, power, and goodness. Philo quotes Epicurus' formulation of the problem: "Is [God] willing to prevent evil, but unable? then he is impotent. Is he able, but not willing? then he is malevolent. Is he both willing and able? whence then is evil?" (*Dialogues*, X)

Whether the reasons for God's existence are taken to be a priori or a posteriori, the problem of evil is a serious theological problem. However, if one can establish God's existence a priori, as Descartes attempted, and as the character of Demea attempts to do, then the problem is only to explain the existence of evil—that is, evil does not count against God's existence, for God's existence has been proved, independent of evil. But for an a posteriori argument, the problem is worse: Cleanthes is attempting to argue from the data to the existence of a perfect designer, yet the data suggest that the designer has some major flaws.

Cleanthes' Response. Cleanthes' response to the problem of evil, however, is to reinterpret the data. He tries to show that what we take to be evil is not really evil at all—or at least, there is not very much of it. Philo, however, disagrees: A very brief, but intense, pain can certainly be much worse than a lot of pleasure. Who would not give up a few hours of pleasure to eliminate five minutes of excruciating pain? Indeed, Cleanthes' claim that the pleasure in the world outweighs the pain seems to be an unsupportable hypothesis.

The Four Circumstances of Evil. Even if we take God's attributes of wisdom, goodness, and power to be finite, it still does not follow from the data that God should have these attributes. Indeed, Philo argues that God could have avoided putting evil into the universe altogether. On his analysis, there are four circumstances of evil, all of which could have been avoided: First, we have a capacity for both pain and pleasure, yet why do we need pain? Could God not have made us to be able to survive in the world without a capacity for pain? Could God not have given us some other faculty to detect those things we must avoid? Second, even if we have the capacity for pain, that does not mean the capacity need be exercised. The only reason it is, is that God has made the universe to behave according to laws—that is, God does not intervene in the everyday workings of things. But why could not God just step in to stop pain when it is about to occur? Third, God was very frugal in designing things. But if God had not been so frugal, there would be less pain, for it would be easier to avoid pain. Moreover, God could have created humans without vices. And finally, God is an inaccurate workman—things go wrong, which causes pain. There are excesses in nature, and in humans: illness, floods, hurricanes, volcanoes. If nature worked well, then these sources of pain would not occur.

Philo's Position on the Argument

Philo does not, of course, think that God is an inaccurate workman, or lacking in perfect attributes, for Philo does not seem to think that there is a God at all. Or at least, he does not think that the argument from design works, for if one truly inspects all the data, then one cannot legitimately infer the existence of the kind of God that Cleanthes wishes. Still, at the end of the *Dialogues*, Philo takes a rather surprising position. He seems to accept the existence of design in the universe. But what he really seems to hold is that we have a natural inclination to interpret the universe as ordered, much as custom leads us to expect that the future will resemble the past.

What Hume shows, then, in the *Dialogues*, is this: The reasoning of the design argument is the kind a scientist would use to support a hypothesis. It is a posteriori. The problem is that it does not support the conclusion that it is supposed to support. Rather, it simply rationalizes what the arguer already believes independently of the data. And thus, he is showing us what really good scientific reasoning should be like: It should not ignore some of the data, even if that data fail to support, or even if they contradict, the hypothesis; and it should not bring supplementary assumptions to the data to help out.

Hume is one of the greatest philosophers of the modern period. While his ideas were not generally accepted when he was alive, their influence in contemporary philosophy is very evident. For example, his view that the meanings of words must be traceable to experience is found in verificationist theories of meaning, such as that of A. J. Ayer. Also, his formulation of the problem of induction posed an important problem for science that philosophers are still grappling with.

What troubled his contemporaries, yet has made him such an important philosopher, is that Hume showed the logical consequences of the empiricist views of his predecessors, notably Locke and Berkeley. He showed that if the meanings of the terms we use must come from experience, then words such as substance, soul, power, cause, *and so, on either have no meaning, or they do not have the meanings we think they do. If we look to our experience, we find that there are no ideas corresponding to these terms. Our belief that there are such things as substance, power, and so on, must be explained in some other way. Part of Hume's task, then, is to show what it is about us that leads us to believe there are such things.*

The main reason Hume's views were not readily accepted was that they led to skepticism about the existence of the material world and about our ability to have knowledge of the future. However, Hume's philosophy was not simply negative; he also undertook an important positive task, namely, constructing a science of the mind relying only upon observation and leaving all speculation and meaningless terms behind. While Hume was not completely successful in his project, he offered many insights about how the mind works; in particular, he showed that reason is not the operative faculty in many of our judgments, beliefs, and so on. Indeed, as we have seen, he showed that our beliefs about what will happen in the future are not determined by any process of reason but instead come from "custom." Similarly, he argued that moral judgments are not the products of reasoning but derive from passion. He thus emphasized the importance of faculties besides reason in our assessments of the world around us and our ability to survive in it, in contrast with Descartes and some of the other rationalist philosophers.

Selected Readings

GENERAL

Ayer, A. J. *Hume*. Oxford: Oxford University Press, 1980.

Bennett, J. *Locke, Berkeley, Hume: Central Themes*. Oxford: Clarendon Press, 1971.

Flew, A. *David Hume: Philosopher of Moral Science*. London: Basil Blackwell, 1986.

Kemp Smith, N. *The Philosophy of David Hume*. London: Macmillan, 1941.

Stroud, B. *Hume*. London: Routledge & Kegan Paul, 1977.

ON CAUSALITY

Salmon, W. *The Foundations of Scientific Inference*. Pittsburgh: The University of Pittsburgh Press, 1967.

ON RELIGION

Kemp Smith, N. "Introduction," *Dialogues Concerning Natural Religion*. New York: Macmillan, 1986.

ON PERSONAL IDENTITY AND THE SELF

Perry, J. "Introduction," *Personal Identity*, ed. by J. Perry. Berkeley: University of California Press, 1975.

16

Thomas Reid

Thomas Reid (1710–1796) was an important philosopher of the Scottish Enlightenment and the main representative of the Common Sense school of philosophy. He was born in Kincardineshire, near Aberdeen. He studied at Marischal College, under a follower of Berkeley. He later studied theology and became a Presbyterian minister. He also became a master at King's College in Aberdeen. In 1763, Reid was granted the Chair of Moral Philosophy at the University of Glasgow that Adam Smith had held.

Reid published only three works: An Inquiry Into the Human Mind *(1764),* Essays on the Intellectual Powers of Man *(1785), and* Essays on the Active Powers of the Human Mind *(1788). Much of his writing was devoted to criticizing the way of ideas. His own views were well received during his lifetime but were later abandoned, and for many years, his works were out of print. Recently, there has been a revival of interest in Reid; many of his ideas foreshadowed those of J. L. Austin and other "ordinary language" philosophers in this century.*

REID'S ATTACK ON IDEAS

Although Reid's early philosophical education was heavily influenced by studying Berkeley, Reid was alarmed at the conclusions that Hume drew from Berkeley's assumptions—for example, that we have no knowledge of the mind, of the material world, or of the continued existence of objects when we are not perceiving them. Thus, much of Reid's work is aimed at criticizing those views. Still, he admired the attempts of the empiricists to provide a scientific, empirically based account of the faculties of the mind and tried himself to find the appropriate starting point to provide a better account of the mind.

Reid's main concern with the conclusions of Berkeley and Hume is that they contradict the beliefs that ordinary people hold and that are reflected in the language we use to describe our experiences of the world. He attributed these mistakes to the way of ideas, tracing its sources to the ancient Greeks. (For a detailed description of the way of ideas, see chapter 13.) In its main assumptions, Reid thinks that the way of ideas is fundamentally opposed to our common-sense views about sense perception. Thus, Reid tries to show where the idea theorists—primarily Descartes, Malebranche, Locke, Berkeley, and Hume—had gone wrong.

Common Sense

In his arguments against ideas, Reid relies heavily on *common sense*. What he means by common sense, however, is not what most people mean. By common sense, Reid means those beliefs that humans have to hold by virtue of their constitution. Reid describes it thus in the *Inquiry*:

> If there are certain principles, as I think there are, which the constitution of our nature leads us to believe, and which we are under a necessity to take for granted in the common concerns of life, without being able to give a reason for them; these are what we call the principles of common sense . . . (*Inquiry*, II, 6)

Our common-sense beliefs are revealed in our language. Reid thinks it is clear that everyone must hold these principles because all languages suppose them. For example, Reid would argue that in all languages, a distinction is made between material objects and ideas in the mind. Hence, it cannot be that material objects are just collections of ideas. Indeed, he thinks that the way of ideas " . . . has led [philosophers] to invent a language inconsistent with the principles on which all language is grounded." (*EIPM*, II, xiv)

THE PROBLEM WITH THE WAY OF IDEAS

The main problem with the way of ideas is its major assumption that the direct objects of perception are ideas in the mind—that is, when we perceive, the objects we are immediately perceiving are ideas. Descartes and Locke thought that we directly perceive ideas, which in turn represent the material objects that cause them. Berkeley and Hume went a step further: They thought we have no evidence that there are any material objects beyond our ideas. In either case, the problem Reid notes is that what we perceive is a mental entity, which he takes to be inconsistent with the way we must think about perception and about the world. That is, by common sense we naturally believe that the objects we perceive exist in the external world, not in our minds. For example, when you perceive this book, you believe that it exists in the world, independently of your mind. You do not believe that it is a mental entity, an object existing in your mind.

One of Reid's strategies to discredit the assumption that what we immediately perceive are ideas is to show that the ideas described by Descartes, Locke, Berkeley, and Hume simply do not exist. He considers two ways we could find evidence that there are such objects of perception, and he argues that neither in fact provides evidence of such mental entites. One way is to see if there is any immediate evidence that ideas exist. We can determine this by introspecting, as well as by considering how we describe the objects we perceive. The other way is to consider the arguments advanced by the idea theorists to show that in perception, the objects we immediately perceive are ideas.

The Evidence of Introspection

First, Reid suggests that if the immediate objects of perception were ideas, then we would certainly be aware of them when we introspect. But we do not find them. What we find when we introspect are mental acts—perceiving, remembering, imagining, willing, judging, and so on—and these acts have objects. But we do not find that those objects are ideas in the mind. For example, when you look at this book, the act of looking is indeed in your mind. But the object of that looking, the book, is not in your mind at all—it is a foot or so in front of your body.

BEING "IN THE MIND"

How we decide whether there are ideas in our minds depends on what we take the phrase "in the mind" to mean. Reid maintains that to say that something is in the mind does not mean that it is located in the mind, for the mind does not take up space. Rather, for something to be in the mind means that its existence is dependent on the mind. So, seeing is dependent on the mind, for there can be no seeing without a mind. However, that does not mean that the objects we see are dependent on the mind. Even if you were to suddenly stop existing, that does not mean the book in front of you also would stop existing—although your act of seeing the book would. That just means that the *book* is not in your mind, while your *seeing* the book is.

In the following passage, Reid makes precisely this point. To say that the objects we perceive are in the mind is incompatible with our ordinary descriptions of them:

> When we see the sun or moon, we have no doubt that the very objects which we immediately see, are very far distant from us, and from one another. We have not the least doubt, that this is the sun and moon which God created some thousands of years ago, and which have continued to perform their revolutions in the heavens ever since. But how we are astonished when the philosopher informs us,

that we are mistaken in all this; that the sun and moon which we see, are not, as we imagine, many miles distant from us, and from each other, but that they are in our own mind; that they had no existence before we saw them, and will have none when we cease to perceive and to think of them; because the objects we perceive are only ideas in our own minds, which can have no existence a moment longer than we think of them. (*EIPM*, II, xiv)

The Continued Existence of Objects. This passage also points to another problem with taking the immediate objects of perception to be in the mind: If the objects we perceive are in the mind, we have to admit that they stop existing when we stop perceiving them. If the book is in your mind, then when you close your eyes for a moment and then reopen them, you would have to say that you are seeing a new object, a new book, for your old idea disappeared when you stopped perceiving it. This was precisely the predicament Berkeley faced, and to solve it, he argued that God is perceiving all ideas all of the time, so that objects do not pop in and out of existence. Hume did not have this option open to him, for he rejected God as well as material substance.

Reid's point, though, is that if we take the way of ideas seriously, we are forced to admit some rather strange things—such as that the objects we perceive are not external to us, that they pop in and out of existence, and so on. It is not a problem to admit that when we close our eyes, the act of seeing stops existing, and when we reopen them, a new act of seeing starts. But Reid thinks we have no reason to hold that the object also ceases to exist when we close our eyes, and a new object begins to exist when we open them. Moreover, it contradicts our way of describing the objects we perceive.

IDEAS AS METAPHORS FOR MENTAL ACTS

Reid is willing to grant that sometimes we say that we have an idea, taking it to be an image of an object. For example, if you are asked to think about the book in front of you, you might describe what you are doing as "having an idea of a book." However, Reid thinks we should not take this to mean that the idea or image you entertain is an object of a mental act. Rather, "having an idea" is a description of the act of mind whereby you think about an object that is outside your mind. The object of this act is not an idea, though. That is, you are not imagining an image—rather, it is the *act* of imagining, not the object of it, that can be thought of as having an image.

The Idea Theorists' Arguments for Ideas

Reid also thinks that there are problems with the arguments advanced by the idea theorists to show that the immediate objects of perception are ideas in the mind. He considers a number of them, but two in particular illustrate where the thinking of the idea theorists goes wrong.

THE CONTIGUITY ARGUMENT

One argument advanced to show that what we immediately perceive are ideas is inspired by the corpuscularian view, according to which change in the material world can only come about by the impulse of corpuscles on each other, in a mechanical fashion. (Corpuscles were thought of as the ultimate particles that make up material objects—like atoms. For a more detailed account, see chapter 13.) Since sense perception is itself a material process—that is, it is caused by the action of a material object on a sense organ, which is also material—it too must be explained by the impulses of corpuscles. But such impulses require contiguity: For one corpuscle to collide with another, they must be contiguous with—adjacent to—each other. What seems to follow is that the ultimate product of the process of sense perception must be contiguous with the objects causing it, namely, corpuscles in the brain. This implies that that product must be an idea in the mind. More formally, the argument could be put thus:

1. Nothing can *directly* act on or be acted upon by another object that is not contiguous with it.

2. The material objects we perceive are not contiguous with our minds.

3. Our minds cannot *directly* perceive material objects.

4. Therefore, what our minds *directly* perceive are ideas.

Reid's Criticism of the Contiguity Argument. Reid thinks that this argument has a questionable hidden premise. That premise is that in perception, the mind either acts directly on material objects, or material objects act directly on the mind. He argues that we have no reason to think that either half of this premise is correct, for in ordinary language we simply would not describe the mind as acting on objects, or objects as acting on the mind, given what we ordinarily mean by *act*.

The real problem, though, is that philosophers have assumed that the activities of the mind follow the same rules that the activities of material objects do, that something like the corpuscularian view must hold for minds as well as for material objects. Reid holds that we have no reason to think so. It is this analogical thinking that has led philosophers into confusion about sense perception and other acts of mind:

> Thought in the mind is conceived to have some analogy to motion in a body; and as a body is put in motion by being acted upon by some other body; so we are apt to think the mind is made to perceive, by some impulse it receives from the object. But reasonings, drawn from such analogies, ought never to be trusted. They are, indeed, the cause of most of our errors with regard to the mind. And we

might as well conclude that minds may be measured by feet and inches, or weighed by ounces and drachms, because bodies have those properties. (*EIPM*, II, xiv)

While Reid thinks that sense perception does require the occurrence of some physical, hence mechanically explainable, events, he does not think that in perception the mind has a physical interaction with an object, or that it is in any sense contiguous with the object. It may be true that the physical process involves impressions made upon the sense organs by material objects, and hence contiguity is required for the mechanical interactions involved. However, the mind is not a physical object, and the act of perceiving is not simply the last event in a serious of mechanical impulses. In other words, Reid thinks that philosophers had gone overboard in admiring the success of the corpuscularian view and the mechanical explanations of phenomena that it offered. Mental phenomena are not subject to exactly the same set of assumptions as are material phenomena.

THE ARGUMENT FROM THE RELATIVITY OF PERCEPTION

Another argument advanced by idea theorists to show that what we immediately perceive are ideas is the argument from the relativity of perception. The argument begins with the observation that an object will have different appearances under different perceptual conditions—for example, color will look different under different lights, water will appear to have varying temperatures to one's hands, depending on their temperature, and so on. The argument is then made that since what we perceive is changing, but the object itself is unchanging, it cannot be the object itself that we see. Reid considers Hume's version of this argument:

1. As I move away from the table in front of me, what I see *directly* appears to change.

2. The real table, existing independent of me, does not change.

3. Therefore, what I see *directly* is not the real table, but rather an idea of it in my mind.

Reid's Criticism of the Argument from the Relativity of Perception. Reid takes this argument to be more formidable than the previous one. However, he dismisses it with a simple observation. He argues that it does not follow from the fact that the properties of an object are constant that their appearance to us must be constant. In the example in the argument, the shape of the table, considered two-dimensionally, changes as the position of the perceiver varies. However, is this not precisely what we would expect to happen? It would be very odd indeed if the appearance of an object did not vary under any circumstances. Reid says:

Let us suppose for a moment, that it is the real table we see. Must not this real table seem to diminish as we remove further from it? It is demonstrable that it must. How then can this apparent diminution be an argument that it is not the real table? . . . Mr. Hume's argument, not only has no strength to support his conclusion, but . . . leads to the contrary conclusion; to wit, that it is the real table we see; for this plain reason, that the table we see has precisely that apparent magnitude which is demonstrable the real table must have when placed at that distance. (*EIPM*, II, xiv)

To make his point, Reid distinguishes real magnitude from apparent magnitude. Apparent magnitude is ". . . measured by the angle which an object subtends at the eye," whereas real magnitude is measured with a yardstick or tape measure. Thus, we can easily see what happens to Hume's table: As the perceiver's distance from the table changes, so does the angle it subtends at the eye, even though its real magnitude does not change. Or consider Descartes' example of the appearance of the size of the sun, which he uses to question the reliability of sensory information. Reid says:

If it be asked, What is the apparent magnitude of the sun's diameter? the answer is, That it is about thirty-one minutes of a degree. But if it be asked, What is the real magnitude of the sun's diameter? The answer must be, So many thousand miles, or so many diameters of the earth. From which it is evident, that real magnitude, and apparent magnitude, are things of a different nature, though the name of magnitude is given to both. The first has three dimensions, the last only two. The first is measured by a line, the last by an angle. (*EIPM*, II, xiv)

The last point is important: The argument trades on failing to distinguish what a two-dimensional image looks like from what the actual three-dimensional object looks like. Clearly a photograph of an object looks different from the object itself. But this result seems inevitable if the objects of perception are taken to be sensations. Visual sensations, in particular, are two-dimensional images.

The Failure to Explain Perception

In addition to arguing that ideas in the philosophical sense—that is, as the objects of perception—do not exist, and that the arguments used to show they do simply do not work, Reid has another reason for thinking the idea theory does not work. It does not explain perception, or any other act of mind. On Reid's view, how or why the mental act of perceiving occurs is a mystery. Trying to give a mechanical account of it does not really help us to understand the mental aspect of it.

Also, introducing ideas that are contiguous with the mind does not relieve the difficulties of explaining mental acts. For we can still ask, "But how do we perceive ideas?" Nor does giving a mechanical explanation explain the occurrence of mental acts. Reid says, "Two things may be in contact without any feeling or perception; there must therefore be in the percipient a power to feel or to perceive. How this power is produced, and how it operates, is quite beyond the reach of our knowledge." (*EIPM*, II, xiv)

REID'S OWN ACCOUNT OF THE MIND

We may wonder, then, what does Reid think can be said about perception and other mental acts? Like the empiricists, Reid, too, wants to give a scientific account of the mind. He thinks that philosophers need to emulate scientific method more closely, starting with the establishment of a firm foundation for science.

Reid's Foundation

To begin his own investigation into the faculties of the mind, Reid starts with a foundation of "clear definitions and self-evident axioms." He does not start, like Descartes, by doubting everything, nor like Hume, by looking first for the objects of study. He thinks philosophers must begin by investigating the starting principles that cannot be doubted and explicating the terms that will be used in the study. He does this by investigating language, as well as by examining evidence from introspection.

THE MEANING OF "MIND"

To establish his foundation, one of the terms Reid discusses is *mind*, which is "that . . . which thinks, remembers, reasons, wills." Reid tells us that we can only know the mind by understanding its operations, just as we can only know material objects by understanding their qualities.

The Mind Is Active. Our descriptions of the mind and its operations in ordinary language tell us that it is active: We perceive, remember, imagine, and so on—all active verbs. This is contrary to the views of some of the idea theorists, who took mental operations to be the having of ideas, thus rendering the mind passive. Hume, for example, tried to show how mental operations differ from one another by looking at the difference between the ideas that characterize them. In Hume's view, when we believe something, we have a more lively idea than when we simply imagine that thing. Reid rejects the view that the mind is passive; he thinks that until philosophers prove otherwise, we must trust to ordinary language and what it reveals about the mind.

Mental Operations Have Objects. Reid also notes that most operations of the mind have objects "to which they are directed and about which they are employed." When you perceive, you perceive something; when you remember, you remember something. This is also in contrast to the implications of the views of some of the idea theorists, according to which mental operations are often reduced to having ideas. For example, to perceive an object is to have a set of sensations; to remember it is likewise to have a certain set of ideas; and so on. Reid thinks it is of the utmost importance to keep the operation of the mind, which is in the mind, distinct from the object, which generally is not in the mind. If the operation is not distinguished from its object, then we end up saying that what we perceive, imagine, remember, and so on, is in the mind. That is, both act and object are said to be in the mind, which Reid takes to be a serious error.

Objects of Mental Acts Need Not Exist. Another important point about objects of mental operations is that they need not always exist. Whether they exist depends on the operation itself. In perception, for example, the objects perceived must exist, otherwise *perception* is not the correct description of the act. When we remember, the object remembered need only have existed at some time in the past. In imagining and hoping, the object need not exist at all.

Reid thinks that one motivation for introducing ideas as the objects of mental acts was that it helped to get around the mystery of how mental acts can have nonexistent objects. For example, suppose you imagine a unicorn. Ordinarily, we would say that unicorns do not exist. But how can it be that you are imagining something that does not even exist? Does it not at least exist in your own mind? Berkeley used a similar line of reasoning to show that we cannot conceive of an object existing outside the mind. Reid thinks, though, that there is nothing more mysterious about imagining nonexistent objects than there is about imagining existent ones. Both are mysterious.

FIRST PRINCIPLES ABOUT THE MIND

Reid also thinks there are certain principles, like axioms, that we must accept. These principles cannot be proved and are themselves necessary in order to reason about other things. Reid thinks philosophers had failed to distinguish between what is in need of proof and what is not, often thinking that everything must be proved. For example, if one thinks that it must be proved that the material world exists, it is inevitable that skepticism will result, for no adequate proof can be mounted. Reid thinks that we can recognize first principles by the fact we cannot help but believe them; there is "universal agreement, among the learned and unlearned, in the different nations and ages of the world." He also calls them "intuitive judgments."

Consciousness as Evidence. One of Reid's first principles is that consciousness provides sound evidence of the occurrence of mental acts. If you thought that consciousness could deceive you—for example, that you could think you are thinking even though you are not—then you would never be able to prove the contrary. Thus, some of Descartes' doubts in the *First Meditation* would be unanswerable, because we can never prove the reliability of consciousness as evidence of our mental acts. We must simply accept it.

Same Thinking Principle. Another principle Reid cites is that the thoughts of which we are conscious all belong to "the same thinking principle." Thus, Reid thinks that personal identity is not something we can prove, but something we must accept. You simply cannot help but believe that it is the same you who has all the thoughts of which you are aware.

Mental Acts Are Distinguishable from Their Objects. Reid also thinks it is a first principle that the objects of mental acts are distinct from the acts themselves. When you look at this book, you cannot help but distinguish between your act of seeing and the book itself—for you surely believe that the book's existence is in no way dependent on your seeing it. In collapsing the distinction between act and object, idea theorists violated a principle that we cannot help holding.

Reid's Account of Sense Perception

As an example of how Reid attempts to provide an account of mental acts, let us consider his account of sense perception. As should be now clear, Reid rejected the accounts of the idea theorists that in sense perception, the immediate object we perceive is an idea in the mind. But what does Reid think we can say about sense perception?

SENSE PERCEPTION AS EVIDENCE OF THE EXISTENCE OF MATERIAL OBJECTS

Reid thinks that sense perception provides us with a kind of evidence for certain of our beliefs, much as reasoning does. The evidence of sense is "good evidence and a just ground of belief" about the world we perceive. Moreover, it would be foolhardy to attempt to prove that what we perceive really does provide information about the material world, because it would be attempting to justify the evidence of one faculty (sense perception) by appealing to the evidence of another (reason). There is no reason to think that we should use the evidence of reason to verify the evidence of sense perception—it would be as silly as using the evidence of sense perception to show the validity of our reasonings. Moreover, Reid thinks there is no superiority to reason as evidence for a belief. Reason and sense perception operate in different ways, provide different kinds of evidence of their objects, and hence have different domains.

Reid's point about sense perception is something like Hume's point about custom. Hume argued that reason is simply not the right faculty to give us knowledge of the future. It can never tell us about matters of fact. Likewise, Reid's position is that reason can never tell us about present matters of fact—sense perception is the faculty that does that, and generally we should trust the evidence with which it provides us.

EXPLAINING SENSE PERCEPTION

Like Hume, Reid looks to Newton's work as an example of how giving a scientific account of the mind should proceed. He finds two points of particular importance: First, the cause assigned to a phenomenon must really exist; and second, it must adequately explain the phenomenon in question. He thinks that the theory of ideas fails on both counts. Regarding the first point, there are no such things as ideas, in the sense of being objects of mental acts; regarding the second point, the theory of ideas fails to increase our understanding of why perception occurs.

Reid himself thinks that perception can only be understood as the result of a power of the mind. He takes sense perception to be a complex mental act, consisting of other mental acts—sensation, belief, and conception. He thinks that real existing material objects cause us to have sensations; but perception is much more than just having a set of sensations. In addition, we have a conception of the object we are perceiving, as well as an immediate conviction, or belief, that it exists. Thus, he says:

> I see a chair on my right hand. What is the meaning of this? It is, that I have, by my constitution, a distinct conception and firm belief of the present existence of the chair in such a place, and in such a position; and I give the name of seeing to that part of my constitution, by which I have this immediate conviction. (*EIPM*, II, xx)

Reid does not think we can really explain how perception itself occurs, beyond understanding the mechanics of sense perception and analyzing the mental operations involved in perception. Because he thinks that the objects we immediately or directly perceive are the material objects that cause our perceptions, his position is called direct realism.

*R*eid is best remembered for his criticisms of the theory of ideas as an account of how we perceive and generally have knowledge of the world. His criticisms focus on the incompatibility of the theory of ideas with the ways in which we normally think about the world and our knowledge of it— our "common sense." (Hume also noted that we have certain beliefs that we cannot help but hold; he attributed such beliefs to "custom.") Our common-sense beliefs are reflected in how we use language. We do not, for example, say that the objects we perceive are in our minds; rather, we describe them as existing independently of us, in the material world.

Another part of Reid's strategy to discredit the theory of ideas is to expose the unfounded assumptions underlying it—for example, that mental events follow the same principles as do events in the material world, and *that our perceptions of material objects should be unchanging because the objects themselves are unchanging. While he sometimes oversimplifies the views of those he is criticizing, Reid's criticisms of the theory of ideas are nonetheless extremely insightful. Moreover, he does manage, more effectively than Berkeley, to preserve our common-sense intuitions, such as that the material world we perceive really does exist.*

Reid's own accounts of the faculties of the mind (such as perception) are insightful, although sometimes not very satisfying, for Reid is unwilling to attempt an explanation that is beyond his conceptual tools— admirably so. For Reid, to understand the mind requires careful introspection and attending to how we use language to describe its activities. We can analyze the elements of mental acts, but we may not be able to explain how they are produced.

In recent years, Reid's insights about the nature of the mental and the importance of attending to how we ordinarily use language have been rediscovered. Reid has thus regained a well-deserved position of importance in the history of modern philosophy.

Selected Readings

Duggan, T. "Introduction" to Thomas Reid, *An Inquiry into the Human Mind*. Chicago: University of Chicago Press, 1970.

Lehrer, K. *Thomas Reid*. London: Routledge & Kegan Paul, 1990.

Reid, T. *An Inquiry into the Human Mind*, ed. by T. Duggan. Chicago: University of Chicago Press, 1970.

_____. *Essays on the Intellectual Powers of Man*, ed. by B. Brody. Cambridge, MA: The MIT Press, 1969.

17

Immanuel Kant

Immanuel Kant (1724–1804) was born in Konigsberg, East Prussia, on April 22, 1724. Descartes had been dead for nearly seventy-five years, and Hume was only thirteen years old. Kant spent his whole life in Konigsberg, now Kaliningrad. He attended the University there, tutored the children of several aristocratic families, soon became an instructor, and eventually, at the age of forty-six, Professor of Logic and Metaphysics at the University of Konigsberg. Kant died in Konigsberg in 1804, having only traveled away from the city once or, perhaps, twice— but never for more than a day or at most two.

Kant was well acquainted with and quite impressed by the work of Isaac Newton, and his interests, besides philosophy, included physics, meteorology, physical geography, and astronomy. Kant's earliest philosophical training came from the Leibnizian school as developed and systematized by Christian von Wolff and Alexander Baumgarten; and his earliest philosophical work belongs primarily to this tradition. But it is not for his early work that Kant has justly earned his fame.

It was not until 1781, when he was already fifty-seven, that Kant published his most important work, the Critique of Pure Reason, *thus marking the advent of so-called Critical Philosophy— the birth of Transcendental Idealism. The* Critique *is concerned with issues at the interface of metaphysics and epistemology. It is an ambitious work of extraordinary vision, subtlety, and difficulty. Indeed, upon its first appearance, it was not well understood— much to Kant's consternation. To this day, it remains one of the most difficult and controversial works in philosophy. To make his ideas more accessible, Kant attempted to provide a more general outline of the Critical program in his* Prolegomena To Any Future Metaphysics that Will

Be Able to Come Forth As a Science *(1783). Kant also substantially reworked some of the central sections of the* Critique *for the second edition (1787).*

During the remaining years of his life, Kant was extraordinarily productive, working out the details of his critical system. Among the most important works of this period are the Critique of Practical Reason *(1787), which was preceded by* The Groundwork of the Metaphysic of Morals *(1785), and followed by the* Critique of Judgement *(1790).*

PRELIMINARIES

Prolegomena
Because of the length and extreme difficulty of Kant's magnum opus, the *Critique of Pure Reason*, it is very rarely assigned to introductory students in philosophy. Instead, it has become standard to assign the *Prolegomena*. A prolegomenon is a critical discussion, usually intended to introduce and interpret—in general, to make more accessible—some more extended, more difficult work, or some set of problems dealt with in such a work. In particular, Kant's *Prolegomena* was intended as a kind of retrospective summary or condensed overview of the central claims and arguments of the *Critique of Pure Reason*.

Though the *Prolegomena* has become the standard introduction to Kant's Critical Philosophy, it is not ideally suited for that role. Kant wrote it primarily for future teachers of the *Critique* and, thus, assumed that most of its readers would have some acquaintance with that work. In consequence, Kant's presentation is occasionally somewhat sketchy, and too often—just when an explanation or argument is most wanted—he refers the reader to passages in the *Critique* where the issues are discussed more fully. Despite its limitations, however, the *Prolegomena* is still perhaps the best primary-source introduction to Kant's Critical Philosophy. Consequently, in this chapter, we shall be concerned exclusively with that work. Moreover, for reasons to emerge shortly, we shall be focusing almost exclusively on the introduction or preface, the preamble, and the first and second parts.

AWAKENED BY HUME FROM HIS DOGMATIC SLUMBER

As Kant makes clear in the preface to the *Prolegomena,* his later philosophy takes as one of its most important starting points the problematic skepticism left by Hume. Having himself been trained in what was essentially a rationalist tradition, Kant found Hume's empiricist attack on the pretensions of rationalism both persuasive and liberating. But he found the apparent skeptical consequences of that attack disturbing and challenging. Hume, Kant says, awoke him from his dogmatic slumber; and in doing so, in effect, set the agenda for much of Kant's mature philosophy.

Indeed, there is arguably no more productive way to approach Kant's views for the first time than to read him as attempting to develop a response to Humean skepticism that would, at the same time, avoid the dogmatic pretensions of rationalism. In fact, the early sections of the *Prolegomena* appear to have been quite self–consciously set up in this way. And it is on just these sections—the sections in which Kant presents and defends his response to Hume's skepticism, culminating with his defense of the objectivity of causal necessity—that we shall focus.

Kant liked to call his alternative to traditional rationalism and empiricism "transcendental idealism" (or, sometimes, "critical idealism"). One of the principal challenges in understanding Kant, as we shall see, is to understand what exactly transcendental idealism is.

As the full title of the *Prolegomena* suggests, Kant was particularly interested in investigating the possibility that metaphysics might, as he puts it, "be able to come forth as a *science*." To qualify as a science, in Kant's sense, is, at least, to be a discipline with a subject matter capable of genuine and systematically justifiable knowledge. So in asking what would be required in order for metaphysics to be a possible science, we can—at least to start with—take Kant to be asking whether, contrary to Hume, there can be genuine metaphysical knowledge. Can there, for example, be genuine knowledge of the Law of Universal Causation, according to which everything is caused in accordance with constant laws of nature? And if there can be such knowledge, how can this possibility be defended against the skeptical arguments of Hume? What precisely Kant understood by *metaphysical* knowledge, and how precisely he understood Hume to have challenged its possibility, are matters we shall investigate more closely below.

THE DISTINCTION BETWEEN ANALYTIC AND SYNTHETIC JUDGMENTS

In order to appreciate Kant's response to Hume, we must first acquaint ourselves with a range of very important distinctions that Kant introduces. Both the rationalists and the empiricists divided all judgments into two kinds: those which, if true, are knowable a priori, that is, knowable without reference to experience (except insofar as experience might be necessary for acquiring the concepts involved), and those which, if true, are knowable only a posteriori, that is, knowable only by reference to experience. Kant also accepted this distinction. But, as we shall see, alongside it, he added a distinction of his own: Kant distinguished judgments he called "synthetic" from those he called "analytic."

Analytic Judgments

Kant, along with Descartes and Hume, also held that any judgment the truth of which is knowable a priori expresses a *necessary* or *universally valid* truth. Kant often calls such truths "apodeictic"—which is to say that they can be known to be necessarily true, with absolute certainty, independently of any sense experience.

Kant was interested in how the possibility of apodeictic knowledge is to be understood. According to Hume, all a priori knowledge can concern nothing more than *relations between ideas*. When true, a mental inspection of the ideas contained in these judgments will show—perhaps with the help of some analysis—that the ideas are indeed related as they are judged to be. What is distinctive about all true judgments concerning relations between ideas, according to Hume, is that their denial will involve a contradiction. Understood in this way, their a priority is a matter of course, and their necessity and universal validity issue from the absolute necessity and universal validity of logic.

In effect, Kant calls "analytic" just those judgments that Hume would say concern relations between ideas. Kant captures Hume's idea that such judgments concern only relations between ideas by saying that analytic judgments express nothing in the predicate of the judgment that has not already been thought in the concept of the subject. So, for example, the judgments "All bodies are extended" and "All bachelors are unmarried" will be analytic judgments. In each case, the predicate concepts—*being extended* and *being unmarried*, respectively—are already "contained in" the relevant subject concepts—*being a body* and *being a bachelor*, respectively. For the concept of being a body is just the concept of being, among other things, something extended; and the concept of being a bachelor is just the concept of being an unmarried adult male.

Moreover, like Hume, Kant insists that what is distinctive about analytic judgments is that they all wholly depend for their truth on the principle of contradiction. In other words, when true, their denial would express a contradiction. According to Kant, then, analytic truths are knowable a priori; and they are knowable a priori for precisely the same reasons that truths concerning relations between ideas were knowable a priori for Hume.

Synthetic Judgments

Analytic judgments are to be distinguished from those Kant calls "synthetic." A synthetic judgment is a proposition the predicate concept of which actually contains more information than is contained or thought in the subject concept. Whereas, in the case of true analytic judgments, the predicate concept merely explicates what is in part or in whole contained within the subject concept, the predicate concept in a synthetic judgment actually amplifies, or adds to, what is contained in the subject concept. For example, we do not suppose that it is part of the concept of being a swan—that is, part of what we know just insofar as we know the meaning of "swan"—that swans should all weigh less than two hundred pounds. Otherwise, the judgment that there are swans that weigh two hundred pounds would be self-contradictory, which it is not. It belongs to the essence of a synthetic proposition that its denial never involves a contradiction.

The concept *being something that weighs more than two hundred pounds* says something more than what is contained in the concept of being a swan. Understanding the concept of being a swan does not, in this case—as it would for an analytic judgment—suffice to enable one to determine that the judgment is true. Nevertheless, it probably is true that all swans weigh less than two hundred pounds. And so, to know the truth of this proposition would amplify, or expand, our knowledge of swans beyond what we know about them just by understanding the concept. And so, to determine the truth of this judgment, we would have to appeal to something beside our understanding of the meaning of "swan." In this particular case, we would, of course, have to appeal to empirical evidence, to experience.

At first, one might get the impression that synthetic judgments are just—or, at least, are very much like—those judgments which, according to Hume, express matters of fact and existence. And indeed, were Kant's distinction available to him, Hume would doubtless have identified the two sorts of judgment. But Hume takes himself to have established that matters of fact or existence are knowable, if at all, only a posteriori. It is precisely here that Kant's new distinction becomes important. For while Kant agrees with Hume that all a posteriori (or empirical) judgments are synthetic, Kant denies that all synthetic judgments must be a posteriori.

Consider again Hume's skeptical challenge vis-à-vis the notion of causation. Hume showed that it is never contradictory to deny that there are any causal regularities. Thus, in Kant's terminology, Hume showed that any general causal principal such as the claim that (necessarily) every event has a cause, cannot be analytic but, rather, must be synthetic. Moreover, Kant accepted that Hume had also successfully argued that no necessity—nor, therefore, any necessary universal truth—could be rationally justified by a posteriori means. Indeed, Kant took this to be one of Hume's most important achievements. But now, if we were to accept Hume's assumption that no synthetic judgment may be known a priori, it would follow that causal knowledge is impossible.

Synthetic A Priori Judgments

Kant noticed that Hume's line of argument can be generalized, with potentially devastating effects. Consider what is involved in traditional metaphysical claims. First of all, they are, as Kant sees them, supposed to be substantive or amplificative in content—they are not, that is, concerned merely with relations between ideas. And so (even though some of his immediate predecessors attempted to argue otherwise) genuinely metaphysical claims are never merely analytic. The denial of any traditional metaphysical claim is never contradictory. Consequently, they must always be synthetic.

Secondly, according to Kant, it is in the nature of genuine metaphysical claims to express only necessary and universal truths. And since Kant accepted Hume's claim that empirical, or a posteriori, knowledge of necessary truths is impossible, he insisted that the truth of a metaphysical claim can only be known a priori.

But now, here is the rub. For Hume, metaphysical knowledge must be impossible precisely because metaphysical claims are both necessary and synthetic. Since, for Hume, synthetic truths can be known, if at all, only a posteriori, and since necessary truths can be known only a priori, it will follow—as Hume sees things—that synthetic a priori knowledge is impossible. And since any genuinely metaphysical judgment will, by its very nature, be a synthetic a priori judgment, it follows that metaphysical knowledge is impossible. There can be no rationally justifiable metaphysical claims or principles.

This argument depends on the Humean views—couched here in Kant's vocabulary—that a priori truths are exhausted by analytic truths, and that a posteriori truths exhaust the synthetic ones. If even the *possibility* of synthetic a priori knowledge could be demonstrated, Hume's skeptical attack on metaphysics would collapse. This, then, sets the agenda for Kant's response to Hume.

The Principal Question: How Is Synthetic A Priori Knowledge Possible?

In order to meet Hume's skeptical challenge, we must, according to Kant, demonstrate the possibility of synthetic a priori knowledge. We must, that is, explain under what circumstances such knowledge would be possible. Of course, a complete answer to the skeptic would be one that demonstrated, not only the possibility of such knowledge, but also its actuality. And in fact, in the *Critique of Pure Reason*, Kant endeavors not only to provide an account of circumstances under which synthetic a priori knowledge would be possible, but also to show that the proposed circumstances are the *only* ways in which such knowledge would be possible and, further, that if they do not obtain we shall be unable to make sense of certain fundamental features of our cognitive lives that even the most ardent skeptic could not coherently deny.

Some of these more ambitious aims are mentioned, and their defense is gestured at, in the *Prolegomena*. But Kant appears there to be concerned primarily with elaborating the circumstances under which, according to him, synthetic a priori knowledge is possible. This more limited task—which shall be the focus of our concern in this chapter—is not trivial. For as we noted above, if Kant can indeed successfully defend the possibility of such knowledge, then—whether or not he goes on to establish its actuality—he will thereby have successfully undermined Hume's general skeptical strategy.

As we have seen, Hume's argument against the possibility of synthetic a priori knowledge depended essentially upon his commitment to two principles:

1. No necessary and universal truth can be established a posteriori.

2. Only analytic truths are capable of being established a priori.

Kant accepted 1. But 2 will be refuted if the possibility of synthetic a priori knowledge could be demonstrated.

HOW IS SYNTHETIC A PRIORI KNOWLEDGE POSSIBLE IN MATHEMATICS?

In Kant's view, there are two important domains of knowledge the possibility of which depends upon the existence of synthetic a priori judgments: mathematics and natural science. Mathematics depends upon this possibility because according to Kant, the judgments of pure mathematics, when properly understood, *are* synthetic a priori. And though most of the judgments of natural science are empirical in nature, their possibility, according to Kant, presupposes certain general synthetic a priori principles, such as the principle of universal causation. These principles make up what Kant calls "pure" natural science.

For the purpose of undermining Hume's challenge, Kant assumes, in the *Prolegomena*, that we possess both mathematical and natural scientific knowledge. He then takes as his task to show how such knowledge is possible. This will involve, first, establishing that each sort of knowledge does indeed depend upon the possibility of certain synthetic a priori judgments. And second, Kant will have to demonstrate how, in each case, the relevant sorts of synthetic a priori judgment are possible.

If Kant is right in supposing that both mathematics and natural science presuppose the possibility of synthetic a priori judgments, then the generalized version of Hume's argument—if sound—would clearly have devastating consequences. Radical skepticism with respect to both mathematics and natural science will, it would seem, be unavoidable.

The Synthetic Status of Mathematical Judgments

Though his views are commonly taken to entail skepticism with regard to most matters that would be of concern to a natural scientist—most matters of fact and existence that transcend immediate experience—Hume never seems to have extended his skeptical reflections to include pure mathematics. Hume never doubted that pure mathematics involves a body of truths that are knowable a priori, with absolute certainty, as necessary and universally valid—that mathematics is, as Kant would put it, an apodeictic science. Of course, Hume believed that the necessity and a priority of pure mathematics are to be accounted for because, in Kant's terminology, mathematical truths are always analytic.

Kant thinks Hume made a serious mistake here. Had Hume reflected more carefully on the nature of pure mathematical judgments, he would have—he *should* have—noticed that they are, in fact, synthetic in nature. In other words, according to Kant, their truth does not follow from the laws of logic; their truth is not ascertained by analysis of the concepts involved. Consequently, the denial of a genuine mathematical truth will never result in a self-contradictory judgment.

If Kant can show that mathematical judgments are, indeed, synthetic and not analytic, as nearly everyone before him seems to have supposed, then, insofar as they are necessary and, hence, are knowable, if at all, only a priori, they will have to be classed among the claims about which Hume *should* have been skeptical. This will put Hume in a peculiar position. If he wants to maintain that mathematics is a genuine science, and if—as Kant does not doubt—he is unwilling to deny the necessity and the universal validity of mathematical truths, then Hume must admit the possibility of genuine synthetic a priori knowledge and, thus, reject his second principle. But without that principle, Hume's general skeptical strategy cannot get off the ground.

All of this, of course, depends on whether Kant can show first that mathematical judgments are indeed synthetic, and second how, despite this, they are knowable a priori. What reasons does Kant give to support his claim that mathematical judgments are really synthetic? Unfortunately Kant's most direct discussion of this in the *Prolegomena* is frustratingly condensed. Kant asks us to consider the judgment that seven plus five equals twelve. Acknowledging that it is tempting to view this as an analytic judgment that follows from the concept of the sum of seven and five, according to the principle of contradiction, Kant nevertheless insists that more careful reflection will reveal that it is in fact synthetic. He points out that the concept of the sum of seven and five "contains" nothing besides the idea of their union in a single number—the particular number itself is not part of or contained in the thought. As Kant insistently puts it, "the concept of twelve is by no means thought by merely thinking of the combination of seven and five; and, analyze this possible sum as we may, we shall not discover twelve in the concept."

Perhaps another example—this time from geometry—may help to illustrate Kant's point further. Consider the concept of a triangle. Presumably, upon analysis, that concept amounts to something like a figure enclosed by three sides and possessing three angles. But surely it is a universally valid geometric truth, knowable a priori, that the sum of the interior angles of a triangle is equal to the sum of two right angles (180°) But now, as Kant writes in a passage in the *Critique of Pure Reason*:

> Suppose a philosopher be given the concept of a triangle and be left to find out, in his own way, what relation the sum of its angles bears to a right angle. He has nothing but the concept of a figure enclosed by three straight lines and possessing three angles. However long he meditates on this concept, he will never produce anything new. He can analyze and clarify the concept of a straight line or of an angle or the number three, but he can never arrive at any properties not contained already in these concepts.

And, in particular, he will not, merely by analyzing the concept of a triangle, arrive at the knowledge that the sum of the interior angles of any triangle is equal to the sum of two right angles.

In case these considerations do not by themselves suffice to convince one of the synthetic status of mathematical judgments, Kant continues his argument by asking us to consider more closely what in fact takes place when we seek to establish the truth of such judgments. According to Kant, in order to ascertain the truth or falsity of a mathematical judgment, we must always go beyond the concepts involved and, as he puts it,

> call to our aid some intuition corresponding to one of them, i.e., either our five fingers, or five points; and we must add successively the units of the five given in the intuition to the concept of seven.

According to Kant, then, analysis of the concept of the sum of seven and five will reveal only that these two numbers are to be combined or added, but this thought contains nothing about what the result shall be. In order to determine this, one must actually go beyond the concepts given and call to our aid some *intuition* such as five fingers, or five stones, or five beads on an abacus. With these intuitions before us, we can then, in effect, "count up" the sum by successively adding each unit to our concept of seven to discover that it is twelve.

Intuitions and Concepts

Essential to Kant's view that mathematical propositions are not analytic but synthetic is his claim that in order to recognize their truth, we must rely not merely on our understanding of the concepts involved but must also appeal to what he calls an "intuition." What precisely Kant means by "intuition" here is a vexed question in Kantian scholarship. One thing should be clear though: He does not mean by it what we mean when we use the word "intuition" in such contexts as "a mother's intuition" or "intuitively speaking." Perhaps an adequate positive indication of what he has in mind can be, for our purposes, obtained by contrasting the notion of *intuition* with that of *concept*, as these two notions get used in Kant's technical vocabulary.

For Kant, concepts and intuitions are two fundamentally different, though functionally complementary, sorts of mental representation. Recognizing the distinction is crucial, Kant thinks, if we are to understand adequately what is involved in that particularly important sort of mental state we call a judgment. When mental representations are related in the way they are when a judgment is made, the result is a commitment, on the part of the person doing the judging, to something being the case: It is essential to judgments that they have the capacity to be true or false.

Consider, for example, a case where someone experiences that such and such is the case—say, that *that* is a chair. Such an experience, according to Kant, involves making a judgment. According to Kant, in order for someone to judge in this way that something is the case, two complementary conditions must be fulfilled. First, something must be given or presented to one's senses, to what Kant sometimes calls the "sensible faculty" or the "faculty of intuition." And second, one must acknowledge what is presented as being of a certain kind. That is, one must in some sense conceptualize it, apply a concept to it—think of it as something of such and such a kind. This is the job of what Kant calls the "faculty of understanding." In Kantian terms, experiencing that something is the case requires both that one have an intuition and that one bring that intuition under a concept.

An intuition, then, according to Kant, is the sensuous feature of our experience taken merely as presenting a particular object. It is, so to speak, that part of our experience for which, if we were to attempt to give it verbal expression, we would have to use some demonstrative expression such as *this* or *that*. And intuition, then, is the direct presentation to the mind, through the senses, of something particular which we can think of as *that*.

Concepts, in contrast to intuitions, do not relate directly or essentially to any particular object or objects but, at best, represent objects in a general way by representing some feature or features which several objects may have in common. It is the essence of concepts to apply ultimately to intuitions, though their application may be mediated by other concepts. Concepts are in this way like predicates, and their deployment in thought requires their application to a subject.

A Priori Intuitions

Returning now to the specific issue of mathematical judgments, Kant's claim, recall, is that in determining the truth of such judgments, the mere analysis of concepts will never suffice; rather, we must also make an essential appeal to some intuition or intuitions. It is by virtue of this apparent need to appeal to intuitions that mathematical judgments can be amplificatory or informative and, hence, synthetic. If we assume, for the time being, that the considerations Kant has presented succeed in making it plausible that mathematical judgments are indeed synthetic, an important new problem emerges.

Kant is assuming that true mathematical judgments are necessary and universally valid. And given his acceptance of Hume's first principle, it follows that mathematical judgments are knowable only a priori. But now that we have seen that our appreciation of the truth of a mathematical judgment depends essentially on an appeal to intuition, the question Kant must face is: How can knowledge essentially grounded on an appeal to intuition issue in an appreciation of the necessity and universal validity of the relevant truths? Alternatively, if our mathematical judgments require an appeal to intuition in order for us to come to know them, then in what sense can we claim that our knowledge of mathematical truths is a priori?

Given that mathematical judgments are knowable a priori and with apodeictic certainty as necessary and universally valid, it follows that no ordinary appeal to empirical intuition will suffice to secure genuine mathematical knowledge. An appeal to empirical intuition will at best provide us with probable knowledge and not with the apodeictic knowledge we claim for mathematics. Plainly then, whatever appeal to intuition we make in evaluating mathematical judgments, this appeal must confine itself to intuitions or features of intuitions given to us a priori, or what Kant sometimes refers to as "pure" intuitions. For if the judgment is to be a priori, then the relevant concepts must be applied to the relevant intuitions "prior to all experience or particular perception." But this will only be possible if the intuitions themselves are given to us "prior to all experience or particular perception."

But how can we make sense of an intuition to which a concept can apply prior to any particular experience when an intuition is just the presentation to experience of a particular? Plainly, the notion of an intuition a priori is not an easy notion to come to terms with. Nor is Kant unaware of this difficulty. Kant's attempt to resolve it appears in a short but exceedingly important paragraph in Section 9 of the *Prolegomena*, where he writes that there is only one way in which

> [m]y intuition [can] anticipate the actuality of the object, and be a cognition a priori, viz., *if my intuition contain nothing but the form of sensibility, which in me as subject precedes all the actual impressions through which I am affected by objects.* For that objects of

sense can be intuited only according to this form of sensibility I can know a priori. Hence it follows that propositions which concern this form of sensuous intuition only are possible and valid for [all] objects of the sense; as also, conversely, that intuitions are possible a priori can never concern any other things than objects of our senses.

Kant is making two important and related points in this passage. First, Kant points out that the only appeal to intuition that will, in fact, preserve the a priori status of those mathematical claims based upon it, must not in any way concern the substance or content of any particular intuition, but rather will concern only the *form* of intuition. We will consider in a moment what Kant means by "form" here. The second important point is Kant's claim, made at the end of the passage, that insofar as a given judgment is knowable a priori by an appeal to the form of intuition, the necessity and universal validity of that judgment can apply only to objects *as intuited*— that is to say, only to possible objects of experience. This, as we shall see later, is a very important point for Kant. Just how it is to be understood and what its significance is, are considerations to which we shall return after we examine Kant's first point a bit more closely.

The Forms of Intuition

What does Kant mean when he says that the only sort of appeal to intuition that can be relevant to establishing the truth of an a priori judgment is an appeal that concerns nothing more than the *form* of intuition? In particular, what does Kant mean by form? At the very least, the idea seems to be that the form or formal features of a particular *type* of thing are just those features which are necessary and universal for and, as such, are determinative of something being a thing of that type. It is, in other words, by virtue of its having the formal features that it has that any particular thing is a thing of the type under consideration. In this sense, notice, the form of an item is always prior to the instances of the item: There could be no instances without the form. This is, of course, not a temporal priority, but rather a logical or conceptual priority.

The form or formal features of intuitions, then, are those necessary and universal features of intuitions by virtue of which they so much as count as intuitions. And so, whenever we intuit a particular object, we intuit something which necessarily conforms to those conditions by virtue of which it is to count as an intuition at all. Something, then, will count as the form of a sensuous intuition only insofar as it is a constitutive feature of our perception of individuals as such, only insofar as nothing could count as an object of sensuous perception unless it possessed that feature.

According to Kant, what we appeal to when we appeal to intuitions in determining mathematical truths is not the particular empirical content of the specific intuitions but the form of intuition itself. In order to see better what Kant might have had in mind here, consider again what actually happens when we calculate a sum—say, seven plus five equals twelve—using our fingers or stones or beads on an abacus. Notice that nothing about there actually being fingers, or stones, say—as opposed to any other sort of particular object that might be presented in intuition—is relevant to the appeal and its success. Nor do we take it to be relevant. On the basis of our calculation, we do not conclude: Well, maybe when you combine five fingers with seven fingers you get twelve fingers; but how do I know that this is true for all things? Rather, we all appreciate that the particular empirical content of the intuitions to which we appeal—there being fingers and not stones, or stones and not beads on an abacus—is irrelevant to the use being made of them. On reflection, it seems clear that any intuition—just insofar as it is an intuition—would do just as well. What is relevant to our appeal is not anything specific to any particular intuition but what is common to, unvarying in—what is constitutive of—all intuitions just insofar as they are intuitions at all. What is relevant, in other words, is the *form* of sensuous intuition itself.

Recognizing that what we appeal to in mathematics is the form of intuition, rather than any specific empirical content, is only half the story. If our appreciation of the form is to be a priori, it cannot be that the form itself is something derived from experience. It must rather be something which, as Kant says, "anticipates" experience.

But how can this be? According to Kant, in order for our appeal to form both to anticipate experience and to guarantee the necessity and universal validity of the mathematical knowledge based on such an appeal, the form of sensuous intuition must be identified with a condition on the very possibility of our sensuously intuiting particulars. It must, however, *not* be a condition imposed by the objects in themselves, for then it could not be intuited a priori. Rather, it must be a condition imposed on any and all possible intuitions by the mind itself, in particular, by the very nature of the mind's faculty of sensuous intuition. In other words, according to Kant, we will be able to explain the possibility of synthetic a priori knowledge in mathematics only if the mind is viewed as being itself the source of those (formal) conditions which must be met by anything that is to be represented as an object of intuition by such a mind.

In the case of the faculty of intuition, then, nothing will count as an object of intuition for us unless it is intuitable by this faculty of intuition. But by virtue of the nature of this faculty, anything intuited by it will be presented to the mind as conforming to certain formal conditions, whose source is the faculty of intuition itself. In this way, all possible objects of intuition, just insofar as they are possible objects of intuition, will conform to these formal requirements. This, as we shall eventually see, is a very important point to understand.

Space and Time as the A Priori Forms of Intuition

Can we say anything more specific about what exactly the form of intuition is? What exactly must objects be like if they are to be possible objects of intuition for us? And how does the fact that they must all conform to these formal demands underwrite our apodeictic arithmetical and geometric knowledge?

For Kant, the answer is plain. Surely no object, whether an inner object (an object of inner sense) or an external object (an object of outer sense), will count as presented to us except insofar as it is presented to us as situated in *time*. And surely no external object will count as presented to us unless it is presented to us as situated in both *space* and time. As Kant says in Section 10 of the *Prolegomena*:

> If we omit from empirical intuitions of bodies and their alternations (motion) everything empirical, i.e., belonging to sensation, space and time will remain, and are therefore pure intuitions that lie a priori at the basis of the empirical.

As Kant sees it, then, it is a condition on the very possibility of intuiting an external thing *as an external thing* that it be intuited as situated in space and time. At the very least, this means that the applicability of spatial and temporal *concepts* to any external intuition—insofar as these concepts are themselves grounded a priori in the pure intuitions of space and time—is guaranteed.

In this view, then, our mathematical judgments, grounded as they are in nothing but the forms of sensuous intuition, concern nothing but the formal features given a priori, on the one hand, of the temporal continuum (time) and, on the other hand, of space. The formal features of the temporal continuum are codified in the mathematics of numbers (where we can imagine them represented in terms of the formal features of the number line); and the formal features of space are, of course, codified in geometry.

Insofar as space and time are the a priori forms of all empirical intuition, it follows that being situated in space and time is required of any object for it even to count as a possible object of experience for us. In other words, conforming to the formal conditions of spatiotemporal configuration, as these are legislated by our faculty of intuition, is constitutive of counting as a possible empirical intuition. No wonder then that any possible object of experience will—of necessity and without exception—accord with the formal properties of space and time as codified in pure mathematics. Consequently, we can never be—and, moreover, we may be assured a priori that we never will be—confronted in experience with counterexamples to the arithmetic and geometric judgments we establish a priori when doing mathematics.

This is not because the claims of mathematics are analytic. For the need to go beyond the concepts and appeal to intuition precludes that. Rather, they are—if Kant is right about that need—synthetic. They are knowable a priori, however, and as necessary and universally valid because they concern only the forms of intuition which are themselves determined by the nature of our faculty of sensuous intuition. This according to Kant, is how synthetic a priori knowledge in mathematics is possible.

If Kant's strategy here is successful, he will at the very least have shown how a certain class of synthetic a priori judgments is possible. The success of his strategy depends on at least two important things. First, it depends upon the success of his argument for the synthetic status of mathematical judgments. And second, it depends upon whether the sort of necessity and universal validity that would be guaranteed by his proposal satisfactorily guarantees the sort of necessity and universal validity we take pure mathematical judgments to possess. If both these conditions are satisfied, then Kant will indeed have established the possibility of synthetic a priori knowledge. And in having done so, he will have successfully undermined the general strategy underlying Hume's skeptical arguments. In particular, he will have proved that Hume's commitment to his second principle—the claim that only analytic judgments can be known a priori—is false, and, hence, any arguments presupposing it are unsound.

Transcendental Idealism

So far, so good. But now, Kant is quite intent on pointing out—and this brings us back to the second important point made in the passage quoted above—that if the possibility of synthetic a priori judgments in mathematics is to be accounted for in this way, then, very importantly, mathematics cannot be taken to tell anything about *things in themselves*, but only about *possible objects of experience, things as they appear to us*. In order to understand this claim and its importance for Kant, we must first understand the contrast that Kant is here intending to draw.

Kant has argued that in order to account for the possibility of the synthetic a priori status of mathematical judgments, our faculty of intuition must be viewed as itself the source of certain formal conditions that must be met by anything if it is to be a possible object of intuition. The relevant conditions, as we saw, consisted of being situated in space and time. Pure mathematics is itself concerned to elaborate and systematize the formal properties of space and time. Since every intuited object must—by virtue of being intuited and given the nature of the faculty of intuition—satisfy the formal conditions imposed by that faculty on its objects, *any* possible object of intuition will be guaranteed to conform to the dictates of pure mathematics.

But since these formal features, which condition the possibility of being an intuited object, derive from the nature of the faculty of intuition in this way, it also follows that mathematics is valid *only* for objects insofar as they appear to us in intuition. Nothing can be guaranteed about objects conceived of in complete and total independence of their being possible objects of awareness for us. Nothing can be guaranteed, that is, concerning objects conceived of *as they are in themselves*. So it is in regard to objects conceived, not as they are *in themselves*, but only as they *appear* to us in intuition that mathematics is necessary and universally valid.

Because it is a consequence of Kant's way of guaranteeing the a priori universal validity of mathematics that being situated in space and time are features of objects contingent upon their being possible objects of intuition, Kant is willing to admit that the possible objects of experience are in a certain sense dependent upon features of the perceiver's mind. And thus he is willing to admit that there is an element of idealism in his view. Kant is emphatic, however, that the sort of idealism to which he is committed is not in any way a problematic or skeptical idealism. Radical idealism of the sort he has in mind here consists in the assertion that nothing exists besides minds, and that whatever objects we take ourselves to perceive in intuition are nothing but representations in these minds with nothing external corresponding to them. In particular, then, Kant claims that his idealism—which he calls "transcendental" or "critical" idealism—does not in any way commit him to denying that the objects of appearance have reality or objective existence independently of our sensuous experience of them.

For Kant, it is important to make a distinction between what we might call *transcendental subjectivity* and *empirical subjectivity*. A feature of experience is transcendentally subjective just insofar as it is a formal condition on the very possibility of empirically objective experience generally. Being situated in space and time, then, are transcendentally subjective conditions of the very possibility of empirically objective experience.

Contrast space and time, however, with color. Seeing objects as having the particular colors they do certainly depends upon features of our sensory apparatus, but it is merely an empirically subjective condition of our visual experience. Nobody supposes that the very possibility of visually experiencing objects depends upon their being perceived as having the colors they are taken by us to have. After all, people who are color-blind are still quite capable of visually experiencing objects. Moreover, the possibility of experiencing objects in general does not even depend upon visually experiencing them at all. People who are blind are still capable of experiencing objects—the same objects we do. So the fact that we see things in the colors we do and even the fact that we perceive things visually at all are empirically subjective conditions on our experience of objects.

Contrast this, however, with our experiencing something in space and time. Surely—Kant would want to say—nothing would count for us as experiencing an object if it was not a presentation of that object in space and time. Given the distinction between transcendental and merely empirical subjective conditions of experience, Kant hopes to be able to allow that while it is true that possible objects of experience must in some sense depend upon features of our transcendental subjectivity, they are wholly independent of our empirical subjectivity—which is just to allow that they are empirically objective.

Consequently, Kant insists that transcendental idealism is fully compatible with what he calls "empirical realism"—which Kant understands to be the claim that the mind can come to possess knowledge of external objects—that is, objects in space and time, which do not depend for their existence on being experienced by us—through experience. Whether, in fact, transcendental idealism fully escapes the charge that it commits Kant to a residual skepticism or problematic idealism will be examined more closely below.

ON THE POSSIBILITY OF AN OBJECTIVELY VALID NATURAL SCIENCE

In order to claim knowledge about any particular, we need to be able to form a judgment concerning that particular. And in order to form a judgment concerning any particular, it is necessary that we be able to intuit that individual. To be a possible object of knowledge requires being a possible object of judgment, which in turn requires being a possible object of intuition and, hence, being situated in space and/or time. But being situated in space and/or time is not the only condition required for being a possible object of judgment. As we noted earlier, in order to form a judgment about a particular, we must also be able to bring our intuition under concepts.

How Are Synthetic A Priori Judgments in Pure Natural Science Possible?

It is this fact, according to Kant, that affords us with the insight we need in order now to go on to show how objective scientific judgments in natural science are also possible. Remember that while ordinary empirical judgments in science are synthetic a posteriori, their possibility, according to Kant, depends upon the possibility of what he calls "pure" natural science. Pure natural science is a collection of synthetic a priori principles or laws without which empirical natural science would not be possible. Kant's principal example in the *Prolegomena* is the Law of Universal Causation—according to which every event is determined by a cause according to constant laws. These principles of pure natural science are, as this example makes plain, precisely the sort of judgments that Humean skepticism takes as its principle target.

In the second part of the *Prolegomena*, in the chapter entitled "Second Part of the Main Transcendental Question" and subtitled "How is Pure Natural Science Possible," Kant attempts both to support his claim for the dependency of empirical science on pure science and to show how knowledge of the relevant synthetic a priori principles is possible. Kant's approach, as we shall see, is to extend the same general transcendental strategy he used to secure the possibility of an objectively valid mathematics to defend the possibility of an objectively valid natural science. Whereas in the case of mathematics Kant appealed to the transcendental conditions on being a possible object of intuition, here Kant is going to appeal to the transcendental conditions on being a possible object of judgment.

Hume would very likely agree with Kant that we have to believe in such a principle as the Law of Universal Causation if we are to do natural science. Moreover, he would certainly agree that we, in fact, do believe such a principle and are not likely to give up this belief. But for Hume, this belief is not justified. At best, it is grounded in the fact that the human mind forms habits of expectation based on experiences of past constant conjunctions. Any necessity we take ourselves to see in the world—in particular, any necessity we suppose to exist in the connection between cause and effect—is really, according to Hume, a subjective necessity, based on a purely contingent subjective compulsion of the mind to expect certain events when experiencing certain others. For Hume, belief in any (nonanalytic) objective necessity cannot be rationally justified.

Against this, Kant wants to defend the possibility of the objective validity of causal judgments and, hence, the possibility of a legitimate natural science. He proposes to do so, at least in part, by arguing for the possibility of synthetic a priori principles, such as the Law of Universal Causation. Kant wants to show—contrary to Hume—both how it is possible for a synthetic principle, such as the Law of Universal Causation, to be objectively valid for all nature and how we can know this a priori.

According to Kant, the necessary universal validity of the Law of Universal Causation can be established if, in some sense, satisfaction of the principle can be shown to be an a priori condition on experiencing anything as an object in nature—in other words, if it can be shown that satisfying the principle is a necessary formal condition of an object's being a possible object of judgment. This will be established, according to Kant, if we can show that for an object to be a possible object of judgment, it must be subsumed under the pure, that is a priori, concept—or, as Kant sometimes calls it, "Category"—of *cause*.

Kant will argue that, just as the nature of the faculty of intuition determines that nothing shall count as an object of intuition unless it satisfies certain formal conditions determined by the nature of that faculty (i.e., being situated in space and/or time), so too the nature of the faculty of judgment, which Kant calls the "understanding," determines that nothing will count as a possible object of judgment unless it is conceived of in accordance with—that is, represented as falling under—certain pure a priori concepts of the understanding, the Categories, one of which is the category of cause. Consequently, the principles based on the Categories amount to formal laws that the understanding "legislates" for all of nature, for all possible objects of judgment.

The Categories are a very special class of concepts. They are to be distinguished from ordinary empirical concepts in that they are a priori and that subsumption of intuitions under the Categories is required in order to render those intuitions suitable objects for empirical judgment. The Categories are the pure forms of judgment. What Categories there are is determined, according to Kant, by the logical forms that judgments can instantiate. If all of this is right, then the universal validity of the relevant synthetic a priori principles will be guaranteed by the fact that any possible object of judgment must, just insofar as it is a possible object of judgment, fall under the Categories.

Kant's specific claim, then, apropos the concept of cause, is that given the nature of the faculty of understanding, it is a formal condition on anything being a possible object of judgment—specifically, a judgment of experience—that it be, among other things, conceived under the Category of cause or causation. And to be conceived under the category of cause will amount, at the very least, to being thought of as subject to the network of causal laws or regularities which it is the business of empirical natural science to articulate. Thus, while we will have to await the results of empirical science to tell us what the specific empirical laws of nature are, we can nevertheless be assured a priori that every possible object in nature, which is to say, every possible object of experience or judgment, will stand in law-governed causal relations to other objects in nature. And, of course, to be assured of this a priori is just to be assured a priori of the necessary universal validity of the Law of Universal Causation.

JUDGMENTS OF EXPERIENCE AND JUDGMENTS OF PERCEPTION

In *Prolegomena*, Kant tries to argue for the claim that subsumption under the concept of cause is a formal requirement on anything counting as a possible object of an objectively valid judgment by examining what he refers to as a distinction between two kinds of empirical judgments which he calls "judgments of perception" and "judgments of experience."

A perception, for Kant, is basically a subjective state of an individual, such as a feeling of warmth, a sensation of red, a salty taste, etc. Perceptions are such as to make no essential reference to any external object. An experience, on the other hand, is always the experience of some feature of an objective reality taken as such. And so, by its very nature, experience involves judgment. When I look at a chair, for example, I have various perceptions of colors in various shapes related in my subjective consciousness. But having these perceptions does not by itself constitute, in Kant's sense, experiencing the chair. To have an experience of the chair is not merely to passively register a variety of sensory stimulations but is to be presented with what one takes (judges) to be an enduring physical object in space and time with certain determinate characteristics, standing in various determinate objective relations to other objects. The perception associated with seeing a chair is just the having of a variety of sensations. Experiencing the chair amounts, in effect, to a visual judgment that what I am seeing is a chair.

According to Kant, judgments of experience possess what he calls "objective validity," while so-called judgments of perception possess only "subjective validity." For Kant, it is obvious that the possibility of empirical natural science requires the possibility of objectively valid judgments and, hence, judgments of experience. Kant's claim is that judgments of experience (unlike judgments of perception) are possible only if the objects of these judgments are subsumed under the Categories.

In the course of his discussion, Kant offers various examples of both sorts of judgments. As examples of judgments of perception, he gives: "The room is warm," "Sugar is sweet," and "When the sun shines on the stone, it gets warm." As examples of judgments of experience, he gives: "Air is elastic" and "The sun warms the stone." Though Kant has in mind here an interesting and important distinction, these examples are quite misleading. Judgments of perception, according to Kant, are not supposed to involve the application of any Category; but each of his examples clearly does. To judge of a room or of sugar or of the sun in the ways suggested requires, at least, the deployment of the Categories of *substance, quality*, and *quantity*. We shall do better, for the time being, to ignore Kant's specific examples and to focus more generally on what is involved in the intended contrast between subjective and objective validity.

Subjective Validity

For Kant, to say that judgments of perception have only subjective validity is to say, at least, that any issue of the legitimacy or correctness of the judgments can in no way depend on how things are outside the subject's own subjective experience. So, for example, if the room feels warm to me now, the same room might feel cold to you now. But the room's feeling warm to me in no way conflicts with or contradicts the room's feeling cold to you. The legitimacy or correctness of my perception—insofar as it even makes sense to speak of it as legitimate or correct—is in no way challenged or contravened by the fact that your perception disagrees with mine, nor is yours challenged by the fact that mine disagrees with it.

Judgments of perception, then, are merely subjectively valid, in the sense that when it seems to me that the room is warm, it may seem to you that the room is not warm, without this "disagreement" raising any objective issue between us concerning which of us is right. The point is that my judgment of perception—thought of as consisting merely in the subjective state of the room's feeling warm to me—makes no claims on an objective external world of any sort that might coherently be challenged by someone disagreeing with me.

Objective Validity

Now contrast the mere subjective validity of judgments of perception, conceived of in the rather thin way I have been suggesting, with what Kant calls the "objective validity" of judgment of experience. Judgments of experience do not possess mere subjective validity, they are not merely valid for the subject in the way feeling warm or tasting sweetness are. Rather, according to Kant, they are necessarily valid for everyone. For example, when I make the judgment of experience that the room is 69 degrees Fahrenheit and if I am correct, then in order for anyone else to be correct about the temperature of the room, they must also judge it to be 69 degrees Fahrenheit.

A judgment of experience is objectively valid in the sense that if you make such a judgment and it is true, then if someone disagrees with you, they must be wrong. In this sense, disagreements between judgments of experience, unlike disagreements between judgments of perception, do raise an objective issue about who is right. Thus, for any two people, if under the same circumstances they make the same judgment of experience, then one of them will be right if and only if the other is right, and one of them will be wrong if and only if the other one is wrong. This is what Kant is getting at when he says that "objective validity" and "necessary universality (for everyone)" are equivalent terms. The necessary universality for everyone of judgments of experience amounts to the fact that the correctness conditions of such judgments—the conditions relative to which they are assessed as true or false—are such that if a given subject's judgment is correct or mistaken, then *necessarily* anyone else who judges the same thing will likewise be correct or mistaken, as the case may be.

The first point Kant wants to make in connection with this distinction between judgments of experience and judgments of perception is that each of us, as an essential part of our conscious experience of the word, does in fact make and recognize contrasting judgments of these two sorts. The distinction is essential to our ordinary experience of ourselves in the world. Indeed, our ability to draw this distinction is even presupposed by the skeptic. After all, the standard conclusion of skeptical arguments is not that no judgments about the external world are possible but that none of the various judgments that we do make can ever legitimately be credited with the status of knowledge.

So, we have before us the distinction between judgments of perception and judgments of experience. The question Kant now feels we must examine is what grounds the possibility of such a distinction. What is at issue, in particular, is how can we have empirical judgments that possess objective validity or necessary universality for everyone.

Kant says that this can never depend merely upon the perceptual or sensuous content of experience given in intuition. This will yield, at best, the sort of subjective validity possessed by judgments of perception. And the clear implication is that Hume's account of judgment can only do justice to judgments of perception, to judgments possessing only subjective validity. Instead, when we consider those of our judgments that possess, by their very nature, objective validity, we shall find, according to Kant, that their doing so always depends upon special concepts—the Categories—which must be superadded to that which is merely presented in perception (cf. Sections 18, 19, and especially 20 of the *Prolegomena*).

Answering Hume's Challenge to the Objective Validity of Causal Judgments

With this much of his general strategy outlined, Kant now feels that he is in a position to answer Hume's skeptical challenge regarding the objective validity of causal judgments. However, Kant wants, first, to emphasize his agreement with Hume on one crucial point—namely, that the concept of cause, when taken to involve the idea of a necessary connection, cannot be an empirical concept. It cannot be derived either directly or by inference from experience, in the way a genuine empirical concept such as *horse* might be; for, after all, it is going to be Kant's point that the very possibility of objective experience already depends upon the prior subsumption of our intuitions under the Categories and, so, under the concept *cause*. Neither can it arise from perception. For all we have in perception is the temporally and/or spatially associative concatenation of sensory images and the like. And, as Hume demonstrated, these resources are insufficient to underwrite any idea of necessary connection such as Kant takes to be an essential ingredient in our ordinary conception of causation. But for Hume, no further resources are available from which our concept of cause may derive.

For Kant, however, there is still the possibility that the concept of cause is an a priori concept which, in virtue of its necessary application to all of our intuitions, renders objective experience possible. This will be the case, though, only if *cause* and the other so-called Categories are purely formal concepts conditioning in general the very possibility of something counting as a possible object of judgment. And, as we have already seen, this is exactly Kant's position. According to Kant, any possible object of experience will, as such, appropriately instantiate the concept of cause and, thereby, be assured to satisfy the related a priori principle, the Law of Universal Causation.

Once again, if all of this makes sense, Kant will have shown how knowledge of a synthetic a priori principle, such as the Law of Universal Causation, is possible and, consequently, how objectively valid causal judgments in general are possible. But what considerations does Kant offer to support his claim that conceiving of an object as entering into causal relations with other objects according to constant laws is in fact a necessary condition for that object being a possible object of a judgment of experience?

Unfortunately, the considerations offered in the *Prolegomena* are, at best, gestures toward the more detailed and quite complex arguments Kant gives in the *Critique of Pure Reason*. The most direct attempt to defend the claim in the *Prolegomena* occurs in Section 28, which is quite condensed and obscure and seems, in any case, primarily aimed at demonstrating the negative conclusion that the Humean story about our causal judgments is inadequate to do justice to their objective validity. Even if this can be established, it would not by itself suffice to show either that being conceived as a cause is a necessary condition of being a possible object of objectively valid empirical judgment or how this is so. Perhaps, however, the following considerations will make Kant's position a little more clear and even somewhat plausible.

Consider first the negative claim that the Humean theory of judgment cannot do justice to the objective validity of causal judgments. Consider the contrast between the judgment of perception involved in a situation where, for a given subject, (1) "It seems that the stone gets warm when it seems that the sun shines on it" and the corresponding judgment of experience that (2) "The sun warms the stone."

Kant wants to insist that the content of the judgment in (2) is importantly different from the content of any mental state which simply represents the temporally contiguous shining of the sun and the warming of the stone, as in (1). At the very least, (2) involves the claim that the warming of the stone is an objective consequence of the sun shining upon it—the latter is a necessary condition of the former—and not merely an accidental temporal concomitant.

How might Hume try to account for this difference? His official story, of course, is that the latter case differs from the former only in that in the latter there is added that impression which is the felt determination of the mind—conditioned by habit—to expect the perception of warmth given the perception of the sun. But for Kant, this plainly will not do. For this is simply to suggest that (2) describes a slightly more complex perception than that represented by (1): It has, in addition to the perception of the stone, sun, etc., the added ingredient of the "reflective" impression of determination. This, though, issues in a slightly more complex judgment of perception; it does not yet issue in any sort of judgment of experience. It does not, that is, result in something plausibly objectively valid.

The Prima Facie Incoherence of Causally Inert Objects of Experience

As we noted before, even if considerations of this sort do successfully challenge Hume's ability to do justice to the objective validity of our causal judgments, they do not by themselves show that subsumption of objects under the Category of cause is required if an object is to be a possible object of experience at all. Kant's critique of Hume's strategy does not, however, require that he establish this—though this is something for which he argues at great length in the *Critique of Pure Reason.*

One way, however, to get at least a preliminary sympathetic feel for why Kant thought this was so is to ask what sense can be made of a wholly causally inert object of experience—an object that is wholly unconditioned by, and is not the condition of, any other object. What would it be like to experience, in Kant's sense, an object which presents itself as uncaused and also as having no causal effects on anything else. It cannot be a solid object—it cannot take up space—for then it would have the effect of excluding other objects from occupying the relevant space. Its existence and nature must be completely causally irrelevant to any other possible object of experience. Nor can it be something capable of causal interaction with our own sensory apparatus—it would have to be "invisible" for every physical sensory modality. In what sense, then, is it an experiencable something, rather than a nothing? In what sense, then, is it something about which it even makes sense to suppose that we could make objectively valid judgments of experience?

If the possibility of synthetic a priori judgments in pure mathematics and pure natural science—judgments about which Hume raised his general skeptical doubts—can be defended along Kant's lines, then Hume's overall skeptical strategy will be shown to be fallacious. Furthermore, if these judgments can be understood as issuing from or constituting nothing more than formal principles of possible experience, then Hume's skeptical doubts cannot even coherently arise. For the objective and universal validity of these principles is guaranteed by the fact that satisfaction of them is constitutive of the very possibility of objective experience. In other words, these principles will be true of any possible object of experience because satisfaction of them is partially constitutive of being a possible object of experience.

Transcendental Idealism, Again

But now, if this response to Humean-style skepticism is to be sustained, we will have to accept—as we already saw in the case of our mathematical judgments—that this knowledge applies only to objects as they might appear to us and never as they are in themselves. A question that we did not ask before, but which needs to be raised, is whether this apparent limitation leaves us with a different skeptical problem. By saying that we cannot know of objects in themselves, whether they are spatio-temporally situated or obey the Categorial principles of the understanding, such as the Law of Universal

Causation, are we admitting a skeptical limitation? By admitting that things in themselves are, as such, not possible objects of empirical knowledge, are we admitting that there are things about the objects which we are not capable of knowing—namely, the way they are in themselves? If so, then in what sense will Kant have successfully responded to a generalized Humean-style of skepticism?

Needless to say, it would be preferable if in accepting Kant's suggestions we did not have to bite the skeptical bullet in this way. But how can we avoid it? Everything depends upon how we understand what Kant means by "cannot" in his claim that we cannot know objects as they are in themselves. If we understand this latter claim, not as the claim that there are features which things possess in themselves about which we cannot hope to acquire knowledge, but as the claim that it simply does not make coherent sense to suppose that a thing conceived of as it is in itself could be an object of knowledge—or, for that matter, an object of ignorance—then, perhaps, we can avoid the skeptical worry. In other words, it could be Kant's view that when we say that we can claim no knowledge concerning things in themselves, we are not claiming that there are some positive facts concerning things about which we are destined to remain ignorant; rather, we are saying that it simply makes no sense to talk about knowledge or ignorance of objects conceived of in that way. If something like this is in fact Kant's view, then to claim that we cannot have knowledge of things as they are in themselves is not skepticism, it is just good sense.

*T*hough we have only explored the preliminary sections of the Prolegomena, *we can easily see what a radical new approach to fundamental issues in metaphysics and epistemology Kant's transcendental idealism involves. Having identified what he takes to be the relative merits and defects of both dogmatic rationalism and radical empiricism, Kant offers an alternative approach which attempts to avoid the defects of both, while retaining their merits. Transcendental idealism is not, however, a mere amalgam of doctrines Kant found acceptable. Rather, it involves a revolutionary new way of thinking about these issues, which promises, if successful, to meet or deflect many of the most fundamental skeptical challenges.*

To what extent Kant is successful at this is not something that we have had time to explore in any detail. Plenty of questions, both substantive and exegetical, remain. Most of them cannot be answered satisfactorily without examining the Critique of Pure Reason itself. In any case, reflection on Kant's Critical program has proven extremely productive in the recent history of philosophy. Philosophy after Kant has been influenced by his views to an extent difficult to overestimate. And even today his views very much remain living philosophical options.

Selected Readings

Kant, I. *The Critique of Pure Reason*, trans. by N. Kemp Smith. New York: St. Martin's Press, 1965.

_____. *Prolegomena to Any Future Metaphysics*, trans. by L. W. Beck. Indianapolis: Bobbs-Merrill, 1950.

18

Thomas Hobbes

Thomas Hobbes was born in England in 1588. Hobbes was greatly impressed with the scientific advances of his time (he was a contemporary of Galileo). He was equally impressed with the horrors of the civil strife that repeatedly broke out in England throughout his life. Hobbes' particular genius lay in his attempt to utilize science to end the political strife through the creation of a science of politics. Although his works in philosophy, and in particular in political philosophy, are Hobbes' greatest legacy, he also made important contributions in fields as diverse as history, optics, and geometry. His political philosophy first appeared in his Elements of Law *in 1640. The two parts of the* Elements *were published in 1650 as two separate treatises,* De Homine *and* De Corpore Politico. *Hobbes' crowning work in political philosophy, however, is his* Leviathan, *published in 1651. Much of his life was spent fleeing to France and back again to England for fear of his life; such were the controversies stirred up by his political and historical writings. Yet his flights from danger were well timed, allowing him to live into his nineties and to remain intellectually active throughout his life.*

HOBBES AND THE TRADITION

Hobbes is properly understood as belonging both to the natural law and social contract traditions of political philosophy. Political philosophers in the social contract tradition maintain that the just political system is the system that would be agreed to by free and equal people in an initial situation often characterized as a state of nature. Political philosophers in the natural law tradition maintain that reason dictates for each of us the basic laws that ought to govern our dealings with other persons. Hobbes embraces these traditions, but he transforms them from within. He brings to the natural law tradition a very specific and, for his time, radical view of human reason. For Hobbes, reason is an instrument or a tool allowing human beings to satisfy their appetites more effectively. Moreover, he adds a radical view of the central human appetites, a view grounded in a quasi-scientific account of humans beings. Specifically, Hobbes argues that each human being will have as his or her primary appetite or desire his or her own continued preservation. Each person's reason will simply tell that individual the most effective means to preserve himself or herself, and the laws of nature are simply the dictates of reason apprising each individual of the most effective way to satisfy the desire for his or her own continued preservation. These laws, in turn, dictate that the most effective way for free and equal beings in a state of nature to preserve themselves is by agreeing to establish a political system presided over by a sovereign whose powers are absolute. Thus, it is rational for free and equal rational beings in the state of nature to agree to a political system governed by an absolute sovereign, preferably, in Hobbes' view, an absolute monarch.

WHAT HUMAN BEINGS ARE

Hobbes' account of what human beings are works on two different levels. The first is an introspective level, upon which Hobbes appeals to the reader to look within his own breast in an effort to discern his central appetites. The second is an explanatory level, upon which Hobbes attempts to provide a scientific explanation of how human beings are constructed, an explanation that establishes what human beings must desire in much the same way that a scientific explanation of carbon establishes how carbon must react in given situations. The introspective account is often obscure. It appeals to central appetites for glory, pleasure, self-preservation, and what Hobbes often terms "commodious living."

The Scientific Account

The scientific explanation is less obscure but more controversial. Hobbes explains that appetites are ultimately nothing but motions in the body. Hobbes identifies the central motion, that which determines all others, as vital motion. This vital motion determines what all of our other appetitive motions will be. The suggestion, in short, is that every appetite one has, one has because it conduces to one's own continued preservation. On this explanatory account, self-preservation is identified by Hobbes as the ultimate end that each person cannot but have, an end to which every other end is directed as a means.

These two levels of Hobbes' psychological account appear to be in considerable tension with each other. Many Hobbes scholars discount the scientific explanation in favor of the introspective account; others discount the introspective account in favor of the scientific explanation. Still others have proposed strategies for reconciling these two levels of Hobbes' psychological account. What is clear, however, is that on one level, self-preservation is at least *a* dominant end, and on the other level, self-preservation is *the* dominant end. Clearly, the central lesson to be learned from Hobbes' psychology is that each individual is naturally led to seek primarily after his or her own continued preservation. Since reason is an instrument for helping each person to get what he or she wants, reason dictates to each person the most effective means for his or her own continued preservation.

THE STATE OF NATURE

Hobbes suggests that human beings in their natural state are free and equal. But the freedom and equality Hobbes has in mind are of a very peculiar sort. Each of us is equal, Hobbes argues in *Leviathan*, because there is greater equality of mind than there is of body, and with respect to equality of body, "the weakest has strength enough to kill the strongest, either by secret machination, or by confederacy with others. . . ."(p. 183) Moreover, each of us is free in the sense that each has a natural right to "use his own power, as he will himselfe, for the preservation of his own nature. . . . " (p. 189) Thus humans in such a state are equal because any person is smart enough and strong enough to kill any other person, and they are free in the sense that it is perfectly reasonable for each to do anything, without constraints, that proves to be necessary for his or her own continued preservation.

State of Nature as State of War

Since the state of nature will invariably be a state of scarcity, Hobbes believes that human beings in such a state will invariably be led into conflict with each other in an effort to preserve themselves. Because there is a scarcity of resources, what I need to preserve myself will often be what you need to preserve yourself. We are thus invariably led into competition over these scarce resources. If you have enough resources for your own continued preservation, moreover, you will be forced to fight to keep these resources. And since it is a bad strategy to simply wait to be set upon unawares or while asleep, it will make sense for you to anticipate others and strike first, even when you have sufficient goods for your own continued preservation. Thus, Hobbes claims that diffidence is a second source of conflict. Finally, some people will be led into conflict for glory, perhaps even when the pursuit of glory conflicts with their own self-preservation. The result is that no matter who you are or what your situation is in the state of nature, your desire for self-preservation will lead you into conflict, which Hobbes describes in *Leviathan* as a war of all against all in which life is "solitary, poore, nasty, brutish and short. . . ."(p. 186) But this leads to a seeming paradox. Each person exercises his or her right of nature to further the end of self-preservation, but the result is a war of all against all which clearly thwarts each person's attempt to preserve him- or herself. If each person does whatever is necessary to stay alive as long as possible, Hobbes is suggesting, we will all die young.

THE LAWS OF NATURE

Reason tells each person to do what is necessary to stay alive, but doing whatever is necessary to stay alive results in early death. It is at this point in the argument of *Leviathan* that Hobbes introduces his Laws of Nature, which are general rules "found out by reason, by which a man is forbidden to do, that, which is destructive of his life, or taketh away the means of preserving the same."(p. 189) Clearly, since war is hostile to our self-preservation, and the laws of nature are rules of reason that dictate the most effective way to further our self-preservation, the laws of nature will tell us to avoid war and seek peace. This is roughly what the first law of nature commands. But here an apparent difficulty develops. Reason dictates peace as a means to self-preservation, but was it not reason that commanded each person to do whatever is necessary to preserve him- or herself, and was it not precisely this command which led to war of all against all in the first place? It seems that reason leads us to a contradiction—it both leads us, ineluctably, to war and commands us to avoid war.

The Reasoning Behind the Second Law of Nature

Here Hobbes proposes an ingenious solution. The right of nature says that we are free to do whatever is reasonable to preserve ourselves. Acting in accordance with this right of nature, however, leads to war, and war thwarts our goal of preserving ourselves. But if doing what is reasonable to preserve ourselves leads to a situation in which we are thwarting our goal of preserving ourselves, is it not then reasonable to agree not to do what is reasonable to preserve ourselves, at least if everyone else agrees to do the same? It is reasoning similar to this that appears to lead Hobbes to his second law of nature, which in its *Leviathan* version holds that "a man be willing, when others are so too . . . as for Peace . . . to lay down his right to all things; and be contented with so much liberty against other men, as he would allow other men against himselfe."(p. 190) Thus, it is reasonable to agree to lay down one's right to all things, one's right to do whatever is reasonable to preserve oneself. Moreover, everyone will want to do what is reasonable, in this case to lay down one's right to do whatever is reasonable to preserve oneself, since everyone wants above all to preserve him- or herself, and reason, in the form of the laws of nature, merely dictates to each individual the most effective way of getting what he or she wants.

THE SOVEREIGN

We are all disposed to agree to lay down our rights to all things, but we are also aware that with selfish, shortsighted, glory-seeking beings such as ourselves, such an agreement or covenant will never hold unless it is backed by the sword. A power must be created to enforce the agreement. Thus, the agreement takes the form of a contract in which we give up our right to all things to an enforcer of the contract, a sovereign, whom we authorize to act on our behalf. Hobbes believes that this sovereign's power must be absolute, roughly because he believes that any attempt to limit the sovereign power will generate different centers of power, with no ultimate power or sovereign above them. Such multiple centers of power, Hobbes believes, are in the same predicament as are individuals in the state of nature. Each center of power will be led ineluctably to seek more and more power in a way that leads to conflict between these factions and, inevitably, to civil war, much as individuals in the state of nature are led, inevitably, to a war of all against all. Hobbes' sovereign, then, must be absolute. To be absolute, the sovereign must never give up his own right to nature. Each individual gives up his or her right to do whatever is necessary to preserve him- or herself to the sovereign, and authorizes all of the sovereign's actions, but the sovereign retains the right to do whatever is necessary to preserve him- or herself.

The obvious objection is that there is nothing preventing such a sovereign from killing any of his subjects on a whim. Hobbes grants that in one sense this is true. Citizens will have authorized the sovereign even to kill each of them. But he suggests that in practice this will rarely occur. This is because for a sovereign interested in his or her own self-preservation, a citizen provides a vital resource for securing such preservation; such citizens, after all, comprise the police force, the army, and the work force that a sovereign must rely upon to preserve the state, and hence him- or herself. The sovereign will thus no more be tempted to kill the subjects than any of the subjects will be tempted to cut off their own finger. In each case, the individual would be depriving him- or herself of a tool useful for his or her own continued preservation, and such an action, except in extraordinary circumstances, is contrary to reason.

Democracy or Monarchy?

One other aspect of Hobbes' political philosophy must be mentioned. Although Hobbes argues that it is preferable that the sovereign be a single person, and at many points perhaps even assumes that the sovereign is a monarch, he allows that the sovereign can also be an oligarchy (a small group) or a democracy (everyone). However, Hobbes clearly rejects the assumption that a democracy gives citizens greater control over their own fate. In a monarchy, the fate of an individual citizen is in the hands of a single person, but in a democracy, the fate of an individual citizen is in the hands of the majority of the populace. Since in either case the citizen's fate is in the hands of others, and a monarch is arguably both more predictable and more efficient, the result would appear to be a clear preference for an absolute monarchy over an absolute oligarchy or an absolute democracy. The point upon which Hobbes insists, in any case, is that whatever form the sovereign power takes, the sovereign must be absolute.

There are several points at which it is tempting to challenge Hobbes' account. First, it can be argued that his individual psychology is false. Although individuals are clearly interested in their own self-preservation, it is not clear, as Hobbes maintains, that individuals are ultimately solely interested in their own self-preservation. Second, it is not at all clear that the solution embodied in Hobbes' second law of nature is workable given his psychology. It is not clear whether individuals who are by nature predominantly self-interested can choose, even for self-interested reasons, not to be predominantly self-interested. Third, it is not at all clear that his arguments for an absolute sovereign are persuasive. Hobbes' views about human nature and the role of a sovereign are extreme. But it is often only at the extremes that the real issues become clear. Hobbes' political philosophy serves as such an extreme, clear alternative in contrast to which subsequent political thinkers, such as Rousseau and Locke, define their own positions.

Selected Readings

Gauthier, D. *The Logic of Leviathan*. Oxford: Clarendon Press, 1969.

Hampton, J. *Hobbes and the Social Contract Tradition*. Cambridge: Cambridge University Press, 1986.

Hobbes, T. *Leviathan*. C. B. Macpherson, ed. Middlesex: Penguin Books Ltd., 1968. (All *Leviathan* citations in the chapter are of this edition.)

Kavka, G. *Hobbesian Moral and Political Theory*. Princeton: Princeton Univeristy Press, 1986.

19

Locke's Political Theory

John Locke presents his positive political philosophy in his Second Treatise *of Government. There are many striking similarities between the position Locke espouses in the* Second Treatise *and the position put forward by Thomas Hobbes in* Leviathan. *Both operate within the natural law and social contract traditions. Moreover, both allow a central role in their accounts for self-preservation. But these superficial similarities obscure profound differences. Although both operate within the natural law tradition, they mean completely different things by "law of nature." For Hobbes, the laws of nature are modeled upon scientific laws. Just as apples cannot but fall from the tree, human beings cannot but attempt to preserve themselves. The laws of nature tell them how best to accomplish this end. For Locke, the laws of nature are modeled not upon scientific laws, but upon civil laws. Just as a government gives its citizens laws that they can break, and be justifiably punished for breaking, so too reason gives all individuals natural laws that they can break, and be justifiably punished for breaking.*

For Hobbes, the state of nature is inevitably a state of war of all against all, which the laws of nature tell us how to escape. For Locke, the state of nature is not a war of all against all; the laws of nature are laws not for escaping the state of nature, but for living in it. For Hobbes, there can be no morality or justice in the state of nature. Morality and justice are created through the contract that allows individuals to escape the state of nature. For Locke, there is both morality and justice in the state of nature. Clearly Locke's contract thus must have an entirely different role than Hobbes's. For Hobbes, the equality in the state of nature is the equal ability of each to kill any other, and freedom is license to do whatever is necessary to stay alive. For Locke, liberty is not license, and equality is equality of rights.

LOCKE'S STATE OF NATURE

Locke's state of nature is a state of perfect freedom, but liberty is not license. Although everyone is bound to preserve him- or herself in the state of nature, Locke also maintains in the *Treatise* that "by the like reason, when his own preservation comes not in competition, ought he, as much as he can, to preserve the rest of mankind. . . ." (par. 6) Such an obligation of each person to preserve, not only himself, but others as well is dictated by reason as a law of nature. Such an obligation, moreover, confers upon all persons a right to their own continued preservation backed by a legitimate claim upon others for assistance in safeguarding that right. All rational beings legislate this law, with its corresponding right, to themselves and to others. Moreover, the executive power, the power to enforce the law of nature, is also conferred upon each rational being in the state of nature.

Reparation and Punishment

Thus, the law of nature gives rise to the right of each person to enforce this law through reparation and punishment. The first, reparation, derives from the right each person has to self-preservation. The second, punishment, derives from the obligation each person has to preserve all of humankind. Clearly, just as each person legislates the law of nature, and each person executes these laws in practice, each person must judge when the laws have been breached and what amount of punishment and reparation is warranted. Thus for Locke, the state of nature functions as a virtual natural government, in which rational beings are each equally the legislative, executive, and judicial branches. Natural liberty is not license, because persons in the state of nature are still under the authority of the laws of nature, and these laws of nature secure each person's right to life and property.

The Right to Property

The extension from a right to self-preservation to a right to property is a very natural one for Locke. To have a property in something, for Locke, is for it to be the case that nobody else has a right to that thing or the use of that thing. Thus, the laws of nature dictate that each person has a property in him- or herself, and that each person is obligated to uphold every other person's right to such a property. But to have a property in oneself is to have a property in one's labor. Therefore, anything in which one has invested one's labor is something that person comes to have a property in. Such a person has brought what is labored upon out of its natural state and intermingled him- or herself, via labor, with it. By virtue of owning one's labor, one has come to own that with which one mingled one's labor.

RESTRICTIONS

Locke places two restrictions upon the legitimate acquisition of property. First, enough and as good of the relevant object (e.g., land, water, food) must be left in common for others. Second, one is only entitled to as much property as one can use without spoilage.

States of War

Such a state of nature is not a state of war, according to Locke. It functions as a virtual natural government. Each person, as a rational being, is aware of the laws (of nature) and empowered to enforce these laws. For Hobbes, the state of nature was inevitably a state of war—it was obvious why human beings should desire to leave such a miserable state. For Locke, the motivation to leave the state of nature is less clear. The state of nature is not a state of war for Locke, but it can all too easily become one. The state of nature becomes a state of war whenever someone threatens the self-preservation of another. Such a threat can either be direct, through designs upon the life of another, or indirect, through designs upon the property of another. An attack upon a person's property is an attack upon that person, for Locke, both because it attempts to deprive the person of things that are needed to preserve his or her life, and because these things are the person's property in virtue of having mingled him- or herself—via his or her labor—with them. To attack a person's property is thus to declare an intention to do with the person as one pleases, including taking the person's life. This clearly violates the laws of nature.

The state of nature will all too easily devolve into a state of war among certain individuals who will invariably allow their own interests to color their determination of when and to what extent the laws of nature have been violated. The consequences will be disputes over property resulting in a state of war between parties. Because there is no independent judge to resolve such disputes in the state of nature, such states of war will persist indefinitely. Locke suggests in paragraph 123 of the *Treatise* that such states of war and the ease with which they can occur in the state of nature will surely threaten rational beings' mutual quest for the preservation of "their lives, liberties and estates, which I call by the general name, property."

POLITICAL SOCIETY

What is necessary, then, are:

1. an established public law free from the bias of individual rational creatures;
2. an indifferent judge with the authority to determine whether this law has been violated and, if so, what reparations and punishments are appropriate; and
3. a power that will reliably and dependably enforce the laws by executing the sentences of the judges.

It is these needs that lead human beings into a commonwealth through the formation of a political society. A political society results when a group of people in the state of nature each give up the legislative, judicial, and executive powers that they have by nature to the group, which in turn makes decisions by simple majority.

The Contract

Such giving up of power by consent simply is the social compact or contract. In par. 99 of the *Treatise* Locke writes, "And thus that, which begins and actually constitutes any political society, is nothing but the consent of any number of freemen capable of a majority to unite and incorporate into such a society." The specific powers that must be given up by compact to the political society are (1) the power of doing whatever each deems appropriate for the preservation of himself and the rest of humankind, and (2) the power of punishing. (pars. 129/130) A person in a political society can no longer act in accordance with his determination of natural law; he or she must abide by the civil law arrived at either directly or indirectly by vote of the majority in the political society. Similarly, a person can no longer assume the power of judging and executing the law; this too must be given up to the political society.

Government

Locke recognizes the impracticality of requiring a political society in its entirety to determine by majority vote what each particular law should be, to decide in each particular case whether a law has been broken, and to enforce the laws in such cases. Clearly, a political society must institute a government to carry out these legislative, judicial, and executive functions in practice. Although Locke expresses certain preferences for specific forms of government, for example an elective parliament to carry out the legislative function, his account allows that whatever governmental form this delegation of functions takes is legitimate as long as it is established by the political society.

Locke takes the legislative function to be more fundamental than the executive and judicial functions of government; the legislative power is the supreme power in every commonwealth. Yet even this supreme power of the government is but a power delegated by the people, the majority of the political society. Thus, Locke claims in par. 149 of the *Treatise* that there "remains still in the people a supreme power to remove or alter the legislative, when they find the legislative act contrary to the trust reposed in them."

Anticipated Objections

There are two objections to Locke's account of the formation of political societies through contract that he takes pains to rebut. The first is that there are no examples in history of such societies formed through consent. Locke responds that in fact there have been such societies, for instance ancient Rome. The reason there have not been even more examples in history is that political society is so advantageous that it has typically been entered into before recorded history. There are not many records of the formation of political societies simply because political societies predate the keeping of written records.

The second objection is that new political societies can seemingly never be formed. Since everyone is already born a member of a political society, no one would seem to be in a state of nature from which a new political society can be formed. Locke responds that citizens are only barred from leaving a political society if they have expressly consented to be members of that political society. In most cases, however, citizens have only given their implicit or tacit consent to living in a political society. Citizens who have only given their tacit consent to live in a political society are free to withdraw from that political society and to participate in the formation of a new society.

CRITICISMS

The Common Good

The proper end of the legislature, according to Locke, is to secure the common good. (par. 131) Yet, the motive that each person has for entering into the political society is in large part to secure his own property, and it is not at all clear that the common good may not best be served in certain situations by redistributing the property of some individuals to others, for instance, in the form of welfare payments and unemployment benefits funded through taxation. Thus, the motive for entering into a political society, the safeguarding of property, will often seem to conflict with what Locke claims to be the proper end of political society and the legislative branch—the pursuit of the common good.

Locke appears to meet this objection by stipulating in par. 138 of the *Treatise* that "the supreme power cannot take from any man any part of his property without his own consent." But by "his own consent" Locke does not mean the consent of each person, but, as he later suggests, "the consent of the majority." (par. 140) If a person enters into political society largely to safeguard his or her property, why would a person agree to a contract that allows the property to be taken away by the vote of a simple majority? Far from resolving the apparent conflict between the pursuit of the common good and the safeguarding of private property, Locke's appeal to the consent of the people seems to exacerbate the conflict.

Other Difficulties

There are other puzzles surrounding Locke's account. For instance, Locke notes in par. 6 that the only time one is obligated to take into account the preservation of others in the state of nature is when his or her own preservation is not at risk. But according to Hobbes, each person's preservation will always come into competition with others in the state of nature. To Hobbes, then, Locke may seem to be nothing more than a Hobbesian wolf in sheep's clothing.

Another puzzle about Locke's account is that it is not clear in what way reason can obligate a person to safeguard the life and property of others, as Locke claims. Locke seems to presume that reason is more than merely an instrument allowing us to get more effectively what we want (Hobbes' account of reason), but he says little about what more reason is. Locke's appeal to a natural right to property and to our supposed natural obligation to safeguard that right is particularly problematic in this respect. For instance, Locke holds that reason dictates that something becomes a person's property if the person mixes his or her labor with it. But if one hoes an acre, does one own only the acre or the field in which the acre is located? Does one even own the acre? Might it not be necessary, not to merely hoe the acre, but to cultivate and harvest it before it becomes one's property? And when this is done, does one own the acre or only the harvest? Reason seems unable to provide the needed answers to these questions. This is an objection which Rousseau develops with considerable force.

Consider also one of the natural limitations that Locke places upon the accumulation of property—his insistence in par. 27 of the *Treatise* that there must be "enough, and as good, left in common for others." This restriction is known as the Lockean Proviso. Difficulties result in the appeal to reason for a natural clarification of this restriction. Can a person only own property if there is as much equally good property left available for each remaining person? This would be an incredibly rigid restriction. If this is not the correct interpretation of Locke's restriction, how is Locke's phrase "enough, and as good" to be correctly interpreted? Again, the appeal to reason to clarify such an interpretation can appear to raise more questions than it answers.

Despite these difficulties, Locke's political philosophy provides a straightforward and in many respects compelling framework for refining and justifying our intuitions concerning such core political concepts as property, rights, and the ultimate sovereignty of citizens. This framework has profoundly influenced the development of liberal democracy, as well as alternatives to liberal democracy, throughout the world.

Selected Readings

Green, T. H. *Lectures on the Principles of Political Obligation.* London: Longmans, Green & Co., 1950.

Locke, J. *Second Treatise of Government.* Indianapolis: Hackett, 1980. (All *Second Treatise* citations in the chapter are taken from this edition.)

Riley, P. *Will and Political Legitimacy: A Critical Exposition of Social Contract Theory in Hobbes, Locke, Rousseau, Kant, and Hegel.* Cambridge, MA: Harvard University Press, 1982.

20

Jean-Jacques Rousseau

The social and political philosophy of Jean-Jacques Rousseau plays at least three crucial roles in the history of political philosophy. First, Rousseau's political philosophy makes novel contributions that are worthy of notice in their own right. Second, Rousseau provides an attack, both implicit and explicit, upon his predecessors, Thomas Hobbes and John Locke. Third, Rousseau anticipates and lays the groundwork for further developments in political thought by such disparate authors as Immanuel Kant and Karl Marx.

Rousseau was born in Geneva in 1712. It was later in Paris, however, that he began to produce his writings in social and political philosophy. The most important of these works include "Discourse on the Origin of Inequality," "Discourse on Political Economy," Emile, *and* On The Social Contract. *The following discussion will focus primarily upon the arguments presented in the "Discourse on Inequality" and in* On The Social Contract.

THE "DISCOURSE ON INEQUALITY"

Rousseau vs. Hobbes and Locke

Like Hobbes and Locke before him, Rousseau returns in his "Discourse on Inequality" to the state of nature. But Rousseau turns the tables on Hobbes and Locke. He argues that man's natural state is neither a state of war nor a state of misery, as Hobbes claims. Indeed, Rousseau argues that the civilized state of human beings is more likely to be one of misery and ceaseless competition. Contrary to Locke's assertions, Rousseau argues that property is non-existent in the natural state. Rather, property is a social invention that leads to civil society and the evils that accompany the radical inequality of civil society. Whereas for Hobbes and Locke civil society is presented as an improvement over the natural state of human beings, for Rousseau the socialization of human beings into civil society is as much a regression as a progression.

For Rousseau, natural humans are solitary; like any other animals in their natural state, they are motivated entirely by natural impulse. The population is small in the state of nature, thus resources are plentiful. Because natural humans are limited to natural impulses, they will have a limited set of natural wants—food, and a cave for shelter. Because resources are plentiful, they will readily be able to satisfy these wants. Such beings will clearly not be in a state of war with each other, as Hobbes mistakenly thought; even though they are primarily self-interested, their interests are few and easily met without resorting to competition. If one source of food is taken, self-interest dictates moving to another source rather than forcing a confrontation. Such natural humans, moreover, are clearly not miserable. Misery, Rousseau suggests, results from the inability to satisfy wants and needs. Because such beings have but few needs and these needs are easily satisfied, they are not miserable. Thus, Hobbes' claims that human beings in their natural state are miserable and in a state of war, all against all, are simply mistaken.

Nor can such humans in the state of nature have any conception of property, as Locke assumes. Property is an abstract social concept. Human beings in their natural state do not have the linguistic abilities to form abstract concepts, nor do they have the social structure necessary to form and implement rules of property. Such beings eat whatever is available when they are hungry and sleep wherever shelter is available when they are tired. Although they differ from other animals in possessing the potential to develop sophisticated language skills, and through them, sophisticated abilities to reason and think abstractly, humans are no more able to think in terms of rights, laws, and property in their prelinguistic natural state than are dogs and cats.

Socialization, Private Property, and the Division of Labor

Such natural human beings are, for all practical purposes, equal. Of course, they have differences. One may be much stronger, another more dexterous, yet another may have perfect pitch. But such inequalities make virtually no difference in the natural state—each wants only to satisfy natural needs, and each spends most of his or her time and resources meeting those needs. With socialization, however, comes language, the tool necessary to develop reason and intelligence. Socialization leads to progressively more complex forms of civil society and progressively greater misery and inequality. The key to the development of civil society, hence of radical inequality and misery, is the development of private property and the division of labor. Thus for Rousseau, Hobbes and Locke could not be more mistaken. Human beings do not leave the state of nature to protect their property, they invent property during the process of socialization. Moreover, human beings do not flee from a natural state of war and misery, they develop from their natural state into a social state of competition and misery.

SOCIALIZATION AND INEQUALITY

Socialization magnifies inequalities. Natural beauty, for instance, is virtually worthless in the natural state, but becomes a great asset in society. Differences in intellect remain merely potential in the natural state, but they become actualized with the development of language. Moreover, socialization leads to the division of labor, and the division of labor further magnifies inequalities. With work divided up into discrete tasks requiring different talents, those with unequal talents excel at tasks which cater to those talents. The beauty that is irrelevant in the state of nature and becomes relevant in society can earn that same person millions as a fashion model in a society with a sophisticated division of labor.

PROPERTY

But although division of labor is necessary, Rousseau suggests in the "Discourse" that the crucial element in the development of civil society is the invention of private property:

> The first person who, having enclosed a plot of land, took it into his head to say *this is mine* and found people simple enough to believe him, was the true founder of civil society. (p. 60)

Rousseau rejects Locke's claim that reason dictates the nature of property rights. According to Locke, mixing one's labor with a thing gives one a property right in that thing. But Rousseau asks, If I build a fence around a field, do I own the ground under the fence, or the ground surrounded by the fence? If I cultivate the land, does such labor entitle me to this harvest, or to all that follow as well? If I pick apples from a tree, does such effort claim the tree as mine? Property and the nature of property rights is not a natural dictate of reason. Rather, it is a social convention exploited by those individuals with unequal advantages through the division of labor to further exacerbate their unequal advantage through the accumulation of assets. The obvious question is why, if property leads to the unequal accumulation of goods in the hands of a few, such a social convention was allowed to develop?

Rousseau's answer is that property is developed as a brilliant con by those who are unequally advantaged to convince the disadvantaged to assist the advantaged in becoming even more advantaged. Those who control much land and wealth convince those who control little that everyone has an equal right to property, specifically to assistance in continuing to control whatever they happen to control. Thus, those who have less are given a right to continue to have less, while those who have more are given a right, enforced by the community, to continue to accumulate more and more. Those who have nothing are thus given a worthless right to continue to have nothing in return for their assistance in securing the ability of those who have everything to continue to have everything. For Rousseau, then, property is not an inalienable natural right, as Locke mistakenly thought, but a social invention, and at its worst, a social scam to perpetuate and exacerbate radical inequality.

INEQUALITY AND MISERY

Because of the division of labor that accompanies socialization, each person is forced to specialize in one or two tasks. Thus, each becomes dependent upon the labor of others to satisfy the entire range of his or her needs. Others will assist you in meeting your needs (for instance, by paying you) only if they perceive you to be of assistance in satisfying their needs. If you are not one of the few who have valued assets, it is thus necessary to appear to have such assets. Moreover, it is necessary to become what others want you to be, whether or not it is what you want to be, in order to interest them in dealing with you. Society has vastly multiplied wants and needs, nor is it any longer a simple business to satisfy even natural needs. Food and shelter, readily at hand in the natural state, now can only be obtained at considerable expense.

Each individual's needs have expanded in society far beyond these natural needs. The ability to satisfy these expanding needs requires an individual to have a good apparent position relative to other individuals, so that others will deal with that individual rather than with others. Thus, each person is naturally led by dependence upon others and expanding needs into a conflict with others for apparent relative position, and the only way one can achieve success in such a struggle is at the expense of others. We are led by socialization into an unending struggle each with all others for apparent relative position. For some to succeed in such a struggle is for most to fail. Since such failure results in failure to satisfiy our wants, and misery is the failure to satisfy one's wants, most of us will be consigned to a miserable existence.

Rousseau has clearly turned the tables on Locke and Hobbes. Property is not a natural right but a social scam. Natural man does not flee away from conflict to society, rather, he becomes embroiled in miserable competition as he becomes more and more socialized. The transformation from natural to civilized beings seems more of a regression that a progression to Rousseau, but it is a regression from which there is no turning back.

THE SOCIAL CONTRACT

In Rousseau's "Discourse on Inequality," he argues that:

> . . . the political state always remained imperfect . . . and, because it had been badly begun, time, in discovering faults and suggesting remedies, could never repair the vices of the constitution. People were continually patching it up, whereas they should have begun by clearing the air and putting aside all the old materials. . . . (p. 71)

In Rousseau's *On The Social Contract*, he undertakes the task recommended in this earlier passage, the task of rethinking the legitimate political state from the ground up. The major shortcoming of the solutions proposed by Hobbes and Locke, Rousseau argues, is that the individual, in order to safeguard his or her self-preservation or right to property, must give up these very rights and goals to an absolute sovereign or to the majority. To secure natural freedom, the individual in the state of nature seems to be required to give up freedom entirely to others. Rousseau suggests in the *On The Social Contract* that these solutions are clearly unacceptable. To be acceptable, a solution must:

> find a form of association which defends and protects with all common forces the person and goods of each associate, and by means of which each one, while uniting with all, nevertheless obeys only himself and remains free as before. . . . (p. 148)

The General Will

Rousseau argues in the *The Social Contract* that the way to accomplish this is by entering into a contract that involves nothing less than "the total alienation of each associate, together with all of his rights, to the entire community." (p. 148) It may seem at first that Rousseau is making the same mistake he identifies in Hobbes and Locke, the mistake of giving up to a sovereign or a majority the very rights and goals the individual is attempting to safeguard. But this is to misinterpret Rousseau's point. To give up rights to Rousseau's sovereign is to give up rights to oneself.

In Locke's political society, the majority ultimately rules, and an individual can disagree with the majority. But on Rousseau's account of a legitimate political system, the society as a whole is the sovereign, and there is a sense in which the individual will never disagree with this sovereign since, as he argues in *On The Social Contract*, "Sovereignty is indivisible . . . either the will is general, or it is not." (p. 154) The sovereign will is a general will, and the general will is indivisible. A majority vote is not acceptable—it merely sets one part of a society against another. Rather, the sovereign will must be a general will free from division. For such a sovereign to will something simply is for each individual to will something. The sovereign's general will is the will of the whole, including, in some sense, all of the individual parts.

But will not individuals often will to act in conflicting ways that resist general agreement? Of course, Rousseau answers, but this is only to point out that the private wills of individuals will often fail to coincide with each other, and with the general will of the sovereign. In such cases, the individual must force him- or herself (or be forced) to act in accordance with the general will and contrary to his or her private will. One must force oneself to do the fair, just, right thing, that which one, as a member of the sovereign body, freely wills, even when this runs contrary to one's own private will. In short, one must force oneself to be free.

LIBERTY AND FREEDOM

What is natural liberty, Rousseau asks, but slavery to appetite? It is moral freedom that we seek. Moral freedom is achieved by developing the capacity to act from the disinterested perspective that we all occupy in our expression of the general will, the perspective in which each person's interests are fairly taken into account without giving preference to others. An action in accordance with the general will rather than with one's private will is thus in some sense an action in accordance with one's better self, one's moral self. Thus, not only do the contractors who alienate themselves and all of their rights to the community remain "free as before," they in fact achieve a greater freedom, moral freedom, where before there was only natural liberty.

A SECOND SENSE OF GENERALITY

The general will is the indivisible will of those who have alienated themselves to the sovereign. But the general will must also be general in a second sense. Not only must the general will be the will of everyone in general, it must be a will that concerns itself with only general matters. The general will can determine, for instance, that anyone who commits murder should be killed, but it cannot determine that a particular murderer should be killed. The reason, Rousseau suggests, is that there would not be a general (i.e., indivisible) will in such particular cases—the murderer, for one, would not will that he be killed. But although a murderer will not will to die after committing a crime, Rousseau contends in *On The Social Contract* that at the time of the initial contract such a future murderer will surely recognize the acceptability of the general rule that "in order to avoid being the victim of an assassin . . . a person consents to die, were he to become one." (p. 159) Rousseau then supports this claim by arguing that:

> Far from disposing of his own life, one thinks only of guaranteeing it. And it cannot be presumed that any of the contracting parties is then planning to get himself hanged. (p. 159)

This second sense of the generality of the general will guarantees that although the sovereign can legitimately legislate general laws, it cannot execute those laws in particular cases. Clearly, it will be necessary to have a separate executive whose function is to implement the dictates of the general will in such particular cases. Moreover, although the general will always wills to establish the right laws, Rousseau suggests that the judgment that guides such a will is not always enlightened. It wills the best, but it is clearly incapable of determining what the best is.

THE LEGISLATOR

Rousseau argues that discovering what the best rules are requires a superior intelligence. He thus recognizes the need for an ideal legislator of superior intelligence. The legislator would recommend laws, but would always be required to obtain the consent of the sovereign general will for the adoption of the laws that he recommends. Such a legislator must often have recourse to appeals to divine authority and other rhetorical devices to convince the sovereign to consent to the best laws.

CRITICISMS

Rousseau's general will is simultaneously one of the most elusive and one of the most suggestive concepts in political thought, past or present. Our present notions of justice and fairness, and our conviction that anyone, regardless of their particular circumstances, ought to be able to determine what is generally fair and ought to act fairly resonate with Rousseau's claim that a sovereign body can indivisibly manifest a general will to which individuals ought to conform their actions. But Rousseau's proposal for a political system built upon the general will gives rise to serious difficulties.

Problems with the Legislator

First, Rousseau creates a radical separation of the legislative and executive functions. He is not at all clear how the executor of the general will is to be held accountable to the sovereignty of the people. Second, Rousseau concedes that although the sovereign people, manifesting the general will, will always want to do the right thing, they will not be able to determine what the right thing is. His answer to this difficulty is the ideal legislator, who must win the consent of the sovereign people, by whatever means possible, to the best legislation that can be willed. But a sovereign people who cannot determine which rules are best surely cannot be expected to distinguish a benevolent ideal legislator from a malicious despot—they will easily be led astray.

Moreover, Rousseau grants that the sovereign people cannot recognize the real reasons why the best legislation is the best; they must be made to consent through appeal to whatever reasons are necessary. But clearly, if the general will can readily be led to endorse the right laws for the wrong reasons, it can be led to endorse the wrong laws for the wrong reasons. The functioning of Rousseau's legitimate political system can seem to depend upon two almost miraculous occurrences—the existence of an executive power that faithfully implements the rules formulated by the general will without usurping the role of the sovereign and the existence of an all-knowing, all-benevolent ideal legislator who is willing to guide the general will, and from whom the sovereign body is willing to take counsel.

Consent

At root, these difficulties stem from Rousseau's loss of faith in the ability of average citizens to judge how best to implement the general will. Locke and Hobbes assume that the consent of individuals to the contract and to the laws implemented under the terms of that contract is, by and large, informed consent. Rousseau assumes that the sovereign body is not capable of informed consent to the laws that will govern them. The ideal legislator is required to obtain the consent of the sovereign, but Rousseau claims that the sovereign body is incapable of understanding the issues relevant to the formulation of legislation. Hence, the sovereign body is incapable of informed consent. This conclusion that human beings in society are incapable of determining their true interests has a profound effect upon later political thought. Nowhere are its effects more profound than in the social and political philosophy of Karl Marx.

Selected Readings

Green, T. H. *Lectures on the Principles of Political Obligation.* London: Longmans, Green & Co., 1950.

Rapaczynski, A. *Nature and Politics: Liberalism in the Philosophies of Hobbes, Locke, and Rousseau.* Ithaca: Cornell University Press, 1987.

Rousseau, J. J. *The Basic Political Writings*, including "Discourse on the Origin of Inequality" and *On The Social Contract.* Indianapolis: Hackett, 1987. (All citations of "Origins of Inequality" and *On The Social Contract* in this chapter are of this edition.)

21

Hume's Moral Theory

Hume presents his moral philosophy in its most comprehensive form in his A Treatise of Human Nature, *but he continued to reformulate aspects of this account throughout his life in various essays and in his* An Enquiry Concerning the Principles of Morals. *In some cases, certain aspects of Hume's account have been substantially altered in the reformulations (e.g., his account of justice in the* Enquiry). *Despite these many reformulations, the main aspects of Hume's moral philosophy as articulated in the* Treatise *remain remarkably constant throughout his work.*

OVERVIEW

Hume launches an attack upon traditional accounts of morality and in particular upon what he takes to be two central assumptions of these accounts:

1. Morality is grounded in human reason.

2. Such reason motivates us to act in accordance with morality and contrary to our desires and other passions.

Morality cannot be grounded in reason, Hume argues, because morality motivates people to act, and reason has no capacity to motivate people to act. Only feelings, desires, and other passions motivate people to act, hence morality must be grounded, not in reason, but in desires and other passions.

Moral conflicts are not conflicts between reason and desire, they are conflicts between the feelings and desires that motivate us to act morally and the feelings and desires that do not. What we do in a particular case depends entirely upon which of our desires and feelings are stronger. The merits of such a view and the consequences of its adoption are issues that dominate the pages of philosophy journals even today.

REASON AND THE PASSIONS

Evidence for this view, Hume suggests, results from a careful look at the distinction between desires and other passions, on the one hand, and ideas, on the other. Hume labels the desires and other passions "impressions of reflection," whereas ideas are the beliefs arising from "impressions of sensation." Impressions of reflection—desires and other passions—clearly motivate us to act. To desire a cheeseburger is to be motivated to get one, and to be angry at a person is to be motivated to act towards that person in certain characteristic ways. However, desires and other passions, Hume argues, cannot be true or false, because they are, in his words, "original existences," rather than "copies." Beliefs, the ideas arising from impressions of sensation, are not in this respect original existences. Unlike desires and other passions, they are copies. A belief is true if it accurately copies the way things really are, and it is false if it does not. A belief that Boston is north of New York is true because such a belief accurately represents, or copies, the way things really are. A belief that Washington D.C. is north of New York is false because such a belief does not accurately represent the way things really are. But desires and other passions are not copies of the way things are; they are original motivating reactions to the way things are. Thus, desires and other passions cannot be good copies (true) or bad copies (false). Desires and other passions can motivate but are original existences that cannot be true or false. Beliefs are not original existences—they are copies that can be true or false. But unlike desires, such beliefs cannot motivate; instead they copy, or represent, the world that desires and other passions motivate us to change. Thus, desires are not true or false, but do motivate; beliefs are true or false, but do not motivate.

Reason

Hume suggests, moreover, that reason is just the discovery of the truth and falsehood of beliefs. Roughly, it is unreasonable to maintain a belief if it can readily be shown to be false and reasonable to maintain a belief that can be shown to be true. Since desires cannot be true or false, they clearly also cannot be reasonable or unreasonable. Moreover, since reason is the discovery of the truth and falsity of beliefs, and beliefs cannot motivate, it seems to follow that reason cannot motivate people to act. Only desires and other passions can motivate, but reason deals with beliefs rather than with such desires and passions, hence reason cannot motivate. Moreover, since only desires and other passions can motivate, the only source of motivation to act contrary to a particular desire or passion has to be another desire or passion.

Objections Considered

Before moving on to the implications of this account of reason and desires/passions for morality, it will perhaps be helpful to consider certain obvious objections to Hume's account of reason and the passions. First, the claim that reason does not motivate can seem false. Surely if reason informs you that there is a bear in the clearing, you are motivated to leave! True, Hume replies, but only because you have a desire not to be mauled by a bear, a fear of bears, etc. If you did have a desire to be mauled by a bear, then you would be motivated to remain in the clearing with the same belief. It is not reason, the discovery of true and false beliefs, that is doing the motivating in such a case: You are motivated differently even though your belief in each case is the same. Clearly, it is the different desires, to be mauled or to avoid being mauled, that motivate in such cases. Second, it may be objected that the claim that desires and other passions cannot be reasonable and unreasonable must be false. You may, for instance, desire to eat a poisonous piece of fruit which you mistakenly believe to be edible. Is this not an unreasonable desire? Again, Hume argues that it is not the desire that is unreasonable, it is the belief that the fruit is edible. The desire is simply a reaction, itself neither reasonable nor unreasonable, to an unreasonable belief.

Hume's Conclusion Concerning Reason

Hume's conclusion in the *Treatise*, then, is that desires cannot be reasonable or unreasonable:

> 'Tis not contrary to reason to prefer the destruction of the whole world to the scratching of my finger . . . (p. 416)

Moreover, reason cannot motivate. What, then, is the relationship of reason to desire? Clearly, each of us has many desires and passions, and we want to satisfy as many of them as possible in the most effective manner possible. Reason, it seems, is best understood as a tool the use of which will allow us to determine the most effective means to whatever ends our sentiments and other passions lead us to desire. If you want a cheeseburger, reason allows you to determine the most effective means for achieving this end, for example, going to the nearest fast food restaurant. Moreover, reason helps to avoid less effective means, for instance, buying and butchering a cow. Thus, reason is the tool that allows us to act more effectively on our passions and desires, whatever those passions and desires happen to be. Hume concludes that properly understood, "Reason is, and ought only to be the slave of the passions. . . . " (*Treatise*, p. 415)

MORALITY AND THE
GROUNDS OF MORALITY

Recall that Hume claims that morality cannot be grounded in reason. Given the account of reason and the passions presented in the previous section, it is clear why Hume takes this to be the case. Hume takes his arguments to have established that reason cannot motivate people to action. But Hume notes in the *Treatise* that "morals excite passions, and produce or prevent actions." (p. 457) Nothing could be more common than the fact that when one recognizes that a particular action violates a moral rule, one is motivated not to perform the action. But since reason cannot motivate, and morality clearly can, Hume concludes that the rules of morality are not conclusions of our reason. Moreover, since morality can motivate, it not only cannot be grounded in reason, it must be grounded in certain of the agent's sentiments that give rise to the desire to act morally. This is the only acceptable explanation of the motivating force of morality. Thus, when moral duty motivates a person to act contrary to his selfish desires, what occurs is a conflict ultimately between certain moral sentiments that lead the person to desire to act morally and certain feelings that lead the person to desire to act contrary to the dictates of morality. Neither course of action is in itself reasonable or unreasonable, and what the person will do in such a case will be determined largely by how strong his or her conflicting desires and passions happen to be.

Moral Sentiment

Morality, Hume argues, is grounded in certain particular feelings that people have, sentiments that generate the desire to act morally. In particular, moral goodness and virtue are manifested by the occurrence of a feeling of satisfaction or pleasure of a particular kind, and moral depravity and vice are manifested by the occurrence of a pain or feeling of disapprobation of a particular kind. Specifically, moral feelings or sentiments are those sentiments of pleasure and pain that cause us to praise in the case of pleasure and condemn in the case of pain. In the case of some moral virtues, such as justice, these moral feelings have arisen entirely through human artifice. In the case of other virtues, such as generosity, these feelings arise through the natural constitution of human beings.

Hume identifies human sympathy as the cause of many of these natural sentiments. Although human beings are motivated largely by feelings of self-love and the resulting desires to further their own interests, human beings also have a natural sympathy, which causes them to feel pain when confronted with the pain of others and pleasure when confronted with the pleasure of others. Much as the plucking of one string on a guitar starts up sympathetic vibrations in other strings, the pain and pleasure of others causes sympathetic pain and pleasure in us. We alleviate that pain in ourselves by alleviating its source, the pain in others. This human sympathy motivates us to demonstrate and approve as virtuous those qualities of human character and action, such as generosity and humanity, that tend to the benefit of other human beings. Sympathy also motivates us to praise as virtuous those human qualities the possession of which conduces to the best interest of society generally, qualities such as temperance and industry. Of course, we have greater sympathy for those closer to us than we do for those who are not our direct concern. The arrest of a friend of mine causes me more pain than does the arrest of a total stranger. But this does not prevent us from developing certain steady points of view that correct for such biases, allowing us to evaluate the characters and actions of others as virtuous or vicious, whether they are close to us or complete strangers.

JUSTICE

Hume follows Hobbes by arguing that justice is an artificial virtue. But on Hume's account, justice arises not through contract, but through convention. In the *Treatise*, Hume's account of the origin of justice is straightforward. Each human being needs society in order to secure the goods that he or she requires to survive and prosper. It is each person's selfish interests that are the force driving him or her into human society. But this very motive that leads each individual into society, the selfish pursuit of goods, also leads each away from society, since others in society can readily unite to deprive a person of his or her goods. Human beings develop conventions of justice as a means of overcoming this obstacle to societal cooperation, thereby making mutually beneficial social cooperation possible. No contract is needed since we are led naturally by our circumstances to establish the conventions of justice, much as two people in a two-person rowboat will naturally each take up an oar and row, the alternative is each merely going in circles.

The conventions of justice establish a system of rules for the acquisition and protection of goods, that is, of property. Thus, the motive to justice is entirely the self-interest of the individuals who will benefit from the social cooperation that justice makes possible. It is justice that eliminates the obstacle—the threat posed by others to a person's goods—that blocks the formation of mutually beneficial human society. Justice is the artifice that human beings develop to make human society possible, in order to derive the considerable benefits of such society. It may be wondered why, on this account, justice has anything to do with morality; it appears to derive entirely from selfish sentiments. Hume's answer is that justice clearly conduces to the public benefit. And though individuals are not led by moral sentiments to establish the conventions of justice, they are led by their sympathy for those who are harmed by injustice, and by their sympathetic approval of anything which conduces to the public benefit, to develop moral sentiments of approval for just characters and actions, and sentiments of disapproval for unjust characters and actions.

Justice in the Enquiry

Hume's account of justice appears to be confronted with a serious difficulty. Hume claims that our selfish interests are the origin of justice, yet clearly, in particular cases it is in our selfish interests to act unjustly. The very motive that leads to the establishment of general rules of justice would appear to lead to the continual violation of justice in particular cases. Nor will it do to point out that you will be punished if you are caught; this only shows that if you are to be an unjust knave, you must be a sensible knave, who only acts unjustly when there is no danger of getting caught. Hume attempts to respond to this challenge to his account of justice, but his response is not entirely convincing. It is thus interesting that in Hume's subsequent discussions of the origin of justice, in the *Enquiry* for example, he downplays the role of self-interest and emphasizes instead the role of utility. Justice, Hume argues, comes about as a result of the social utility, or usefulness, of such a set of conventions governing property. And although self-love motivates us in large part to adopt what is socially useful, our sympathetic love of others also motivates us to adopt conventions that benefit those with whom we associate. This account of justice may allow Hume to explain more effectively why we will not all be sensible knaves. Whereas the selfish sentiments that lead to justice may in particular cases lead us away from just actions, the sympathetic sentiments that also lead us to justice may lead us to resist our selfish tendencies in such cases and to persist in acting justly.

HUME'S SUBJECTIVISM

One consequence of Hume's grounding of morality in moral sentiment rather than reason is his apparent subjectivism. There are at least three different aspects of Hume's subjectivism.

Rational Subjectivism

The first can be termed Hume's rational subjectivism. It has already been demonstrated that for Hume, sentiments and the desires and actions that result from them cannot ultimately be reasonable or unreasonable. To be rationally justified in claiming that an action is the moral action to perform in a given situation is to demonstrate that it is an action that effectively gives expression to our moral sentiments, sentiments that are not themselves reasonable or unreasonable. What is it, however, to demonstrate that an action is a reasonable action for any particular person to perform? Since the person's sentiments and corresponding desires are not themselves reasonable or unreasonable, his or her actions are reasonable as long as they are effective means of satisfying the individual's own subjective desires and passions, whatever these happen to be. Thus, whether it is reasonable for a person to act morally in a particular case depends upon whether or not acting morally is the most effective means of satisfying his or her own subjective desires. There is no objective justification—justification that no rational person can reasonably reject—for acting morally. Whatever justification there will be for acting morally depends upon the relative strengths of the various sentiments and desires that an agent happens to have, hence rational subjectivism. Consider again Hume's claim that it is not contrary to reason to prefer the destruction of the world to the scratching of one's little finger. It is certainly wrong to destroy the world, countless lives, etc., just to avoid scratching your finger, but Hume's rational subjectivism appears to commit him to saying that it may be reasonable for a particular subject to do what is wrong.

Linguistic Subjectivism

A second form of subjectivism often attributed to Hume can be termed linguistic subjectivism because it focuses upon moral language. We typically take moral statements to differ greatly in meaning from statements about our respective feelings and desires. Thus, the statement "Murder is wrong," we assume, means something very different from the statement "I am led by certain of my desires and feelings to disapprove of unprovoked killing." The first states an objective moral fact; the second states a fact about my own subjective state of mind. But Hume appears at points in the *Treatise* to suggest that the claim "Murder is wrong" means just the same thing as the claim "I am led by certain of my desires and feelings to disapprove of murder":

> When you pronounce any action or character to be vicious, you
> mean nothing, but that from the constitution of your nature you have
> a feeling or sentiment of blame from the contemplation of it. (p. 469)

Thus for Hume, moral statements of fact seem to turn out to *mean* the same as statements about my subjective feelings.

Metaphysical Subjectivism

A third aspect of Hume's subjectivism can be termed his metaphysical subjectivism. When you assert that a table is round, you ascribe a property, roundness, to an object, a table. Similarly, when you assert that an action, say willful murder, is vicious, it seems that you ascribe a property, viciousness, to the action, murder. But Hume suggests in the *Treatise* that the latter case differs significantly from the former:

> Take any action allow'd to be vicious: Wilful murder, for instance. Examine it in all lights, and see if you can find that matter of fact, or real existence, which you call vice. In which-ever way you take it, you find only certain passions, motives, volitions, and thoughts. There is no other matter of fact in the case. The vice entirely escapes you . . . till you turn your reflex into your own breast, and find a sentiment of disapprobation, which arises in you, towards the action. (p. 468)

Hume is arguing that there is no viciousness, or wrongness, or rightness, in the world. Rather, these are feelings of disapprobation that arise in me when confronted with certain events in the world. Thus, viciousness is not, like roundness, an objective property in the world, it is rather a subjective reaction to non-moral objective occurrence in the world. We are led into error on this point because human beings tend to *project* value onto actions, much as a movie camera projects images onto the screen. The viciousness is really a reaction on my part to events that take place in the world, but I project it onto the world as a property of those events. There is a fact, but it is not a fact about a moral property in the world, it is a fact about one of my psychological states. In this respect, Hume takes moral properties to be similar to color properties. Hume believed, as many scientists still do, that objects in the world are not really colored. Rather, objects merely absorb and reflect different frequencies of light waves (in our science, not Hume's), and different animals' minds supply different colors corresponding to different frequencies of these light waves. Colors are not in the world, they are in the mind. Yet animals see colors as being in the world. The explanation offered is that human animals project colors onto the world, much as they project values onto the world.

Subjectivity Summarized

Hume's rational subjectivism maintains that there are no justifications of moral actions that can be grounded in anything other than the desires and sentiments of a particular subject. The linguistic subjectivism sometimes attributed to him maintains that there are no moral statements that cannot be reduced to statements about the desires and feelings of particular human subjects. His metaphysical subjectivism maintains that there are no moral facts that cannot be reduced to facts about human subjective desires and feelings. Each of these aspects of Hume's subjectivism is controversial (including whether he actually maintains some of them) and in certain respects counterintuitive. Yet, each can seem to follow more or less straightforwardly from Hume's compelling account of reason and the passions, and their relationship to morality.

COMMENTS AND CRITICISMS

Values and Colors

There are many sources of difficulty with Hume's views. One such difficulty Hume brings upon himself, with his projectivist analogy between value properties and color properties. Assume Hume is right that human beings project colors onto the world. There nonetheless seem to be everyday facts of the matter concerning whether, for instance, this page is black or white. It is true that the page is white and false that it is black. In short, whether or not colors are projected properties, there appear to be objective standards for colors, and those who hold beliefs that violate these objective standards hold beliefs that are false and unreasonable. Similarly, even if value properties such as viciousness are projected by people onto actions, there seems to be a fact of the matter about whether or not a murder is vicious. Just as there are objective standards for colors that we project onto the world, are there not objective standards for values that we project onto the world, such that those who disagree about such issues have moral beliefs that are false and unreasonable? Hume actually presents such an argument for the existence of objective standards of taste, for example, of beauty, in his remarkable essay "The Standards of Taste." But if Hume's account of beauty as grounded in the sentiments allows for objective standards of beauty, then why does not Hume's account of morality as grounded in the sentiments allow for objective standards of morality?

Truth and Reasonableness

There is yet another aspect of Hume's subjectivism that seems deeply problematic. For Hume, to say that the mass-murderer Charles Manson acted immorally is to say that we have a sentiment of disapproval regarding what Charles Manson did, a sentiment which leads us to be outraged by what he did. There appear to be two problems with such an account. First, is it not the case that we are outraged because what Manson did is wrong, not that it is wrong because we are outraged? If this is the case, then Hume has gotten the story exactly backwards. Second, Manson himself was not outraged by what he did, and Hume appears to concede that on his account of reason, Manson may have been acting rationally. But can we put someone to death or imprison them for trying to effectively satisfy their desires and sentiments simply because those desires and sentiments happen to be different, or simply differing in strength, from our own? It seems to be of crucial importance to us that Manson's sentiments were not only different, and such as to give rise to disapproval in us (our sentiments, after all, may well give rise to disapproval in Manson), but were moreover *unreasonable* sentiments, sentiments that he can thus be blamed for acting upon. Thus, although Hume is clearly right that desires and other passions cannot be true or false, we seem deeply committed to holding that they can nonetheless be reasonable or unreasonable, and in a way that cannot be explained away as the unreasonableness of related beliefs. It is reservations such as these that Kant develops into a deep critique of Hume's moral philosophy.

*D*espite these and many other puzzles concerning Hume's moral philosophy, the central claim put forward by Hume seems to many today as obvious as it did to Hume then. If morality motivates, and beliefs and reasoning about beliefs do not, then any acceptable account of morality, it seems, must be grounded not in our reason but in our sentiments and the desires and other passions to which they give rise.

Selected Readings

Baier, A. *A Progress of Sentiments.* Cambridge, MA: Harvard University Press, 1991.

Flew, A. *David Hume, Philosopher of Moral Science.* New York: Blackwell, 1986.

Hume, D. *A Treatise of Human Nature.* Oxford: Clarendon Press, 1978. (All *Treatise* citations in this chapter are of this edition.)

22

Kant's Moral Theory

David Hume begins his account of morality by demonstrating that morality cannot be grounded in reason, and concludes that it must be grounded in the passions—desires and sentiments—instead. Kant begins his account of morality by demonstrating that morality cannot be grounded in desires, sentiments and other passions—in Kant's terminology, inclinations—and concludes that morality must be grounded in reason instead. Indeed, Kant goes a step further, arguing that anyone who believes that morality is grounded in inclination, Hume for instance, is mistaken in the conviction that he or she is doing moral philosophy at all. Such a person is mistaking the study of practical anthropology for the study of morality. In segments of his Critique of Pure Reason, *as well as in his* Foundations of the Metaphysics of Morals *and his* Critique of Practical Reason, *Kant attempts to demonstrate how real moral philosophy is done. The most accessible presentation of his moral philosophy occurs in his* Groundwork of The Metaphysic of Morals, *in which Kant analyzes two concepts that play a crucial role in morality, the concepts of freedom and duty.*

DUTY

The Argument From Inclination   Each of us, Kant points out, has a sense of duty. Moreover, we realize that the only actions that have moral worth are actions that persons perform not merely *in accordance with* duty, but *from* duty. What is this distinction? Kant identifies people acting merely in accordance with duty as those who perform moral actions because they want to—because performing such actions satisfies their natural desires and inclinations. Such people, Kant argues, are motivated to act in exactly the same way as are those who perform immoral actions. People who act immorally perform the actions they do because they want to—because performing such actions satisfies their natural inclinations. The difference between people who act morally because they happen to want to and those who act immorally because they happen to want to is merely a difference between the situations they happen to be in and the inclinations they happen, by nature, to have.

The person who gives to the poor because it gives him or her pleasure is motivated in exactly the same way as is the person who spends everything on him- or herself because it gives him or her pleasure. Each is motivated by the desire for pleasure. But just as the person who spends everything on him- or herself because it gives him or her pleasure deserves no moral credit, so the person who spends much of his or her money on others because it gives him or her pleasure deserves no moral credit. Each is simply doing whatever he or she happens to be naturally inclined to do. It just so happens that what one is naturally inclined to do is what a moral person would do in that situation, and the other is not so inclined. Clearly if it is a person's inclinations—desires, sentiments, and passions—that motivate him or her to act morally, such actions can have no moral worth.

Note the results of this argument for an account of morality such as that offered by Hume. Since for Hume everyone acts only from his or her inclinations, and Kant claims to have shown that actions motivated by inclination never have moral worth, it follows that if Hume were right, no one's actions could ever have moral worth—no one would ever merit praise or blame for what he or she does. If people do perform actions that have moral worth, and Kant is right that such actions cannot be motivated by inclination, then Hume must be wrong in claiming that only inclination motivates us to action. This is precisely what Kant will argue.

Reason and Motivation

The beginning of Kant's account of why Hume is wrong—his argument that reason can motivate—can be discovered in his analysis of what is involved in acting, not merely in accordance with duty, but *from* duty. What makes an action morally worthy is clearly not *what* the person does—the person acting merely in accordance with duty performs the same action—but *why* the person does what he or she does. The person who acts from duty is motivated to perform the action he or she does not because he or she is inclined to, but because it is the right thing to do—because it is commanded by morality. It is not people who do the right thing because it satisfies their wants whose actions have moral worth. Rather, it is those persons who are motivated to do the right thing because it is the right thing who are acting *from* duty, and whose actions are deserving of moral praise. This is why Kant opens the *Groundwork* with the claim that the only thing that is good unconditionally is a good will. A good will is a will that motivates a person to do the right thing because it is the right thing. It is this good will, this good motivation, that is the source of whatever moral worth an action has.

Moreover, Kant points out that each of us is aware, for the most part, of what duty requires. Do not lie. Do not break promises. Do not murder. Do not steal. Even the most dimwitted of us recognizes that these are the dictates of morality, and that they are binding upon everyone regardless of his or her particular inclinations. Morality does not command us not to steal if we do not want to; it commands us not to steal regardless of what we want to do. To perform an action with moral worth is to peform an action because it is so commanded. These universal and objective commands of duty clearly do not arise from natural inclination, which can vary from subject to subject. Rather, they are dictated to us by reason. It is in virtue of being rational beings that we are aware of the moral commands. Indeed, Kant maintains that reason itself provides us with a test that readily determines, for any proposed rule of conduct, or maxim, whether it is a moral rule. Following a rule because it is a moral rule, that is, out of respect for the moral law dictated by reason (regardless of our inclinations), is what gives an action moral worth. Note that Kant is arguing that a condition for any action's having moral worth is that it must be motivated by reason rather than desire—a possibility which Hume, Hobbes, and many others since them have denied.

The Categorical Imperative

Reason supplies a test to determine whether any particular action is a moral action. The test first requires a person to determine the rule that his proposed action will be in accordance with. Thus, you are considering breaking a promise that you made, because it is convenient to do so. The rule (or in Kant's terminology, the "maxim") that you are acting in accordance with is thus the rule that promises can be broken whenever it is convenient to do so. Reason supplies the following test of the morality of any such maxim. If you can consistently act in accordance with the maxim, and at the same time will the maxim to be a universal law for all to follow, then actions in accordance with such a maxim will be moral actions. To the extent that such actions are motivated by respect for the dictates of reason as manifested in this test, they will have moral worth. The way of determining whether a maxim can consistently be willed to be a universal law is straightforward. The question reason asks you is: Can you consistently will to act in accordance with the maxim that you are proposing to act in accordance with and will that everyone else act in accordance with this maxim too? Assume then that your maxim of breaking promises when convenient is universalized, that everyone breaks their promises whenever it is beneficial to do so. Clearly, Kant claims, you can not benefit from breaking your promise in such a situation.

TWO INTERPRETATIONS OF THE CATEGORICAL IMPERATIVE

Kant seems to have one of two things in mind here. It may be that he thinks that in such a situation, it would be *logically* impossible to break a promise, because promises are by definition agreements that one must keep even if it is not convenient to do so. Hence in a situation in which no one kept a promise unless it was convenient to do so, there would be no promises. It may also be that he thinks that in such a situation, it would be *practically* impossible to benefit from breaking your promise. If everyone broke promises whenever it was convenient to do so, then no one would expect anyone else to keep their promises. But the only way you can benefit from breaking a promise is if someone made such a promise expecting you to keep it, and you disappointed their expectation. Given the assumption that no one ever expects you to keep a promise unless it is convenient to do so, no one will never accept a promise from you unless he or she believes it is convenient for you to honor it. On either interpretation, Kant's point is clear. Reason demands consistency, and the only way that one can break a promise when it is beneficial to do so is if one inconsistently acts in accordance with a rule that one realizes other similarly situated people cannot at the same time act in accordance with. Indeed, to benefit from breaking a promise one must make oneself an exception to the rule that others are following, namely, "keep your promises even when it is not beneficial to do so." The test sketched above is an implementation of the command, generated by pure practical reason, that each agent act only "in such a way that I can also will that my maxim should become a universal law." (*Groundwork*, p. 70) Kant labels this command the categorical imperative.

Kinds of Imperatives

This may all seem a bit fishy. After all, did Hume not demonstrate that reason cannot ground morality, and did he not prove that reason functions as a tool or an instrument for satisfying desires and inclinations? How can Kant reconcile his claims that reason itself gives moral commands and motivates us to act in accordance with these commands to Hume's arguments purporting to establish that reason cannot motivate at all? Kant agrees with Hume that many of the commands of reason (in Kant's terminology, "imperatives") are commands that tell us the most effective means of satisfying particular inclinations. These are commands that are binding upon us, hence capable of motivating us, only if we happen to have the relevant inclination.

But Kant disagrees with Hume's assumption that these hypothetical commands are the only commands of reason. If they were, then no actions would have moral worth; the commands of reason would only be telling us the most effective means to satisfy our inclinations, and the force of the commands would originate, not in reason itself, but in the inclinations that reason is telling us how best to satisfy. Kant maintains that in addition to such commands of reason that are conditional on the presence of a particular inclination, there are other commands that are not conditional upon having a particular inclination. These commands, unconditioned by any desire/inclination, are commands of pure reason, commands that do not depend upon what a particular person wants. They are commands that are binding no matter what a particular person wants. These commands Kant labels categorical imperatives; they are precisely those commands that pass the categorical imperative test sketched above. Thus, although "eat beets" is an unconditional command, it is not a categorical imperative that will pass the categorical imperative test. Only such unconditional commands as "do not lie" and "do not murder" will pass this test. Moral commands are precisely those categorical imperatives that pass the test of the categorical imperative, the test that shows them to be dictated by pure practical reason unconditioned by any inclination. Actions that have moral worth are precisely those actions that are motivated by respect for the moral law, the categorical imperatives dictated by pure practical reason in the form of the test dictated by *the* categorical imperative.

Autonomy and "Ends-in-Themselves"

Kant's point can be put in a somewhat different way. A being who can only act so as to satisfy its natural inclinations can neither be praised nor blamed for what it does. Such a being is a slave to natural inclinations, just as for Hume reason itself is a slave to passions. Such a being cannot be praised for acting in accordance with duty, or blamed for acting contrary to duty. In each case, it can do nothing but what it is inclined to do, and nature has determined what she is inclined to do. A being of this kind can only treat other beings as means to the satisfaction of its own inclinations. Moreover, it can only treat itself as a means to the satisfaction of its own natural inclinations. If it is inclined to kill itself or others, then it cannot but do so.

Kant's point is that we are not such beings motivated only by inclination, beings who can treat ourselves and others only as means to satisfying our inclinations whatever they happen to be. Rather, we are motivated as well by reason, and reason commands us to treat ourselves not as means only, but as ends. Thus, commands of reason are commands that rational beings give themselves, commands that forbid them to treat themselves as means only. The command not to lie, for instance, prevents me from using others, by lying to them, as means for accomplishing what I desire. A will that is motivated by reason is thus an autonomous will, a will motivated by a command that I give to myself. A will that is motivated by inclination is what Kant labels a heteronomous will, a will motivated by a command that derives its force from outside of us, from the inclinations that nature has given to us.

Only rational beings with autonomous wills are persons, ends-in-themselves capable of treating others as ends-in-themselves, rather than mere things such as rocks and cows. Cows are beings that can only do what they are inclined by nature to do; we are persons, "ends-in-themselves" capable of acting in accordance with laws that we give to ourselves, even when such laws conflict with the dictates of natural inclination. Only such rational beings are persons with unconditional value (dignity) rather than things with merely conditional value (price). Rational beings autonomously command themselves, in the form of the categorical imperative, to treat themselves and others not merely as means to the satisfaction of their natural inclinations, but as "ends-in-themselves." Thus Kant presents the following as an alternative formulation of the categorical imperative:

> Act in such a way that you always treat humanity, whether in your own person or in the person of any other, never simply as a means, but always at the same time as an end. (*Groundwork*, p. 96)

FREEDOM

All of the above components of Kant's account have arisen from his analysis of our sense of moral duty. In the third section of the *Groundwork*, Kant reinforces and deepens his account with an analysis of our sense of freedom. We believe that we have free wills, that we make the choices that we do in a way that is not determined by outside causes. Indeed, it is hard to imagine how we can make choices unless we think there are at least two different things it is in our power to do, even given the outside forces that have shaped us. A person who is thrown out of a window does not choose to fall; he or she simply falls. This is because the person has no choice; the laws of nature cause him or her to fall regardless of his or her choices. But a being that can be motivated only by inclination, Kant suggests, is no more free to choose than is the person thrown from the window. Such a being's inclinations are determined to be what they are by nature, in accordance with natural laws, and the actions of such a being are caused by its inclinations. Thus, its actions are determined by natural forces outside of itself—it is not free.

Freedom and the Moral Law

But although such a being whose behavior is entirely dependent upon outside causes is not free, neither is behavior free that is not dependent upon any causes. Imagine what such a truly uncaused action would be like. Suddenly, completely to my surprise and for no reason, I find myself striking out at the person next to me. Such an action may be uncaused, but it clearly is not an action that I have freely chosen to do, hence that I am responsible for doing. Nor is a will free that is entirely dependent upon more than one outside cause; it is merely determined to act in accordance with the strongest of the forces external to it. A free will, then, must be caused, but must be capable of willing independently of outside causes. A free will must be determined in accordance with laws, since this is what it is to be caused, but it must be capable of determining itself to act independently of natural laws, such as those that determine our inclinations. But the only law that we autonomously give to ourselves, unconditioned by inclination, is the moral law dictated by reason in the form of the categorical imperative. Kant concludes that the only way that we can have free wills, which we cannot help but believe we do (every time we make a choice), is if we are capable of determining our wills in accordance with the moral law which we, as rational beings, autonomously give to ourselves.

Freedom of the will presupposes the capacity to will to act from the moral laws dictated by reason in the form of the categorical imperative and contrary to inclination as manifested in hypothetical imperatives. This does not demonstrate why we should choose to act in accordance with the moral law, nor is it clear how such a practical necessity can be reconciled with the fact that we appear to be caused to do what we do by the natural forces that have shaped us. Nor has Kant demonstrated how reason can motivate us, but only that in order to be able to act from duty, hence to choose freely, we must be capable of determining our will, or motivating ourselves, to act in accordance with reason.

COMMENTS AND CRITICISMS

Reason and Motivation Reconsidered

Kant attempts to demonstrate that in order to be free persons capable of acting from duty, as we take ourselves to be, we must be capable of being motivated entirely from reason. How this can occur is a great difficulty for Kant's account, especially in light of Hume's arguments. If, for instance, reason motivates the will by giving rise to an inclination to follow it—a solution some take to be suggested by Kant's remarks about the moral feeling and motivation to act out of respect for the moral law—then reason appears to be no more than one among a person's inclinations, much as Hume's moral sentiment is. What Kant has in mind is clearly more subtle than this, but whether it can ultimately avoid Hume's criticisms is not clear.

Problems with the Categorical Imperative

A second set of difficulties with Kant's moral philosophy surrounds the categorical imperative. There are, in all, three different versions of the categorical imperative (only the first two have been discussed above). But none of them appears to be equivalent to the others. These reformulations, then, may turn out to be subtle but important alterations in Kant's position. Moreover, the first version of the categorical imperative, the test for maxims, does not appear to establish the morality of the rules that even Kant takes for granted as moral rules. It is clear enough how the test works in cases such as promising and lying, but Kant's efforts to demonstrate that the test prohibits suicide and commands benevolence to others seem to involve misapplications of his own test. This appears to leave Kant with two choices. Either suicide is not wrong and benevolence is not right, because they fail the test of the categorical imperative, or suicide is wrong and benevolence is right, and Kant has gotten the wrong test.

Puzzles About Freedom

The problems with Kant's account of freedom are also immense. The account can be read as suggesting, for instance, that we are only free when there is a moral component to our choices, since only in such cases do we have an alternative offered by the moral law to oppose our inclinations. Moreover, even if Kant is right that a person is only free if he or she is capable of acting in accordance with the moral law, it is still not clear why the person should freely choose to do so. Kant's efforts to answer these questions require appeals to aspects of his metaphysics and epistemology that have proved to be particularly problematic.

*D*espite all these problems, Kant's stands as a compelling and in many respects persuasive argument that on any account of morality that takes moral duty and human freedom seriously, reason cannot simply be a slave to the passions. Rather, reason itself must provide the tools for determining whether actions in accordance with desires and passions are justified or unjustified.

Selected Readings

Allison, H. *Kant's Theory of Freedom.* Cambridge: Cambridge University Press, 1990.

Herman, B. *Morality as Rationality: A Study of Kant's Ethics.* New York: Garland Press, 1990.

Kant, I. *Groundwork of the Metaphysic of Morals.* New York: Harper and Row, 1964. (All citations of the *Groundwork* in the text are of the edition.)

O'Neill, O. *Constructions of Reason: Explorations of Kant's Practical Philosophy.* Cambridge: Cambridge University Press, 1989.

23

The Utilitarians

*J*ohn Stuart Mill made important contributions in many areas of philosophy, politics, and economics. His most influential philosophical contribution is his advocacy of the moral theory known as utilitarianism. Mill is not the first of the utilitarians—that honor goes to Jeremy Bentham. Nor is Mill the most subtle of the utilitarians—Henry Sidgwick perhaps best merits that honor. Nor is Mill the most eclectic of the great utilitarians—that honor goes to G. E. Moore. Rather, Mill is the most influential of the great utilitarians, and this influence is largely the result of the clarity with which he is able to lay out the major components of his view. Mill was born in London in 1806 and was educated at home by his father, James Mill. In the 1820s, Mill encountered and was profoundly influenced by the utilitarianism of Jeremy Bentham. By the end of the decade, he had given utilitarianism his own peculiar twist and developed the position that he expounded in his pamphlet Utilitarianism. Mill's other great work in moral and political philosophy is his essay On Liberty, in which he presents his account of human freedom and autonomy and attempts to reconcile this account to his fundamental utilitarian commitments. Throughout most of Mill's adult life, he worked for the East India Company, rising to a position of great importance in the company. He died in 1873.

THE GENERAL ORIENTATION OF UTILITARIAN THEORIES

Immanuel Kant attempts to demonstrate that moral worth accrues to actions only indirectly. What makes an action morally worthy for Kant is not so much what is done, but why it is done. Utilitarians argue the exact opposite. For the utilitarians, what makes an action morally worthy is not so much why it is done, but what is done. This focus upon what actions are done, rather than upon why actions are done, results from the utilitarians' interpretation of a simple and extremely plausible claim, the claim that the right action to perform in a particular situation is the action that will bring about the best state of affairs. How could it not be right, after all, to do what is best? The right action, then, simply is the action that brings about the best state of affairs. Why someone performs the action does not make it any more or less right since no matter why it is performed, if it brings about the best state of affairs, it is the right action.

The Utilitarian Strategy

The strategy that utilitarians propose for discovering which actions are the right actions appears to follow directly from the realization that the right action in a given situation is the action that brings about the best state of affairs. The strategy is simply to determine what the best state of affairs is in a given situation; the right action in that situation is the one that brings about the state of affairs thus determined. The key, then, is to determine what the best state of affairs is. Again, utilitarians take the strategy for making such a determination to be relatively straightforward: First, identify the feature or features of states of affairs that make them good; then, determine which of the possible states of affairs that can be brought about will bring about the most of this feature. The state of affairs that brings about the most of this good feature will be the best state of affairs. For Jeremy Bentham it is obvious what the feature of states of affairs is that makes them good—pleasure. The best state of affairs, then, is the state of affairs that brings about the most pleasure, and the right action is the one that brings about the best state of affairs, that is, the state of affairs with the most pleasure. To determine what it is right to do, then, Bentham suggests that you simply must determine which of the states of affairs that you can bring about will result in the greatest overall pleasure. This is the best state of affairs, and the right action is the action that brings about this state of affairs. There are certain troubling features about Bentham's proposal, the most obvious of which are his assumptions that all that we value can ultimately be cashed out in terms of pleasure and that all pleasures are on a par.

MILL'S UTILITARIANISM

Like Bentham and the other utilitarians, Mill agrees that the right action is the action that brings about the best state of affairs. But his account of the feature of states of affairs that should be maximized to bring about the best state of affairs is considerably more complicated than Bentham's. For Mill, the feature of states of affairs to be maximized by right actions is identified initially not as pleasure, but as happiness:

> Actions are right in proportion as they tend to promote happiness; wrong as they tend to promote the reverse of happiness. (*Utilitarianism*, p. 7)

I say initially, because Mill goes on to define happiness itself as "pleasure and the absence of pain." Thus, to maximize happiness is just to maximize pleasure and minimize pain, on Mill's account. Moreover, to maximize happiness, according to Mill, is just to maximize utility. Happiness, pleasure, and utility appear to be treated as virtual synonyms by Mill, and each purports to capture that single feature of states of affairs that an action must bring about the most of in order for the action to be the right action.

Objections Considered

Mill suggests that most objections to utilitarianism are based upon misconceptions about and oversimplifications of the theory. For instance, the major criticism of Bentham's utilitarianism is that it maximizes quantity of pleasure, without regard to the quality of the pleasures that are being maximized. Thus, Bentham is led to conclude that pushpin, the equivalent at the time to our relatively mindless game of tic-tac-toe, is as good as poetry. Indeed, if pushpin gives more pleasure, it is not clear why it should not be deemed morally superior to poetry. Moreover, it is not clear why, if mere quantity of pleasure is our ultimate goal, we should not simply spend our lives hooked up to a pleasure machine (if one were to become available) that directly stimulates the pleasure center of the brain. Yet, most of us would reject such a life of mindless pleasure. Mill responds that such objections result from Bentham's own oversimplification of utilitarianism. In maximizing pleasure, Mill suggests, one must weigh not only the quantity of pleasure but the quality of pleasure as well. Some pleasures are better than others, and even smaller quantities of such pleasures are to be preferred to greater quantities of lower quality pleasures. Mill concludes in *Utilitarianism* that it is "better to be Socrates dissatisfied than a fool satisfied," (p. 10) since it is better to have fewer of the higher quality pleasures, as does Socrates, than it is to have more of the lower quality pleasures, as does the fool. Who determines which pleasures are higher and lower? Clearly those persons who have experienced both (such as Mill), and can compare the two.

A second misunderstanding charges that utilitarianism requires us to continually act as moral saints since it requires us always to bring about the greatest happiness of the greatest number of people, regardless of the consequences to ourselves. Thus, utilitarianism seems to require you to throw yourself on the hand grenade to save others, even if you could readily find safety behind a table—after all, an action that saves more lives will typically maximize happiness. Mill's response is that such cases in which your own happiness and the happiness of the greatest number clearly diverge seldom arise. In most cases, the best strategy for maximizing overall happiness is to concentrate upon maximizing the happiness of those whose needs, goals, and aspirations you understand the best, your own and those of people close to you. Thus, bringing about the greatest happiness of the greatest number will typically involve bringing about your own greatest happiness and the greatest happiness of those closest to you, such as your friends and children. Occasionally, you will be morally required to make personal sacrifices and even potentially great sacrifices, but is this not clearly what morality demands in some cases, and is it not a virtue of utilitarianism that it provides a way of identifying what those cases are?

Third, the utilitarian claim that we are always required to do what we believe will bring about the greatest happiness seems to many to lead to moral chaos. Specifically, it seems that we are morally required to lie, cheat, break promises, steal, and even kill innocent persons if we believe that such actions maximize happiness in a particular situation. Indeed, if the only way to maximize happiness is to kill an innocent person (assume there are no maximizing alternatives), then according to utilitarianism, it would be wrong not to kill the innocent person. Clearly, must not any view with such a result be mistaken? Again, Mill suggests that this objection merely results from an oversimplification of utilitarianism. Although it is always right to do what brings about the greatest happiness, it may well maximize happiness to adopt certain rules, such as "do not lie" and "do not steal," and follow them even in particular cases in which it is not expedient to do so. Thus, it may maximize happiness to tell the truth even when it is expedient to lie, because adherence to such a rule (except in the most extreme cases) maximizes happiness in the long run.

Mill's Proof of Utilitarianism

These arguments by Mill are attempts to fend off objections to utilitarianism. In Chapter Four of *Utilitarianism*, Mill offers what he takes to be a positive argument for utilitarianism. The argument appears to presuppose that right actions are the actions that bring about the best states of affairs—how could it not be right to do what is best? The argument attempts to prove that the best state of affairs is the state of affairs with the greatest happiness. The proof has two stages.

STAGE ONE

In the first stage, Mill argues that happiness is a "good" for everyone, that is, that everyone finds happiness desirable as an end. This proof is straightforward. Mill suggests that just as the only evidence that something is visible is that people see it, so too the only evidence that something is desirable is that people desire it. Since Mill takes it as obvious that everyone desires his or her own happiness, he takes it to be established that each person's happiness is desirable as a good to that person. He also takes this to establish that the general happiness is desirable as a good for the aggregate of people.

STAGE TWO

The second stage is somewhat more complicated, and its conclusion more controversial. In this stage, Mill argues that happiness is not merely desirable as a good for each person, but that each person desires only his or her own happiness as an ultimate end. This seems simply false—people often pursue virtue, for instance, for its own sake, whether or not acting virtuously makes them happy. Mill grants that people do pursue virtue for its own sake, but suggests that such pursuit is derived originally from the pursuit of pleasure, hence is properly understood as a part of happiness. Mill suggests in *Utilitarianism* that virtue must be desired ultimately as a means to the pursuit of pleasure because properly understood, "desiring a thing and finding it pleasant . . . are . . . two different modes of naming the same psychological fact . . . to think of an object as desirable . . . and to think of it as pleasant are one and the same thing. . . ." (p. 38) Thus, since maximizing happiness simply is maximizing pleasure and minimizing pain, and finding something desirable is just finding it pleasurable, maximizing the satisfaction of our desires is just maximizing our pleasure, and maximizing our pleasure is just maximizing our happiness—we can do no other. It is possible, Mill allows, that we can, as Kant suggested, will to do other than we desire. But Kant's explanation was mistaken. The will can diverge from desire only because the will is susceptible to the effects of habit. We can thus develop habits that will lead us to do what we do not want to do, in much the same way that a drug habit will lead us to take drugs even after we want to stop. Even in such cases, Mill contends, the original source of such habits of the will is the agent's quest for the ultimate end of happiness. Everyone desires his or her own happiness, and no one ultimately desires anything but his or her own happiness. Happiness is the ultimate good, and the right action to perform is the action that brings about the best state of affairs, the state of affairs with the most good in it. Thus, Mill concludes that he has demonstrated that the best state of affairs is the state of affairs that maximizes happiness.

Justice   Mill identifies justice by first marking off those inexpedient actions that are properly labeled immoral actions, then identifying those immoral actions that are properly labeled unjust actions. An action is right to the extent that it maximizes happiness. Any action that falls short of maximizing happiness Mill labels "inexpedient." In most such cases, however, punishing someone for performing an inexpedient action will cause more unhappiness than it will prevent. Immoral actions, however, are those inexpedient actions for which punishment is appropriate, that is, actions the punishment of which will cause more overall happiness than unhappiness. Moral actions are thus actions that individuals are taken to have a duty to perform, actions that people will be punished for failing to perform.

There are, moreover, two different sorts of duties, known as duties of perfect and imperfect obligation. Duties of imperfect obligation are those "in which, though the act is obligatory, the particular occasions for performing it are left to our choice," whereas duties of perfect obligation are "those duties in virtue of which a correlative right resides in some person or persons." (*Utilitarianism*, p. 48) Thus, I have an imperfect duty to give to the poor, because although I must give to the poor, there are no particular occasions upon which I am obligated to give and no particular poor persons to whom I am obligated to give. By contrast, I have a perfect duty to respect the property of each person all the time, a duty which correlates with their right to own property. Unjust acts are those immoral acts that involve failure to carry out duties of perfect obligation, and such failures always correspond to violations of the rights of others. Justice requires the existence of rules of conduct that establish certain rights, rights that "society ought to defend me in the possession of" (*Utilitarianism*, p. 52) through punishment of the offenders.

JUSTICE AND RIGHTS

It may seem, however, that rights pose a serious difficulty for utilitarianism since for whatever right is in question—freedom of speech, life, property—it seems that the utilitarian must say that it is right to violate such a right when doing so will maximize happiness. But a right that can be set aside whenever it maximizes overall happiness to do so, it seems, is not a right at all. Such an objection, Mill suggests, is again based upon an oversimplification. The most vital of all human interests, Mill argues, is the human interest in security. Without security, human beings cannot be happy. But rights are necessary for security; only an enforced right to property will make me secure in my possessions, and only an enforced right to free speech will make me secure in my freedom of speech. Thus, security is necessary to maximize happiness, and rights are necessary for security.

THE SENTIMENT OF JUSTICE

Mill believes that our "sentiment of justice," our outrage at violations of rights and our corresponding thirst for revenge, can readily be accounted for within this framework. First, human beings sympathize with their fellow human beings and are naturally outraged at harm inflicted upon such innocent human beings in violation of established rules of conduct. Second, each person realizes that someone who will violate the rights of a fellow citizen will not hesitate to violate his or her rights as well. Thus, an impulse of self-defense leads to the demand that action be taken against anyone who would violate rights by ignoring duties of perfect obligation and by violating established rules of conduct. These two sentiments, sympathy and the impulse of self-defense, are sufficient, Mill argues, to account for the strength of the sentiment of justice.

COMMENTS AND CRITICISMS

Mill's version of utilitarianism may well be the most criticized moral theory ever. These criticisms for the most part fall into three different categories.

Criticisms—
Category One

In the first category are criticisms of Mill's account of how the best state of affairs is properly determined. Such criticisms are offered both by utilitarians and by their opponents. Thus, the famous utilitarian G. E. Moore argues that Mill's attempt to identify that feature of states of affairs that makes them good—in Mill's case happiness understood as pleasure maximization—is simply mistaken. Moore claims that the right action is the action that brings about the best state of affairs, but argues that goodness is a simple property that cannot be further defined in terms of happiness, utility, or pleasure. It is an "open question," Moore argues, whether a state of affairs that maximizes happiness is the best state of affairs. But this is sufficient to demonstrate that "Does it maximize happiness?" and "Does it bring about the best state of affairs?" are not the same question asked different ways, as Mill claims, but two different questions.

Objections have been raised, as well, against specific components of Mill's argument for utilitarianism, namely, the claim that happiness is the only thing desirable as an end. First, it is not at all clear that what maximizes pleasure, happiness, and utility is one and the same, as Mill seems to assume. If you bought the most pleasurable car, the car that would make you the happiest, and the most useful car, it is not at all clear that they would all be the same car. Secondly, Mill's proof claims that "desirable" and "pleasurable" are merely two names for the same thing, but people often desire to do things that are less pleasurable, even to cause themselves great pain—is the most pleasurable thing for them the most painful thing? Clearly there is something wrong with this aspect of Mill's argument. Finally, there appear to be difficulties with his appeal to quality as well as quantity of pleasure. Bentham defines goodness in terms of pleasure, but Mill defines goodness in terms of high quality pleasures, that is, in terms of good pleasures. Is Mill not clearly using goodness in a definition of goodness?

Criticisms—Category Two

The second category of criticisms allows that there must be some way of determining what the best states of affairs are, but denies that the right action is always the action that brings about the best state of affairs. Our intuitions appear to support these claims in many cases. If a doctor can save five patients by killing one basically healthy patient, and no other options present themselves, two facts seem clear: The best state of affairs is one in which five lives are saved and one lost, rather than one saved and five lost, and the right thing for the doctor to do is to allow the five patients to die and to refrain from killing the healthy patient. Yet, this suggests that the right action in this case is not the action that brings about the best state of affairs. Rights seem to provide evidence for such a claim as well, since to have a right to free speech, for instance, seems to mean precisely that it is wrong to deprive people of the ability to speak freely, even in cases in which it may be beneficial to society overall to shut them up—for instance, white supremacist skinhead rallies.

Criticisms—Category Three

The third category of criticisms focuses upon the fact that on utilitarian theories such as Mill's, the rational thing for each person to do is to maximize his or her own happiness, whereas the right thing to do is to maximize the general happiness. Their answer to the question "What reason do I have for doing the right thing?" seems to be: "Often none." In cases in which what maximizes your own happiness maximizes the general happiness, it is rational to do the right thing. But in cases in which your happiness and the general happiness diverge, and such cases appear to be quite common, you seem not only to have no reason to be moral, but to have good reason to be immoral. Mill suggests in Chapter Two of *Utilitarianism* that psychological and external punitive sanctions can be created to bring the two closer together, but this only pushes the question back a step further. Why is it reasonable to adopt such external punitive sanctions? Henry Sidgwick, perhaps the most subtle and profound of the utilitarians, concedes in his *Methods of Ethics* that it is not. There is no rational argument to convince an individual to do the right thing in cases in which the right thing and the thing that maximizes his or her happiness diverge. Such a concession, however, seems to violate one of our most fundamental convictions about morality—that it is ultimately reasonable to be moral.

The criticisms of utilitarianism are many, and they are telling. Yet despite the effectiveness of these criticisms, utilitarianism has persisted to this day as one of the dominant moral theories. The source of this staying power, it seems, is that utilitarianism is grounded upon an intuition that seems virtually impossible to deny, that the right thing to do in a given situation is the thing that brings about the best state of affairs—how could it ever be wrong to do what is best?

Selected Readings

Berger, F. R. *Happiness, Justice, and Freedom: The Moral and Political Philosophy of John Stuart Mill.* Berkeley: University of California Press, 1984.

Gray, J. *Mill on Liberty: A Defence.* London: Routledge and Kegan Paul, 1983.

Mill, J. S. *Utilitarianism.* Indianapolis: Hackett, 1979. (All citations in the text are of this edition.)

Schneewind, J. B. Ed. *Mill: A Collection of Critical Essays* Garden City: Doubleday, 1968.

Sidgwick, H. *The Methods of Ethics.* Indianapolis: Hackett, 1981.

24

Karl Marx

Karl Marx (1818–1883) was born and educated in Prussia, now a part of Germany. His economic, social, and political views led him into conflict with the government, however, and he was forced to move to Paris. Difficulties with the French government led to his relocation, in 1845, to Brussels and, in 1849, to London. Marx was trained as a philosopher, but his political, philosophical, and economic writings have had a profound impact upon every arena of human inquiry, from history and literature to the sciences. The following remarks will focus entirely upon those aspects of Marx's thought that constitute the central tenets of his social and political philosophy. Moreover, they will focus upon these major tenets of Marx's thought as they are presented in his relatively concise earlier works, The Economic and Philosophical Manuscripts *(1844),* The German Ideology *(1846), and* The Communist Manifesto *(1848), rather than in his great later work,* Capital *(1867).*

REAL HISTORY

History is often presented primarily as the history of the development of religious, philosophical, and political ideas. These political, religious, and philosophical developments are taken to explain, in large part, the behavior of individuals and nations. Thus, for example, it is such factors as Constantine's religious conversion that are taken to have profoundly influenced the course of development of the Roman Empire, and the development of natural rights and social contract theories is often cited as a cause of the American Revolution.

Marx maintains that such a political/philosophical/religious approach to history is fundamentally skewed. Real history, according to Marx, is economic history, the history of the development of productive forces and the relations of production. Religious, political, and philosophical ideas are best understood not as causes of these economic changes, but as themselves the products of these "material" economic developments:

> Morality, religion, metaphysics, all the rest of ideology and their corresponding forms of consciousness, thus no longer retain their semblance of independence. They have no history . . . ; but men, developing their material production and their material intercourse, alter, along with this their real existence, their thinking and the products of their thinking. (*The German Ideology*, p. 155)

Unlike religion, philosophy, and politics, economics is a science grounded in *real* premises, premises subject to empirical confirmation or disconfirmation. These real economic premises explain real (economic) history and allow for the prediction of the real future.

Real Premises

In *The German Ideology*, Marx attempts to pierce through to what he takes to be the "real" premises driving economic development. Marx points out first that human beings must be able to live, and that to do so, they must produce what is necessary to satisfy their basic needs. Such satisfaction of needs, Marx suggests, naturally leads to the creation of new and more complex needs. The satisfaction of these new needs generates still newer and more complex needs, and onward in an upward spiral. Moreover, human beings reproduce, and such reproduction requires at least the basic social structure of the family. Reproduction guarantees that human beings are essentially social, and the ever expanding nature of human needs guarantees that human beings will be led to develop ever more sophisticated social relations (productive relations) in order to develop the more and more sophisticated forces of production necessary to satisfy their continually expanding needs. From these few simple "real" premises, Marx takes it to be clear that real history will be the history of the continual expansion of the productive forces necessary to meet the continually expanding needs of individuals. This expansion of productive forces will dictate the continual development of social relations in whatever ways will most effectively facilitate the expansion of these forces.

Language and Labor

Human language, and with it human consciousness, is itself a product of these productive pressures. The productive pressures require more and more sophisticated forms of social intercourse; language is produced as a tool to facilitate such intercourse. Thus, language and, with it, consciousness itself are produced by the real conditions of life. This same pressure to expand productive forces leads to ever more sophisticated division of labor—first through a separation of industrial and commercial labor from agricultural labor, then through a separation of commercial from industrial labor. Marx argues, moreover, that this evolution of the division of labor is simply the evolution of property relations.

Labor, Property, and Classes

Division of labor among segments of the populace manifests itself as division into classes, historically, into minority propertied classes that oppress and majority propertyless classes that are oppressed. The oppressor classes control the forces of production, including the products of the labor of the oppressed majority. The nature of that oppressive control manifests itself as the form of property in existence at a given time. The history of the development of ever more sophisticated productive forces is thus a history of class struggle between the minority oppressors and the majority oppressed. These class relations are simply the productive relations that have been generated by the productive forces at a given time. Whether the oppressors and the oppressed are citizens and slaves, aristocracy and serfs, or the bourgeosie and the proletariat, the productive relations have ever taken the form of minority oppressor classes and majority oppressed locked in struggle for the control of the materials and products of production.

When a set of productive relations has become outmoded, that is, has lagged behind the development of productive forces, it has historically been overthrown in a revolution. But the new productive relations that have resulted from such revolutions have until now merely instituted a new oppressor class in place of the old. For instance, with the dramatic changes in productive forces brought about by the industrial revolution and expansion of trade, the modern bourgeosie has (largely) overthrown the aristocracy. Yet for Marx, this was merely another case of a new oppressor class (the bourgeosie), better suited to the new productive forces, replacing the old oppressor class (the aristocracy).

Estrangement

Marx argues that as productive forces become more and more sophisticated, human beings become ever more estranged from their labor and the products of their labor. The situation is worse for members of the oppressed class, who are literally estranged from the products of their ever more menial labor, products that are siphoned off by the members of the oppressor class. But even members of the oppressor class are enslaved to the onward march of productive forces and the productive relations that are shaped by those forces. Marx argues that the alienation and estrangement of human beings from the products of their labor has become particularly acute with the advent of capitalism. Capitalist societies are driven to maximize profits.

Profits are comprised largely of the difference between the actual worth of the labor invested in a good and the wages paid to the laborer for that good. Thus, the system is premised upon paying laborers—the proletariat—far less than what their labor is actually worth. The oppressor class, the bourgeosie, lives off the profits. These profits accumulate as capital. The larger the amount of capital accumulated by the ever-shrinking bourgeosie, the easier the accumulation of even more capital by this smaller, wealthier bourgeosie.

Individuals in such a society, Marx argues, cease to be thought of as "ends-in-themselves," and come to have value only as means to maximize profits. A good capitalist closes a plant if it maximizes the company's profits to do so—no thought is given to the lives ruined by such a closing. Individuals are thus reduced to the level of machines in modern capitalist society, tools of production that are utilized as long as they are useful, and discarded when the are not. Because capital generates more capital, Marx believes that capital will become increasingly concentrated in the hands of the few, and more and more people will become members of the proletariat as the class gravitates slowly towards bare subsistence level and ever less satisfying, more dehumanizing tasks.

MARX'S RESPONSE TO HIS CRITICS

On Marx's account, the oppressing class controls mental as well as physical production. Thus, this class rules "also as thinkers, as producers of ideas . . . their ideas are the ruling ideas of the epoch." (*The German Ideology*, p. 173) The political writings of Locke, Hobbes, and even Rousseau, are thus properly understood as nothing more than mental products of the current oppressor class produced to rationalize the continued oppression of the majority—the proletariat—by their bourgeosie oppressors. Their "justifications" of a right to private property are on Marx's account no more than rationalizations of the continued exploitation of the majority proletariat by the minority bourgeosie. That such "justifications" can involve appeal to democratic principles is merely an indication, for Marx, that the proletariat can be duped by such rationalizations into playing a role in its own continued exploitation.

Freedom and Private Property

To the claim that at least people are free in a capitalist society, Marx responds in *The Communist Manifesto* that the only true freedom in a capitalist society is freedom of the market and free trade. Humans are enslaved to others through their labor. Like slaves, the proletariat is compelled to perform menial labor for long hours for their continued subsistence. Unlike masters with their slaves, however, the bourgeosie takes no responsibility for the welfare of the proletariat. Members of the proletariat are discarded (fired) like machines as soon as they are no longer needed.

To the response that capitalist societies safeguard rights, and in particular the right to property, Marx argues that capitalist societies are premised upon depriving the vast majority of the population (the proletariat) of property, which must be concentrated in the hands of the few (the bourgeosie). Marx is clear, both in *The German Ideology* and *The Communist Manifesto*, that he is advocating, not doing away with property, but doing away with capitalist private property, an inherently unfair form of property "the necessary condition for whose existence is the non-existence of any property for the immense majority of society." (*The Communist Manifesto,* p. 486)

Motivation and Individuality

Against the claim that capitalism is necessary to foster individual motivation, Marx responds that those who work hardest in a capitalist society, the proletariat, acquire nothing for their efforts, while the bourgeosie, who accumulate more and more capital, do not work but live off the labors of the proletariat.

Finally, against the claim that capitalism is necessary to foster individuality, Marx argues that capitalism systematically reduces individual human beings to their exchange value and to the level of mere machines. The goal of capitalism is to find progressively simpler, more machine-like tasks for employees that make such employees easier to replace, for instance, tightening a screw on an automobile assembly line instead of building an entire car. Such tasks, however, are progressively more and more dehumanizing.

THE COMMUNIST REVOLUTION

From real premises generating real history, Marx has generated an economic account that purports to explain why any political system operating in a capitalist society, whether it be monarchical or liberal democratic, cannot but be a product of productive forces that are generating greater and greater oppression of more and more of the population. This real history, the history of productive forces unfolding in accordance with economic principles, not only allows Marx to explain the past, it allows him, as does any good scientific theory, to predict future occurrences. Inevitably, Marx argues, the economy will develop into a world economy, and more and more people will be forced into the propertyless class of the proletariat.

There will only be two classes, one extremely small class, the bourgeosie, controlling all of the property, and one vast propertyless class, the proletariat. The communist revolution that will occur when this situation has been reached will differ from past revolutions in that the class that overthrows the bourgeosie will not be yet another small oppressing class, but the proletariat itself. With the overthrow and the virtual obliteration of the extremely small bourgeosie by the immense proletariat, no new oppressor and oppressed classes will result. Rather, what will remain is a single class composed of every member of society, a class that will control the forces of production. The result, in short, is a classless society freed from capitalist private property, a society in which the property owners, the former proletariat, and the laborers or producers, again the former proletariat, are for the first time one and the same.

Such a state of affairs will result from the inevitable unfolding of productive forces in accordance with economic laws and will result in a state of affairs in which "society regulates the general production and thus makes it possible for me to do one thing today and another tomorrow, to hunt in the morning, fish in the afternoon, rear cattle in the evening, criticise after dinner, just as I have a mind, without ever becoming hunter, fisherman, shepherd, or critic." (*The German Ideology*, p. 160) After the communist revolution, estrangement and alienation from labor and the products of labor will simply cease, and the state as a tool of the oppressing class will simply wither away. Insofar as real history, moreover, is properly understood as the history of class struggles generated by the ever expanding forces of production, the emergence of a classless society is, in an important sense, the end of history.

The most common criticism of Marx is one which he, in many respects, invites upon himself. Marx claims to put his social and political philosophy upon a scientific basis, and it is this scientific basis, he claims, that gives it its predictive power. Yet, a theory in science that makes false predictions is taken to be a false theory. Thus, given that the unfolding of communism predicted by Marx has not come about, it may be argued with some plausibility that the inaccuracy of Marx's own predictions testifies to the falsity of his own theory. Such criticisms, however, are far too simplistic. It could be argued, for instance, that the development of a world economy, a development which Marx claims is necessary for the onset of the communist revolution, is only now coming about. Recent failures of so-called communist governments could then be seen as inevitable precisely because productive forces have not yet developed to the point at which a true communist revolution can occur.

Marx's social and political philosophy has serious difficulties. But these problems with Marx's system have been celebrated to such an extent that his extraordinary insights are often overlooked. Marx's criticisms of traditional property rights, for instance, must be taken seriously. Like Rousseau, Marx asks what worth a right to property has to a person whose circumstances of birth, etc., virtually guarantee that, through no fault of his or her own, the person will never own any property? If resources are unfairly distributed, will not property rights simply perpetuate such unfairness? Moreover, Marx forces us to take seriously the possibility that concentrated economic power can subvert the purported principles and goals of a political system. Even elected politicians can be bought, and money influences elections, now perhaps more than ever.

Selected Readings

Cohen, G. A. *Karl Marx's Theory of History*. Oxford: Oxford University Press, 1978.

Elster, J. *Making Sense of Marx*. Cambridge: Cambridge University Press, 1985.

Tucker, R. C., ed. *The Marx-Engels Reader*. New York: W. W. Norton & Co., 1978. (All citations in this chapter from *The German Ideology* and *The Communist Manifesto* are of this edition.)

25

G. W. F. Hegel

G. *W. F. Hegel (1770–1831) was born in Stuttgart, into a family of modest means. At university, in Tubingen, his closest associates were the philosopher-to-be, Schelling, and the poet-to-be, Holderlin. Hegel was profoundly influenced by these two thinkers; but however profound that influence was, it was Hegel who was to become the most eminent and famous German idealist, the arch-rationalist philosopher, whose influence upon the modern world can hardly be overestimated.*

Hegel's most important works are The Phenomenology of Mind *(1807),* The Science of Logic *(1812–16), the* Encyclopedia of the Philosophical Science *(1817), and the* Philosophy of Right *(1821). Many of his earlier works and his many lectures were published posthumously.*

CENTRAL HEGELIAN THEMES

Hegel is not easy to comprehend. Indeed, it is often hard to ignore the suspicion that he is a philosopher whose writings are the product of willful obfuscation. Still, it is a relatively straightforward matter to isolate the fundamental aspects of his work.

Hegel and Idealism

In important respects, Hegel's work can be viewed as a radicalization of Kant's transcendental idealism. Central to that vision is the view that it is we who give structure to the objects of awareness. More than this, the entire distinction between the subject and the object of experience is rejected by Hegel. The knowing experience is a unity of subject and object. In addition, Hegel rejects Kant's notion that there is but a single set of categories by which human experience is fixed. According to Hegel (here he was influenced by the philosopher Fichte), there are various forms of consciousness. Each of these forms of consciousness sets its own agenda, as it were, and structures experience and truth in its own fashion. Thus, there are different perspectives, each of which, we may say, has a partial grasp on the truth. Yet Hegel is no relativist. It is not as though there are different forms of consciousness, different perspectives, and that is the end of the matter. Rather, from some other and more complete perspective, it can be seen that these various forms of consciousness, in offering some partial grasp of the truth, are themselves an essential part of the Absolute, which includes and completes these other perspectives.

The Dialectic

We are beginning to characterize Hegel's famous notion of the dialectic. It is sometimes said that the dialectic is Hegel's method. Though there is truth to this, we are on firmer ground if we conceive of the dialectic as Hegel's conception of the way things themselves are (or rather, develop). The dialectic is the way of reason, in the sense that it is rationality at work in the world.

THESIS, ANTITHESIS, SYNTHESIS

Consider: Two different forms of consciousness will make incompatible claims. Each offers its own particular truths and its own conception of what makes for truth. We have, in the language of Hegel's dialectic, "thesis" and "antithesis." What must be emphasized is that for Hegel, not only do things not end with the assertion of incompatible claims, but, necessarily, they do not so end. Rather, there must be some other, some more complete, inclusive, or (in awkward language) "truer" perspective which will supplant the two previous perspectives and in some important way reconcile the two perspectives. In some sense, the new perspective can be seen to be the completion of the earlier, less complete perspective. This new movement—the "synthesis," in the jargon—will then be, in virtue of its *own* incompleteness, challenged by some incompatible vision. And the process begins anew.

The synthesis, then, does not simply discard thesis and antithesis. For Hegel, the process of reason, indeed the structure and being of what exists, is one of negation and mediation. The new form of consciousness, the new concept, must be understood to include and to make use of the previous forms of consciousness. Yet this process is not interminable; it necessarily comes to some conclusion. This is the Absolute. This whole process of negation and mediation is conceived by Hegel as the development of Spirit.

SPIRIT

Characterizing Hegel's notion of Spirit is no mean feat. In one sense, it is subjectivity or consciousness rather than, as with Spinoza, substance. But like Spinoza's notion of Nature, Hegel's notion of Spirit has religious connotations. In this sense, Spirit is the divine, the rational soul of the universe. This, however, suggests too strongly that Spirit is wholly distinct from the world. For Hegel, this is not so. Rather, in ways that are very hard to fathom, Spirit puts forward the world of material things and finite spirits (i.e., us) as part of its own development. Indeed, History is the development of Spirit in time. Spirit cannot exist apart from the cosmos.

In this way, Hegel's "absolute idealism" is not like earlier forms of idealism which are, ultimately, ways of denying the reality of the material world. Rather, the world, through its essential connection to consciousness, is itself, at bottom, Spirit. And, as we shall see, the purpose of the universe, made manifest in the dialectic, is the self-consciousness of Spirit.

Much of this will sound very odd and unfamiliar. Still, it is not hard to appreciate the grandeur (not to say grandness) of the Hegelian project. What is ultimately real for Hegel is Spirit or Mind, this necessary process of development. And Hegel's own work is not just a description of this process; rather, Hegel conceives of his philosophical work as the Absolute itself made real.

THE PHENOMENOLOGY OF MIND

The Phenomenology of Mind is the history of the development of Spirit—the story of its development through the process of negation and mediation. We have already seen that there is much about this project which will strike us as unfamiliar. It is important to recognize that *this* thought is itself a very un-Hegelian one. Hegel views the *Phenomenology* precisely as the overcoming of familiar epistemological and metaphysical problems. Two remarks from the introduction to the *Phenomenology* are worth noting. First, Hegel attacks Kant's notion that there must be a "thing-in-itself," which is as it is, independently of consciousness. Hegel argues, in a way which startlingly recalls Berkeley's arguments, that such a notion involves contradiction. Any such distinction, according to Hegel, must be a form of what he terms "being for consciousness;" thus, the distinction between what is given to consciousness and what is independent of consciousness must be drawn within consciousness. It cannot serve to characterize, to pick out, what is independent of consciousness.

Second, Hegel is deeply suspicious of a kind of philosophical project with a long history in the West. This project takes as its subject matter the scope and limits of the human mind. For Hegel, this is a self-defeatingly circular project. The human mind, whatever its powers, must be the instrument by which such a project is carried out. Thus, the adequacy of the mind is being assumed from the very start.

Many of the fundamental issues relating to the study of Hegel emerge here. It is precisely because thinkers who have pursued this project sharply distinguish between concept and object that Hegel's charge is a serious one. Once this distinction has been erased, as it is in Hegel's account, the worry, indeed the whole setting of the Cartesian skeptical problematic, can be seen to be groundless. According to Hegel, the standards by which we evaluate human cognitive endeavors are not static and unchanging. They too emerge and develop with the subject of consciousness. This is a natural result if, like Hegel, we think that world and subject—concept and object—constitute a seamless whole. For if this is so, one can raise no worry about how and whether the mind is an adequate knower of some independent world.

The Path of the Phenomenology

The *Phenomenology*, Hegel writes, is the explication of the dialectical process. The *Phenomenology* was itself to be part of a much larger project, some of it carried out in the *Logic*, and much of the rest outlined in the *Encyclopedia*. What is important to emphasize is that in the *Phenomenology* we are meant to see the ways in which various forms of consciousness contain within themselves the source of their own incompleteness; each form of awareness signals and foreshadows some other, more complete, form of consciousness. This history of consciousness is the story of reason and Spirit.

The *Phenomenology* is the development and the history of the various forms of consciousness. But given Hegel's view of the essential unity of mind and object, it is more than this. Since it is the history of the development of Mind or Spirit, it is also the history of what *is*. Since there is ultimately no distinction between concept and object, it must be the story of the dialectical development of Idea–Nature–Spirit. Science, for Hegel, is precisely the coming to awareness of this whole process of development which ends in the Absolute. "Truth," Hegel writes, "is the whole. The whole, however, is merely the essential nature reaching its completeness through the process of its own development. Of the Absolute it must be said that it is essentially a result, that only at the end is it what it is in very truth; and just in that consists its nature which is to be actual. . . ."

In the preface to the *Phenomenology*, Hegel notes that "Spirit is alone reality. It is the inner being of the world." So, when Hegel writes that substance is essentially subject, he is at once overturning a philosophical tradition which holds that substance is the fundamental ontological category and rejecting a distinction, fundamental to philosophical reasoning since Descartes, between the subject and object of consciousness.

OVERCOMING THE SUBJECT/OBJECT DISTINCTION

For Hegel, there is no subject of consciousness without an object (content) of consciousness, and there is no object (no content) without subject. The two develop simultaneously. What is finally overcome in the Absolute is the very distinction between the subject and object of knowledge. Absolute knowledge is consciousness knowing itself. We can, with some justification, understand this in the following way: If there is no distinction between subject and object of awareness, then ultimately all knowledge is a kind of self-knowledge. The realization of this, the clear-sighted awareness that thought thinks itself, is science, and it is precisely the philosophy of Hegel. More than this, since the story of the cosmos is the story of increasing self-consciousness carried out though the understanding of finite spirits, it is also the story of freedom. In coming to an understanding that all knowledge is self-knowledge, that the cosmos is but a manifestation of the dialectic of Mind or Spirit, the universe and its finite subjects come to understand themselves as wholly what they are, as fully self-realized, and hence free.

FORMS OF CONSCIOUSNESS

The *Phenomenology* carries us through the development of these various forms of awareness. We cannot here do justice to the intricacy of Hegel's discussion. We shall give some attention to Hegel's discussion of one of these forms of consciousness—sense certainty—and then briefly characterize some of the others.

Sense Certainty   Hegel's discussion of sense certainty can be regarded as a criticism of certain forms of empiricism. Sense certainty claims to be the most direct and immediate form of knowledge. "[I]t seems to be the truest, the most authentic form of knowledge; for it has not yet dropped anything from the object, it has the object before itself in its entirety and completeness." Thus, sense certainty claims to be immediate and direct. It is what another philosophical generation would term "knowledge by acquaintance." The important issue for Hegel is that sense certainty by virtue of its immediacy represents itself as unmediated by concepts.

Hegel points out that the immediacy of sense certainty is illusory. The absolute unity of subject and object is not to be achieved by sensory experience. There is the fact that there are two, in Hegel's terminology, "thises": the object of experience and the I, who is appeared to in thus and so a manner. This fundamental distinction undermines the immediacy of sense certainty and leads to its demise.

SENSE CERTAINTY CONSIDERED

As Hegel had already noted in the preface, sense experience is fundamentally characterized by the non-identity of subject and object. So, whatever immediacy is to be found in sense certainty must be found in either the subject or the object.

Let us consider the object of sense certainty. It is meant to be the immediately given world, the world just as it is. But Hegel at once challenges this conception by, in a nutshell, asking just what sense certainty can know. "Sense certainty itself has . . . to be asked what is the This?" Whatever is given immediately is the "This." We can characterize it only as "This" because, recall, sense certainty is meant to be prior to conceptualization. We cannot characterize what is given as "tall" or "brown" or "red," etc. So what is the thing which is given without conceptual mediation and about which the subject has immediate knowledge? In short, Hegel asks sense certainty to *say* what it knows, to characterize the object of its knowledge in some determinate fashion. If it can say nothing, then we are surely right to conclude that it is empty. Sense certainty can do no more than point to this or that.

According to Hegel, the "This" to which sense certainty points is not some particular "this"; that would require conceptual mediation (in order to distinguish this "This" from that "This," etc.). What was meant to be the most particular is the most universal. The "This" in general is the most abstract universal, it is just being in general.

The important point is that there is, for Hegel, no knowledge without mediation. Indeed, there is no making sense of consciousness at all without mediation. "Consciousness, we find distinguishes itself from something to which at the same time it relates itself." Without mediation, there is no particular thing from which consciousness is able to distinguish itself. Only at the end of the dialectic, when consciousness is its own object, can such immediacy be achieved.

Other Forms of Consciousness

The rest of the *Phenomenology* tells the remaining story of the dialectic. Next, we encounter difficulties with conceptual or mediated consciousness. Many of these are familiar philosophical difficulties which have their basis in the relation between substance and attribute. In any case, an understanding of some one thing, as the thing that it is, demands more than can be present in sensory awareness. It demands something like the concept of law or natural law. In brief, the kind of thinking we find in the physical sciences is necessary. But this kind of consciousness, Hegel thinks, demands self-consciousness or self-knowledge. In going beyond what is given to sensory experience and in seeking to resolve the contradictions of that stance, self-consciousness is generated. In some way or other, Hegel seems to think that it is apparent that the object of such thinking is itself consciousness.

SELF-CONSCIOUSNESS

It is in the sections devoted to a discussion of self-consciousness ("The True Nature of Self-Certainty") that some of the most famous passages from Hegel are to be found. Fundamental to the view presented here is the notion that self-consciousness demands another self-consciousness. The self-conscious self is, in a fundamental way, a socially constituted being.

Part of the discussion here hinges upon the notion that theoretical and practical reasoning are united in the notion of desire. Understanding and consciousness seek to control, to dominate, nature. Thus consciousness urges control and domination of its object.

LORDSHIP AND BONDAGE

Hegel illustrates these claims in the section entitled "Lordship and Bondage." This section has exerted an extraordinary influence on the modern mind. It is told as the story of two consciousnesses meeting and engaging in a struggle for power and recognition. One will be master and one will be slave. The point is that the consciousness of the slave is essential to the self-consciousness of the master. There is established, in fact, something like a symbiotic relationship. My own self-consciousness demands recognition by some other. There are, as is true with much of Hegel's social philosophy, echoes of Rousseau here. The crucial claim (as with Rousseau's notion of "living outside of oneself") is that I am who I am only insofar as I am understood to be so by some other. The self that I am is nothing which exists in isolation of other self-conscious selves. The self is essentially social in its very construction.

STOICISM, SKEPTICISM, "UNHAPPY" CONSCIOUSNESS

Next are various efforts to mediate the relation between mastery and slavery. First, we have Hegel's account of Stoicism. Here, according to Hegel, thought itself realizes that it is free in the practice of thought itself. This is a wholly abstract freedom, one which seeks to isolate itself from the concreteness or particularity of the world. Hegel characterizes Skepticism as the negation of this. The freedom of thought of the Stoic can be pushed farther; that freedom can be pushed to an examination of thought, and so of freedom, itself. The freedom of the Stoic offers no final resting place.

The uneasy effort to unify these two forms of self-consciousness is termed by Hegel, "The Unhappy Consciousness." Hegel's discussion is a sensitive treatment of the effort of consciousness both to recognize the situatedness and particularity of the subject and to make a place for the freedom and universality of the individual. The basic contradiction here is that the individual is both *an individual* and somehow a part of, or connected to, the universal. This kind of unhappy consciousness is exemplified by Christianity with its doctrine that a human being is somehow dual-natured.

REASON

The recognition of the unity of the particular and the universal can only be achieved by reason. It is at this point that Hegel's transitions become especially difficult to follow; in consequence we shall move rapidly.

In these sections, Hegel is chiefly interested in the ways in which consciousness can seek to find its categories and laws in its own investigations. This stage of mind, reason, is for Hegel, idealism. Perhaps we can do no better than Hegel's own words here:

> [Reason] is certain its self is reality, certain that all concrete actuality is nothing but it. Its thought is itself *eo ipso* concrete reality; its attitude toward the latter is thus that of *Idealism.*

There are discussions of reason's observation of inorganic and organic nature as well as discussions of psychology and the psycho-physical. Additionally, there is an account of some portions of ethics. Needless to say, this is a diverse collection of topics. If there is any coherence to this discussion, it is to be discovered in the fact that, with reason, the individual is seeking to understand the order of the cosmos by imposing upon it its own order, rationality. (Only in this way can the views presented here be understood as idealist.) In this sense, reason makes its world and is the world of its understanding. This kind of thinking is essentially self-conscious. It strives to understand what is by looking for reason, order, laws, categories, etc., within itself. This demands awareness of self.

So, perhaps, it is reasonably clear why reason is an important stage in the gradual overcoming of the duality of subject and object, and particular and universal. However, these contradictions cannot, as we might have expected, be mediated at this level of consciousness. Some commentators have characterized the difficulty by saying that Hegel regards Reason as too subjective. But this can be seriously misleading. The problem is not that Reason is too subjective; indeed, in its own sphere of investigation it is adequate. Rather, the problem is that it is too individualist.

From Reason to Spirit

It is this concern which explains what might otherwise seem a startling change of the subject when we move to the section of the *Phenomenology* entitled "Spirit." Now we are no longer concerned with individual consciousnesses but with the organization of consciousnesses into larger units. Thus, in these sections, we read about the ethical order and about the march of history. The failure of reason to resolve the dualities noted above demonstrates that the individual consciousness is not the appropriate tool whereby Spirit is completed or realized.

Hegel's discussion of ethics, of political and social history focuses on the ways in which the individual consciousness points to the larger Spirit, to infinite consciousness. This is not surprising since, as we said before, Spirit posits finite awarenesses in order to realize, to complete, itself. These larger political, social, and ethical orders are the manifestations of Spirit. If before, Spirit moved through the development of individual consciousnesses, now the individual develops through the movements of the larger social, political, and religious orders. As a result, the individual consciousness comes to understand itself as essentially constituted by the larger framework of which it is a part. Hegel's discussion of the ways in which the individual is transcended in larger political and social units recalls Rousseau's notion of the "general will." At this stage, the individual will is submerged into, and constituted by the will of the larger order.

RELIGIOUS CONSCIOUSNESS

Next, Hegel discusses religious consciousness. There is much insightful—even if not historically accurate—discussion of the movement from natural religion (God as manifest in the natural world), through religion as a kind of art (the religion of the Greeks), to revealed religion (the completion of which is Christianity). Hegel, as we will by now expect, gives an account of how the earlier forms of religious consciousness give shape to the later. What is important for our purposes is that in religious consciousness there is a self-conscious awareness of the Absolute.

But religious consciousness, however far it is taken, cannot resolve the contradictions we have been following. For this we need speculative philosophy, Absolute Knowledge.

Absolute Knowledge

Here, self-consciousness is aware of itself as its own object. This is accomplished only if individual consciousnesses come to self-consciousness, in the sense that they recognize that they are the means by which Spirit comes to self-consciousness. Absolute Knowledge is Spirit's self-consciousness. In this way, the whole of the *Phenomenology* and an appreciation of it as the necessary expression of Spirit, is Absolute Knowledge. It is Spirit appreciating itself, fully realizing itself.

We can close our discussion of the *Phenomenology* by noting that it is at this stage that the struggle between subject and object, particular and universal, is overcome with the self-realization and freedom of Spirit. Spirit is free in that it is now fully what it is. Having made the journey, we, as individuals, are free as well since we recognize ourselves in the infinite Spirit. In broad terms, we are not too distant from Spinoza's intellectual love of God. What began as our effort to understand the world, can finally be seen to have been all along Spirit's effort to know itself.

*P**erhaps enough has been said to give some glimmer of the nature of Hegel's thought. We should mention here that Hegel pursues the program begun in the* Phenomenology *in his* Logic. *His* Logic *(both in the work of that name and in the "lesser logic" of the* Encyclopedia*) is an effort to characterize the concepts which are essential to understanding anything. But though this recalls Kant's work, we must recall that, since in Hegel one has a unity of subject and object, Hegel's* Logic *is also an account of the dialectical structure of reality itself. What this means is that the* Logic *of Hegel is an effort on the part of philosophy to demonstrate the logical or conceptual structure of what is. Given our survey of the* Phenomenology, *we will not be surprised to learn that the* Logic *ends with the Absolute Idea, in which subject and object are revealed as one.*

Still, if the reading of Hegel is very often frustrating, we would do well to keep in mind that his influence on our times has been enormous. Marx's dialectical materialism is but Hegel's dialectic altered. Hegel's discussion of lordship and bondage has influenced, perhaps even more profoundly, Marx and legions of Marxists. Hegel's influence can also be seen in analytical philosophical circles; his discussion of sense-certainty neatly anticipates much that epistemologists have said about the "given" in experience. It would be an easy matter to detail the ways in which Hegel's thought has had and continues to have an immense impact on the intellectual history of the West. Nonetheless, his influence, by and large, is the result of the brilliance of isolated portions of his system rather than the brilliance of the system as a whole.

Selected Readings

Gadamer, H. *Hegel's Dialectic*. New Haven: Yale University Press, 1976.
Kojeve, A. *Introduction to the Reading of Hegel*. Ithaca: Cornell University Press, 1969.
Taylor, C. *Hegel*. Cambridge: Cambridge University Press, 1975.

26

Sören Kierkegaard

From the perspective of an observer, it is not difficult to relate the essentials of Kierkegaard's life. He was born in Copenhagen, in 1813, into a very comfortable household. His father had risen from poverty and peasantry, had married a servant, and had achieved great wealth. All of this left its predictable mark: Kierkegaard's father was a stern and, in a quite literal fashion, a God-fearing man. Sören Kierkegaard in his youth was something of a bon vivant; he was quite the social butterfly. Not surprisingly, he and his father were estranged. In 1840, he became engaged to Regine Olsen, many years his love. But, in a way that would reflect much of his later thought, he suddenly broke off the engagement. It is this event that begins the immensely productive period of Kierkegaard's life. He died in 1855. From this rather unexceptional sounding life, emerged a thinker who is often regarded as the first existentialist.

Kierkegaard's chief philosophical works are Either/Or *(1843),* Fear and Trembling *(1843),* The Concept of Dread *(1844),* Philosophical Fragments *(1844),* Concluding Unscientific Postscript *(1846),* Edifying Discourses *(1847), and* Sickness Unto Death *(1849).*

KIERKEGAARD'S PHILOSOPHICAL COMMITMENT

Throughout much of the history of philosophy, the emphasis has been upon the human being as a potential knower—the human being as knower of some independently existing world. Here the relevant questions are: What can I know? What are the standards of knowledge? And so on. However we answer such questions, we are apt to take the third-person stance in asking and answering them. That is, we are apt to regard our worries about what and whether we know to be a matter which is appropriately settled by appeal to objective standards. And even the priority of such questions assumes a picture of the human being as situated in a world independent of him or her. We may, like Hegel, one of Kierkegaard's chief targets, regard the world as essentially rational and thus something which can be known by subjects like ourselves. Or we may, like Kant, regard the "thing-in-itself" as situated beyond the scope of human reason. But, in any case, such questions presuppose that our chief interest as human beings lies in discovering the objective truth: Something is as it is quite independently of what any particular human subject thinks or feels.

Kierkegaard regards all of this as something of a sham. The chief question for Kierkegaard is not "What can I know?" but "What shall I do?" Of course, in order to answer this question *I must choose*. According to Kierkegaard, though we can choose in many different fashions all human choice produces "dread," or "despair." I must choose; no answer from the third-person, or objective, point of view can be anything more then self-deception or bad faith.

On Selfhood

Part of Kierkegaard's reason for such a view—that truth is subjectivity—stems from his view of what it is that the human being is. In language which startlingly anticipates the twentieth-century existentialists, Kierkegaard writes:

> Man is spirit. But what is spirit? Spirit is the self. But what is the self? The self is the relation which relates itself to its own self, or it is that in the relation [which accounts for it] that the relation relates itself to its own self; the self is not the relation but [consists in the fact] that the relation relates itself to its own self. Man is a synthesis of the infinite and the finite of the temporal and the eternal, or freedom and necessity, in short it is a synthesis. A synthesis is a relation between two factors. So regarded, man is not yet a self.

So, according to Kierkegaard, I am not a self. Rather, being a self, a chooser and a doer, is an achievement. It is a burden that must be taken up. This at once makes clear that the point of Kierkegaard's philosophical work is not to tell us, to inform us of, the truth. Rather, its point is to improve us, to "edify" us. His goal, ultimately, is to show us that if we are to become choosers, real selves, if we are to escape dread, we must become Christians of a peculiar sort. For just as the goal of the philosophical framework that emphasizes the human being as knower is knowledge, so the goal of Kierkegaard's view of human being as chooser is faith.

DECISION AND DREAD

So then, for Kierkegaard, we must choose. This choice, it must be emphasized, is not just a matter of choosing what to do, what act to perform now; it is also a matter of choosing what to believe. This, too, is a practical matter which cannot be settled by appeal to some objective standard. Kierkegaard here stands against a tradition in which beliefs are regarded as something which are compelled by evidence or canons of reasoning. What I come to believe is as much an act of mine as what I do in the more familiar sense. And since there is nothing to rely upon in such choosing, and since we must choose, we are in dread.

Why is choice accompanied by dread, why is selfhood such a burden? Here, we must appeal to Kierkegaard's conception of the self, or rather the self-conscious self. When I choose self-consciously, unlike the innocent animal, I pick some one alternative about which I think there is something to be said. But in having chosen, I have ruled out the other alternatives. And since I am self-conscious, I can imagine that I chose in this other way. And since I can imagine these other possibilities, since I am not actually constituted by what I do choose, since what I am is as much possibility as actuality, I can always doubt that this choice was best. But the point is deeper than this. Whatever we think about free and responsible choice, it is common ground that we want such choice to reflect *who* we are. Autonomous choice, we might say with Kant, depends on nothing but my core self. But since, according to Kierkegaard, there is nothing that I am as a matter of objective fact—since I am essentially a synthesis of the finite and the infinite, the eternal and the temporal, of the possible and the actual—all such efforts at autonomous choice must be self-defeating. For if I seek to act on those aspects of my core self, those aspects of myself which are really and fundamentally me, my effort must be a failure. There is no core, no fixed center, to the human self.

To illustrate briefly: Let us say that you must choose between two courses of action. As such decisions sometimes go, you are torn. So how are you to choose? Well, you might ask yourself what you *really* want to do or what you *really* ought to do. And here the goal seems to be to discover those aspects of yourself (preferences, desires, values) which are somehow central or fundamental to who you are. But why should any of those aspects so discovered be central or fundamental to what you are? Why should those aspects constitute who you are? Any such choice seems arbitrary. Not just because in reflecting on and evaluating any such aspect of yourself it is made manifest that that aspect does not constitute you, but also because any such choice that that aspect does constitute you must make it apparent that you might have chosen otherwise—that you are not just that aspect, since you are possibly some other. Indeed, Kierkegaard identifies dread with the very possibility of freedom.

Faith as the Solution

What then is the cure, what can end the dread? Only faith, which at once ends the dread and makes of us selves. Why should this be? Here, Kierkegaard's point seems to be that any effort to choose by relying upon myself must in various ways display the groundlessness of that choice. Only God, only an infinite being, can be the proper object of that sort of passionate commitment which can produce a self.

HOW IS IT THAT ONE CHOOSES?

According to Kierkegaard, there are three ways in which we can approach choice or decision: The Aesthetic, The Ethical, and The Religious.

The Aesthetic Life

In the aesthetic mode of approaching choice, I do not regard my choices as anything but the immediate result of my desires. I do not appeal to principles or standards against which I measure my action. In this kind of choice, I either lack or refuse to employ a certain kind of self-reflection which would seem to be essential to what Kierkegaard regards as full-bodied choice. In aesthetic choice, I may ask myself what to do, but the answer to such a question is provided by my desires, by my heart. But what I do not do is to go on to ask the question: Ought I to be moved by my heart, by my desires, in this way? Or, perhaps more to the point; do I want to be the sort of creature that acts upon such desires? The thinking reflected in these questions demands a kind of self-criticism in which normative standards play a role. I must take such standards seriously in order to raise these questions; and in the aesthetic way of choosing, either I lack such standards or I do not take them seriously. This explains why it is that Kierkegaard writes that an aesthetic choice is no choice. Choice reflects commitment of a self and with the aesthetic way of life, the person is moved by immediate desires and cannot formulate some principle by which she commits herself to choice.

The Ethical Life

The ethical way of life does appeal to standards against which the individual measures herself. Such a chooser does engage in the sort of self-criticism the aesthetic chooser lacks. Such a chooser has a will which is constituted by her principles, and such principles provide at least the beginnings of the commitment necessary for the appreciation of selfhood. Thus, in characterizing the distinction between the aesthetic and the ethical, Kierkegaard writes:

> It is, therefore, not so much a question of choosing between willing the good *or* the evil, as choosing to *will*, but by this, in turn, the good and evil are posited. He who chooses the ethical chooses the good, but here the good is entirely abstract, only its being is posited, and hence it does not follow by any means that the chooser cannot in turn choose the evil in spite of the fact that he chose the good.

Choice is here regarded as a serious matter; indeed, everything depends upon it in the ethical life. It is here that one is apt to find the most self-conscious dread. Here, one gives one's allegiance to a principle or standard, but until one reaches the religious, one has not given one's allegiance to a thing which is the proper object of one's allegiance. It must be emphasized that it is not easy to characterize Kierkegaard's thinking. But it is clear that there is a kind of commitment which the ethical chooser cannot attain. This is for the very reasons noted above during our consideration of the dread that choice or decision must involve. Only with faith, only with a commitment to God, to the infinite, can one achieve the sort of core to one's self that other sorts of choosing patently lack.

Religious Choosing

But faith and the religious mode of choice are not just a matter of replacing one sort of principle with another—that would be to understand the religious mode of choosing as a mere variant of the ethical. In ethical choosing, we act on universal principles; we regard them as objective and as applying to all human beings. It is very likely that we can supply—indeed most of ethical theory is devoted to this project—an argument in favor of our particular ethical theory. This argument will give us good or sufficient reason for taking our ethical principles to be, as a matter of fact, the correct ethical principles. But for Kierkegaard, faith is precisely the "leap of faith." There is no certainty and so I must just will to believe while at the same time recognizing the objective uncertainty of God's existence. It is only this kind of leap which makes for the commitment necessary for religious choice. It is only this kind of commitment, this sort of passion, which makes of the chooser a self. It is precisely the awareness of the objective uncertainty involved in my commitment to God and in my committing myself to him, that makes faith, faith. One who believes on the basis of historical reasoning or speculative philosophical argument does not have faith. The passionate inwardness of faith demands an awareness of objective uncertainty.

There are worries about Kierkegaard's doctrine of the leap of faith. The chief worry here is a simple one: Do we have the capacity to do what Kierkegaard's doctrine demands? If his view is correct, then it must be true that I can alter my beliefs at will. If I am to have faith, it must be the case that I will to believe against the evidence. But it just is not clear that human psychological subjects possess the capacity to leap to a belief as a result of a simple act of the will.

THE TELEOLOGICAL SUSPENSION OF THE ETHICAL

We can perhaps get a better handle on the religious mode of choosing and its relation to the ethical by considering Kierkegaard's notion of the teleological suspension of the ethical. In *Fear and Trembling*, Kierkegaard retells the story of God's request that Abraham sacrifice Isaac—a particularly dramatic instance of religious choosing, which displays the teleological suspension of the ethical.

The ethical mode of choosing, we know, is rooted in the universal, in the sense that one's moral standards are regarded as applying to all, at all times. The ethical is precisely that which is not to be violated in choosing. In the story of Abraham and Isaac, there is an ethical principle at work: That a father shall love his son more dearly than himself. Thus, insofar as Abraham chooses after the ethical, he must not slay his son. But Abraham is willing to kill his son. What makes Abraham great, Kierkegaard notes, is not moral virtue but personal virtue. Why then is Abraham willing to act so?

> For God's sake, and (in complete identity with this) for his own sake. He did it for God's sake because God required this proof of his faith; for his own sake he did it in order that he might furnish the proof. . . . What ordinarily tempts a man is that which keeps him from doing his duty, but in this case the temptation is itself the ethical—which would keep him from doing God's will.

This, then, is the teleological suspension of the ethical. Abraham acts from faith, and he violates universal ethical norms in doing so. And he acts in objective uncertainty of the facts. This is the religious way of choosing. It should, then, be clear why, for Kierkegaard, faith is the passion and the miracle which unifies and makes whole a human life.

TRUTH IS SUBJECTIVITY

These views about the nature of the self, choice, and the role of faith give rise to an extraordinary doctrine that truth, at least so far as the existing individual is concerned, is subjective not objective. In some of his most important philosophical writings Kierkegaard seeks to show that the picture of the human being as a disinterested, impartial seeker after the truth is a fiction. It is a fiction, not just because certainty in the epistemological realm is impossible to achieve, but because this conception of the human being as an impartial seeker after objective truth must result in our becoming centerless, soulless, creatures.

Much of Kierkegaard's point can be seen straightforwardly as a continuation of a certain skeptical tradition. If we seek certainty, then we must be disappointed; at best, we can achieve the probable. Speculative philosophical argument, or historical or scientific research cannot get us certainty. About this, Kierkegaard writes:

> Anything that is almost probable, or probable, or extremely or emphatically probable, is something [the seeker after objective truth] can almost know, or as good as know, or extremely and emphatically almost know—but it is impossible to believe.

Kierkegaard's worry is, as we have emphasized throughout, how it is we are going to live and to choose. If we are not to be deeply and fundamentally alienated and fractured in our lives and choices, we must *believe* that by which we measure our lives and direct our choices. But any objective approach to these worries must leave us deeply divided: Such an approach— whether philosophical, scientific, or historical—can take us only to the probable. And the probable is not a fit object of belief. Limiting ourselves to the pursuit of objective truth, we must remain alienated from our lives and principles. Truth, if it is to play a role in directing my life, if it is something to which I can give my allegiance, must be a passionate inwardness. It must be subjective; it must be faith.

*I*t is easy to dismiss Kierkegaard as merely a religious thinker, with little to say to our age. This would be a mistake. Through the writings of existentialists, like Jean Paul Sartre, Kierkegaard's influence on our age is enormous. It is true, of course, that many of us will reject his solution— faith—for our lives. Nonetheless, the current age finds his characterization of what that problem is—the problem of the particular existing individual— compelling.

Selected
Readings

Hannay, A. *Kierkegaard.* New York: Routledge and Kegan Paul, 1984.
Sontag, F. *A Kierkegaard Handbook.* Atlanta: John Knox Press, 1988.

27

Friedrich Nietzsche

Friedrich Nietzsche (1844–1900) was born in Rocken in Prussia. Nietzsche's early passion was for the classics; and though he is one of the most important philosophers of modernity, he was trained as a classical philologist. He studied at Leipzig under the famous classical scholar Ritschl. Even before he had completed the doctorate, he was appointed to a chair at the University of Basel. It was at Basel that he began his stormy relationship with the composer Ricard Wagner. A profound loathing for the professional academic life led Nietzsche to resign his position in 1879.

Nietzsche's works have exerted a truly extraordinary influence upon our age. He is perhaps the most iconoclastic of thinkers—one of his works is subtitled How to Philosophize with a Hammer. *He attacks traditional metaphysics, Christianity, morality, the notion of the self, and the view that there is one true world.*

Nietzsche's main philosophical works are: The Birth of Tragedy *(1872),* Untimely Meditations *(1873–76),* Human, All-Too-Human *(1878–79),* Dawn *(1881),* The Gay Science *(1882; the fifth part of this work was completed in 1887),* Thus Spake Zarathustra *(1883–85),* Beyond Good and Evil *(1886),* A Genealogy of Morals *(1887),* The Will To Power *(1883–88; this work was left unfinished),* The Case of Wagner *(1888),* Nietzsche Contra Wagner *(1888),* Twilight of the Idols *(1888),* The Anti-Christ *(1888), and* Ecce Homo *(1889). By early 1889, Nietzsche was suffering from a complete mental breakdown; he never recovered.*

CENTRAL THEMES

Even those who know little of the history of philosophy are likely to know of Nietzsche's famed proclamation of the "Death of God." Although this is certainly meant by Nietzsche to have theological implications, its significance is more than theological. For with the death of God depart not only theism and theistic ethical systems, but also the possibility of there being a *God's-eye view* of the world. There is, for Nietzsche, no one way that the world is. There is no *the* truth about the world.

Very often readers mistake Nietzsche's views for nihilism—the belief that since there are no facts, moral or otherwise, one should believe in nothing. Emphatically, Nietzsche is not a nihilist. Nihilism *can* result from coming to believe that God is dead. But, in Nietzsche's view, this moral will be drawn only by the weak, who cannot survive without belief in some fixed, eternal truth. In fact, though the death of God makes possible great things, it is also a great danger precisely because it can produce lifeless, bored and boring, nihilistic creatures.

Nietzsche's own view of truth is *perspectivism*. This is the view that everything is interpretation. The claims of philosophy, science, etc., are not true third-personally, and objectively. Rather, claims are true *for* particular individuals and peoples. Truth is not *given*, it is made.

This view is clearly at odds with philosophical tradition. Most philosophers, (most thinkers in fact), understand themselves to be engaged in the pursuit of the objective truth, a truth which is independent of their own particular perspectives. It is a fundamental claim of Nietzsche's that our truths, metaphysical and moral, are but a reflection of our own biases and committments. Truth is perspectival. This claim raises serious questions about Nietzsche's own work: If everything is interpretation, what is the status of the claim that everthing is interpretation?

Notwithstanding this concern, the claim that truth is perspectival is a fact that few serious readers of Nietzsche can forget. Very often, Nietzsche's philosophical styles—he has many—strike the student of philosophy as bizarre. He writes in aphorisms, poetry, songs, stories. These styles are, however, surely an appropriate way to express the fact that truth is perspectival—the result of who one is. Nowhere in his works is the disembodied voice of reason to be found.

Genealogy

With some justice, we can say that Nietzsche's method is genealogy. Genealogy is a way of uncovering the roots or genesis of something—a way of displaying how it is that something came to be. In Nietzsche's hands, genealogy displays how it is that various concepts and claims are the product of interpretation and not simply given. Genealogy is, then, a historical enterprise; more than this, genealogy displays as the product of a contingent history concepts and propositions that we very likely take as fixed and given. Such an enterprise can show that something we regard as unchanging is, in fact, quite accidental—it might have been otherwise. In this way, genealogy can make us aware of alternatives and possibilities in places where we thought there were none.

MORALITY

A genealogy of morals will provide us with an understanding of the circumstances which gave birth to moral values. The genealogy is necessary if we are to provide what Nietzsche understands to be essential to our survival, a critique of moral value. What must be called into question, says Nietzsche at the start of the *Genealogy of Morals*, is the value of these values. What is the connection between genealogy and critique? A genealogy of morals will force us to understand that our values are not *given*, they are the result of particular interests; they are the product of interpretation.

Good and Bad, Good and Evil

According to Nietzsche the history of value is a history of the struggle between two opposing evaluative schemes: Good and Bad, on the one hand, and Good and Evil, on the other. Nietzsche draws on philological evidence to suggest that "good" is closely related to the noble, the powerful, the aristocratic, and that "bad" derives from the base, weak, plebeian, and powerless. In any case, the first scheme, Good and Bad, is the older, primordial one. The nobility's "good" amounts to the capacity to be happy, to thrive and to flourish in this world. These values, Nietzsche writes:

> Presupposed a powerful physicality, a flourishing, abundant, even overflowing health, together with that which serves to preserve it: war, adventure, hunting, dancing, war games, and in general all that involves vigorous, free, joyful activity.

It is important to emphasize that this mode of valuation is unselfconscious and spontaneous. The activities and characters that it values spring directly from joy and mastery in the things of this world; there is a naturalness to this notion of "good."

The "bad" or base, on this conception, comes as something of an afterthought. The "bad" are the lowly and despised, the weak and the powerless. They are those who cannot do what the powerful can do.

The Slave Revolt in Morality

According to Nietzsche, glimmers of the Good and Bad valuational scheme are still present in our talk about value. But, by and large, this has been supplanted by the victory of the slave revolt in morality which has succeeded in reversing these values.

The lowly slave suffers much at the hands of the world and at the hands of the powerful. This gives rise to *ressentiment,* a venomous hatred, for the strong. This *ressentiment* is however, a creative force. Since the weak cannot express their desires effectively in the real world, they take refuge in the interior world. They have, Nietzsche writes, *squinting* souls, but it is precisely the weak and powerless who become self-conscious and clever. They take delight in *imagined* assaults on the strong.

The "good" (or the strong) is the *evil one* for the weak. Whereas the values of the strong amount to a "Yes" to life, the slave or *herd* morality is a ringing "No" to this life and world. And whereas, the strong arrive at their conception of the good spontaneously and almost naturally, the weak construct their valuational scheme as a reaction and response to suffering and frustration. Indeed, the reasoning of the weak proceeds in something like the following fashion: "You the strong, since you cause us pain, you are evil. And since we are not at all like you, we are good." Thus the morality of good and evil, paradigmatically Christian morality, is the slave's revenge.

Both valuational schemes, Good and Bad, and Good and Evil, are interpretations, of course. Neither is *given*, both are made to suit the interests of the lives they support. It is, however, clear where Nietzsche's sympathies lie.

IMPLICATIONS OF THE SLAVE REVOLT

But how could the slave revolt succeed? How could anyone take seriously the claim, "I am good!" in the mouth of the pathetic and weak? Before such an effort can be made, it is necessary that one have at one's command a notion of the self or subject. This self must be understood to stand apart from the rest of the world. This is, of course, very much a traditional conception of the self. But this conception, too, is for Nietzsche an interpretation; all things are, for Nietzsche, connected to every other thing—the world is a becoming and not a being. That we pick out anything as a *single, independent thing* is always the result of interpretation. This holds true of the self. But the weak's conception of the self as an independent thing permits them to understand behavior as a matter of *will* or *choice.* Thus, the weak are able to view their own behavior and that of the strong as reflecting choice and so virtue and vice. As a result, the necessary effects of weakness (impotence, etc.) are transformed into a "meritorious deed," and the necessary effects of strength (vitality, etc.) are transformed into viciousness.

THE WILL TO POWER

Both moralities are an expression of the *will to power*. Nietzsche puts this fundamental notion to work in many ways in his works. He sometimes speaks of the world and everything in it as *being* the will to power. In this usage, he is influenced by the philosopher Arthur Schopenhauer (1788–1860). More frequently, and more comprehensibly, the will to power is the fundamental instinct of life; it is this force which drives us in all that we do. As the phrase would indicate, the will to power is a drive to live, to control, to dominate. Our values, our metaphysics, our sciences, these are all, for Nietzsche, the expression of the will to power. The world our sciences display is not the world as it is, but the world as it must be if we are to live—this world, our world, is an expression of the will to power.

Ascetic Ideals and the Will to Power

Christian asceticism, and Christian morality in general, would seem to constitute a difficulty for Nietzsche's view of the universal role for the will to power. To see why consider the difference between this radical form of asceticism and artistic or philosophical asceticism. The artistic ascetic might well deny him- or herself certain aspects of life that most of us regard as very valuable; and his or her evaluative scheme might have it that those things are to be positively dis-valued. Yet this kind of morality is clearly in the service of life and the will to power. This kind of ascetic practice denies certain parts of this world because it seeks to concentrate upon, and to maximize, what is, by its lights, most valuable in this world—for example, artistic creation.

But Christian asceticism says "No!" to life as a whole, or so it seems. According to this scheme, this world and this life are to be wholly rejected. What is most valuable is the heavenly life; all must be sacrificed to that. This evaluative scheme would appear to be "life against life." Yet Nietzsche's doctrine of the will to power would seem to be able to make no sense of this. All forms of life must be devoted to the increase of power and vitality.

There is, says Nietzsche, only the appearance of paradox here. The weak, recall, suffer horribly; their desires are frustrated. This life holds nothing for them. But one can endure anything so long as it has meaning. And that is just what Christianity confers on the lives of the weak. In claiming that our sufferings are deserved, in claiming that we are guilty before God, and in claiming that this world is without value, Christianity makes, for the many powerless and pathetic, continued life possible. "This ascetic priest," Nietzsche writes, "this apparent enemy of life, this *denier*—precisely he is among the greatest *conserving*, and, yes, creating forces of life."

If this is so, what explains Nietzsche's great antipathy for Christian morality? Nietzsche's claim is that Christian morality can succeed in sustaining the lives of the weak only if it represents itself as being *the truth*. Thus, it is a pre-condition of the efficacy of Christian morality that it be universal and eternal; it must represent itself as something which is precisely *not* an interpretation. And so, Christian morality destroys life for the strong. The strong must be told that they are sinners, that they must repent, and become like the weak if they are to be good. This is the real brilliance of the Christian priest. The result, according to Nietzsche, is that the well of life is poisoned for everyone.

THE OVERMAN

One of the most notorious and misunderstood aspects of Nietzsche's thought is the *Übermensch* or Overman. But the overman is, for Nietzsche, a regulative ideal for humanity. It is something to strive for in the midst of the falling idols of the age. The overman is precisely the individual who recognizes that the world is pure flux, essentially becoming. He understands that values are not found or given, they are created. Consequently, he understands that he himself is not given, but that he too must be made, affirmed in a creative process.

Eternal Recurrence

Perhaps something of the character of the overman emerges through a consideration of Nietzsche's puzzling doctrine of the *eternal recurrence*. At Section 341 of *The Gay Science*, Nietzsche writes:

> *The Greatest Weight.*—What, if some day or night a demon were to steal after you into your loneliest loneliness and say to you: "This life as you now live it and have lived it, you will have to live once more and innumerable times more; and there will be nothing new in it, but every pain and every joy and every thought and every sigh and everything unutterably small or great in your life will have to return to you, all in the same succession and sequence—even this spider and this moonlight between the trees, and even this moment and I myself. The eternal hourglass of existence is turned upside down again and again, and you with it, speck of dust!"

In other works, especially *The Will to Power*, Nietzsche discusses the eternal recurrence as a real cosmological hypothesis. Indeed, he suggests that the eternal recurrence follows from the conservation of energy, and he calls it the "most scientific of hypotheses." But whatever the status of the eternal recurrence as cosmology, it plays a clear role in Nietzsche's characterization of the overman.

For consider, how would you respond to the revelation of the eternal recurrence? With terror, perhaps. But insofar as one could respond with joy, insofar as one could affirm eternal recurrence, that would indicate one's nearness to the ideal of the overman. For this would indicate not only that one had somehow succeeded in forging some coherent, satisfying, and compelling self for oneself, but also that one had come to recognize that one can be nothing other than what one makes of oneself each day.

It is immensely difficult to classify Nietzsche's work. Metaphysics, ethics, epistemology, psychology, and anthropology mix, in ways which can produce great unease. Furthermore, though Nietzsche is often classified among the existentialists, he is as much naturalist as existentialist. His prespectivism and genealogy are increasingly influential in philosophy and literary criticism. And his devastating critique of received views about morality is likely to be an enduring achievement.

Selected Readings

Danto, A. *Nietzsche as Philosopher*. New York: Macmillan, 1965.

Hayman, R. *Nietzsche: A Critical Life*. New York: Oxford University Press, 1980.

Nehamas, A. *Nietzsche: Life as Literature*. Cambridge, MA: Harvard University Press, 1985.

Schacht, R. *Nietzsche*. London: Routledge and Kegan Paul, 1983.

28

Jean-Paul Sartre

To the man or woman on the street, there are few philosophers as famous as Jean-Paul Sartre (1905–1980). There are, no doubt, many reasons for this fame. Perhaps one is that, in addition to writing works of academic philosophy, Sartre was also a richly talented novelist, dramatist, and social critic. This, however, is very likely not the entire story. Among relatively contemporary philosophers in the continental tradition, few have sought to detail and to examine what we might call the "human condition" with the verve and richness of Sartre. Even in his difficult Being and Nothingness *(a work much influenced by the German philosopher Martin Heidegger), there is much which strikes with the force of revelation.*

Sartre's literary works are too numerous to mention here. His early novel Nausea *is a useful introduction to his work. His major philosophical works are* The Transcendence of the Ego *(1937),* Being and Nothingness *(1946), and the* Critique of Dialectical Reason *(1960).*

NAUSEA

Antoine Roquentin, while in the city of Bouville (Mudville) doing research, is, over the course of some time, struck by "nausea." This is no ordinary illness. It is, rather, the recognition that things, phenomena, do not come in ready-made categories, nor do they have, as a result, any intrinsic meaning. The nausea is the gradual falling away of cultural, social, and philosophical efforts to impose an order or meaning on things and the self.

What is revealed is the bare existence of things, their brute "facticity." It is this awareness that serves to ground the existentialist credo that "existence precedes essence."

The Burden of Freedom

Along with the awareness of the brute facticity of things comes the recognition that one is wholly free. For it is not just the case that whatever meaning the things of experience have must be supplied by one's own free acts; in addition to this, one also recognizes that the social or cultural self is also a construction. We are anything we choose to be.

The comprehension of this absolute freedom and absolute responsibility is not easy to bear. As the hero of another of Sartre's novels has it: "Freedom is exile." It is exile precisely because, once one has been struck by the nausea, everything, the world and oneself, is unfamiliar and strange. Whatever one is and whatever the world means cannot be discovered, it must be made through choice and action.

BEING AND NOTHINGNESS

Being and Nothingness is Sartre's major philosophical work. It is a work that Sartre describes as an "essay on phenomenological ontology." It is an effort to describe the most fundamental aspects of being. And for Sartre, this means that what must be described is the being of consciousness and the being of phenomena—or that which appears to consciousness.

Sartre's Relation to Husserl

In approaching this massive work, some mention should be made of Sartre's indebtedness to Edmund Husserl (1859–1938) and to his phenomenological method. For the phenomenologists, all consciousness is intentional, that is, all consciousness of "consciousness-of." It is consciousness of what appears, or consciousness of phenomena. It is with these assumptions that Husserl begins something like Descartes' search for certainty, for a scientific foundation for knowledge. But Husserl rejects both the epistemological importance of Descartes' distinction between appearances and things, as well as Kant's distinction between phenomena and noumena, or "things-in-themselves."

For if consciousness, as Husserl has it, is consciousness of objects, then what we need to do is to investigate carefully and to describe these phenomena. This, for Husserl, is carried out by "bracketing" or setting aside the issue of the existence of things and limiting oneself to an examination of the objects of consciousness themselves. So, phenomenology is the search for accurate descriptions of the objects of consciousness.

According to Husserl, what is revealed in the correct application of the method is the real nature of the things themselves. And more than this, attention to our consciousness of objects makes clear that there exists a "transcendental ego," something which unifies and relates the various different consciousnesses of, say, a banana. (Now I see the banana from above, now from below, and so forth; something must serve to unify these various consciousnesses into a consciousness of *the banana*.)

There is much that Sartre takes over, in whole, from Husserl. But for our purposes we must emphasize the important disagreements.

ON CONSCIOUSNESS AND THE EGO

First, for Sartre, what is made manifest in consciousness is not the essence or nature of the object but the fact of its brute existence. A proper application of the phenomenological method does not reveal the nature of the objects of consciousness, but rather just the fact of the *being* of the objects of consciousness. Second, Sartre is at pains to argue against Husserl's notion of the transcendental ego. Sartre's arguments in the *Transcendence of the Ego* as well as in *Being and Nothingness* are complex, and his language is picturesque. Much of his point seems to be that a transcendental ego would, as it were, fill up every act of consciousness, it would make consciousness "opaque," and "heavy." But according to Sartre consciousness is pure "consciousness-of," wholly about an object; but this could not be so were the structure of consciousness to include a transcendental ego. Consciousness must be "translucent," a pure "emptiness."

The I, or ego, Sartre argues, is *transcendent*. It is an object of consciousness, not a part of consciousness. (As we will soon see, matters are more complicated than this.) Indeed, Sartre goes on to argue that all "consciousness-of " is, indirectly at least, self-consciousness. But it is not the case that, for example, in your current consciousness of the words on this page, there is also, and in addition, your consciousness of something else: your self, or ego. No, the point is that your consciousness of the words on this page must be, just by virtue of being a consciousness of the words on the page, self-consciousness.

THE INTRODUCTION TO BEING AND NOTHINGNESS

The "pursuit of being" is, as we have already announced, the study of the being of consciousness and the being of phenomena. In this way, Sartre's study is a contribution to the study of a traditional and familiar philosophical problem: the relation of consciousness to reality. Much of the difficult introduction to *Being and Nothingness* is an effort to display the errors of idealism and Husserl's phenomenology (though of course, Sartre agrees that phenomenology has done much to overcome the dualism of consciousness and object). As a way of making this clear, we may say that, for Sartre, the being of any phenomenon, any thing that appears, implies the existence of two "transphenomena:" consciousness, or the subject of phenomena, and the brute existence of the object of consciousness. In calling these "transphenomena" Sartre means to point out that these are not objects for consciousness, though there would be no phenomena but for these transphenomena.

Sartre's arguments for these conclusions are difficult. We have already said something about why it is that consciousness is a transphenomenon, never given as a phenomenon, but translucent, a pure emptiness. Part of Sartre's reasoning behind his claim that anything known must transcend our awareness of it is that any object that I grasp has a unity to it. But what makes it a unity is that it has an infinitude of phenomenal manifestations; and these cannot be grasped as a unity in any consciousness of phenomena. Sartre goes on to argue that when, for example, I am aware of an apple, it is not just the case that I intend some particular "applish" appearance or other. Rather, the being of the apple is present, but this being of the apple cannot be present to consciousness as a phenomenon, since it is precisely that which I am not aware of, the apple's unseen backside, and interior, etc., which grounds its being as an existent. Thus, objects are transphenomenal. This is the comprehension of the brute existence of things recognized in nausea.

"Being-in-Itself"

This transphenomenon, the brute existence of things, just is "being-in-itself." There is not much to be said about being-in-self; that is the nature of the beast. Sartre writes, for example, that "Being is. Being is in-itself. Being is what it is." Perhaps a bit more helpful is the following: "Uncreated, without reason for being, without any connection with any other being, being-in-itself is *de trop* for eternity." Thus "being-in-itself" is beyond the categories we bring to phenomena in seeking explanation and understanding. "Being-in-itself" simply is.

"Being-for-Itself"

If "being-in-itself" simply is, then "being-for-itself," consciousness, "is what it is not and is not what it is." We must return to this difficult and obscure formulation of the nature of the "for-itself." But we must note that for Sartre, it is consciousness, the "for-itself," that introduces nothingness into being.

Non-being, or nothingness, is something, Sartre tells us, that arises only with human beings. In a famous phrase: "The being by which Nothingness comes to the world must be its own Nothingness." Although nothingness is the product of human judgment, expectation, etc., it is not the case that nothingness is a mere abstraction, or fiction. In a puzzling way, Sartre wishes to characterize "concrete nothings." If we have a taste for paradox (and this is something we must cultivate in the reading of Sartre), we may say that nothingness is a real aspect of being.

THE 'FOR-ITSELF' AND NOTHINGNESS

How is it that the "for-itself" introduces nothingness into the heart of being? Fundamentally, the "nihilating" nature of the "for-itself" is present in the structure of consciousness itself. Every consciousness is, we have seen, a "consciousness-of," thus it must be an appearing to some subject of awareness. But what this makes apparent is that every consciousness is a consciousness of the "not-me." (Even reflective consciousness—in which I self-consciously try to make of myself an object of awareness—does not catch the "me" as its object, since there must a subject of consciousness who enjoys the consciousness of the object of awareness.) In this fundamental way, consciousness is a "not" in the heart of being.

This aspect of consciousness is, in fact, what generates the concrete nothings by means of human judgment and expectation. Thus, if I walk to the cafe expecting to meet Pierre, and he is absent, that absence is, for Sartre, a real thing. Consciousness is a "nihilator" and it introduces nothingness into the world, in this case, in the form of Pierre's absence.

NOTHINGNESS CONSIDERED

Still, if consciousness introduces nothingness into the world, its most fundamental "nihilating" activities are best seen when we turn those activities against consciousness itself. Consciousness is, for Sartre, itself a concrete nothing. In this way we may crisply characterize the distinction between the "in-itself" and the "for-itself." Consider, then, the case we mentioned above in which I may be said, in reflective consciousness, to attempt to have myself as an object of consciousness. I bring to awareness the fact that I am a male, a husband, a philosopher, a procrastinator, etc. But what this kind of effort makes clear is that there is essentially a cleavage between consciousness and its object. For the subject of awareness can never catch that subject as an object of consciousness. The thing reflecting is not identical with the thing reflected upon. And any property I attribute to myself in reflective consciousness is always open to question—just by virtue of this non-identity. What any particular consciousness is, as a result, is not a matter of discovery but a matter of choice, of free choice.

**Nothingness
and Freedom**

Here we have the connection between nothingness and freedom. Insofar as consciousness is spontaneous, a nothing, it is necessarily free—its existence precedes its essence. Thus, its being is always a question. For while an "in-itself" is what it is (a rose is a rose is a rose) this, as we have just seen Sartre arguing, is not true of the "for-itself." Thus, I am what I am not because I am, possibly, what I recognize I am not (e.g., I am possibly conscientious, etc.) and I am not what I am just because no fact about me, my past, etc., constitutes me. This double negativity is revealed in the simple fact of consciousness.

BAD FAITH

The "nihilating" activity of consciousness against itself is perhaps best seen in Sartre's discussion of bad faith. The phenomenon of bad faith (typically called "self-deception") is a familiar one. Sartre's discussion of it is among the most brilliant portions of *Being and Nothingness*.

We often find people believing what we also believe they believe to be false. We speak of people, in some way or another, lying to themselves. Some examples spring to mind: The alcoholic, his life in ruins, who believes he is not an alcoholic, the anorectic, in the face of illness and decay, believing that she has no eating disorder. We might spell out the cases in detail; but the point is, in any case, how can one believe one's own lies, how can one believe what one also believes one has no good reason for believing? (It should be mentioned that before Sartre provides his own account of bad faith he considers appeals to the unconscious in order to explain this phenomenon. His criticism and rejection of Freud has proved to be one of the more enduring achievements of this work.)

**Explaining
Bad Faith**

Sartre's explanation of bad faith hinges on his conception of the "for-itself" as a being who is what it is not and is not what it is. Thus, for Sartre, the human being is an uneasy amalgam of facticity and transcendence. I am facticity in so far as it is a fact about me that I am a white American male, that my body is constituted as it is, etc. But I am, for Sartre, at the very same time, transcendence; I am not these things, for all these are the product of my interpretation and, he says, my choice. I am able to transcend these, to leave these behind, to constitute myself differently. And again, that this is true is manifest in my reflective consciousness and in the cleavage between subject and object of consciousness.

In bad faith, one exploits the fact that one is simultaneously facticity and transcendence; one holds the two apart or makes of transcendence, facticity or of facticity, transcendence. Consider a simple example: A long-time smoker may say to himself that, since he has failed to quit many past times, he is a smoker. He concludes that there is no point in trying to quit. Or he may say that, though he currently smokes, he can nonetheless quit anytime he wants, and so there is no point to quitting now. Both of these attitudes reflect bad faith; the first makes transcendence into facticity and the second makes facticity into transcendence.

FACTICITY AND TRANSCENDENCE

But since the human being is fundamentally just this uneasiness of facticity and transcendence, how is it that bad faith is to be avoided? Sartre's answer seems to be that it is a matter of recognizing that one is simultaneously facticity and transcendence. There is always disintegration at the center of the "for-itself." There is, and essentially so, no stability for the "for-self." In good faith, we recognize this fact, we recognize the nothingness at our core and realize that we must decide to be what we are. Thus Sartre writes:

> Good faith seeks to flee the inner disintegration of my being in the direction of the in-itself which it should be and is not. Bad faith seeks to flee the in-itself by means of the inner disintegration of my being. But it denies the very disintegration as it denies that it is itself bad faith.

Bad faith flees from the disintegration while at the same time exploiting it. Good faith flees from it as well, but it does not flee in order to escape, since it recognizes clear-headedly that such escape is not possible. Good faith comprehends that it is absolute freedom. It must flee toward being in order to be at all, but it understands that it is not this being towards which it flees.

FREEDOM

Our discussion of bad faith and the ways in which the "for-itself" both is and generates nothingness has emphasized Sartre's preoccupation with freedom. Given the view that the subject of consciousness is a concrete nothing, it follows that there is no substantival or secure self. One *is* only insofar as one chooses and acts. We are, according to Sartre, a choice in the making. And since there is never a firm grounding for such a choice, such choice is absurd. In holding that such choice is unconditioned and without base of support, Sartre points to the fact that I am absolute, spontaneous, choice.

This is a radical view. Such a view of free action has it that the basis of choice is not to be found in what I am (conscientious, prim, virtuous, etc.)

or in the requirements of reason, or, as according to the currently popular therapeutic sensibility, in my past (my parents' treatment of me, my socioeconomic status, etc.). There is, in a literal fashion, no basis for whatever I choose; and whatever I point to as grounding that choice must be, ultimately, some other choice.

It is in virtue of this view that Sartre sometimes speaks of my choosing and being responsible not only for myself but also for the world. Any situation I find myself in is my creation. What matters to me, what I must balance in any decision, is the result of my freedom, my choice. I create my world, and the situations that I face in my world, by supplying the meanings, the interpretations, and the significance for things. (Recall, here, that being simply *is*.) Since this world is the product of my choice, I, and I alone, bear responsibility for this world. I might choose some other.

Sartre's is a conception of our freedom and responsibility as absolute. And it can be no surprise that according to Sartre, most of us try to flee, in bad faith, the anguish of such freedom. Sartre, of course, wants to view our responsibility for the world and ourselves as absolute just because such choice is wholly spontaneous and without support. It is important to note that we might draw a contrary conclusion. For how, if such choice is, in fact, baseless, could it be anything but arbitrary and a matter of chance? But, perhaps in addition to being an expression of bad faith (as Sartre would surely say), this is not quite fair to Sartre. His real point may be that the effort to ground our fundamental values and preferences, our notions of the good life, in something outside of ourselves is doomed to failure; the only real basis to our values and their only support could be our continuous choosing to affirm them in action.

*O*ur *treatment of Sartre has, of necessity, been selective. We have not discussed what is essential to his notion of the facticity of the for-itself, his treatment of the body. Nor have we considered his version of Hegel's Lordship and Bondage dialectic, "The Look." Both of these discussions are of central importance in Sartre's phenomenological ontology. Even so, we have characterized what is peculiar to Sartre's conception of the human situation. We should close by noting that later in his life Sartre turned more and more to political activism and to Marxism. There are suggestions that Marxism interiorized, or internalized, is a kind of existentialism.*

Selected Readings

Catalano, J. *A Commentary on Jean-Paul Sartre's Being and Nothingness.* Chicago: University of Chicago Press, 1980.

Warnock, M. *The Philosophy of Sartre.* Oxford: Oxford University Press, 1965.

29

American Pragmatism

*T*he philosophical movement known as American Pragmatism originated in the United States at the end of the nineteenth century and reached the height of its influence (to date) in the first half of the twentieth century. The three greatest exponents of American Pragmatism are its originator Charles Sanders Peirce (1839–1914), William James (1842–1910), and John Dewey (1859–1952), who gave pragmatism its most systematic expression. Other notable figures in the development of American Pragmatism are George Herbert Mead (1863–1931) and C. I. Lewis (1883–1964). One of the most remarkable features of American Pragmatism is that three thinkers with such disparate training, temperaments, and interests as Peirce, James, and Dewey could plausibly come to be understood as advocating many of the same basic philosophical doctrines. Whereas Peirce took as his source of historical inspiration the philosophy of Immanuel Kant, James built his views upon the foundation of British empiricism, and the most abiding influence upon Dewey was the thought of Hegel. Peirce was primarily interested in mathematics, logic, and the philosophy of science, while James demonstrated broad humanistic interests often focusing upon religious issues, and Dewey demonstrated broad interests in the social sciences and the humanities.

The common threads that unite these disparate intellects into a single movement are their convictions (1) that human thought, intelligence, and reason are properly understood as tools for bringing about more and more effective control of our environment in the discovery and pursuit of the ends we value, and (2) that the experimental method utilized by the empirical sciences, with its emphasis upon the role of practical activity, is a paradigmatic example of the optimal method for employing these tools. Although *the label pragmatic is borrowed by Peirce from a technical distinction made by Kant, the pragmatists are truly pragmatic in their approach to philosophy. Theories are good if they effectively facilitate activity in practice; bad if they do not. True beliefs allow us to gain greater control of our experiences as means to more effective and satisfying action; false beliefs do not.*

PEIRCE

The first formulation of certain pragmatist themes appears in Peirce's essay "How to Make Our Ideas Clear." In this essay, Peirce argues that "beliefs," properly understood, are really "rules for action," and that "the rational purport of a word or other expression, lies exclusively in its conceivable bearing upon the conduct of life." To see what Peirce means by these claims, consider that in science, one belief is shown to be superior to another in part by the demonstration, through experimental activity, that effects predicted by the first belief occur, while effects predicted by the second belief do not. The assumption clearly is that a belief which is in this respect more predictively powerful ought to be accepted in preference to another, less predictively powerful belief. Each candidate for belief is a proposed rule for experimental actions that yield certain effects, but the superior belief provides better rules for action, rules that allow for more extensive and accurate prediction of the effects of actions, thereby allowing for greater manipulation and control of those effects in the pursuit of our ends. Peirce argues that what is true for scientific beliefs is true for beliefs generally. Beliefs are rules for action. To believe that it will surely rain today, for instance, simply is to commit to such rules of action as that if you have a picnic, it will be ruined, if you leave the car window open, the interior will get wet, and so on. Moreover, Peirce's theory of meaning suggests that what is true for beliefs is true for the meanings of words and expressions.

JAMES

Peirce develops these pragmatic themes for application (for the most part) in the relatively constrained realms of logic, philosophy of language, and the philosophy of science. It is William James who appropriates these themes for application to broader issues in philosophy and in the attempt to reconcile apparent conflicts between science and values. His pragmatic metaphysics and epistemology find their most developed formulations in his collection of essays entitled *Essays in Radical Empiricism*, although many aspects of this account are anticipated in his *The Principles of Psychology*, one of the great founding texts of the modern science of psychology. His pragmatic inquiry into the relationship of science to values is presented in his collection of essays entitled *The Will to Believe* and in his book *The Varieties of Religious Experience*. A succinct and accessible summary of many of these aspects of James' account appears in his collection of essays entitled *Pragmatism*.

James on Truth

The central component of James' epistemological and metaphysical theory is his account of truth. According to James, since the purpose of thought and ideas is to allow us to gain greater control of our experience in the pursuit of ends we value, the claim that an idea is true is simply a claim that it is a useful "instrument," that it "will carry us prosperously from any one part of our experience to any other part, linking things satisfactorily, working securely, simplifying, saving labor." (*Pragmatism*, p. 30) A belief is false if it is not such a useful instrument. Thus, the belief that there is no gravity is false because such a belief will not link things satisfactorily. It will fly in the face of many of our particular experiences, for instance, the experience of falling when dropped, and will result in much wasted labor (not to mention serious injury). The belief that there is gravity is true for the opposite reasons. Utilizing the tools of pragmatism, specifically the criterion that beliefs are true only if they are useful instruments for more effective prediction of the consequences of action, James concludes that many traditional philosophical debates are mere pseudodebates since which side is accepted makes no difference for predicting the consequences of particular actions in the process of living our lives. For other such philosophical debates, however, James concludes exactly the opposite—that which side of the debate we accept as true profoundly effects our ability to successfully comprehend and predict the consequences of our actions, hence to discover and accomplish the ends for which we live our lives.

The Will to Believe

It is in James' famous essay "The Will to Believe" that he develops another extremely controversial result that he takes to flow from pragmatism. According to James, pragmatism demonstrates that in certain key cases we have the right to choose what to believe. Most of our beliefs cannot, of course, be chosen. My belief that I am less than seven feet tall is not the result of choice but of evidence—it is ridiculous to suggest that I can choose to believe otherwise. But with many candidates for belief of great importance to us, for instance our belief in human freedom and our belief in God, James argues that evidence through appeal to particular effects and consequences simply does not decisively determine the issue one way or the other. Yet whether one believes in human freedom or in God can have a profound impact upon the life one leads and the satisfactions one derives from leading it. Nor is it legitimate to refrain from choosing in such cases because of a lack of sufficient evidence. Not choosing *is* a choice. To refrain from choosing to believe in God, for instance, is effectively to choose not to believe in God. Moreover, often the only way to get evidence for one's belief is to choose to adopt the belief in the first place. Consider, for example, that in athletics the belief that one will win is often a crucial component in winning, hence in producing evidence that the belief was a true one. In such cases, James argues, individuals have a right to choose or to will to believe in God, freedom, etc., and there are compelling practical reasons for doing so, most notably the satisfaction and purpose that such beliefs will contribute to individuals' lives.

DEWEY

Although James expands the focus of pragmatism, he does so in a haphazard and relatively unsystematic fashion. It is in the writings of John Dewey that pragmatism receives its most carefully articulated and systematic formulation. Though Dewey is perhaps better known as a social reformer, educator, and political theorist, his writings in these areas are best understood as specific implementations of his own articulation of the pragmatic tradition that he inherits from James and Peirce. Like James, Dewey takes as the primary challenge to philosophy the task of reconciling the intransigent conflict between science and values, broadly construing the latter as including aesthetics and politics as well as ethics. In true pragmatic fashion, Dewey attempts to demonstrate that this conflict is the inevitable result of a radical and unwarranted disconnection of philosophical inquiry from practical activity. In place of this separation, Dewey presents a theory of inquiry and a corresponding epistemology and metaphysics that are essentially grounded in practical activity.

Dewey on the History of Philosophy

The constructive components of Dewey's brand of pragmatism are built, in large part, upon his systematic criticism of the Western philosophical tradition. In *The Quest For Certainty*, Dewey argues that the philosophical quest through history is characterized by an interrelated and systematically misguided set of epistemological, metaphysical, and methodological commitments. The epistemological commitment is to a quest for the attainment of *certain* knowledge. The metaphysical commitment is to the attempt to locate the proper objects of knowledge in a higher reality, an unchanging realm of pure being. The methodological commitment is to a method of inquiry that completely rejects any role for practical activity. The interconnection of these three traditional philosophical commitments can be made readily apparent. Practical activity is by its nature uncertain; it deals with individualized situations that are never exactly duplicable. All such activity, moreover, essentially involves change. Practical activity involves change and uncertainty; the quest of traditional philosophy is for certain knowledge of an unchanging reality. The method of philosophical inquiry appropriate to this quest thus must not concern itself with the inherently uncertain realm of practical action. It must focus instead upon the certain knowledge of an unchanging realm that is accessible only through reason and pure intellection.

Dewey argues that it is precisely the radical uncertainty surrounding action, the constant peril of acting in an almost completely uncontrolled and unpredictable environment, that first led primitive men to the postulation of a supernatural realm the secrets of which were accessible only through oracle and omen. It was only later, with the Greek philosophers, that this supernatural realm began a process of transformation to a realm of pure, unchanging being, a realm of which certain knowledge is held to be available through the exercise of pure intellection and reason. Metaphysically, the realm of action is demoted to a realm of mere appearance and becoming, as opposed to the realm of reality and being.

Epistemologically, the realm of action is demoted to a realm of which only belief and opinion, as opposed to knowledge, are possible. Methodologically, the method of inquiry appropriate to the formation of mere opinions governing actions in the realm of appearance is ignored in favor of the method of inquiry appropriate to the rational attainment of knowledge of reality.

SCIENTIFIC METHOD

Dewey argues that although thinkers from the seventeenth century on continue to endorse the fundamentally skewed metaphysical, epistemological, and methodological commitments of the Greeks, they do abandon the Greeks' teleological approach to science, an approach governed by a method of inquiry divorced from practical activity, in favor of modern science. The most distinctive feature of modern science is its adoption of a method of inquiry, the experimental method, that establishes an intrinsic connection between scientific inquiry and practical scientific activity. It is the scientific method, Dewey argues, that holds the key to unlocking the systematic errors of traditional philosophy.

Method provides the key because, although the scientific method is one which essentially connects the quest for scientific knowledge to experimental activity, the knowledge obtained through the use of this method is nonetheless taken by scientists and philosophers to be certain knowledge of an unchanging reality. The method links knowing to practical activity, but the account of knowledge and reality continues to be one built upon the denial of such a linkage. It is this fundamental inconsistency, on Dewey's view, that leads to the intractable conflicts between science and values that have dominated philosophy since the seventeenth century. Philosophers allow that there are values of which we can have certain knowledge, and allow that scientific inquiry reveals ultimate reality. But scientific reality, the deterministic reality of matter in motion, allows no place for values. The commitment to science thus leads philosophers to a denial of values, while the commitment to values leads philosophers to a reality fundamentally incompatible with that dictated by science.

Dewey's Constructive Account

Dewey attempts to utilize this account of the problem of philosophy through its history to motivate his pragmatic resolution of the problem. Clearly, he maintains, it is the quest for certain knowledge of ultimate reality and the radical separation between knowledge and practical activity that this quest involves that has led philosophy into its current morass. Science points the way for Dewey, not because it discloses certain knowledge of a true reality, but because it employs a method of inquiry that intrinsically links knowledge and practical activity, hence that implicitly rejects the quest for certainty attainable only through a methodological rejection of a role for practical activity. Dewey's championing of the scientific method is the championing of the adoption, in a particular area of inquiry, of a method which on Dewey's view ought properly to be extended to all areas of inquiry—a pragmatic method of inquiry that forges an intrinsic connection between knowledge and practical activity.

In *Logic: The Theory of Inquiry*, Dewey articulates an account of inquiry according to which inquiry is understood as "the controlled or directed transformation of an indeterminate situation into one that is . . . determinate in its constituent distinctions and relations . . ." (p. 104) Inquiry begins in doubt and is successful when such doubt is successfully removed. Knowledge, according to Dewey, is the product of successful inquiry; the mistake of traditional accounts was to demand that knowledge be certain, hence that it be placed upon a more solid foundation than inquiry can provide. Dewey's theory of knowledge constitutes an abandonment of the claim that the task of epistemology, hence of a theory of knowledge, is to determine what we can know for certain (and how we can come to know it). A determinate situation may become indeterminate in the face of new developments or in the face of new and superior methods of inquiry. But far from viewing this potential revisability of all knowledge as a shortcoming of his theory of knowledge, Dewey sees this as a necessary feature of any account of knowledge that pretends to include the continually evolving outcomes of inquiry concerning the things that humans claim to know.

Just as Dewey's theory of knowledge is a pragmatic attack upon the quest for certain knowledge, and his theory of inquiry is a pragmatic attack upon the traditional method of inquiry employed in the pursuit of that knowledge, so too his metaphysics is a pragmatic attack upon the traditional philosophical quest to discern the true, unchanging reality which is held to be the proper object of certain knowledge. In his *Experience and Nature*, Dewey argues that there is no unchanging realm of being, no antecedent reality, which it is the unique office of philosophy to uncover. It is this commitment to a reality transcending the realm of practical activity which has systematically skewed most, if not all, of the defining dualisms of traditional metaphysics, including those between subject and object, mind and body, form and matter, and appearance and reality. Dewey's metaphysical writings are thus largely taken up in efforts to demonstrate that these dualisms, properly understood, are dualisms both components of which can be comprehended within the natural realm of practical activity, not dualisms between one component within the natural realm (e.g., body) and another existing in some higher realm (e.g., mind).

Dewey developed the consequences of his pragmatism for politics and education (Democracy and Education), ethics ("Towards a Theory of Valuation"), and aesthetics (Art as Experience). Throughout these works and the works of the other pragmatists, there is a continued effort to demonstrate that because philosophy should be less than has been previously thought—it should not be a quest for certain knowledge of an unchanging realm of being—it can be more than has previously been thought; more relevant to understanding the world in which human beings live and how that world can be made better. The pragmatic insistence that theories must make a difference to practice insures that philosophical theorizing will be relevant to practice. Though this pragmatic movement waned in popularity through the middle of the twentieth century, it has recently been revived in the writings of such noted philosopherrs as Richard Rorty, Hilary Putnam, and Wilfrid Sellars.

Selected Readings

Dewey, J. *The Quest For Certainty*. New York: C. P. Putnam's Sons, 1960. (All citations of this text in the chapter are of this edition.)

_____. *Logic: The Theory of Inquiry*. New York: Holt, Rinehart and Winston, 1938. (All citations in the chapter are of this edition.)

James, W. *Pragmatism*. Indianapolis: Hackett, 1981. (All citations in the chapter are of this edition.)

Schlipp, P., ed. *The Philosophy of John Dewey*. Chicago: Northwestern University, 1939.

Sleeper, R.W. *The Necessity of Pragmatism*. New Haven: Yale University Press, 1986.

30

The Origins
of Analytic Philosophy

At the turn of the century, both in Germany and (only slightly later) in England, what we today call analytic philosophy was being born. One should not suppose, however, that analytic philosophy emerged all at once and fully mature at some determinate time. More importantly, one should not suppose that analytic philosophy is characterized by a fixed and unique essence—some unified and tightly organized set of defining doctrines, interests, or methodology. The analytic tradition has evolved steadily, though quite gradually over the last century; and there has always been a great deal of diversity — even sharp antagonism — among the views of the various subgroups or individuals that are typically collected under this label. Nevertheless, there are loosely related concerns and strategies that do tend to be more characteristic of the analytic approach than others. These were especially prominent in the earliest manifestations of the analytic approach.

THE FUNDAMENTAL STATUS OF LOGIC AND THE ANALYSIS OF LANGUAGE

Crucial to the origin and character of analytic philosophy was the emergence of a renewed concern with the nature and status of *logic*—a concern which, though lively for the Greeks and the Scholastics, was rendered marginal when, as a result of Descartes' influence on European philosophy, epistemological questions achieved an explanatory priority over all other philosophical enquiries. At the turn of the century, however, a growing number of philosophers began to view logic as one of the most fundamental, if not the most fundamental, concern of philosophy. The emerging attitude seems to have been this: Unless we possess a clear understanding of the nature and status of logic—of those principles which structure our very understanding of truth and reason—what hope can we have of achieving a satisfactory philosophical understanding of the diverse issues raised in any other area of philosophical enquiry?

Correlative with this new emphasis on logic, and of at least equal importance for the development of analytical philosophy, was a growing conviction that the most promising way (indeed, for some, the only way) to achieve a philosophically illuminating account of logic—and with it, of rational thought generally—is through an adequate philosophical account of *language*. The reasons for this new emphasis on language are diverse and difficult to trace with accuracy. It is worth noting, however, that in the most interesting cases the increased focus on language was not unrelated to the sorts of concerns that led directly to the new priority accorded logic in the philosophical hierarchy.

THE REJECTION OF IDEALISM AND PSYCHOLOGISM IN LOGIC

Suffice it to say that those philosophers chiefly responsible for founding the analytic movement, Gottlob Frege and Bertrand Russell, came to believe that certain central features of the two philosophical perspectives that dominated the scene during their early careers—classical empiricism and neo-Hegelian idealism—committed the proponents of those perspectives to wholly untenable views about the nature and status of logic. In particular, as we shall see in more detail when we examine Frege's views below, these earlier views were seen as involving or promoting a conception of the mind and the nature of thought—specifically, the nature of judgement—that was overly psychologistic. Because of this, they were regarded as incapable of providing a satisfactory account of the nature of judgement or of doing justice to what Frege called the "objectivity" of thought. In consequence, they were viewed as incapable of doing justice to the nature and status of logic.

The earliest analytic philosophers came to feel that by an appropriate shift of focus away from the mind and its immediate contents to language—the public medium of thought and the exchange of ideas—the deficiencies of psychologism could be more readily exposed, and the demands placed by an adequate conception of logic on our understanding of thought and judgement could be more clearly seen. Emphasis on the analysis of language spread quickly. Eventually, traditional philosophical problems generally came to be viewed as the result of linguistic confusions, and the proper method for their solution, or dissolution, as laying in a logically adequate analysis of the language involved. For only thereby could the confusions be adequately exposed and overcome.

The impact of this way of thinking on twentieth-century philosophy—for good or ill—must not to be underestimated. Though today some of the more fundamental presuppositions of the analytic approach are coming under challenge, the movement is not likely to die a quick death. And so, it is incumbent on anyone wishing to understand contemporary Anglo-American philosophy to become familiar with the general outlines of the analytic approach. The chapters that follow aim to acquaint the reader, in at least a preliminary way, with two of the principal figures and some of the central issues responsible for the emergence of analytic philosophy.

31

Gottlob Frege

*G*ottlob Frege (1848–1925) was a German mathematician, logician, and philosopher. Frege was a professor of Mathematics as the University of Jena, but most of his published work belongs to philosophy rather than to mathematics. And even in mathematics, the bulk of his mature work is in logic. His philosophical interests were quite limited, being confined to philosophical logic, the philosophy of mathematics, and what we today call the philosophy of language.

Frege's earliest major work of philosophical interest is Begriffsschrift (Conceptual Notation), *published in 1879. This was followed, in 1884, by his masterpiece,* Die Grundlagen der Arithmetik (The Foundations of Arithmetic). *In 1893, the first volume of his unfinished magnum opus,* Die Grundgesetze der Arithmetik (The Basic Laws of Arithmetic), *appeared. The second volume appeared in 1903, and the third remained unwritten—no doubt primarily because he was unable to see his way around a contradiction in his system that the British philosopher/logician Bertrand Russell pointed out (see chapter 32). In addition to these books, Frege also published a series of seminal articles on topics in philosophical logic and the philosophy of language, including* "Funktion und Begriff" ("Function and Concept") *in 1891,* "Uber Sinn und Bedeutung" ("On Sense and Meaning") *in 1892,* "Uber Begriff und Gegenstand" ("On Concept and Object") *in 1892, and his three* Logische Untersuchungen (Logical Investigations)— "Der Gedanken" ("Thoughts") *in 1919,* "Negation" *in 1919, and* "Gedankengefuge" ("Compound Thoughts") *in 1923. Most of Frege's unpublished writings on philosophical topics have also been collected and published together as* Nachgelassene Schriften (Posthumous Writings).

During his lifetime, Frege's writings were typically ignored or misunderstood. Not until Russell, and then Ludwig Wittgenstein, drew attention to them, expressing their own profound admiration of them, did they begin to achieve the critical notice and respect they so clearly deserve. Today, their impact is so pervasive that they can be said, with little exaggeration, to have set the agenda for or otherwise shaped the methodology of nearly every area of contemporary analytic philosophy.

BACKGROUND

Frege's Logicism

The guiding project of Frege's professional career was his concern to show that it is possible to reduce the truths of mathematics (excluding geometry, for reasons that need not concern us) to truths of pure logic. Frege contended that true mathematical propositions do not have their own special and irreducible subject matter, and thus mathematics is not to be thought of as just another special science such as physics, chemistry, or biology. Neither are true mathematical propositions synthetic a priori, as Kant had believed. Nor, finally, are they empirical, as John Stuart Mill argued. Rather, according to Frege, true propositions in mathematics express truths of pure logic. It is precisely in virtue of this that mathematics possesses the distinctive epistemological and metaphysical status that it has.

The thesis that pure mathematics is really nothing but logic, and hence is reducible to logic, is standardly known as *logicism*. Given Frege's commitment to logicism, it is not surprising that he should have been deeply concerned to understand the nature of logic. After all, if one's aim is to demonstrate (1) that all mathematical expressions are definable in terms of purely logical notions, and (2) that all mathematical truths are provable from these definitions and purely logical first principles, then one had better have a fairly clear and compelling conception of what does and does not belong to the domain of logic. In particular, one had better have a clear view of what counts as a genuine proof based exclusively on logical principles.

The notion of logical proof or deductively valid inference plays a central role in Frege's conception of his foundational investigation. It was essential to the success of Frege's project that any purported proofs of the basic mathematical laws from purely logical first principles be rigorous, fully explicit, and gap-free. If a proof were imperfectly rigorous, the possibility would always exist that it depended upon hidden assumptions—assumptions whose truth may be open to dispute, or whose status as purely logical may be questionable. Unless this possibility were excluded, one would have no right to be confident that one had correctly identified the fundamental principles on which mathematics rests, let alone to have shown them to be exclusively logical in nature.

The Begriffsschrift: A Logically Perfect Language

It was in the context of these demands that Frege wrote his *Begriffsschrift*. Frege regarded ordinary language as too imprecise to support the kind of logical rigor he required. He felt that he could proceed only by constructing a logically perfect artificial language and by devising a formal system of inference designed to ensure the accuracy and explicitness of proofs carried out in that language.

In the *Begriffsschrift*, Frege set out to design a language which allowed for the expression of only what is essential for logic, as opposed to the various logically distracting expressive and rhetorical properties of ordinary language. As far as possible, all logically relevant similarities and differences between sentences in our ordinary language were to be captured directly, and without rhetorical residue, by purely formal or syntactic similarities and differences in the allowable sentences of the *Begriffsschrift*, and any logically irrelevant syntactic differences between sentences must be guaranteed to play no role in the construction and evaluation of inferences. Rules of inference were then to be designed that attend only to those syntactic features of *Begriffsschrift* sentences that are logically relevant, and in such ways as to guarantee the validity of the inferences they license. Finally, a number of *Begriffsschrift* sentences must be identified which, when their meaning was made clear, would clearly be recognized as expressing fundamental logical truths and which, consequently, could serve as axioms for his system. Frege's hope was that once this was accomplished, all logical relations between sentences could be determined purely by inspection, according to fixed rules, of the formal features of the sentences involved. The result was an extraordinary achievement: the first rigorous formal axiomatic logical theory, incorporating, it turns out, truth-functional logic and first- and second-order quantification theory.

LOGIC AND THE OBJECTIVITY OF THOUGHTS

The Fundamental Normative Status of Logical Principles

Frege's project in the *Begriffsschrift* required that he be clear about what features of our ordinary sentences are and are not logically relevant. And this required, in turn, that he be clear about the nature and status of logic itself.

For Frege, the nature of logic is revealed, in the first instance, by reflecting on its normative status. In particular, it is revealed by reflecting on those of our cognitive and linguistic practices for which the principles of logic provide constitutive standards against which their success or failure is evaluated. Reflection reveals that logic specifically sets standards that govern those of our cognitive and linguistic practices that essentially concern themselves with the *truth*. Indeed, for Frege the principles of logic are nothing less than the "laws of truth"—they express the very content of the concept of truth.

In particular, then, logic sets standards that constitutively govern our practice of judgment, assertion, and inference. Judgment or belief essentially aims at the truth. Judgments are, in the first instance, correct or incorrect, successful or unsuccessful, just insofar as they are or are not true. Assertion is just the outward expression of judgment. And inference essentially subserves judgment. When inferring, we start with judgments as premises and aim to justify a judgment as conclusion. An inference is successful or valid only insofar as the truth of the premises guarantees for us the truth of the conclusion. In this respect, inference, too, essentially aims at the truth. The principles of logic impose the ultimate standards of consistency on our thinking and speaking, standards we cannot opt out of and still consider ourselves to be making judgments or assertions. The "laws of logic" are, as Frege puts the matter in the introduction to The *Basic Laws of Arithmetic*, "the most general laws, which prescribe universally how one ought to think if one is to think at all."

The logician's task is to articulate these laws in a rigorous and systematic way. To do this, he must provide a detailed account of precisely those features of our judgments and assertions by virtue of which they are subject to logical appraisal in the systematic ways that they are. He must, in other words, provide an account of that by virtue of which our judgments and assertions are subject to evaluation as true or false, by virtue of which our beliefs are consistent or inconsistent, by virtue of which our inferences are valid or invalid.

Distinguishing Judgments from Their Contents

For Frege, the essential first step in any such account was to distinguish clearly judgments or assertions, qua mental acts or states, from their contents—that which is judged or asserted. To judge is to acknowledge the truth of a propositional content—what Frege came to call a *Gedanken* (which I will always translate as Thought, with a capital T). But Frege insisted that the content of a judgment—the Thought—must be viewed as, in some sense, independent of the act of judging.

Appreciating this independence is required if we are to do justice to the distinction between merely grasping or entertaining a Thought and actually acknowledging its truth. And unless we recognize this distinction, we shall not be able to do justice to the various ways in which our judgments and the judgments of others are subject to comparative logical appraisal in the ways that they are. For example, unless we admit the possibility of grasping a Thought that we are not obliged to admit as true, we could make no sense of our ability to recognize—and our attendant logical obligation to respond to—intersubjective disagreements and intrasubjective inconsistencies in judgment. To understand what is asserted by a person with whom I disagree, I must be able to entertain the Thought—the same Thought—that he or she asserted, even though I am not willing to acknowledge its truth. The Thought we both grasp, and which the other person acknowledges as true and I do not, cannot be essentially dependent on his or her judging it. It is available for both of us to entertain, though it is, in some sense, independent of either of our doing so.

The point is that in order for our judgments, assertions, and inferences to be subject to logical appraisal (as they must be if they are even to count as judgments, assertions, or inferences), it is required that we be able to recognize the same Thought again—sometimes asserted by ourselves, sometimes asserted by others, sometimes denied, and sometimes occurring as an unasserted component in a complex Thought which may itself be asserted, denied, or queried. (This latter would be the case, for example, with disjunctive Thoughts, Thoughts of the form "P or Q." Since I may be unsure which is the case, I may be willing to commit myself to the truth of the disjunctive Thought that either John went to the store or he went to the movies, without being willing to commit myself to the truth of either the Thought that John went to the store or the Thought that John went to the movies individually.) If some feature of a possible judgment or assertion is such that logic requires us, in these sorts of ways, to recognize its presence again, that feature is, according to Frege, to be assigned to the content of the judgment, the Thought.

For Frege, it is Thoughts, then, that are the primary relata of logical relations and the primary bearers of truth value (that is, what are, in the first instance, to be evaluated as true or false). Frege conceived of Thoughts as mind-independent abstract objects in their own right, distinct from either external material objects or from such inner mental objects as pains, images, and tickles. They were objects to which minds of an appropriate complexity could stand in various cognitive relations—grasping, judging, doubting, querying, etc.

Even so, it would be a profound mistake to suppose that what lies behind Frege's repeated insistence on the objectivity of Thoughts amounts to no more than his insistence that they possess this sort of mind-independent ontological status. Indeed, as we have already begun to see, for Frege, appreciating the objectivity of Thoughts means appreciating their independence from the mental acts of judging or asserting, which in turn involves appreciating the special sense in which the same Thoughts may be entertained by different people or by the same person at different times. Appreciating the objectivity of thoughts in this sense is required if we are to respect the way in which our judgments are constitutively subject to logical appraisal in the ways that they are. The intimate connection between Frege's insistence on the objectivity of Thoughts and his conception of the demands of logic is, perhaps, best appreciated by considering what remained throughout his life a central feature of his approach—his anti-psychologism.

FREGE'S ANTI-PSYCHOLOGISM

Distinguishing the Logical from the Psychological

In the introduction to *The Foundations of Arithmetic*, Frege lays down three related methodological principles that he felt were essential to any well-conceived investigation into the nature of logic, language, and thought. These principles are:

1. Always separate sharply the psychological from the logical, the subjective from the objective.

2. Never ask for the meaning of a word in isolation, but only in the context of a sentence.

3. Never lose sight of the distinction between concept and object.

In the first of these principles, Frege is rejecting any insinuation of psychologism into the study of logic. What exactly Frege understood psychologism to be will emerge momentarily. The principle makes it clear, however, that the problem with psychologism—however Frege understood it—is that it in some way undermines, falsifies, or otherwise fails to respect the distinction between what is objective and what is subjective. Its failure to respect this distinction is not distinct from its failure, as Frege puts it in other places, to do justice to the centrality of the notion of truth in logic.

In the beginning of his late essay "Thoughts," for example, Frege writes:

From the laws of truth there follow prescriptions about asserting, thinking, judging, inferring. And we may very well speak of laws of thought in this way too. But there is at once a danger of confusing different things. People may very well interpret the expression "law of thought" by analogy with "law of nature" and then have in their mind general features of thinking as mental occurrence. A law of thought in this sense would be a psychological law. And so they might come to believe that logic deals with the process of thinking and with the psychological laws in accordance with which it takes place. That would be misunderstanding the task of logic, for truth has not been given its proper place.

This passage reveals that at the core of psychologism, for Frege, is the tendency—either explicit or implicit—to identify logic with the science of human thinking, to view the laws of logic as, at bottom, those laws of nature in accordance with which human thinking takes place. This conflation, according to Frege, results from a failure to do justice to the place of truth in logic and, consequently, in an inability to sustain a coherent distinction between the subjective and the objective.

Psychologism's Failure to Respect the Subjective/ Objective Distinction

If we are to understand Frege here, getting clear about the contrast between subjective and objective, as he intends it, is crucial. For Frege, objectivity is not something we can understand or define independently of logical considerations. There is no assessing the objectivity of something except from a perspective that gives substance to the contrast between something being the case versus its merely seeming to be the case—the contrast between true and false judgment. And such a perspective is provided only by a point of view antecedently committed to accepting the normative governance of logic. When we say, "it is objectively the case that P" (where P, here, stands for any indicative sentential complement), we are, in effect, doing no more than asserting that P, that is, accepting that it is true that P. If the circumstance that P can be asserted to obtain, then the circumstance that P is an objective circumstance. The connection between truth, assertibility, and objectivity could not be more intimate.

This being the case, our appreciation of the distinction between the subjective and the objective issues from and is manifest in our appreciation of and sense of responsibility to the norms of logic in our practice of judgment, assertion, and inference. Those features of our cognitive and linguistic practice that exhibit this commitment are so intimately connected with the essence of logic that any attempt to characterize that essence which failed to do justice to such features would *ipso facto* fail to be a satisfactory characterization of logic. Frege's most fundamental critique of psychologism, then, is an argument that the conception of logical laws endorsed by the promoter of psychologism (the psychologician, as I shall call him) fails in just this way.

Frege's most sustained attacks on psychologism are to be found in the Introduction to *The Basic Laws of Arithmetic* and in his essay "Thoughts." We will focus on a line of argument extractable from Frege's discussion in the Introduction to *The Basic Laws of Arithmetic*.

Frege's claim that psychologism fails to respect the subjective/objective distinction amounts to the claim that it fails to do justice to the fact that our practice of assertion, judgment, and inference is by its very nature subject to evaluation in accordance with the principles of logic. Such a failure will be revealed if it can be shown that accepting psychologism would preclude us from accounting for any of the features of our linguistic and cognitive practice which directly manifest this constitutive governance. It is just this that Frege proposes to show.

What are some of these features? The central features of our practice are, of course, that we make judgments and that we use language to make assertions. That is, we think and speak in ways such that what we think and what we say can be evaluated as true or false and can stand in logical relations with each other. Remember, as Frege saw things, nothing could count as a judgment or assertion unless it had a content that could be evaluated as true or false and was capable of standing in logical relations with the contents of other judgments or assertions in accordance with the dictates of the laws of logic.

Part and parcel of this practice, then, is the fact that some of what we judge to be the case requires or allows that we accept something else as true as well; or that two or more of our beliefs may be inconsistent and, thus, be such that they cannot both be true. We are, consequently, logically obliged to give at least one of them up. There is also the salient fact that our own judgments or assertions may be inconsistent with, consistent with, or in full agreement with the judgments or assertions of others. We use language to communicate with others in ways that enable us to recognize agreements and disagreements and to adjudicate, rationally, intersubjective conflicts in beliefs. In other words, we recognize that not only our own claims and beliefs stand in logical relations with each other, but that our claims and beliefs also stand in logical relations with the claims and beliefs of others.

The Argument Against Psychologism in Frege's Basic Laws of Arithmetic

Frege's argument in the *Basic Laws* is that the psychologician, by identifying the laws of logic with psychological laws, has placed out of reach any account of the principles of logic capable of accommodating the peculiar truth-value-relevant normative force they have over our practice of judgment, assertion, and inference. In consequence, they will be unable even to do justice to the fundamental contrast between genuine, logically relevant judgment and other psychological processes over which logic has no normative control.

According to Frege, by identifying the laws of logic with empirically determinable generalizations about psychological processes, the psychologician commits himself to the intelligibility of encountering and recognizing beings whose own thought processes are "governed" by different laws of thinking from those which correctly describe our own. To use Frege's example, we might encounter beings who do not "accept"—i.e., who do not think in accordance with—one of our own most fundamental logical laws: the principle of identity, which states that everything is identical with itself. These logical aliens would be creatures who sometimes or always denied statements of the form "A is identical with A," statements we unhesitatingly affirm. Indeed, if the psychologician is right, it must be intelligible to suppose that even we, or our heirs, might over time evolve into just such beings.

The psychological theory that correctly describes our current thought processes will evidently include a law stating something like, as Frege suggests, "It is impossible for people living in the year 1893 to acknowledge an object to be different from itself." And the psychological theory that correctly describes the aliens will deny that this law holds of them. Since each of these theories will be suitably relativized to apply only to the relevant population, there will be no inconsistency between them. But surely there is an important sense in which we and the logical aliens disagree that this view of the matter does not satisfactorily capture.

To bring out what is at stake here, Frege asks us to consider what we should do were we in fact to confront such logical aliens. He writes:

> The psychological logician could only acknowledge the fact and say simply: those laws hold for them, these laws hold for us. I should say: we have here a hitherto unknown type of madness. Anyone who understands the laws of logic to be laws that prescribe the way in which one ought to think—to be laws of truth, and not natural laws of human beings' taking a thing to be true—will ask, who is right? Whose laws of taking-to-be-true are in accord with the laws of truth? The psychological logician cannot ask this question, if he did he would be recognizing laws of truth that were not laws of psychology.

Frege's point here is that if we admit the intelligibility of logical aliens, as the psychologician must, then for us the question must inevitably arise: Whose inferences are correct, ours or theirs? But this, it seems clear, is an *extrapsychological* question. Neither the laws describing the logical aliens' psychological habits nor the laws describing our own so much as address the question of whether objects are self-identical. This being the case, the psychologician cannot admit the legitimacy of the question, except on pain of conceding the legitimacy of an extrapsychological study of inference. Conceding this, however, would undermine his own position.

But why should not the psychologician simply dig in his heels here and reject the legitimacy of this question? Would this not effectively avoid the self–defeating consequences just noted? Frege, though, asks us to consider the consequences of the psychologician's doing so—in particular, the consequences for that feature of our ordinary cognitive practice which involves the possibility of agreeing and disagreeing with others in our judgments.

By denying the very legitimacy of the question, "Whose inferences are correct, ours or theirs?," the psychologician is effectively placing out of reach the very possibility of recognizing a genuine truth-value-relevant disagreement between us. What we recognize as a disagreement, the psychologician is now forced to recognize as merely a species of contingent psychological difference. If viewing logical laws psychologistically precludes us from raising the question. "Which of us is right?," then the logical space, so to speak, within which genuine disagreements in judgment can be recognized at all has been removed.

But if the disagreement between ourselves and the logical aliens cannot, from the psychologistic point of view, raise an issue of correctness between us, then in what respect can the psychologician give substance to the idea that there can be genuine disagreements in judgment even between you and me? To be fully consistent, the psychologician is also obliged to treat any disagreement between you and me as a species of mere psychological difference, a species of psychological idiosyncrasy with respect to which no issue of correctness, and so no issue of truth, can arise. But if no issue of correctness can arise between you and me when we are not in agreement, then our disagreement cannot be a disagreement in *judgments*.

For Frege, it is the fact that the psychologician is forced to an understanding of disagreement along these lines that exposes his or her inability to do justice to the distinction between the subjective and the objective. In effect, the psychologician's position forces him to treat disagreement in truth evaluable judgment on a par with disagreement in subjective taste. Frege allows that there certainly are disagreements in taste such that, for example, "A soup that tastes pleasant to one person may be nauseous to another." But this sort of disagreement is not—in the logically relevant sense—a disagreement in judgment or belief. While there is a clear sense in which these two persons can be said to disagree, it is also clear that the state of mind that the one person gives expression to with "Yum!" does not logically contradict or even disagree in truth value with the state of mind the other person gives expression to with "Yuk!". Indeed, no question of right or wrong, correct or incorrect, truth or falsity is raised here. Such subjective responses or judgments of taste are simply not constitutively subject to the normative governance of logic. But then judgments of taste, so-called, are not judgments in any logically relevant sense. Nor are our subjects' "Yum!" and "Yuk!" genuine assertions.

Psychologism's Failure to Respect the Fundamental Normative Status of Logical Laws

Frege's point, of course, is that the psychologician's conception of the laws of logic as mere generalizations about certain psychological processes of the human mind does not provide him or her with the resources to draw a coherent contrast between genuine objective judgment and assertion and the mere having and venting of subjective, non-truth-evaluable states. Thus, on the basis of the materials the psychologician allows, no distinction between the subjective and the objective can be coherently drawn. An adequate conception of logic must do justice to the way in which logical principles provide constitutive standards for the correctness and incorrectness of judgments, assertions, and inferences, while emphasizing the central role played by the notion of truth in setting those standards. It will, in other words, decisively underwrite the subjective/objective contrast as Frege understood it. Consequently, the psychologician's inability to support the distinction between genuine truth-value-relevant disagreements or agreements in judgment and mere disagreements or agreements in taste vividly exposes the bankruptcy of the psychologician's conception of logic.

FUNCTION AND CONCEPT

Accounting for the Logical Complexity of Judgable Contents

For Frege, there is no understanding what a judgment or assertion is except as something aiming at the truth and subject to evaluation in accordance with the principles of logic. Understanding this fact in the right way will require, as we have seen, that we distinguish the contents of our judgments or assertions from the judgments and assertions themselves. For Frege, the contents of two judgments will differ—in particular, they will differ in what we might call their *logical potential*—whenever the judgments themselves differ in their potential for logical appraisal. Once the need to distinguish judgments from their contents is appreciated, the logician's principal task will be to provide a systematic account of those features of the contents that makes sense of the ways in which judgments differ in their potential for logical appraisal. To understand different judgments as having, by virtue of their different contents, different logical potential, we must think of judgable contents as logically complex.

Frege insisted that a satisfactory account of the logical structure of judgable contents must be governed by our prior and more primitive understanding of the practice of judgment and the different sorts of logical commitments that attach to judgments with different contents. In requiring this, Frege was, in effect, rejecting the traditional approach to such matters. Traditionally, attempts were made to understand and explain the nature of judgments and their contents by appeal to a supposed prior understanding of some such notion as *concepts* or *ideas*. Concepts or ideas were treated as the building blocks out of which all of our more complex thoughts were constructed by various psychological principles of association or synthesis. These concepts or ideas were themselves given to us by a primitive psychological process of abstraction or were viewed as the dim residue of prior and more vivid sensory impressions. Frege viewed this traditional approach as hopelessly backward. According to Frege, if the notion of a concept is to play a useful role in characterizing the logical complexity of judgable contents, our understanding of that notion will have to presuppose and subserve a prior understanding of our practice of judgment and inference.

For, after all, it is judging that is the fundamental activity to which logical standards apply.

An adequate account of the logical structure of judgable contents will make sense of the systematic ways in which judgments differ in their potential for logical appraisal. As Frege saw things, providing such an account will involve devising a language in which precisely the different sorts of logical commitments that attach to different possible judgments can be directly read off from features of the symbols provided by that language for expressing the contents of those judgments. In this context, Frege's insistence on the priority of judgments over concepts is concisely expressed by the second of the three methodological maxims mentioned earlier—never ask for the meaning of a word in isolation, but only in the context of a sentence. After all, it is, in the first instance, through the assertory utterance *sentences* that we express our judgments. The *Begriffsschrift*, as we have already seen, represents Frege's first attempt as constructing the required sort of language.

Respecting the Semantic Unity of Judgable Contents

Approached in this manner, the project of providing an adequate account of the logical complexity must accomplish two things. First, it must characterize the logically relevant contributions made by the different parts of the sentences of one's logically perfect language in such a way as to respect the essential *semantic unity* of the judgable contents those sentences are designed to express. To say that a judgable content is semantically unified is just to say that it possesses a fixed truth value determined by a unique and determinate set of truth conditions. So an account of the logically relevant contributions made by different sorts of subsentential expressions must characterize their contribution in such a way as to underwrite the possession of a determinate set of truth conditions by the sentences in which they occur. Moreover, and of equal importance, this first task must be accomplished in a way that reveals how, on the basis of the contributions made by the subsentential expressions, the judgable contents expressed by the sentences in which they occur have the logical potential that they do.

Traditional approaches to the analysis of thought fare extremely poorly in the face of these desiderata. If a judgable content is thought of as essentially a complex entity composed of concepts or ideas, and if these constituents are viewed as logically prior to and independent of the sorts of contents that they figure in, then it is difficult to understand the nature of their composition in a way that makes sense of the fact that, *qua* composed, they are truth-evaluable, judgable wholes.

Consider, for example, the proposal that the contents of judgments are complexes composed of different concepts (or ideas), where concepts (or ideas) are thought of as forming an ontologically homogeneous class of entities. Now consider the thought that Socrates is mortal. According to the view under consideration, this thought consists in some combination of the concept (or idea) of *Socrates* and the concept (or idea) of *mortality*. But how are we to think of these two concepts (or ideas) as related in such a way that the result is the truth-evaluable thought that Socrates is mortal? We cannot merely think of them as concatenated in the mind in the way, say, two words might be concatenated on a page. For it is hard to see how the mental concatenation of two concepts (or ideas) can result in a determinate set of truth conditions any more than the mere concatenation of two words on a page, say,

Socrates, mortality

results in a determinate truth-evaluable sentence. In order to view these two concepts (or ideas) as determining truth conditions, they must, it would appear, be viewed as related in some logically appropriate way. Plato might have said, for example, that the former must be thought of as related to the latter by means of some sort of "instantiation" or "participation" relation.

What is really thought when one thinks that Socrates is mortal is something like, that Socrates instantiates (or falls under, or participates in) mortality. If this is right, then the original thought is evidently composed of three concepts (or ideas) and not merely two, namely, *Socrates, mortality*, and *instantiation*. But how can adding another concept (or idea) help matters here? For now we simply have three, instead of our original two, concepts (or ideas) to combine. We face the same problem as before. It is no easier to see how the mental concatenation of three concepts (or ideas) can issue in a determinate set of truth conditions than the mere concatenation of three words on a page,

Socrates, instantiation, mortality

results in a determinate truth-evaluable sentence. And so it is no clearer how three concepts (or ideas), rather than two, can be combined in the mind to result in a truth-evaluable thought. It will obviously not help matters to suggest at this point that the real content of our original thought is that Socrates is related by instantiation to mortality. Here we have simply added a fourth concept, relation. And the original difficulty begins all over again.

Clearly then, if we are to respect the semantic unity of judgable contents, the logically relevant contributions made by the different sorts of subsentential expressions out of which the sentences of our language are composed must be so characterized that it is clear from *their very nature* how they relate with each other in such a way as to issue in determinate truth conditions. And if we are to satisfy our second requirement, the way in which the logically relevant contributions made by the different sorts of subsentential expression determine those truth conditions must also make the logical potential of the relevant judgable contents clear.

Composition- ality with Respect to Logically Relevant Content

Central to Frege's conception of how logical complexity is to be repre- sented in a logically perfect language was his fundamental commitment to a principle of *compositionality* with respect to logically relevant content. According to this principle, the substitution in a sentence of one expression for another with the same logically relevant content must leave unchanged the logically relevant content of the sentence as a whole:

> *Compositionality.* For any complex expression E containing an expression e, the logically relevant content of e is the same as the content of another expression e' if and only if the complex expres- sion E' that results from substituting e' for e in E has the same logically relevant content.

On this way of viewing the matter, identifying the logically relevant content of an expression amounts to no more nor less than identifying what, on the one hand, has to be the same between it and any other expression if the one is to be allowed to substitute for the other in complex expressions without affecting the logically relevant content of those complex expres- sions; and, on the other hand, it is that feature of complex expressions which remains the same whenever a constituent expression is replaced by another with the same logically relevant content.

Function and Argument

Frege's commitment to *compositionalism* underwrote, in turn, what was unquestionably one of Frege's most important and fruitful innovations—his proposal that the logical complexity of the contents of judgments be under- stood on the mathematical model of function and argument. Frege proposed that the relationship between the logically relevant content of a sentence and the logically relevant content of its components be modeled on the relation- ship between the value had by a mathematical function for a particular argument and the particular function and arguments involved.

Consider the following example from Frege's paper "Function and Concept." Each of the following complex mathematical expressions stands for a specific number:

$$2\cdot 1^3+1$$
$$2\cdot 4^3+4$$
$$2\cdot 5^3+5.$$

The first stands for 3, the second for 132, and the third for 255. (Frege always emphasized that we must take care to distinguish the symbolic expression from what the expression stands for. The name "Frege" and Frege the person are clearly different things. Likewise, the expressions "$2\cdot 1^3+1$" and "3," though different, both stand for the same number.) Despite their differences, it is easy to recognize in these expressions a common pattern. Each expression appears to be formed by filling in the gaps of the expression,

$$1 \cdot (\ )^3 + (\ )$$

by different numerals. It is obvious that the number designated by the complex expression varies systematically depending upon the number designated by the numerical expression used to fill the gaps. This suggests that in determining what is designated by the completed complex expression, what is relevant is not only the number designated by numerical expression used to fill the gaps, but also what the "gappy" expression itself stands for.

It is common in mathematics to call such "gappy" expressions *function expressions* or *functors* and to think of them as standing for or expressing functions. The gaps are usually referred to as the argument places of the function expression and are standardly indicated by the presence of variables, thus—

$$1 \cdot x^3 + x.$$

When we think of a particular number as the number designated by the expression occupying the argument places of the function expression, we call that number an *argument* for the function. And we call the number designated by the complex expression, once the argument for the function is determined, the *value* of the function *for that argument*. Thus, the value of the function expressed by "$1 \cdot x^3 + x$" for the argument designated by "5" is 255. For a given argument (or sequence of arguments, if the function has more than one argument places), a function will always yield exactly one value; though, for different arguments, a function may yield the same value.

Now, what Frege noticed was that certain nonmathematical expressions operate just like function expressions. For example, when we remove the proper names "Sweden" and "William" respectively from the expressions "the capital of Sweden," or "the father of William," the result is the two "gappy," or *incomplete*, expressions "the capital of ( )" and "the father of ( )." These expressions behave very much like function expressions; for when their gaps are filled with argument expressions of the appropriate sort, they systematically determine a unique object as the object for which the completed expression stands. We can, accordingly, identify the content of such incomplete expressions with the functions for which they seem to stand, and the content of the argument expressions with the objects for which they stand. The content of the completed complex expression may then be viewed as the value of the relevant function for the given argument.

Frege then points out that we can even view standard indicative sentences—the sorts of sentences we standardly utter when making assertions—as completed function expressions. Consider, for example, the sentence "Napoleon is dead." According to Frege, we can think of the subject of this sentence, "Napoleon," as an argument expression designating

Napoleon and of the predicate of this sentence as the incomplete expression, "( ) is dead," which stands for a function. To distinguish incomplete expressions of the predicative sort from other function expressions, Frege called them "concept expressions"; and the functions for which they stand he called "concepts."

Concepts and Objects

Over the course of Frege's career, he changed his mind about how best to understand the nature of concepts. Early in his thinking, during the time of the *Begriffsschrift*, he tended to view concepts as functions whose values for appropriate arguments are judgable contents—the judgable contents expressed by the sentences formed by completing them with appropriate argument expressions. By 1891, however, for reasons we shall examine below, Frege proposed that concept expressions are best thought of as standing for functions which, for appropriate arguments, take truth values— either the True or the False—as values. In Frege's mature thought, the label "concepts" is used only for those functions that yield truth values for appropriate arguments.

Frege regarded the analysis of logical complexity in terms of function/argument structure as one of his principal theoretical insights. And it was, indeed, this feature of his approach that enabled him to achieve the monumental technical advances in logic which have earned him the title of founder of modern mathematical logic. But Frege's attraction to the function/argument analysis of logical structure also had a more purely philosophical motivation. The analysis of logical structure in these terms not only enabled Frege systematically to characterize the logical potential of different judgable contents with a generality never before achieved in the history of logic, but it enabled him to do so in a way that perfectly satisfies the first of the requirements mentioned previously that any such analysis do justice to the semantic unity of judgable content.

Adopting the function/argument conception of logical complexity leaves no room for a question how things might hold together in such a way as to yield truth-evaluable contents. If we understand the role played, for example, by "Napoleon" and "is dead" in the sentence "Napoleon is dead" along the lines Frege recommends, it is no longer a mystery how when the function expression is completed with the argument expression—in this case, a proper name—the whole thing possesses a truth value. Moreover, understanding the semantic role of these expressions as standing for an object and a concept, respectively, makes the truth conditions of the sentence explicit. The sentence is true only insofar as the concept designated by the concept expression yields the value True for the argument designated by the argument expression; it is false only insofar as that concept yields the value *False* for that argument. Or in plain

English, the sentence is true if and only if Napoleon is dead and false otherwise.

Frege was quite insistent that in order to appreciate what is genuinely involved in the having of a value by a completed function expression—including, of course, sentences—we are obliged to regard the contribution of the functional expression as fundamentally distinct from the contribution of any argument expressions. We must, consequently, think of functions—and, so, concepts—as a fundamentally different sort of entity from objects. Hence, Frege's third methodological maxim: never to lose sight of the distinction between concept and object.

Frege often says of functions that they are "incomplete" or "unsaturated" entities and contrasts them with objects which he characterizes as "complete" or "saturated." By this he means to point out that it is the nature of a function to be the sort of thing that yields a value when "completed" by an appropriate argument. It is the nature of a concept, consequently, to yield a truth value when completed by appropriate arguments. The values of functions are always themselves complete entities; they no longer yearn for completion. They are, consequently, objects. Thus, according to Frege, we must also view the truth values, the True and the False, as objects.

While Frege allows that certain "higher-level" functions can take certain "lower-level" functions as arguments, there must be functions which take as arguments entities which are not themselves functions—entities which are, so to speak, pure arguments. Conceived in this way, what I have just called pure arguments must be complete entities—objects. They are typically what ordinary proper names, such as "Socrates" or "England," and such other singular terms as "George Washington's father" or "the smallest prime number," stand for. Frege calls those functions whose nature it is to take as arguments only objects "first-level" functions, those functions which take as arguments only first-level functions are "second-level" functions, and so on.

Because of the fundamental distinction between functions and objects, and between functions of different levels, the analysis of logical complexity in terms of function/argument structure enabled Frege to account for how our sentences can express semantically unified, which is to say, truth-evaluable contents and, moreover, to do so in a way that provides a general and systematic account of the logical potential of such contents. The problems faced by what we earlier labeled the "traditional" approach simply do not arise here.

SENSE AND MEANING

In the *Begriffsschrift*, as we noted earlier, Frege proposed that concepts—the logically relevant content of predicate expressions—be identified with functions whose values, for appropriate arguments, are judgable contents. He also tended, during this early part of his career, to identify judgable contents with just those circumstances the obtaining or not obtaining of which decides the truth or falsity of the judgment. Frege, however, immediately noticed that this way of viewing things raises a prima facie difficulty when it comes to expressing the identity of contents. If two expressions *a* and *b* have the same content, and if, as one would ordinarily suppose, the identity symbol "=" is to be understood as having as its content an ordinary relation (a two-place concept, so to speak), then according to the principle of compositionality, the sentence "*a=b*" must express the same judgable content as the sentence "*a=a*." For Frege, however, it was obvious that sentences of the form "*a=b*" and "*a=a*" typically express different judgable contents. Since we cannot have it both ways, it looks as if we have a serious problem.

A bit later, we will consider the criteria to which Frege appeals when he supposes that two sentence express different judgable contents. It will be useful for now, however, simply to remember Frege's tendency, at the time, to identify the judgable contents expressed by a sentence with the circumstances that would have to obtain if that sentence is to be true. Thus, in supposing that a pair of identity sentences of the relevant sort differ in their judgable contents, Frege will naturally have been led to assume that they must also differ in what circumstances must obtain in order for each to be true. With this in mind, the solution proposed by Frege in the *Begriffsschrift* to the above difficulty will not be altogether surprising.

Frege proposed that the content of "=" must be such that sentences of the form "*a=b*" do not, as we initially assumed, express a relation between the contents of the expressions *a* and *b*, but rather between the expressions themselves. He writes:

> The identity of content differs from conditionality and negation by relating to names and not contents. Although symbols are usually only representatives of their contents—so that each combination [of symbols usually] expresses only a relation between their contents—they at once appear *in propria persona* as soon as they are combined by the symbol for identity of content, for this signifies the circumstance that the two names have the same content.

Since the circumstance that the expression *a* has the same content as the expression *b* clearly differs from the circumstance that the expression *a* has the same content as the expression *a*, the original difficulty appears to have been eliminated.

A Different Approach

By 1891, however, Frege had become quite dissatisfied with various features of his *Begriffsschrift* views, including the treatment of identity. In "Function and Concept," he details a number of the more systematic changes and refinements that he believed were necessary in order to do better justice to the requirements of logic. There are two principal and intimately related changes with respect to which nearly all of the others are either adjustments or direct consequences. The one central to our concern is Frege's introduction of a distinction between *Sinn* (sense) and *Bedeutung* (reference/Meaning). The second is the substitution of truth values for judgable contents as the principle semantic values of sentences. In "On Sense and Meaning," after severely criticizing his *Begriffsschrift* treatment of identity, he provides an extended and systematic defense of these two principal innovations.

(It is a matter of some controversy how one should translate into English Frege's term "*Bedeutung*" and its cognates—especially after it takes on the important theoretical status that it does after Frege introduces his distinction between *Sinn* and *Bedeutung*. For some time, the tradition had been to translate "*Bedeutung*" as "reference." Recently, however, translating "*Bedeutung*" more literally as "meaning" has gained favor; and nearly all standard additions of Frege's work in English have adopted this practice. I will follow current practice, but I will always capitalize "Meaning" in order to remind the reader that Frege's own use of "*Bedeutung*" during this period was quasi-technical and, consequently, much more restricted in intent than the English word "meaning" suggests.)

Frege came to see that a deep conflict existed between (1) his commitment to compositionalism, (2) his view that judgable contents are the values of concepts for appropriate arguments, (3) his conception of judgable contents as the objective circumstances that must obtain if the judgments, whose contents they are, are to count as true, and (4) his understanding of the demands that logic places on the individuation of judgable contents in terms of their logical potential.

Consider, for example, the concept that would, for Frege, constitute the content of a predicate expression such as " ( ) is a planet with a shorter period of revolution than the Earth." No function, and so no concept, can yield different values for the same argument. But if, following Frege, we allow that the content of the expression "Phosphorus" is just Phosphorus and the content of the expression "Hesperus" is just Hesperus, then (since Phosphorus is identical to Hesperus), whether one appeals directly to compositionality or to the nature of functions, the value of our concept for Phosphorus as argument must be the same as the value of that concept for Hesperus as argument. In particular, the circumstance that is required to obtain in order for the sentence, "Phosphorus is a planet with a shorter period of revolution than the Earth" to be true is just the same as that which is required for "Hesperus is a planet with a shorter period of revolution than the Earth."

And yet, by whatever criteria Frege felt logic obliges us to individuate judgable contents, the judgable contents expressed by these two sentences are not the same. Consequently, judgable content cannot be the values of those concepts that take objects as their arguments.

This is, in essence, Frege's argument in "On Function and Concept," from which he concludes, for the first time in print, that we must distinguish the *Meaning* of a sentence from its *sense*—the *Thought* it expresses.

> If we say that "the Evening Star is a planet with a shorter period of revolution than the Earth," the Thought we express is other than the sentence "the Morning Star is a planet with a shorter period of revolution than the Earth"; for someone who does not know that the Morning Star is the Evening Star might regard the one as true and the other as false. And yet the Meaning of both sentences must be the same; for it is just a matter of the interchange of the words "Evening Star" and "Morning Star," which have the same Meaning, i.e., are proper names of the same heavenly body. We must distinguish between sense and Meaning.

The difficulty this argument takes as its starting point turns out, on reflection, to be a simple generalization of the difficulty with identity statements already noticed by Frege in the *Begriffsschrift*. It is hard to imagine, though, how one might coherently generalize the *Begriffsschrift* solution to cases of this more general sort. In consequence, the solution offered here must be different.

In the famous opening passage of "On Sense and Meaning," Frege explicitly links his rejection of his earlier solution with his reasons for introducing the distinction between sense and Meaning. He writes:

> Equality gives rise to challenging questions which are not altogether easy to answer. Is it a relation? A relation between objects, or between names or signs of objects? In my *Begriffsschrift* I assumed the latter. . . . What we apparently want to say by a=b is that the signs or names "a" and "b" designate the same thing, so that those signs themselves would be under discussion; a relation between them would be asserted. But this relation would hold between the names or signs only insofar as they named or designated something. It would be mediated by the connection of each of the two signs with the same designated thing. But this is arbitrary. Nobody can be forbidden to use any arbitrary producible event or object as a sign for something. In that case, the sentence a=b would no longer refer

to the subject matter, but only to its mode of designation; we would express no proper knowledge by its means. But in many cases this is just what we want to do.

What is Frege's objection here? In *Begriffsschrift*, Frege had hoped that by proposing a different account of what the sentences are *about*—of what circumstances have to obtain in order for them to be true—he could satisfactorily sidestep any conflict between his view that the judgable contents of the two sorts of identity sentence differ and his view that judgable contents are the compositionally determined semantic values of sentences. But this sort of solution is plausible only if the particular metalinguistic circumstances hypothesized to be the real contents of identity statements genuinely reflect what we take—what logic obliges us to take—such statements really to be about. It is just this that Frege now denies.

Frege's Puzzle

Frege came to appreciate—no doubt, in part by reflecting on the fact that the problem is general, affecting forms of sentences besides identity sentences—that his previous proposal simply did not do justice to the truth conditions of the sentences. If informative identity statements are taken to be about the expressions rather than the Meanings of the expressions, then these sentences would not really convey the information we take them to convey. At best, upon learning that two expressions denote the same thing, we learn a linguistic fact—a fact that simply does not directly concern the objects the relevant expressions are normally taken to stand for, to Mean.

For example, when we learn that the Morning Star is the very same object as the Evening Star, we ordinarily take ourselves to have learned something about a certain astronomical body. But on Frege's earlier proposal, this would not be the case. The information would not concern the planet Venus at all but only the words that we happen to use to refer to that planet. And since it is an arbitrary convention which expressions we use to refer to objects, it is clear that the identity claim could be true whether or not the terms involved were actually used to refer to Venus at all—just so long as whatever they were used to refer to was the same. Had we chosen to use the relevant two names to refer to different things, then the very same sentence with the very same content would have been false, even though Venus would remain identical with Venus.

If we are to do justice to the truth conditions of identity sentences, we have no serious choice but to suppose that the constituent names contribute just those objects that they ordinarily designate to determining the circumstances that must obtain if the sentences in which they occur are to be true. But this, Frege noticed, leaves us with a new, though related, puzzle, namely, how can two sentences that require, in order to be true, that the same circumstances obtain—that precisely the same object or objects fall under the same concept or relation—nevertheless differ in the logically relevant way that Frege continues to suppose such sentences as "a=a" and "a=b" differ? To solve this puzzle, Frege felt obliged to distinguish the sense of a sentence—the Thought expressed by it—from its Meaning, which Frege identifies with its truth value.

Distinguishing Cognitive Significance from Referential Truth Conditions

Let us say of two sentences that differ in the way that two sentences differ when, according to Frege, they express different Thoughts that they differ in their *cognitive significance*. And let us call those features of a sentence that are accounted for by the theory of Meaning the sentence's *referential truth conditions*. Since Frege held that differences in cognitive significance reflect logically relevant differences between sentences, and since sentences can differ in their cognitive significance even when they fail to differ in their referential truth conditions, Frege insisted that we must recognize a logically relevant feature of sentences and subsentential expressions over and above any features that can be accounted for by appeal to the resources available from a theory of Meaning. It is just this feature then— however it is to be understood—that Frege is now calling sense.

In order to understand adequately the challenge that Frege took his puzzle to pose, and thereby to get a clearer picture of the work that the notion of sense is required to do, we need to understand better the sorts of consideration on which Frege relied when insisting that the cognitive significance of sentences like 1 and 2 above, or "a=b" and "a=a," differ. Unfortunately, Frege nowhere offers a sustained and systematic discussion of these matters. He seems to have thought that his readers would have no trouble appreciating why he insisted on distinguishing cognitive significance where he did. And even in the various passages where he does offer explicit reasons for his distinctions, he tends to appeal to criteria which advert to general features of our cognitive and linguistic practice without making explicit the underlying logical relevance of these features.

The principal criteria to which Frege appeals when distinguishing cognitive significance can be accurately summarized as follows:

Cognitive Significance. Two sentences will express different judgable contents only insofar as it is possible for a linguistically competent and rational speaker, who is acquainted with all the expressions in both sentences,

    (i)   to extend his or her knowledge by coming correctly to believe what would be expressed by (literal) utterance of one, despite his or her already knowing the truth of what would be expressed by the (literal) utterance of the other; and/or

    (ii) to believe what would be expressed by the literal utterance of one, while, without changing his or her mind, failing to believe—either disbelieving or suspending judgment on—what would be expressed by the other.

To avoid serious misunderstanding, the notion of *possibility* being used in these criteria must be correctly understood. Plainly, given Frege's anti-psychologism, it cannot be a matter of psychological possibility. Rather, given the centrality of Frege's concern with logic, it should be clear that what is possible, according to Frege, when two sentences differ in cognitive significance is that a competent speaker may, without violating any logical norms, extend his or her knowledge by learning the truth of what is expressed by one while already knowing the truth of what is expressed by the other; or, alternatively, he or she may, without violating any logical norms, believe what is expressed by one while failing to believe, perhaps even disbelieving, what is expressed by the other. Frege's puzzle, then, is how is it possible for two sentences which possess the same referential truth conditions nevertheless to differ in such a way as to admit these possibilities?

Distinguishing Sense from Meaning

To solve this puzzle, we must, according to Frege, simultaneously recognize a logically relevant respect in which sentences such as 1 and 2, or "a=a" and "a=b," are the same and a logically relevant respect in which they differ. As Frege, in retrospect, came to see things, his *Begriffsschrift* understanding of judgable content had involved a confused conflation of these two features. We can now see, however, that they must be clearly separated. Whatever logical considerations originally compelled us to distinguish the judgable contents of sentences like our 1 and 2, or "a=a" and "a=b," are now taken to individuate the Thoughts that they express. Whereas that respect in which we are obliged to regard such sentences as the same—i.e., in respect of their Meaning—we are now asked to identify with their truth value. And while the content of subsentential expressions was previously identified univocally in terms of its compositional contribution to the judgable contents of the sentences in which it occurs, we must now distinguish between that feature of their content by virtue of which they contribute compositionally to the Thoughts expressed by those sentences—their *sense*, and that feature of their content by virtue of which they contribute compositionally to determining the truth values of those sentences—their *Meaning*.

Two sentences will differ in their sense—in the Thought they express—just insofar as they differ in cognitive significance. Two expressions will differ in sense just insofar as the substitution of one for the other in a sentence would alter the cognitive significance of the sentence. In other words, Frege endorses a principle of compositionality for sense precisely parallel to the one he had earlier endorsed for logically relevant content. He also endorses a principle of compositionality for Meaning. The substitution of one expression for another with the same Meaning must leave unchanged the Meaning of the sentence. Frege reserved the function/argument analysis of logical complexity for the theory of Meaning. The Meanings of singular terms are objects, the Meanings of predicate expressions are concepts. And, as we mentioned earlier, concepts are now thought of as functions from appropriate arguments to truth values. Thus, for Frege, the Meaning of a sentence is its truth value.

How, though, did Frege understand the notion of sense so that an appeal to a difference in the senses of two expressions could plausibly account for differences in the cognitive significance of the sentences in which they occur? Unfortunately, Frege did not have a great deal to say about this. What he does say, however, can be summarized roughly as follows.

In Frege's view, the sense of an expression determines its Meaning. Though one and the same Meaning may be determined by different senses, there can be only one Meaning determined by a given sense. The sense of an expression is, as Frege puts it, a "mode of presentation" of—a way of thinking about—the Meaning. There will always be more than one way to think about any given object such that it will not be logically self-evident that the object thought about in one way is the same as the object thought about in the other way. To each of these different ways of thinking about an object there corresponds a sense. It is upon this fact about senses that Frege depends when he appeals to senses in order to solve his puzzle.

Understanding an expression consists in *grasping* its sense. The sense of an expression is what is (or would be) grasped by anyone sufficiently familiar with the language. It is what is communicated when someone understands the sentence uttered by another. When we grasp a sense, we think about the relevant Meaning—we do not think about the sense. Perhaps the best way to put the matter is to say that we think *with* the sense *about* the Meaning. This is not to say that we cannot think about senses. When we think about a sense, however, we do not do so by grasping that very sense. Rather, we grasp another sense that determines the original sense as its Meaning. Senses are assumed to be *cognitively transparent*. This means that if two expressions have the same or different senses, and if one understands both expressions, there can be no question that they have the same or different senses. Unless senses are assumed to be cognitively transparent in this way, it is quite unclear how an appeal to a difference in senses could account for a difference in cognitive significance.

In grasping a sense, one is not guaranteed that there is a Meaning. Thus, in grasping a Thought, one is not guaranteed that the Thought possesses a truth value. A Thought will fail to possess a truth value if, for example, it is the sense of a sentence that contains an expression which itself fails to have a Meaning. Since Odysseus does not really exist, the name "Odysseus" fails to refer to anything, fails to have a Meaning. Thus, the sentence "Odysseus was set ashore at Ithaca while sound asleep," while expressing a Thought, fails to possess a truth value. A sentence will fail to express a Thought only if one of its constituent expressions fails to have a sense. Such a sentence will evidently express nonsense. These are immediate consequences of the compositionality of Meaning and the compositionality of sense.

Some Unanswered Questions About Sense

Though Frege's efforts to elucidate the notion of sense are quite limited, they do help us to see both what features the senses of expressions must possess and what, in outline, a theory of sense would have to look like in order for an appeal to differences in sense satisfactorily to explain differences of cognitive significance in the puzzling cases. But Frege's remarks raise as many questions as they provide answers. How, for example, are we to understand his claim that senses determine meaning? By what sort of mechanism is this accomplished? And what is it to *grasp* a sense, where this does not involve thinking about it? In other words, what sort of object—and remember that, for Frege, senses are objects—can we think *with* without thinking *about*? And what must senses be like such that when we think with them we manage thereby to think *about* the objects, concepts, and other functions that are their Meanings? How are we to understand the cognitive transparency of senses—especially since, according to Frege's views, they are only transparent when we think with them, though not when we think about them? Whether these and other questions like them can be answered satisfactorily—indeed, whether these are even legitimate questions—is the topic of a great deal of current debate in the philosophy of language and mind.

Belief Sentences: A Challenge to the Compositionality of Meaning

Questions about the nature and status of senses are not the only ones raised by Frege's views. Indeed, a *prima facie* quite challenging difficulty is also raised by Frege's commitment to the compositionality of Meaning. According to the principle of compositionality for Meaning, recall, the exchange within a sentence of one expression for another with the same Meaning ought to leave the Meaning of the sentence—namely, its truth value—unaffected. Since George Eliot is the same person as Mary Ann Evans, the two names "George Eliot" and "Mary Ann Evans," though they differ in sense, have the same Meaning. Thus it would seem that in any sentence in which the name "George Eliot" appears, we ought to be able to substitute "Mary Ann Evans" without affecting the truth value of the sentence. But this seems not always to be the case. Here is a clear case in which such a substitution would fail to preserve truth value.

Suppose that Adelheid does not know that Mary Ann Evans and George Eliot are the same person. She knows of George Eliot as the author of several famous novels, and she has met a women she knows as Mary Ann Evans at many social events. She does not know that they are one and the same. Given this information we can suppose that the following sentence is true:

(1) Adelheid believes that George Eliot is a famous novelist.

But, surely, we can also be confident that the following sentence is false:

(2) Adelheid believes that Mary Ann Evans is a famous novelist.

Sentence 2, though, is derived from 1 by substituting the co-referential *Mary Ann Evans* for *George Eliot*. According to the compositionality of Meaning, therefore, it ought *not* to be possible for 1 and 2 to differ in truth value.

Indirect Sense and Indirect Meaning

Frege was well aware of this apparent difficulty and discusses it at length in "On Sense and Meaning." But his recognition of sense as an additional objective semantic component of expressions, over an above their Meaning, provided him with a way around this problem. To see how, consider the sorts of sentence in which co-referential substitution will generally fail to preserve truth value? They will usually be ones in which various cognitive attitudes toward Thoughts are attributed to individuals, sentences involving such *propositional attitude* verbs as "believes," "says," "knows," "hopes," "desires," etc. Frege's suggestion is that such verbs do not generally stand for relations between the subjects of such attitudes and the Meanings of the sentences we use to express the contents of their Thoughts, but rather between the subjects of such attitudes and the Thoughts themselves. What is important to the truth value of such sentences is that we correctly identify the Thought the subject believes is true, hopes is true, knows is true, says is true, etc. Focusing on indirect speech, Frege puts the matter this way in "On Sense and Meaning":

> In indirect speech one talks about the sense, e.g., of another person's remarks. It is quite clear that in this way of speaking words do not have their customary Meaning but designate what is usually their sense. In order to have a short expression, we will say: In indirect speech [as well, of course, as in reports of other propositional attitudes], words are used *indirectly* or have their *indirect* Meaning. We distinguish accordingly the *customary* from the *indirect* Meaning of a word; and its *customary* sense from its *indirect* sense. The indirect Meaning of a word [or sentence] is accordingly its customary sense.

Frege calls the Meaning that an expression ordinarily has its "customary Meaning," the sense that an expression ordinarily has is its "customary sense." But now, according to Frege, we need to notice that when an expression occurs in the subordinate clause of a propositional attitude ascription, it will no longer have the same sense or the same Meaning that it customarily has. Rather, in these contexts, expressions will have as their Meaning what Frege calls their "indirect Meaning"—which he identifies with their customary sense. So the contribution made by an expression, occurring in the subordinate clause of a propositional attitude ascription to compositionally determining the Meaning of the sentence as a whole is not its customary Meaning, but its indirect Meaning, that is, its customary sense.

Consequently, if we are to evaluate fairly whether the principle of compositionality for Meaning holds in these cases, we must be sure to attend to what the Meanings of the relevant expressions are—given that they appear in the relevant subordinate clauses. Thus the Meaning of the name "George Eliot" when it appears in such a clause is the customary sense of that name. And the Meaning of the name "Mary Ann Evans" when it appears in such a clause is the customary sense of that name. But since these names have different customary senses, the substitution of one for the other in these clauses will be an illegitimate test of compositionality. A legitimate test would be one that allows only the substitution of expressions which in these contexts have the same Meaning—expressions that, in other words, have the same customary sense. And this is clearly not the case in the present example. Thus, what appeared to be a counter-example to the principle of compositionality for Meaning turns out not to be one after all.

Another Challenge to the Compositionality of Meaning: Meaningless Names

There remains, however, another challenge to the principle of compositionality for Meaning, which is not so easily avoided. We have already noted that a consequence of this principle is that if a sentence contains an expression which fails to have a Meaning, then the sentence must also fail to have a Meaning—which is just to say that it cannot possess a truth value. But if this is right, how are we to understand sentences of the form "N does not exist," where "N" is a proper name or other singular term?

If the name "N" does not have a Meaning, that is evidently because there is no N; but in this case, we cannot truthfully say that N does not exist. Since one of its constituent expressions fails to have a Meaning, the sentence "N does not exist" cannot have a Meaning—a truth value. Thus, if a sentence of the form "N does not exist" has a truth value at all, it must always be false; for it will only have a truth value when "N" has a Meaning, in which case, it will be false to say that N does not exist.

Moreover, it turns out that a sentence of the form "N *does* exist" can never be false. If "N" fails to have a Meaning, the sentence is without truth value. Thus, if it has a truth value at all, it will always be true. This is plainly unacceptable, for it is surely the case that we often successfully do use negative existential statements to convey information, and it is not clear how we could do that unless they could be, at least on occasion, true. Moreover, we certainly do not find positive existential statements trivial when they are true, and it is not clear how this could be unless they could be, at least on occasion, false. Unfortunately, Frege offers no clear way around this problem. Whether there is a way of dealing with this difficulty that is consistent with Frege's general outlook is still a matter of serious philosophical dispute.

In the foregoing, we have examined a selection of Frege's central doctrines and some of the arguments he offered in their favor. There is much that we have had to leave out, not the least of which is an examination of his formal achievement in logic or a more detailed discussion of his logicism and its subsequent failure. And much of what we did cover, we could only examine in a quite preliminary way. The complexity and sweep of Frege's thought is no doubt apparent. And yet, despite the challenges presented by various features of his approach, Frege's achievement is staggeringly impressive. Nearly all of contemporary philosophy of language and a great deal of the contemporary philosophy of mind is, in one way or another, indebted to him. The views of most contemporary philosophers in these areas can be understood as reactions to — either as attempts to refine, repair, or otherwise reject — some version or feature of Frege's position. Whatever one's ultimate views about the correctness of this or that aspect of his approach, the impact of Frege's views must be taken into account, not only if one wishes to understand the history of analytic philosophy, but if one seriously wants to approach and to understand contemporary work in philosophical logic, the philosophy of language, the philosophy of mind, metaphysics, and epistemology.

Selected Readings

PRIMARY SOURCES

Frege, G. *The Basic Laws of Arithmetic: Exposition of the System*, trans. and ed. by M. Furth. Berkeley: University of California Press, 1964.

_____. *Collected Papers on Mathematics, Logic, and Philosophy*, ed. by B. McGuinness. Oxford: Basil Blackwell, 1984.

_____. *Conceptual Notation and Related Articles*, trans. and ed. by T. W. Bynum. Oxford: Clarendon Press, 1972.

_____. *The Foundations of Arithmetic: A Logico-Mathematical Enquiry into the Concept of Number*, trans. by J. Austin. Oxford: Basil Blackwell, 1974.

SECONDARY SOURCES

Bell, D. *Frege's Theory of Judgment*. Oxford: Oxford University Press, 1979.

Currie, G. *Frege: An Introduction to His Philosophy*, Brighton: Harvester, 1982.

Dummett, M. *Frege: The Philosophy of Language*. Cambridge: Harvard University Press, 1973.

_____. *The Interpretation of Frege's Philosophy*. Cambridge: Harvard University Press, 1981.

Haaparanta, L., and Hintikka, J., eds. *Frege Synthesized*. Dordrecht: D. Reidel, 1986.

Sluga, H. *Gottlob Frege*. London: Routledge and Kegan Paul, 1980.

32

Bertrand Russell

*B*ertrand Arthur William Russell (1872–1970) was a British philosopher, logician, and promoter of social reform. An extremely prolific writer, he authored more than sixty books and a vast number of articles. He was elected to a Fellowship in philosophy at Trinity College, Cambridge, in 1895, later to a Lectureship, and then returned as a Fellow in 1944. Unlike Frege, much of Russell's writing received immediate recognition and had widespread influence during his lifetime. Though his most important philosophical work was in the same general areas and addressed the same general concerns as Frege's, Russell's total philosophical interests and writings cover a much broader range of issues and questions, including epistemology, metaphysics, the philosophy of mind, the philosophy of science and even issues in ethics, religion, and in social and political philosophy. In 1950, he earned the Nobel Prize for literature.

Russell's most original and important work in philosophy was produced in the period immediately after the publication of his early A Critical Exposition of the Philosophy of Leibniz *in 1900 and before the outbreak of the First World War.* The Principles of Mathematics, *his first attempt to articulate and defend logicism, appeared in 1903. This was followed by a series of important papers, including what is doubtless his most widely recognized work, "On Denoting," which appeared in 1905. "Mathematical Logic as Based on the Theory of Types" was published in 1908, and "Knowledge by Acquaintance and Knowledge by Description" in 1911. Then, in 1910, 1912, and 1913, respectively, each of the three volumes of Russell's collaborative effort with Alfred North Whitehead, the monumental* Principia Mathematica, *appeared.* Principia *is unquestionably Russell's greatest work and, next to Frege's* Begriffsschrift, *quite possibly the most important philosophical work in logic in the twentieth century.*

After 1911, having completed the bulk of his contribution to Principia Mathematica, *Russell turned his attention more directly toward issues in metaphysics and epistemology.* Problems of Philosophy *(1912) provides a lively and accessible sketch of his early views on these matters.* Our Knowledge of the External World *appeared in 1914. In 1918, Russell published his "The Philosophy of Logical Atomism."* An Introduction to Mathematical Philosophy, *a useful overview and introduction to the views of his earlier work, appeared in 1919. Between 1919 and his death, Russell's most important philosophical works included* The Analysis of Mind *(1921),* The Analysis of Matter *(1927),* An Inquiry into Truth and Meaning *(1940), and* Human Knowledge: Its Scope and Limits *(1948).*

BACKGROUND

The Rejection of Idealism

Russell was one of the very few philosophers who recognized the importance of Frege's work early on. He liked, in fact, to credit himself—and not wholly unfairly—with having rescued Frege's ideas from the widespread neglect they had received prior to Russell's discussions of them in his own works. Russell received a copy of Frege's *Begriffsschrift* around 1896 but claimed not to have understood it until he made some of its discoveries for himself some years later. Like Frege, Russell began his career with a primary interest in mathematics. He was also a logicist, and as such, he found himself preoccupied from a very early stage in his career with issues about logic and the logical analysis of language. Unlike Frege, however, Russell's earliest philosophical explorations involved a serious flirtation with neo-Hegelian idealism.

Russell entered Trinity College, Cambridge, at the age of eighteen on a mathematics scholarship and spent the major part of his first three years studying mathematics. During his fourth year, his interests turned toward philosophy. The prevailing philosophical perspective at both Cambridge and Oxford during this time was neo-Hegelian and idealist; the views of John M. E. McTaggart dominated at Cambridge and those of Francis H. Bradley dominated at Oxford. Russell was soon seduced.

During this time, Russell first became acquainted with the slightly younger G. E. Moore, whose subtlety of mind and intellectual honesty Russell greatly admired. Moore too had fallen under the spell of the prevailing idealism. But, for reasons not wholly unrelated to those that underwrote Frege's anti-psychologism, he soon became dissatisfied with the idealist's conception of judgment and launched a sustained critical campaign. Russell quickly followed suit. The idealism being promoted at this time not only made everything radically mind-dependent, which offended Moore's sense that judgment must be of objective states of affairs, but it was radically monistic, requiring that everything be essentially related with other things in a manner that offended Russell's sense of the logic of relations. Russell and Moore countered the dominant idealist monism with an alternative realist or Platonist pluralism.

Logicism After Frege

Apart from the abandonment of idealism, the next most important formative event in Russell's early career was his meeting with the Italian logician and mathematician Guiseppe Peano. The rigor and precision of the logical notation that Peano had developed greatly impressed Russell. The possibility of demonstrating the reducibility of mathematics to logic now presented itself as an attainable goal. Russell's discussions with Peano also awakened his interest in Frege; Russell was by this time already in possession of a copy of *Begriffsschrift*. In *The Principles of Mathematics*, Russell sought to combine and promote his newfound realism together with his commitment to logicism. It was while working on this book that Russell came fully to appreciate the magnitude of Frege's accomplishment, and he devoted a lengthy appendix to discussing and critically comparing Frege's views with his own. Even though Russell found himself disagreeing with Frege on many points, he shared with him not only his commitment to logicism, but a philosophical outlook that both accorded to logic a certain pride of place in the philosophical hierarchy and gave central importance to the use of logical analysis for addressing and solving philosophical problems.

The period that followed, up through the publication of *Principia Mathematica*, was the most concentrated and philosophically fertile period of Russell's career. During this time, he discovered a deep problem in the way Frege had attempted to implement his logicist program, a contradiction that has come to be known as "Russell's Paradox." We shall examine this paradox more closely below. Overcoming or avoiding Russell's Paradox immediately became a *sine qua non* for any foundational investigation in the philosophy of mathematics. Russell himself developed his famous Theory of Types in order to overcome the paradox.

During this period Russell also set forth what is doubtless his most familiar and enduring philosophical contribution, the Theory of Descriptions. The young Cambridge philosopher Frank Ramsey later called the theory a "paradigm of philosophy." Whether or not Ramsey was right, Russell's Theory of Descriptions is certainly a paradigm of *analytic* philosophy, and we shall examine it in some detail.

For Russell, one of the most important events of this period was the occasion, in 1912, of his first contact with the young Austrian, Ludwig Wittgenstein. Wittgenstein had been greatly impressed by Russell's *Prin-*

ciples of Mathematics. On the advice of Frege—of whom he had first learned from reading Russell's book—Wittgenstein went to Cambridge to study with Russell. Their close relationship lasted until the outbreak of the First World War, and the influence they had on each other is inestimable. Russell came quickly to view Wittgenstein as his successor, as the person most likely to solve the outstanding problems in philosophical logic that he himself would not solve. And Wittgenstein, in his pioneering monograph, *Tractatus Logico-Philosophicus*, credits Russell and Frege with being the two philosophers who most influenced his thinking. Wittgenstein eventually came to feel that he outgrew Russell, but the trajectory of Wittgenstein's philosophical career would have been very different indeed had it not been for this early and formative contact with Russell.

Metaphysics and the Theory of Knowledge: Russell's Ontological Conservatism

Though Russell recognized better than most the importance of logic for philosophical work, a concern with pure logic in and for its own sake was not the principal driving force behind his philosophical inquiries. Rather, Russell viewed clarity in logic as essential if he were to make any progress in the two areas where his principal interests did lie: metaphysics—in particular ontology—and the theory of knowledge. The deep motivation underlying nearly all of Russell's philosophizing were his twin interests in (i) determining *what there is*, in providing some justified account of the fundamental types of things that make up reality, and in (ii) determining by what methods, by what arguments or inferences, we can legitimately establish the truth of our beliefs. His approach to these questions, however, was always guided by his conviction that the only hope of getting a clear view of the nature of reality is through a rigorous and perspicuous logical analysis of the sentences we use to talk about reality, the sentences we use to express and to challenge our beliefs.

Not unrelated to this, and also extremely important for understanding the motivation behind Russell's views (in particular, after *Principles*), is Russell's commitment to a methodological principle that is often called Occam's Razor—the maxim that entities are not to be posited beyond necessity. Given his interest in ontology, Russell tended to view the process of logical analysis as largely aimed at uncovering the underlying ontological commitments of various of our claims. His methodological commitment to ontological parsimony required that one should always proceed in the task of analysis with an eye toward exposing the absolute minimum ontological commitments necessary to do justice to the semantic properties of the items being analyzed. Thus, for example, while our ordinary talk often appears to involve reference to entities we call numbers and, therefore, an ontological commitment to the existence of such entities, Russell would argue that a proper analysis of the sentences in which our talk involves this ostensible reference to numbers will reveal that no such reference is really involved. And thus, we are not committed to including numbers in our ontology.

Throughout his philosophical career, Russell held that through the proper logical analysis of our language we should aim to expose the ultimate constituents of reality—the logical atoms out of which the world as we ordinarily experience it and talk about it is composed—and the principles in accordance with which this composition takes place. Not surprisingly, he liked to call this conception of philosophy "Logical Atomism."

RUSSELL'S PARADOX

Frege was not merely a logicist, but he was also a realist about numbers. He believed that numbers are genuine objects. Numbers exist and are no less objects than rocks or molecules, they are just a different sort of object—abstract ones, existing outside of time and space. This realism about numbers placed a special burden on the defense of his logicism. For if mathematics is just logic, and if numbers exist as objects, then we must, it seems, be able to establish their existence from purely logical first principles. They must be genuine logical objects.

Eventually, Frege came to identify numbers with what are in effect certain classes or sets. For Frege, classes were to be identified exclusively with the *extensions of concepts*, where the extension of a concept may be thought of as the collection of all items which, when taken as arguments for the concept, yields the value True (cf. discussion of Frege's notion of concept on pp. 385–388). It is, in other words, the class of all those things of which the concept can be truly predicated. Frege then proceeded to identify the number *one*, for example, with the extension of the second-level concept expressed by "( ) is a first-level concept true of exactly one object." (Frege, however, showed how to express this second-level concept using only logical vocabulary, thus avoiding any need to rely on the numerical expression "one.") Thus, in effect, he identified the number *one* with the class of all concepts which are true of exactly one thing. The number *two* was identified with the extension of the second-level concept expressed by "( ) is a first-level concept true of exactly two objects," in other words, the class of all concepts which are true of exactly two things, and so on.

In order to justify this construction on purely logical grounds, Frege found himself obliged to accept as a logical axiom a principle which, in effect, guarantees that for any concept there is an extension of that concept containing all and only the things of which it is true. At first glance, such a principle would seem to be perfectly in order. In fact, however, it is Frege's need to rely on just such a principle that leads to the contradiction in his system that Russell was to expose.

Russell's Paradox arises as follows. Plainly, the extensions of some concepts are not members of themselves, while the extensions of others are. For example, the extension of the concept designated by "( ) is a man" is not a member of itself; for classes are not men. On the other hand, the extension of the concept designated by "( ) is not a man" is a member of itself. The extension of this concept contains all and only those objects that are not men. Since no class is a man, the class which is the extension of the designated concept will be a member of that very extension.

But now consider the extension of the concept designated by "( ) is the extension of a concept whose extension is not a member of itself "—or, more compactly, "( ) is a class that is not a member of itself." Let us call this the Russell Concept. The Russell Concept would appear to be a perfectly good concept; after all, we have just seen that it can be predicated truly of certain extensions and falsely of others. But now consider the extension of the Russell Concept itself. Is the extension of this concept a member of itself? In other words, is this concept true of its own extension?

If all concepts have extensions, then the Russell Concept must also have an extension. And if it does, then either the Russell Concept is true of it, or it is not true of it. The extension of the Russell Concept must either be a member of itself or not—plainly, it cannot be both. But what Russell pointed out was that neither case is possible. First, assume that the extension of the Russell concept is a member of itself. But in order to belong to the extension of the Russell Concept, a class must not be a member of itself. So, the extension of the Russell Concept can be a member of itself only if it is not a member of itself—a manifest contradiction! Suppose, then, that the extension of the Russell Concept is not a member of itself. But if it is not a member of itself, then the Russell Concept is true of it; and, consequently, it belongs to the extension of that concept. So the extension of the Russell Concept can fail to be a member of itself only if it is a member of itself—another contradiction! In other words, the extension of Russell's Concept is a member of itself if and only if it is not a member of itself, a manifest impossibility. Clearly something must be wrong with our original assumptions about the relations between concepts and extensions. But as noted earlier, these were assumptions that Frege felt he needed to underwrite his particular number-realist brand of logicism.

The discovery of Russell's Paradox irreparably undermined the way in which Frege hoped simultaneously to provide a logicist and a number-realist foundation for mathematics. After several perfunctory attempts to get around the difficulty, Frege eventually abandoned logicism completely and spent the better part of his late career trying to extract and consolidate those of his views on the nature and status of logic that remained untouched by the failure of his logicism. In the meantime, overcoming Russell's Paradox became the primary hurdle for logicism as well as for other foundational programs in the philosophy of mathematics. Russell himself struggled in the ensuing years to find a satisfactory way around it. The significance of Russell's Paradox is not to be underestimated, for it was very largely through the efforts of Russell and other logicians and mathematicians to come satisfactorily to terms with this paradox that modern axiomatic set theory achieved its maturity.

THE THEORY OF DESCRIPTIONS

Rejecting Frege's Distinction Between Sense and Meaning

Russell's Theory of Descriptions is, in the first instance, a proposal about how best to understand the logical structure of sentences containing certain occurrences of definite descriptions—expressions of the form "the *F*," where *F* stands for some descriptive phrase such as "father of George Washington" or "tallest man in Toledo" or "smallest prime number." Thus the phrases "the father of George Washington," "the tallest man in Toledo," and "the smallest prime number" are all definite descriptions. (Russell treated plural and generic definite descriptions, such as "the roses in the vase" or "the whale," as in "the whale is a mammal," separately.) The motivations behind the Theory of Descriptions are actually quite complex. There are, however, two that were central, both connected with the ontological conservativism engendered by Russell's commitment to Occam's Razor.

Definite descriptions would appear to be referring expressions, or singular terms, whose semantic value is the object, if any, that satisfies the condition expressed by the descriptive phrase. Indeed, this was precisely how Frege viewed them. If this is right, then in order for a definite description to discharge its semantic duty, there must in fact be an object to which it describes. It must, in Frege's terminology, have a Meaning (*Bedeutung*). But what, then, are we to say about sentences that contain definite descriptions that fail to designate anything? For example, what is the proper semantic account of sentences such as

(1) The present king of France is bald.

(2) Yesterday I met the present king of France.

Since there is no king of France at present, it seems to follow that the definite description occurring in each of these sentences fails to designate anything, fails to have a Meaning. But if it fails to have a Meaning and, thereby, fails to discharge its semantic duty, how are we to account for the fact that sentences 1 and 2 seem, nevertheless, to be perfectly meaningful?

Let us call descriptions like "the present king of France," which fail to describe any actually existing thing, empty descriptions. The question is, then, what is the proper semantic analysis of sentences containing empty descriptions?

For Frege, of course, this is no particular problem. He would certainly allow that the failure of the description to have a Meaning suffices to guarantee that the sentence as a whole will not have a Meaning. But because the description plainly does have sense, the sentence as a whole can be credited with expressing a Thought. According to Frege, then, our judgment that these sentences are perfectly meaningful amounts to no more than our appreciation that they express Thoughts—even if they are without truth values.

Russell, however, found Frege's doctrine of sense a mystery. In any case, he felt that it would be preferable, in general, if our analyses of sentences did not have to postulate two levels of semantic description—one in terms of Meaning or reference and one in terms of sense—but could make do with a single level of description. According to Russell, senses were both ontological and explanatory extravagances. In effect, Russell wanted to argue that a purely referential semantics must suffice. And it was in large part to this end that he proposed the Theory of Descriptions.

If, however, we are not allowed to appeal to something like Frege's theory of sense and must rely only on a compositional referential semantics, we seem to face another problem—and an even greater offence to Russell's ontological conservatism. The difficulty arises the moment we ask ourselves how, if we allow ourselves only a referential semantics, can we account for the apparent meaningfulness of sentences like our 1 and 2, given that they contain empty descriptions? If we restrict ourselves, as Russell insists, to a compositional referential semantics and continue to suppose that definite descriptions are singular terms, then the only way in which sentences containing descriptions can be genuinely meaningful is if the constituent descriptions manage successfully to designate something. Thus, unless we are willing to give up our assumption that 1 and 2 are in fact genuinely meaningful sentences—and Russell is not willing to do so—we seem obliged to suppose that, contrary to initial appearances, the description "the present king of France" does in fact have a referent. But what can it be? Not, of course, any actually *existing* present king of France—for we all agree there is no such thing. Rather, it must be some more ethereal *subsisting* entity, say, a possible present king of France, or something like that.

While Russell may have found some such suggestion quite congenial during the period of *Principles of Mathematics*, by the time he came to write "On Denoting," any such suggestion deeply offended his ontological scruples. Think of all the bizarre sorts of entities we would have to countenance in our ontology if we supposed that every description—even those that prima facie describe nothing that exists, for example, "the round square," "the largest prime number," "the fountain of youth"—possessed a referent! On the one hand, Russell wants to provide an analysis of sentences containing empty descriptions that does justice to the fact that such sentences can be perfectly meaningful. On the other hand, he wants to do so without appeal to any notion like Fregean sense and without committing himself to a vast number of bizarre subsisting entities. But how is this possible? Russell's solution was to deny that definite descriptions are in fact singular terms at all. And the Theory of Descriptions was his alternative account of how to understand the semantic properties of sentences containing them.

Russell's proposal, as we have seen, was based in large part on his rejection of Frege's distinction between sense and Meaning. In particular, he rejected the need to postulate a level of semantic description over and above the referential. Of course Russell was aware of the sorts of puzzle that motivated Frege's introduction of the notion of sense. But it was his view that puzzles of this sort—as well as puzzles that Frege seems unable to solve, such as the puzzle about negative existential statements—could be handled without introducing any notion like sense. He argued that what is needed is a more refined analysis of the referential truth conditions of the sentences that lead to Frege-style puzzles.

Cognitive Significance and Information Content

Frege felt compelled, recall, to introduce a notion of sense over and above his notion of *Bedeutung* in order to solve the following puzzle. He noticed that two sentences could differ in their cognitive significance even though they possess precisely the same referential truth conditions, that is, even though what is required for them each to be true is that precisely the same objects fall under precisely the same concepts or relations. Since Frege regarded differences in cognitive significance as logically relevant differences, he felt that it was the obligation of an adequate semantic theory to account for them. He also felt that in order to account for such differences, an adequate semantic account of such sentences must postulate something over and above what is handled by the theory of Meaning—what we are here calling the theory of reference. Thus, the theory of sense was born.

According to Frege, two sentences, A and B, will differ in their cognitive significance just insofar as it is possible for someone to extend his or her knowledge by coming correctly to believe what is expressed by A despite his or her already knowing the truth of what is expressed by B. But now what puzzled Russell was this. If this is what it is for two sentences, A and B, to differ in cognitive significance, then it must be that A expresses or semantically encodes different information about the world than B does. For if they expressed the same information, how could one extend one's knowledge by coming correctly to believe what is expressed by one sentence while already correctly believing what is expressed by the other? So it would seem that two sentences can differ in cognitive significance only if they express or encode different information about the world.

But now Russell would have us ask: How can two sentences semantically encode different information about the world without differing in their referential truth conditions—that is, without differing in what they each require the world to be like in order for them to be true? If two sentences both required, in order to be true, that precisely the same state of affairs obtain in the world, how could one of them convey information about the world distinct from that conveyed by the other? So it would seem that two sentences can differ in the information they encode or express only if they differ in their referential truth conditions. But if all of this is right, it immediately follows that two sentences can differ in cognitive significance only if they differ in their referential truth conditions.

This, though, immediately undermines the whole basis of Frege's puzzle. For as Frege understood the matter, what is puzzling is precisely the supposed fact that two sentences with the *same* referential truth conditions can differ in cognitive significance. It is just this supposition that the above line of argument purports to undermine. Unless there can be differences in cognitive significance where there are no differences in referential truth conditions, there will be no differences to explain that are not already captured by the theory of reference. And so there can be no need for any theory of sense.

Of course, if one is to take this line—as Russell plainly did—then one is obligated to provide an account of the differences in referential truth conditions wherever there is a difference in cognitive significance. As we saw in the previous chapter, Frege's reasons for supposing that puzzling pairs of sentences do indeed possess the same referential truth conditions seemed quite compelling. Consequently, a philosophically satisfying account of how such sentences in fact differ in their referential truth conditions ought to enable us to see, not only where Frege's mistake was, but also how it was so easy to make it. This was just what Russell proposed to do in the case of sentences containing definite descriptions.

Russell saw that one can surely extend one's knowledge, in a sense relevant to differences in cognitive significance, by coming correctly to believe what is expressed by the sentence

(3) The inventor of bifocals is dead.

despite already correctly believing what is expressed by

(4) The original publisher of *Poor Richard's Almanac* is dead.

And this, despite the fact that the inventor of bifocals is the same person as the original publisher of *Poor Richard's Almanac*, namely, Benjamin Franklin. But Russell did not find this fact puzzling at all. For him it just indicated that, contrary to what Frege would have supposed, 3 and 4 must have different referential truth conditions. But how did Russell propose we analyze such sentences in order to expose this difference?

Before turning directly to this question, let us first consider one more puzzle that Russell hoped his Theory of Descriptions would solve. We have already seen that Russell was particularly concerned to account for the meaningfulness of sentences containing empty descriptions and how the rejection of a theory of sense would seem to make this especially difficult. The problem raised by empty descriptions becomes especially acute when we consider them in negative existential statements of the form "the *F* does not exist," as, for example,

(5) The fountain of youth does not exist.

We saw in the previous chapter that Frege had considerable difficulty with negative existential statements. Indeed, it was not at all clear how he could successfully deal with the problem. The difficulty, recall, was that according to the principle of compositionality for Meaning, if a component expression in a sentence fails to have a Meaning, then so will the sentence. This leaves it a mystery how to account for the fact that we often do express true Thoughts by means of negative existential sentences. For if the Thought is true, that means that there is nothing for the relevant singular term—in our example, "the fountain of youth"—to refer to, in which case it fails to have a Meaning. But if it fails to have a Meaning, how can the sentence containing it have one?

This is a problem for Russell because he also endorses the principle of compositionality for reference that underlies this difficulty. How can sentences which *appear* to contain non-referring singular terms—in particular, negative existential sentences—nevertheless convey truth-evaluable information about the world? I have emphasized the "appear" in our statement of this puzzle to suggest what Russell's strategy is going to be. Russell will propose that whenever we have a meaningful, truth-evaluable negative existential statement with an apparent singular term as subject, we must analyze that statement in such a way as to reveal that the semantic role played by that term is not that of a singular term after all. He begins with sentences that contain definite descriptions, and then, as we shall see, he generalizes his solution there to other *prima facie* singular terms.

Indefinite Descriptions

It is now time to examine how exactly Russell does propose that we analyze sentences containing definite descriptions. Russell, in fact, approaches this issue somewhat indirectly by first considering *indefinite* descriptions. An indefinite description is a descriptive phrase that begins with the indefinite article "a(n)" instead of the definite article "the." "A women," "an elephant," "a salesperson" are all indefinite descriptions. Now consider the sentence

(6) A bird is on the fence.

In order for this sentence to be true, all that is required is that some bird or other be on the fence. It is clearly not required that some specific bird be on the fence—any bird will do. Thus, it should be clear that the expression "a bird," as used in this sentence, is not functioning as a singular term. To be a singular term, it would have to have some unique object as its referent. But as we have just noted, since there is no specific bird that must be on the fence in order for 6 to be true, "a bird" cannot be functioning as a singular term.

Notice, however, that under certain circumstances, those circumstances where there is some one specific bird—call him "Tweety"—on the fence, we can, in a sense, say that it is Tweety's presence on the fence that makes 6 true. Under these imagined circumstances, we could say that what makes the sentence

(7) Tweety is on the fence.

true, also makes 6 true. But plainly, 6 and 7 do not say the same thing—they have different truth conditions. In order for 7 to be true, the only bird whose presence on the fence is relevant is Tweety's. Whereas for 6 to be true, any bird would do. Sentence 7 requires Tweety's presence on the fence in order to be true—no other bird will do. Though Tweety's presence on the fence is sufficient to make 6 true, it is, as we have seen, not required. Thus, the sense in which, under the imagined circumstances, the truth of 6 depends upon Tweety's presence on the fence and the sense in which the truth of 7 depends upon Tweety's presence on the fence are quite different.

We can bring this out by noting that in order to state the truth conditions of 7, we are obliged to mention Tweety, whereas in order to state the truth conditions of 6, no mention need be made of any specific bird. Rather, the truth conditions of 6 are given by the requirement that at least one bird (it does not matter which) be on the fence. In other words, in order to state the truth conditions of 6, we need only mention two properties, *being a bird* and *being on the fence*; what is required for 6 to be true is that these two properties be co-instantiated.

What does this tell us about the semantic role played by indefinite descriptions in sentences such as 6? According to Russell, we note right off that they do not play the role of singular terms. But is there anything that we can count as their Meaning? The question involves a mistake. If we are tempted to look for the Meaning of an indefinite description at all, it can only be because we are mislead by the fact that they are grammatically similar to singular terms—they too can appear in the subject position of subject/predicate sentences. But once we reflect on their role in determining the truth conditions of the sentences in which they appear, we see that it is a mistake to attempt to associate some specific Meaning with them. Rather, sentences of the form "an *F* is *G*" seem best thought of as expressing a relation between the two concepts or properties designated by *F* and *G* respectively. According to Russell, such sentences say of two properties that one of them bears the relation of being instantiated by at least one object that instantiates the other. Thus, though it is not plausible to suppose that indefinite descriptions themselves have a Meaning, there is no mystery in how sentences containing them can have determinate truth conditions.

Most of this should be uncontroversial; it is not likely that anyone would have mistaken the semantic role of an indefinite description for that of a singular term. The reason Russell goes through this, however, is that he is about to argue that something very similar is true for definite descriptions. He is about to argue that, contrary to superficial appearances (and *pace* Frege), definite descriptions are also not singular terms.

Definite Descriptions

According to Russell, definite descriptions differ from indefinite descriptions only in their requirement that the descriptive phrase be uniquely satisfied. Whereas a sentence of the form "an *F* is *G*" will be analyzed as saying "there is at least one thing which is both *F* and *G*," a sentence of the form "the *F* is *G*" will require this and, in addition, that there be no more than one *F*. Thus, Russell proposes that the proper analysis of a sentence of the form "the *F* is *G*" requires that (i) there be at least one *F*, (ii) there be at most one *F*, and (iii) whatever is *F* is *G*.

As in the case of sentences that contain indefinite descriptions, the truth of a definite description sentence of the form "the *F* is *G*" may depend upon some particular object satisfying the condition designated by *G*—namely, whatever object uniquely satisfies the condition designated by *F*. But just as in the case of indefinite descriptions, the manner in which the truth of this sentence concerns that object is not of the appropriately intimate variety necessary for the description "the *F*" to count as a singular term.

Consider, for example, the true sentence

(8) The author of *Waverly* was Scottish.

Given the circumstances that actually obtain, we can, in a sense, say that this sentence is made true by the same circumstances that make the sentence

(9) Sir Walter Scott was Scottish.

True. But if Russell is correct in his analysis of sentences containing definite descriptions, it will not be the case that these sentences say the same thing; they will not have the same truth conditions. The situation here is parallel to that in our previous example concerning the indefinite description. There, despite the fact that it was—under the imagined circumstances—Tweety's presence on the fence that made 6 true, we saw that the truth conditions of 6 did not actually concern themselves directly or essentially with Tweety at all. Likewise, here, despite the fact that—given the circumstances that actually obtain in the world—it is Sir Walter Scott's being Scottish that makes 8 true, the truth conditions of 8 also do not directly or essentially concern Sir Walter Scott. Had any other Scotsman uniquely authored *Waverly*, 8 would have been just as true. Consequently, it cannot be correct to view the semantic role played by the definite description "the author of *Waverly*" in 8 as that of a singular term.

As before, we can bring this out by noting that in order to state the truth conditions of 9, we are obliged to mention Sir Walter Scott, whereas, if Russell is right, in order to state the truth conditions of 8, no mention need be made of any particular person. Rather, the truth conditions of 8 are given by the requirement that *someone* uniquely authored *Waverly* and *whoever* that was, was Scottish. In other words, in order to give the truth conditions of 8, we are only obliged to mention the two properties, *authoring Waverly* and *being Scottish*—what is required, according to Russell, is that one of them (*authoring Waverly*) bears the relation of being uniquely instantiated by an object which also instantiates the other one (*being Scottish*). No *reference* to any specific individual occurs.

There is, to be sure, a sense in which definite descriptions can more reasonably be viewed as "picking out" a particular object than indefinite descriptions—at least when there is one that uniquely satisfies the conditions specified by the descriptive phrase. But, if Russell is right, it is a mistake to regard this object as the Meaning, the semantic value, of the description. To mark this distinction, Russell introduces the special notion of *denoting*. A definite description is said to denote the object, if any, that uniquely satisfies the description. That object, when it exists, will be called the *denotation* of the description. If no object satisfies the description, the description will fail to have a denotation, it will not denote anything. But, importantly, unlike with genuine singular terms and their referents, the failure of a description to have a denotation will not have the result that the sentence containing the empty description is without a truth value. A definite description that fails to denote anything, an empty description, can nevertheless successfully carry out its semantic role. Accordingly, definite descriptions cannot be singular terms. We can now see precisely where, according to Russell, Frege made his mistake. Frege mistakenly took the fact that definite descriptions are denoting expressions for their being referring expressions. And since it is not hard to see how easy it might be to make this error, we can appreciate why Frege's assumption that sentence pairs of the puzzling sort have the same referential truth conditions seemed to be intuitively compelling.

APPLICATIONS

Accounting for Differences in Cognitive Significance Without Using Senses

How does this proposal help Russell solve the difficulties discussed earlier? First, how does this analysis of sentences containing definite descriptions enable us to account for the differences in cognitive significance between such sentences as our 3 and 4 above? We saw that in order to account for this problem without invoking a notion of sense, Russell's theory will have to assign to these sentences different referential truth conditions. According to the present proposal, this is precisely what results. Sentence 3 will be true if and only if there is one and only one person who invented bifocals and that person is dead; and 4 will be true if and only if there is one and only one person who first published *Poor Richard's Almanac* and that person is dead. Whereas both sentences concern themselves with the property of being dead, 3, unlike 4, concerns itself with the property of inventing bifocals, while 4, unlike 3, concerns itself with the property of publishing *Poor Richard's Almanac*. Neither, notice, concerns itself directly with Benjamin Franklin. Franklin does not, as Russell would put it, "occur as a constituent" in either of the propositions expressed by these sentences. These two sentences are about different aspects of the world, they require in order to be true that different states of affairs obtain. In this way, Russell supposes he has accounted for their difference in cognitive significance without appeal to Frege's notion of sense.

Dealing with Empty Descriptions

So much for the difficulty raised by differences in cognitive significance of the sort that Frege believed required the postulation of a theory of sense. How about the difficulties raised by empty descriptions? Here, too, Russell feels that he has provided an efficient and intuitively correct solution. In the first place, once it is denied that definite descriptions function semantically as singular terms, it no longer follows directly from the fact that they fail to be uniquely satisfied by something, that the sentences containing them are meaningless. Consider the problem of negative existential sentences with definite descriptions as subjects. According to the current proposal, there is no longer anything puzzling about them. Sentence 5, for example, will now be analyzed as saying that it is not the case that there is one and only one fountain of youth. In other words, it says that it is not the case that the property of being a fountain of youth is uniquely instantiated. And this is true, just as we would expect.

And what about sentences like our 1 and 2? According to the Theory of Descriptions, 2 should be analyzed as saying that there is one and only one present king of France and that I met him. Since these truth conditions are not satisfied, the Theory of Descriptions declares that 2 is false. This seems perfectly right in this case. Sentence 1, however, is a different story.

According to Russell, 1 should be analyzed as saying that there is one and only one present king of France and that he is bald. Since there is no present king of France, the Theory of Descriptions will require that we treat 1 as false also. But many have found this counter-intuitive. Not, however, because they think that 1 is true, but rather because they agree with Frege that sentences like 1 are best regarded as neither true nor false. After all, intuitively, it seems that in order for 1 to be false, the present king of France must fail to be bald; but if there is no present king of France, there is no clear sense to make of *his* failing to be bald, and so there would seem to be no clear sense to be made of the sentence's being false. We need not try to decide how to accommodate these intuitions here. But it is worth knowing they exist—you may feel them yourself. If Russell's proposal is to be fully satisfactory, he must be able to show that the considerations which underlie such intuitions are not semantically probative.

So far, we have examined the motivations for Russell's Theory of Descriptions; we have seen what the theory itself involves and have witnessed its apparent success in addressing the various puzzles and difficulties Russell set out to solve. It provides the resources to account for differences in cognitive significance between sentences such as our 3 and 4 exclusively in terms of differences in their referential truth conditions and thus without having to appeal to anything like Frege's notion of sense. Moreover, the manner in which the theory assigns truth conditions is such that even sentences containing empty definite descriptions get assigned determinate truth conditions—and without having to admit into our ontology any queer subsisting entities. There is, consequently, no longer any mystery how such sentences can be meaningful. Nor, if Russell's proposal is adopted, will the puzzle remain about how to account for true and informative negative existential statements—a difficulty, recall, Frege appears unable to solve.

DIFFICULTIES

What About Incomplete Definite Descriptions and Ordinary Proper Names?

Russell's proposal is not, however, without its own difficulties. First of all, notice that the puzzles, which seem so nicely resolved by Russell's theory, do not arise exclusively in the case of sentences containing definite descriptions. We have seen, for example, that it is also possible for two different, but co-referential ordinary proper names to differentially affect the cognitive significance of the sentences in which they appear. According to Frege's criteria, the sentences

(10) Superman can fly.

and

(11) Clark Kent can fly.

will differ in cognitive significance. For it is plainly possible for someone who already believes what 10 expresses to extend his or her knowledge by coming to learn what 11 expresses. Moreover, problems precisely parallel to those that arose in connection with sentences containing empty descriptions arise in connection with sentences containing "empty"—that is, non-referring—names. The Theory of Descriptions does not address these problems. Does this mean that we will need to resort to a Fregean notion of sense to deal with differences of cognitive significance in these sorts of cases or to explain how sentences with empty names can nevertheless seem meaningful? If so, then the Theory of Descriptions will hardly present us with a general alternative to Frege's two-tiered semantic theory.

Notice also that by far and away the greatest number of definite descriptions that we use in everyday discourse do not contain descriptive phrases which plausibly specify uniquely satisfied conditions. I ask for the book on the table. But I am under no illusion that there is one and only one book or one and only one table. I notice that it is time to make an appointment at the dentist. But, again, I am well aware that there is more than one dentist in the world. Suppose, on the day that my telephone bill arrives, I say, as anyone might, "The telephone bill arrived today." Surely, under the circumstances, what I said will be true. But if we are to analyze this sentence in accordance with Russell's theory, it seems we must suppose that it is true just in case there is one and only one telephone bill and it arrived today. And so, since there is obviously more than one telephone bill in the world, what I said would turn out to be false!

Let us call a definite description with a descriptive phrase that fails to be satisfied uniquely an incomplete description. Thus, such descriptions as "the book," "the table," "the dentist," and "the telephone bill"—indeed, as I said before, most of the descriptions we ordinarily use—are incomplete descriptions. So if Russell's theory is to be applied in a straightforward manner to all of the definite descriptions that occur in ordinary discourse, it will turn out that most of what we say using sentences containing descriptions will be false. If, however, it is a direct consequence of the proposed semantic analysis of some very commonly used type of expression that most, or even all, of the competent utterances of sentences containing expressions of that type turn out to be false, and if, furthermore, no reasonable explanation is available of why speakers should be in error so often, so consistently, and on so many diverse occasions, then surely we have ample reason to reject the proposal.

Incomplete Descriptions

Russell was not unaware that precisely the same difficulties and puzzles that affect sentences containing definite descriptions also affect sentences that contain ordinary proper names. Nor was he unaware of the problem with incomplete descriptions. Russell had specific proposals about how to deal with each of these problems.

Russell's way of dealing with the problem of incomplete descriptions is fairly straightforward. According to Russell, when a speaker is fully aware that the description he or she is using is incomplete, uses of such descriptions are to be counted as truncated or abbreviated versions of more complete descriptions that the speaker has in mind. We allow ourselves to use these incomplete descriptions on the occasions we do because, according to Russell, we expect the necessary completing qualifications to be evident to our audience from the context of utterance. Thus, when I say something like, "I have an appointment with the doctor today," I usually mean that I have an appointment with the doctor whom I regularly see, assuming that there is one and only one doctor that I regularly see. Or when I say, "I got the telephone bill today," I usually mean I got my telephone bill for this month today. On such occasions, I expect my audience to understand these qualifications without my having to make them explicit. It would, after all, be an immense conversational burden to have to make all of the uniquely individuating conditions one has in mind explicit; and so, according to Russell, we truncate or abbreviate our descriptions when we expect the necessary further qualifications will be understood.

The point is that it would be overly legalistic to insist that the Theory of Descriptions be applied strictly to our actual words, for it is a common and useful feature of our conversational practice that we often use sentences that in some manner or other abbreviate what we intend to communicate. In such cases, we reasonably expect that the context of utterance will enable our audience to fully understand what it is that we intend to be saying. When the Theory of Descriptions is applied to the fully explicit description sentences whose meanings we intend to convey by uttering sentences containing incomplete descriptions, we find ourselves no longer obliged to assess most of what we say on those occasions as false. And so, according to Russell, the difficulty raised about incomplete descriptions is not a genuine difficulty at all.

How satisfied should we be with this response? We cannot, unfortunately, explore the matter very fully here. Suffice it to say that if this response is to be adequate, it must be the case that whenever we knowingly use an incomplete description, we actually do have in mind some specific complete—that is, uniquely individuating—description which we intend our uttered description to abbreviate. Is this really always the case? Moreover, if we are to avoid reintroducing problems or puzzles of the sort the Theory of Descriptions was designed to solve, we must be assured that the complete descriptions that we are supposed to have in mind do not themselves contain expressions which, though making the same contribution to the referential truth conditions of the sentences in which they occur, differ in cognitive significance. Which brings us to our problem about ordinary proper names.

Ordinary Proper Names

How does Russell propose to deal with the issue raised by the fact that the same puzzles that motivated the Theory of Descriptions also arise with respect to sentences that contain ordinary proper names? As Russell saw things, if the Theory of Descriptions was to fulfill its promise in a general way, we would be obliged to view ordinary proper names as, in effect, disguised, or abbreviations for, definite descriptions. In other words, upon analysis, sentences containing ordinary proper names really possess the same logical structure, the same sort of referential truth conditions, as sentences that contain definite descriptions. As in the case of incomplete descriptions, Russell assumes that when we use ordinary proper names we have in mind a complete description for which we use the name as a conventional abbreviation. Even ordinary proper names, then, are not, from a purely logical point of view, singular terms!

So, for example, when I utter the sentence

(12) Benjamin Franklin invented bifocals.

what I am really expressing, according to Russell, is a proposition that would be more explicitly expressed by a sentence of the form "*the F* invented bifocals." His idea was that in thinking about Benjamin Franklin, I must have in mind some description which I believe uniquely individuates him—how else will my thought concern precisely him and not some other object? My intention, then, in using the sentence is to speak about whoever uniquely satisfies the relevant descriptive condition. It is this description, then—whatever it is—that I use the name "Benjamin Franklin" to abbreviate. Thus, according to Russell, if I wanted my thought to be more explicit, I would utter a sentence in which the occurrence of "Benjamin Franklin" was replaced by the relevant definite description. If I wanted my thought to be perfectly explicit, I would utter a sentence fully analyzed in accordance with the Theory of Descriptions—in other words, a sentence of the form "There is one and only one *F* [where *F* is the uniquely individuating descriptive condition I have in mind] who invented bifocals."

If something like this is correct, then the solutions provided by the Theory of Descriptions to our various difficulties and puzzles as they arose in connection with sentences containing descriptions can now be applied *mutatis mutandis* to those difficulties and puzzles as they arise in connection with sentences containing ordinary proper names. But working out this application of the theory in satisfactory detail turns out not to be such an easy matter.

Acquaintance and Logically Proper Names

First of all, notice that if the original puzzle about differences in cognitive significance are not to be reintroduced at a different level, the predicates making up the descriptive phrases in these underlying descriptions cannot themselves be allowed to contain any expressions which, though having the same meaning or reference as some other possible expression, might nevertheless differentially affect the cognitive significance of sentences in which they appear. Needless to say, this also goes for the complete descriptions that are supposed to back up our ordinary uses of incomplete descriptions.

For Russell, the only expressions about which we can be assured that this is not the case are those expressions our understanding of which consists in our being, as Russell called it, "acquainted" with the items they stand for. It turns out, as Russell was clearly aware, that in order for his notion of acquaintance to serve as intended, to exclude the forbidden expressions, that notion will have to satisfy the following condition: If one is acquainted with X and is also acquainted with Y, and if X is identical to Y, then it will be impossible for one to fail to recognize that they are one and the same. Russell labeled the permitted expressions "logically proper." Thus, for example, a name is a logically proper name only if its referent is something I am acquainted with; a predicate expression is a logically proper predicate expression only if the property or concept for which it stands is one I am acquainted with. Obviously, ordinary names are not logically proper names.

On Russell's view, then, sentences that contain ordinary proper names—indeed, all sentences—turn out, upon logical analysis, to be directly about only features of the world with which we are immediately acquainted. But given what is required for acquaintance, it turns out, according to Russell, that we can only be acquainted with such purportedly epistemically intimate things as sense data, certain universals, and perhaps ourselves. Thus, it is a consequence of generalizing the Theory of Descriptions to cover sentences containing ordinary proper names (and any other "apparent" singular terms which can differ in their contribution to the cognitive significance of the sentences containing them), plus Russell's commitment to the view that all fully analyzed sentences will contain only logically proper expressions, that our sentences (indeed, even thoughts) can never—contrary to what we might have supposed—directly concern or be about any objects with which we cannot be acquainted. Consequently, according to Russell, our thought and talk can never directly concern or refer to such ordinary and familiar items as tables, chairs, members of our family, our lovers, our teachers, or even our own hands and feet! These things may be the denotations of our sentences, but because they are not the sorts of things with which we can be directly acquainted (in Russell's sense), they are not the possible referents of any logically proper names that we can understand.

The objections to this aspect of Russell's view have been legion. Though we cannot explore them here, suffice it to say that many philosophers have objected to the ontology of sense data and the variety of foundationalist epistemology that goes with it. Moreover, the notion of acquaintance that Russell needs turns out to be extremely difficult, if not impossible, to spell out and defend coherently. But for the majority, perhaps the most pressing difficulty is that the last mentioned consequence of Russell's proposal manifestly fails to remain faithful to what we intuitively take sentences containing ordinary proper names to be essentially about. The extent of this last failure is, for example, forcefully argued for by the contemporary philosopher Saul Kripke, in his important book *Naming and Necessity*, where he details the various ways in which, according to him, description-based approaches to the semantics of proper names fail to do justice to various fundamental semantic, metaphysical, and epistemological intuitions associated with our use of proper names. The point is that Russell's Theory of Descriptions, the problems it aimed to solve, as well as the problems it seems itself to engender, are all still very much topics for contemporary philosophical debate.

In the foregoing we have examined only a very small selection of the diverse and often conflicting doctrines that Russell promoted at different times over the course of his long and distinguished philosophical career. With the exception of our discussion of Russell's Paradox, we have had to leave out any discussion of his technical accomplishments in logic and in the foundations of mathematics. We had occasion (in our discussion of his notion of acquaintance) only barely to touch upon Russell's ever-evolving views on epistemology. And our brief remarks on his ontological conservativism and the impact this had in motivating the Theory of Descriptions is just the surface of a rich legacy of reflection on metaphysical issues. Nevertheless, the selection of Russell's views we have examined, besides representing some of the most well known and influential, provide an especially clear example of Russell's analytic methodology and the general tenor of his overall concerns. Russell's impact on subsequent philosophy has been incalculable. He has left such a rich and diverse legacy of ideas that nearly everyone will find something challenging, insightful, and provocative in his works.

Selected Readings

PRIMARY SOURCES

Russell, B. *Logic and Knowledge: Essays 1901–1950*, ed. by Robert Marsh. London: Allen and Unwin, 1956.

_____. *Mysticism and Logic*. New York: Barnes and Noble, 1917.

_____. *The Principles of Mathematics*. New York: W. W. Norton and Co., 1903.

_____. *The Problems of Philosophy*. Oxford: Oxford University Press, 1912.

SECONDARY SOURCES

Ayer, A. J. *Bertrand Russell*. London: Fontana, 1972.

Hylton, P. *Russell, Idealism, and the Emergence of Analytic Philosophy*. Oxford: Clarendon, 1990.

Pears, D. F. *Bertrand Russell and the British Tradition in Philosophy*. London: Fontana, 1967.

Sainsbury, M. *Russell*. London: Routlege and Kegan Paul, 1979.

Savage, C. W., and Anderson, C. A., eds. *Rereading Russell: Essays in Bertrand Russell's Metaphysics and Epistemology*. Minneapolis: University of Minnesota Press, 1989.

Index

Index

Ethics (Spinoza), 140–143, 149
Edaimonia (Aristotle), 59
Eudaimonism, Socratic, 24
Euthyphro, 19, 20, 21, 23
Evil, St. Augustine on, 78–79
Experience, Kant on judgments of, 266–272

F

Facticity and transcendence, Sartre on, 358
Faith
   Kierkegaard on, 341
   St. Anselm on, 80–82
Fear and Trembling (Kiekegaard), 338
"Final Argument" (Plato), 35
"Five Ways" (Aquinas), 91–92
Flux, 6
Form, Aquinas on, 88–89
Formal causes, Bacon on, 101
Forms
   Bacon on, 101
   Plato on, 33–37
Foundations of Arithmetic (Frege), 370
Four causes, Aristotle's doctrine of, 54–55
Fourfold division, Aristotle on, 48–49
Franklin, Benjamin, 408
Freedom
   Hume on, 225–226
   Kant on, 309–310
   Leibniz on, 156–157
   Marx on, 324–325
   Rousseau on, 291
   Sartre on, 353, 358–359
   Spinoza on, 150
Free will
   Descartes on, 131
   Hume on, 223–227
   Stoics on, 68
Frege, Gottlob, 370–371
   on anti-psychologism, 375–380
   background of, 371–372
   on function and concept, 380–386
   on logic and the objectivity of thoughts, 372–375
   logicism of, 371–372
   on sense and meaning, 387–396, 404–406
Function, Frege on, 380–386

G

Galileo, influence on Leibniz, 153
Gassendi, Pierre, 84
Gaunilo, 84
Gay Science (Nietzsche), 345, 350
Genealogy, Nietzsche on, 346–347
Genealogy of Morals (Nietzsche), 345
General will, Rousseau on, 290–292
Geometry (Descartes), 107
German Ideology (Marx), 321, 322, 325, 326
Glaucon, 38–39
God
   Aquinas on, 90–93
   Berkeley on, 203–204
   Descartes on existence of, 116–123
   St. Augustine on, 77
Good, ultimate, 59
Goods, classification of, 38–39
Gorgias, 11, 23
Gorgias (Socrates), 24
Great Instauration (Bacon), 98–99
Groundwork of the Metaphysic of Morals (Kant), 249
Gyges' ring, 39

H

Happiness, Aristotle on, 58–61
Hedonism, 65
Hegel, G. W. F., 328
   on absolute knowledge, 336–337
   on the dialectic, 329
   on forms of consciousness, 332–337
   and idealism, 328–329
   on lordship and bondage, 334
   on the phenomenology of mind, 330–332
   on reason, 335
   on religious consciousness, 336
   on self-consciousness, 334
   on sense certainty, 332–333
   on the spirit, 330
   on Stoicism, 334
Heraclitus, 5–7
Herodotus, 22
Hesiod, 1
Hintikka, Jaako, 112
Hippias, 11

OTHER BOOKS IN THE HARPERCOLLINS COLLEGE OUTLINE SERIES

ART
History of Art 0-06-467131-3
Introduction to Art 0-06-467122-4

BUSINESS
Business Calculus 0-06-467136-4
Business Communications 0-06-467155-0
Introduction to Business 0-06-467104-6
Introduction to Management 0-06-467127-5
Introduction to Marketing 0-06-467130-5

CHEMISTRY
College Chemistry 0-06-467120-8
Organic Chemistry 0-06-467126-7

COMPUTERS
Computers and Information Processing 0-06-467176-3
Introduction to Computer Science and Programming
    0-06-467145-3
Understanding Computers 0-06-467163-1

ECONOMICS
Introduction to Economics 0-06-467113-5
Managerial Economics 0-06-467172-0

ENGLISH LANGUAGE AND LITERATURE
English Grammar 0-06-467109-7
English Literature From 1785 0-06-467150-X
English Literature To 1785 0-06-467114-3
Persuasive Writing 0-06-467175-5

FOREIGN LANGUAGE
French Grammar 0-06-467128-3
German Grammar 0-06-467159-3
Spanish Grammar 0-06-467129-1
Wheelock's Latin Grammar 0-06-467177-1
Workbook for Wheelock's Latin Grammar
    0-06-467171-2

HISTORY
Ancient History 0-06-467119-4
British History 0-06-467110-0
Modern European History 0-06-467112-7
Russian History 0-06-467117-8
20th Century United States History 0-06-467132-1
United States History From 1865 0-06-467100-3
United States History to 1877 0-06-467111-9
Western Civilization From 1500 0-06-467102-X

Western Civilization To 1500 0-06-467101-1
World History From 1500 0-06-467138-0
World History to 1648 0-06-467123-2

MATHEMATICS
Advanced Calculus 0-06-467139-9
Advanced Math for Engineers and Scientists
    0-06-467151-8
Applied Complex Variables 0-06-467152-6
Basic Mathematics 0-06-467143-7
Calculus with Analytic Geometry 0-06-467161-5
College Algebra 0-06-467140-2
Elementary Algebra 0-06-467118-6
Finite Mathematics with Calculus 0-06-467164-X
Intermediate Algebra 0-06-467137-2
Introduction to Calculus 0-06-467125-9
Introduction to Statistics 0-06-467134-8
Ordinary Differential Equations 0-06-467133-X
Precalculus Mathematics: Functions & Graphs
    0-06-467165-8
Survey of Mathematics 0-06-467135-6

MUSIC
Harmony and Voice Leading 0-06-467148-8
History of Western Music 0-06-467107-7
Introduction to Music 0-06-467108-9
Music Theory 0-06-467168-2

PHILOSOPHY
Ethics 0-06-467166-6
History of Philosophy 0-06-467142-9
Introduction to Philosophy 0-06-467124-0

POLITICAL SCIENCE
The Constitution of the United States 0-06-467105-4
Introduction to Government 0-06-467156-9

PSYCHOLOGY
Abnormal Psychology 0-06-467121-6
Child Development 0-06-467149-6
Introduction to Psychology 0-06-467103-8
Personality: Theories and Processes 0-06-467115-1
Social Psychology 0-06-467157-7

SOCIOLOGY
Introduction to Sociology 0-06-467106-2
Marriage and the Family 0-06-467147-X

Available at your local bookstore or directly from HarperCollins at 1-800-331-3761.